SHAPING STRATEGIC CHANGE

SHAPING STRATEGIC CHANGE

Making Change in Large Organizations

The Case of the National Health Service

ANDREW PETTIGREW
EWAN FERLIE
LORNA McKEE

SAGE Publications
London • Newbury Park • New Delhi

SAGE Publications Ltd
6 Bonhill Street
London EC2A 4PU

SAGE Publications Inc
2455 Teller Road
Newbury Park, California 91320

SAGE Publications India Pvt Ltd
32, M-Block Market
Greater Kailash – I
New Delhi 110 048

British Library Cataloguing in Publication Data

A catalogue record for this book is available from the
British Library

ISBN 0 8039 8778 1
ISBN 0 8039 8779 X pbk

Library of Congress catalog card number 92–50540

Typeset by Mayhew Typesetting, Rhayader, Powys
Printed in Great Britain by The Cromwell Press Ltd,
Broughton Gifford, Melksham, Wiltshire

Contents

Acknowledgements

We are grateful to many people for their assistance in the development of this book.

The research underpinning the manuscript was co-financed by the then National Health Service Training Authority (now the NHS Training Directorate) and a consortium of eight Regional Health Authorities in England. These authorities were: Mersey RHA, North East Thames RHA, North Western RHA, North West Thames RHA, Oxford RHA, South West Thames RHA, West Midlands RHA and Yorkshire RHA.

The goals of the research sprang from the implementation of the Griffiths general managerial reforms and a pilot project around the management of change undertaken by Andrew Pettigrew in 1984–5 in three Regions. The subsequent desire of the funders to generate larger-scale research findings which would help to develop practice formed the starting point for the project.

The project team at the Centre for Corporate Strategy and Change, Warwick Business School, consisted of Andrew Pettigrew, Ewan Ferlie and Lorna McKee. The fieldwork for the project began in early 1987 and extended into 1990. Lorna McKee went on maternity leave in February 1989, but has continued on a part-time basis to work as a team member. The secretary to the project was Gill Drakeley, who should be thanked not only for her secretarial skills, but for acting as librarian and administrative back-up for the project.

Philip Marsh, then Director of Manpower in North East Thames RHA and now Director of Personnel at the Open University, played an invaluable role in championing the need for quality management research in the NHS. His role was crucial in pulling together the consortium of Regions which co-financed the work. Philip also chaired the steering group which guided the project through its various phases. Public thanks of this form can only capture part of the gratitude the Warwick team feel for Philip's long-term practical support.

We are also grateful to Derek Cumming, General Manager of St Helens and Knowsley District Health Authority. Derek was one of the eight District General Managers (DGMs) who allowed us access to his working environment. He was also a faithful attender of steering group meetings, and on Philip Marsh's departure from the Service he took the role of Chairman of the group. Latterly Derek has played a constructive role in encouraging the dissemination of our findings throughout the NHS.

Bob Dearden was Chief Executive of the NHSTA at the time this project was launched. We thank him for his support and encouragement at the outset of the work and also the series of NHSTA staff who linked with us throughout the four years of the project. Collective thanks are also due to the Regional representatives who devoted time to the steering group in a period of great pressure in the Service.

Empirical research of the kind reported in this book requires the considerable long-term support and cooperation of the participating organizations. We are deeply indebted to all the individuals who helped us carry out the research in our eight Districts. It is certainly invidious to mention only a few names, but nevertheless we thank: Alasdair Liddell, Tim Matthews, Louis Smidt and Cathy Walter of Bloomsbury DHA; Maggie Burnett and Ron Spencer of Bromsgrove and Redditch DHA; Trevor Hallett, Tony Keighley and Peter Woods of Huddersfield DHA; Peter Catchpole of Mid Downs DHA; Andrew Donaldson and Julian Pedley of Milton Keynes DHA; Barbara Young and Deirdre Cunningham of Paddington/Parkside DHA; Richard Cummins of Preston DHA; and Derek Cumming of St Helens and Knowsley DHA.

While this project on managing service change in the NHS was getting off the ground at the Centre for Corporate Strategy and Change, so other related work on strategic change and competitiveness and human resource change was developing. We are grateful to all our Centre colleagues, but particularly to Richard Whipp for dedicating time to join the project steering group and in other ways supporting our efforts to understand public policy change.

At various times we have benefited from conversations and correspondence with colleagues from our wider academic network. Thanks are due to Chris Ham, Armand Hatchuel, David Hunter, John Kimberly, Leif Melin, Christopher Pollitt and Gerard de Pouvourville.

As is ever the case, we the authors are responsible for the accuracy of our data and the soundness of our conclusions.

Abbreviations

A and E	Accident and Emergency
AHA	Area Health Authority
AIDS	Acquired Immune Deficiency Syndrome
ATO	Area Team of Offices
ATU	Assessment and Treatment Unit
BMA	British Medical Association
CE	Commissioning Executive
CEO	Chief Executive Officer
CHC	Community Health Council
CITC	Care in the Community
CLASH	Central London Action on Street Health
CMHT	Community Mental Handicap Team
CNO	Chief Nursing Officer
CPRS	Central Policy Review Staff
CT	Commissioning Team
DA	District Administrator
DCIC	District Control of Infection Committee
DCO	District Commissioning Officer
DCP	District Community Physician
DCPT	Dependencies Care Planning Team
DDU	Drug Dependency Unit
DGH	District General Hospital
DGM	District General Manager
DHA	District Health Authority
DHMC	District Hospital Medical Committee
DHSS	Department of Health and Social Security
DMB	District Management Board
DMO	District Medical Officer
DMT	District Management Team
DNA	District Nurse Adviser
DNO	District Nurse Officer
DPG	District Policy Group
DTO	District Team of Officers
ESMI	Elderly Severely Mentally Infirm
ESRC	Economic and Social Research Council
FMI	Financial Management Initiative
GNP	Gross National Product
GP	General Practitioner
GUM	Genito-Urinary Medicine

HA	Health Authority
HAS	Health Advisory Service
HIV	Human Immunodeficiency Virus
HMAC	Hospital Medical Advisory Committee
HMC	Hospital Management Committee
HRM	Human Resource Management
ICI	Imperial Chemical Industries
ILEA	Inner London Education Authority
JCPT	Joint Care Planning Team
JMC	Joint Medical Committee
LA	Local Authority
MBC	Metropolitan Borough Council
MEC	Medical Executive Committee
MHPT	Mental Handicap Project Team
NA	Nurse Adviser
NAHA	National Association of Health Authorities
NAO	National Audit Office
NDT	National Development Team
NHS	National Health Service
NHSTA	National Health Service Training Authority
NUPE	National Union of Public Employees
OD	Organizational Development
OPCS	Office of Population, Censuses and Surveys
PAC	Public Accounts Committee
PESC	Public Expenditure Survey Committee
PSO	Public Sector Orientation
RAWP	Resource Allocation Working Party
RCN	Royal College of Nursing
RHA	Regional Health Authority
RMI	Resource Management Initiative
RTO	Regional Team of Officers
SAMO	Senior Administrative Medical Officer
SCM	Specialist in Community Medicine
SMOs	Social Movement Organizations
SSD	Social Services Department
STD	Sexually Transmitted Diseases
UCH	University College Hospital
UGC	University Grants Committee
UGM	Unit General Manager
UMB	Unit Management Board
UMT	Unit Management Team
VAT	Value Added Tax

1
Introduction

'Restructuring' was a common experience in the Britain of the 1980s, in both the private and the public sectors. The pace of change seemed to accelerate, and to be driven from the top in a way which would not have seemed possible in the 1970s, when all the talk was of ungovernability, government overload and the power of the periphery. While many of these changes were rooted in the new Thatcherite political economy, at the same time they also addressed some much longer-term problems and issues. Within the public sector in general and the NHS in particular, line management was strengthened throughout the decade, perhaps in reaction against the previous perception that human service agencies should be seen as 'frontline' organizations where relatively junior resource allocators made the real decisions through the operation of discretion and the construction of standard operating procedures.

This book examines the processes of strategic change which have been evident in one key sector of British society, namely the National Health Service. Admired abroad yet criticized at home, the NHS represents a hugely complex test bed for the introduction and study of these change processes. The introduction of general management within the NHS in 1984/5 represents the most visible attempt to managerialize the NHS, yet this reform sits in the context of a much wider raft of measures which became more evident as the decade wore on. Nor was the introduction of general management by itself sufficient to achieve radical change, but only the beginning of a long haul. One estimate was that it would take ten years before general management could be expected to make a major impact. Securing periodic structural changes was increasingly seen as of secondary importance as compared to changing deeper rooted attitudes and behaviours within public sector agencies.

Intellectual Agenda and Key Themes

This book reports final results from a study of the management of strategic service change processes within the National Health Service which took place between 1986 and 1990. The study of management reforms in themselves would have been interesting, and provided a more contained field for investigation, but in our view management changes should not be seen as an end in themselves, but rather as a means to an end. What, in other words, is general management for? The examination of strategic service changes – many of them taking place in waves of long duration – provided one way of connecting the management agenda with actual health care services. Strategic service change is a particularly interesting grey area where both clinicians and the emergent cadre of general managers might be expected to claim territory. At a theoretic level, the project represents an opportunity to extend generic work on patterns of organizational change into the health care sector. Hospitals were neglected in Britain in the 1980s as sites for the study of strategic change processes, although analyses of health care settings in the past have been influential in building organizational theory. For example, the study of an innovative medical school contributed to the formation of an organizational 'life cycle' perspective (Kimberly and Miles, 1980). Hospitals also provided research settings for contingency theorists (de Kervasdoue, 1981), and students of professionalized organizations (Bucher and Stelling, 1977).

We are in essence rekindling a long history of organization theoretic research in health care settings. The questions of the 1990s are of course different and relate more to the study of strategic change. The public sector, like the private sector, is increasingly interested in questions of performance, the ability to manage longer-term change, the impact of the political economy on organizations and the role and nature of leadership (Pettigrew and Whipp, 1991). Other studies (Pettigrew, 1985a) have explored the debate between incremental and discontinuous models of strategic change in the private sector. Kanter (1985, 1989) similarly explores – within a private sector context – processes of renewal in large organizations. Pascale's study (1990) of organizational transformation in the private sector highlights the importance of constructive tension, creativity and adaptability. Grinyer et al.'s studies (1988a, b) of 'Sharp-benders' in the private sector examines why it was that the rate and pace of change varied between firms, and why it was that some succeeded in self-transformation. Hospitals are also interesting and complex research sites and may themselves produce a more generic model that can in turn be used to inform work on the private sector. We indeed attempt to develop such a model.

At the outset the team also identified a number of key themes at a more operational level. The first, as we have indicated above, was to specify the focus of a potentially vast topic in terms of tracking the influence of a particular managerial innovation (general management) on ongoing strategic service change processes. As work went on it became more and more apparent that the introduction of general management itself was but one force in a highly complex situation, and there could be many other reasons which could explain why change processes took the form that they did. The fundamental unit of analysis is thus the strategic change process: all the results reported from the empirical chapters relate to long time frames. Some (such as the closure of asylums) have their roots in the Victorian era when these institutions were constructed; the issue with the shortest time frame is HIV/AIDS but even here it is important to go back to the late 1970s when the early research groups emerged around hepatitis B which were subsequently to shift across to HIV.

Secondly, we decided to focus on 'high change' Districts and include in the sample Districts which were tackling major strategic issues. The sample may not therefore reflect the 'average' District, and one should be careful in extrapolating from the sample to the population. The decision to select 'high change' Districts was made for two reasons. First, questions of managerial capacity to handle change would stand out in much sharper relief in these Districts where changes of major substantive importance were proceeding and in which critical dramas would be likely to emerge which could condense and illuminate wider processes of negotiation. Secondly, such change processes were of great societal interest in their own right: the closure of Victorian asylums and the construction of new District General Hospitals set stern and visible tests for general managers.

Thirdly, we wished to study and identify motors of, and barriers to, strategic change. We wanted to interrogate the case material to identify facilitating and inhibiting factors. What drove change and what prevented it? This is a much wider question than assessing the impact of general management on change, as general management may play a positive role in some case studies, yet a marginal or even a negative role in others. We therefore need a conceptual framework which will alert us to a much wider array of potential sources of change.

Fourthly, we wanted to explore the skills associated with change management. While we expected great variability, some of the reasons for a faster pace of forward movement could relate to process as well as structure. Action could play a role as well as context. Such skills may either be explicit change management skills, or more implicit and intuitive, but are important to track and to analyse. Of course we should not assume that in such a pluralist organization as the NHS general managers represent the only source of change, and in some of the cases the role of clinical product champions was found to be crucial.

As time went on the explanation of local variability in the achievement of strategic service change seemed more and more interesting. Why was it that the rate and pace of change varied so much either between localities processing the same issue or within the same locality but across different issues? Why did closure processes in asylums seem to generate their own pace and personality? Why was it that within the same DHA one issue could receive favoured status and another be regarded as largely intractable? The derivation of a more general model of change (the metaphor of receptive and non-receptive contexts which we develop in Chapter 9) was the outcome of this increasing concern to develop more generic thoughts across the mass of case material.

Methodology

The project has contained a major empirical element, although the empirical analyses were linked with more theoretical material. A four cell

matrix was used to select issues and Districts divided into service base
(acute sector *vs* priority group) and the status of the issue in terms of
growth *vs* retrenchment. A case study methodology has been used,
although one which is more longitudinal, processual and comparative in
nature than conventional single case work. The derivation of a plurality
of perspectives through the interviewing of a wide range of stakeholders
has been emphasized. Historical antecedents and the chronology of
change are considered vital. The fundamental design choice in this study
has been to conduct intensive analyses of a relatively few cases (about 400
interviews were conducted in the course of the study, supplemented with
attendance at meetings, examination of archival material and informal
observation), rather than the more superficial analyses of a larger
number. Such are the complexities both of the strategic change issues and
of the host systems that such superficial analyses would be in danger of
missing key components of the explanation. The Appendix contains fuller
details of the sample and of the methodology.

Plan of the Book

The book moves from the theoretical to the empirical, and then back to
the theoretical. In Chapter 2 we review a range of different literature
which has been used to study organizational change processes and explain
why an approach based on the study of organizational transitions and
adaptations is to be preferred. In Chapter 3 the focus switches to the
British political economy of the 1980s and the top-down pressure that has
been evident to secure restructuring within the public sector. Many of the
themes apparent in the NHS are paralleled in the higher ranks of the
British Civil Service or in the world of local government. The question of
whether it is possible to restructure deep behaviours within institutions or
whether this is an overambitious and essentially illusory goal is addressed.

Next comes a suite of empirical chapters (Chapters 4–8). While each
addresses a different change issue, the format is similar, namely an
explication of some of the analytic themes embedded in the cases,
followed by individual case study material, comparative case study
analysis and finally more general reflections. Each of the empirical
chapters seems to throw up some distinctive theoretical issues, as well as
more general ones. The final chapter (Chapter 9) develops a more generic
model for understanding strategic service change based on the metaphor
of receptive and non-receptive contexts and speculates about its potential
relevance for the new agenda of the 1990s.

2

Understanding the Process of Organizational Change

In the Britain of the 1980s, restructuring processes were evident in the public and private sectors alike, but nowhere were such processes of strategic change more apparent than in the National Health Service. Strong top-down commitment to change challenged the cultural continuity (although combined with recurrent changes to formal structure) apparent since 1948. A common theme was the perception politically that public sector management was underperforming and that concepts, models and indeed personnel should be exported from the private sector into health care. This politically generated shift obviously has had implications in academic analysis, although the immediate importance of this policy based agenda perhaps acted to disguise some important backstage shifts that were proceeding in organizational and management theory.

Organizational, managerial and service change processes alike have emerged as key empirical themes of the NHS in the 1980s, but these are themes which have been highly action-driven and much less subject to analysis or reflection. In part this reflected the action orientation of the new order, in part also the legacy of the public administration literature with its insistence on difference, its ghetto status and its reluctance to generate theory which had made it difficult to tie any understanding of change processes apparent within the NHS into broader literature. The immediate preoccupation was with the process of sectoral transfer – which was hotly debated.

One function of this chapter will be to address the question of sectoral transfer. We will argue that concepts derived from the private sector should not be mechanistically trundled across the sectoral divide (as significant differences remain between the two sectors particularly in the degree of politicization and the power and social position of the professionals), but also that a wider theoretic openness may illuminate change processes occurring within the NHS. There are therefore similarities as well as differences. Interest in organizational culture as a shaper of organizational performance, for example, originated in private sector analyses in the early 1980s but has subsequently found resonance in analyses of the NHS. We will secondly explore the literature which can move the discussion on from a relatively narrow and limited debate about sectoral base.

Subsequent chapters will examine a range of strategic change processes empirically, but there is also a more theoretic question of how such change processes are to be understood, and in particular there is an important and developing literature in the field of organization theory which needs to be accessed. There is no shortage of theory in the field and indeed the choice of perspective is sometimes bewildering, as this chapter will explore. In the first section below we outline our starting position, which represents a plea for a more process based and 'contextual' mode of research where the organization is seen as embedded in its social, cultural, political and historical context. The following section outlines the introduction of general management and a third section pulls together and reviews various streams of literature. Finally, further implications for the development of our own theoretical perspective and methodology are discussed.

Analysing Change Processes in Context

In a broad review of the literature on business and organizational change made elsewhere (Pettigrew, 1985a), the point is made that, with a few limited and noteworthy exceptions (Berg, 1979; Kervasdoue and Kimberly, 1979), much research on organizational change is ahistorical, aprocessual and acontextual in character. There are remarkably few studies of change that allow the change process to reveal itself in any kind of substantially temporal or contextual manner. Where the change project is treated as the unit of analysis the focus is often on a single event or a set of discrete episodes somehow separate from the immediate and more distant antecedents that give those events form, meaning and substance. Such episodic views of change not only treat innovations as if they had a clear beginning and a clear end, but also, where they limit themselves to snapshot rather than time series data, fail to provide data on the mechanisms and processes through which changes are created. Studies of organizational change are, therefore, often preoccupied with the intricacies of narrow *changes* rather than the holistic and dynamic analysis of *changing*.

The starting point for our analysis of change in the NHS is the notion that having 'correct' policies for change is not sufficient; an organizational capacity to change is also necessary. Indeed a fundamental problem in the 1970s was the development within the NHS of service policies for massive change, without building up the organizational capacity to translate this ambitious change agenda into practice. Perhaps this perception of 'implementation failure' has fuelled attempts in the 1980s to reduce perceived immobilisme in the NHS. For example, achieving change in psychiatric service provision requires massive adjustments to the structure and ethos of interorganizational planning and liaison. The managerial skills needed to effect such shifts certainly do not readily fit with simplistic conceptions of rational process and top-down directives but are likely to engage a broader range of political skills.

Thus, theoretically sound and practically useful research on change should involve the continuous interplay between ideas about the context of change, the process of change and the content of change together with skill in regulating the relations between the three (Pettigrew, 1985a, 1990). Each of these three areas and their interconnections contain a series of research themes and issues.

Content refers to the particular area or areas of transformation under study. Thus in sequence, or more likely in parallel, a District could be seeking to contract acute services while expanding the community based services for priority groups. The content of change can also be classified according to a set of more abstract features which may affect adoptability: some changes will be radical, others incremental; some technological (where there is some evidence of premature diffusion) and others centred on changes to roles (where there may be important barriers to rapid diffusion). There are links here with issue analysis (Hall et al., 1975), where it is argued that the nature of the organizational response may be shaped by the characteristics of the issue that is being processed.

Analytically, it is helpful to distinguish between inner and outer contexts for change. Outer context refers to the national economic, political and social context for a DHA as well as the perception, action and interpretation of policies and events at national and Regional levels in the NHS. The changing national political economy has clearly exerted major top-down pressure on the NHS in the 1980s, and these themes will be developed in the next chapter. Social movements and long-term professionalization or deprofessionalization processes also form important aspects of the outer context. Inner context, by contrast, refers to the ongoing strategy, structure, culture, management and political process of the District which help shape the processes through which ideas for change proceed. Perhaps a weakness of much of the generic organizational change literature is an over-reliance on the inner context, which has led to a neglect of wider issues.

The process of change refers to the actions, reactions and interactions of the various interested parties as they negotiate around proposals for change. The strongest material is that which can tie this process down to observed or documented behaviour in context, as opposed to general statements of attitude. Each of the different stakeholders may, of course, provide a distinctive account of the process of change. Broadly speaking, the What of change is encapsulated under the label 'content', much of the Why of change is derived from an analysis of 'inner and outer context', and the How of change can be understood from an analysis of 'process'.

The neglect of context and the role of powerful groups within it has produced a situation in which myths abound about rational problem solving processes and linear implementation. While some recent research in a number of different disciplines has moved away from classical models of rational and formal long-range planning and of non-problematic top-down implementation, this research has still to filter through many of the textbooks used on teaching programmes. But in our view change should be seen as a consequence not just of problem solving processes, nor of the weight of technical evidence and analysis, nor of managerial drives for efficiency and effectiveness, though on the surface the custom and practice of persuasion may dictate that initiatives for change are publicly justified in such ways. Rather, changes are also a product of processes which recognize historical and continuing struggles for power and status as motive forces, and one needs to consider the *'cui bono?'* question: how do interest groups and individuals gain or lose as proposed changes surface, receive attention, are consolidated and implemented or fall from grace before they ever get off the ground?

However, it is not our aim simply to substitute rational linear theories with political process theories. The task is more eclectic and rather to identify the varied causes of change, to assess against the evidence alternative accounts such as rational, incremental, political and cultural views of process, quests for efficiency and power, the role of exceptional people and extreme circumstance, the untidiness of chance, unintended consequences and counterproductive actions.

Such an eclectic and processual view requires an ability to handle different and perhaps competing explanations. Analysts need to be sensitive to both continuity and change, action and structure, endogenous and exogenous factors, and the role of chance and surprise as well as purposeful action. In the view of the present authors, and indeed in the theoretical writing and empirical work of others (Normann, 1977; Pfeffer, 1981; Hardy, 1985; Greenwood and Hinings, 1986; Wilson et al., 1986; Johnson, 1987), a view of process which combines rational, political and cultural elements has real power in explaining organizational continuity and change.

The interest in culture directs attention to sources of coherence and consistency in organizational life, to the dominating beliefs or ideologies which provide the systems of meaning and interpretation which filter in and out environmental and intra-organizational signals. The recognition that culture can shape and not merely reflect organizational power relationships directs attention both to the ground rules which structure the political process inside DHAs, and the assumptions and interests which powerful groups shield and lesser groups may only with fortitude challenge.

The acts and processes associated with politics as the management of meaning represent conceptually the overlap between a concern with the political and cultural analyses of organizations. A central concept linking political and cultural analyses essential to the understanding of continuity and change is legitimacy. The management of meaning refers to a process of symbol construction and value-use designed to create legitimacy for one's own ideas, actions and demands and to delegitimate the demands of one's opponents. If one sees major change processes at least partially as a contest about ideas and rationalities between individuals and groups, then the mechanisms used to legitimate and delegitimate particular ideas or broader ideologies are crucial. Equally, the resolution of such contests about ideas needs to be sensitive to questions of power and control in the organization. Structures, cultures and strategies are not just neutral, functional, constructs connectable to some system need such as efficiency or adaptability; those constructs are viewed as capable of protecting the interests of dominant groups. As Normann has so aptly put it, 'the only way to bring about lasting change and to foster an ability to deal with new situations is by influencing the conditions that determine the interpretation of situations and the regulation of ideas' (1977, p. 161).

The analytical challenge is to connect up the content, contexts and processes of change over time to explain the differential achievement of change objectives. Perhaps the most critical connection is the way actors in the change process mobilize the contexts around them and in so doing provide legitimacy for change. Changes in the outer context can also be mobilized to fashion change. Thus John Harvey Jones used the rapidly changing economic conditions facing ICI in the late 1970s to help win support for a new company strategy (Pettigrew, 1985a). Indeed securing a better understanding of how the environment was changing was a key part of the management of strategic change in such private sector settings as Jaguar Cars (Pettigrew and Whipp, 1991). The contexts in which change operate are not inert or objective entities. Just as managers and other actors perceive and construct their own versions of those contexts, so do they subjectively select their own versions of the environment around them and seek to reorder the District change agenda to meet perceived challenges and constraints.

In our view, this analytical approach could provide a novel framework for researching the problem of management of change in the NHS. We now test the distinctive and additive character of our approach against an extensive but still selective review of the different literatures.

Understanding Public Sector Management

First we intend to explore the literature on the introduction of general management and the rise of a managerial ideology sometimes seen as associated with its introduction. We then consider the question which has exercised much of the literature in the 1980s – is sound organization theory-generic or sector-specific? – before suggesting that this may be a partial and perhaps unhelpful debate.

General Management and the New Managerialism

Historically, hospitals have been seen as almost an ideal typical case of the professionalized organization (Bucher and Stelling, 1977), characterized by shifting and organic professional segments largely autonomous of a marginal administration. The whole nature of health care systems came under challenge with the introduction of general management in the mid

1980s, with a strengthening of line management vis-à-vis the professionals. Initially central government was also anxious to increase the proportion of general managers drawn into the NHS from the private sector, although such attempts met with very limited success.

Little research was commissioned on the introduction of general management, and such as there was often focused on the renegotiation of roles within particular localities as a way of getting a practical handle on these complex change processes. So the empirical focus was often on changes to the roles of professional groups such as nurses (Glennerster et al., 1986; Strong and Robinson, 1988) or doctors – Harrison et al. (1989a) found little change in doctor–manager relations after the introduction of general management. Sometimes the analysis was at a broader District level where the earlier pluralist assumptions could still come into play. On the basis of earlier (pre general management) case study analysis in seven districts, Thompson (1987) argued that the NHS is characterized by a number of powerful occupational coalitions whose interactions can produce conflict as they struggle for scarce resources and speculated about the possibility of a new general managerial coalition emerging. The negotiation of managerial roles was also a theme of the Templeton College DGM tracer study (Stewart et al., 1987a, b), but this analysis was not linked to the study of specific and issue based managerial behaviour through time. Harrison et al. (1989a) adopted a multi-case study design in their attempt to assess the impact of general management, but early analysis conflated data across the sites and did not attempt to uncover local logics within particular sites, although the dominant tone was one of scepticism about major change.

Other writers have however taken a rather broader view in trying to unpick the rise of general management in the public services, for example, Petchey's speculative and critical piece (1986) attempted to locate the ideological roots of general management in the changing political economy. General management, in this view, should not be seen simply as a technique, but as the expression of the rise of a new ideas system which accorded special status to 'managers' as an elite, decision making group within society. General management was a change imposed by the centre, not only frustrated by the performance of professionals and anxious to import private sector models, but also attracted to a new managerial ideology:

> General management rests on the argument that there are profound similarities between all large organizations, regardless of their particular activities, workforce or clientele. Anywhere and everywhere you look, so it is claimed, much the same practical problems occur, problems which are most effectively solved by a common set of managerial methods. Every effective business or service organization needs firm leadership, the systematic specification of goals, the detailed measurement of individual and group performance and a battery of rewards and punishments. (Strong and Robinson, 1990)

For Pollitt (1990, p. 83), a particular subset of managerial ideas – 'neo-

Taylorism' after the original American writer who favoured formal, rationalistic and measurement-orientated management methods – characterized attempts to restructure public sector services in the 1980s as much in Whitehall as in the NHS. The rise to prominence of such an ideas system across different public services could be seen within this analysis as an ideological movement, from which there were clear winners (including the emergent general managerial function) and losers. Signs and symptoms of neo-Taylorism include recourse to such measures as: tight cash limits and cash planning; staff cuts; the introduction of performance indicators which stress economy and efficiency; staff appraisal and merit pay systems; more budgetary devolution to line managers; concrete short-term targets; and a (so far largely rhetorical) emphasis on responsiveness to consumers. Certainly, such a managerial reform movement could be seen as incorporating only a very limited set of ideas about how to run organizations. For Pollitt, therefore, the key question is that of the degree of appropriate sectoral transfer, and his critique of the appropriateness of such private sector models for the management of public services implies the need to develop alternative models, the leading candidate perhaps emerging as the 'Public Service Orientation' model which was developed as a way of ensuring commitment to high quality services which reflected customer and citizen (not the same category at all) preferences and values.

Organization and Management Theory: Generic or Sectorally Specific?

The extent to which generic models of management can be developed has formed a long running debate throughout the 1980s, as the last section has highlighted. Famously, and in his 1983 Report which led to the introduction of general management in the NHS, Sir Roy Griffiths argued that the differences that existed between private and public sector organizations were much overstated. Such a view has, however, been far more influential in the policy making process than in the research community. Some have questioned whether a generic model can be developed even within the private sector (Hales, 1986), given the immense diversity of work. Any contextualist analysis would a priori be sceptical about such attempts to develop abstract and highly general models, divorced from their work setting. Others have seen public services as a separate form of work organization. Thus Ackroyd, Hughes and Soothill (1989) argue that public services have sufficient in common to be treated as a relatively homogeneous group, where management style (and typically managers have been recruited from the ranks of professionals) revolves around the residual role of defending customary forms of provision rather than securing major change (so much the worse for them, some might argue), although not much evidence from health care settings after the introduction of general management is considered in their analysis.

Analyses of particular functions come up with similar reservations. As far as strategic management is concerned (Smith and Perry, 1985), a range of differences have been identified between public and private organizations (such as openness, multiple publics and symbolic rather than substantive government policies) which complicate the task for public sector strategic managers. Pollitt (1990) supplies a long list of reasons for why, in his view, the characteristics of public sector organizations remain very different from those apparent in the private sector. For example, users of public services are not only consumers but also possess an important additional role as citizens.

In part this is a disaggregation problem. A major argument for difference is the greater degree of politicization apparent in the public sector, yet such differences may be expressed on a spectrum rather than through a binary divide. There are for example parts of the private sector (pharmaceuticals, oil) which also operate in a complex political environment and where the lobbying of government ministers is a key task. The closure of large plants in single industry towns may have parallels with hospital closure processes and also pose difficult political issues. Nor should we assume that these sectoral categories are static and that health care organizations will always be located in the public sector: the American health care system has always exhibited a major private sector element; British long-term residential care is now located more in the private than the public sector; the voluntary sector has expanded its service provision role; and the setting up of NHS self-governing trusts has been justified in terms of the relaxation of top-down control mechanisms within the public sector and the mimicking of market based mechanisms.

In part this is also a question of which bodies of knowledge are being transferred. As Harrow and Willcocks argue (1990), the highly formalistic models of management being exported to the public sector have themselves been undermined by private sector research (Mintzberg, 1973; Kotter, 1982) which paints a very different portrait of the manager as a more intuitive decision maker, with complex tasks, and operating through personal contacts and 'soft' information, taken at a hectic pace.

One 'halfway house' response has been the development of a public organization or public management approach which is more open to generic theory, while still alert to the dangers of mechanistic transfer from the private to the public sector. Stewart and Ranson (1988) developed their 'Public Sector Orientation' (PSO) model which borrowed from the private sector literature a stress on 'strong cultures' to emphasize the delivery of high quality and consumer-responsive services. In some respects (such as management in a highly politicized environment), there could be examples of excellence in the public sector which could be transferred to the private. Gunn's development of this position (1989) argues that there are processes and skills generic to management (such as agenda setting or influencing skills), which become more similar the higher one goes in the managerial hierarchy.

From an American 'public organization theory' perspective, Rainey (1983) also notes a convergence of the literature on public bureaucracies and generic organizations and comments on the resulting increased interest in questions of structure, behaviour and management within the public sector. At the same time, organizational analysts working in public sector agencies would need to explore the impact of such factors as the absence of economic markets for their products and the political and institutional forces in their environments.

Within the British context, there are at least three possible sources for commonality which could underpin the development of a more generic approach. The first concerns generic issues (such as human resource management) which are important in both sectors. The second refers to a common context, such as changes in the national political economy, which have forced the question of restructuring in both the private and public sectors. The third refers to common managerial and organizational processes and competencies such as strategy making, networking and political skills. There is both an intellectual challenge to link these possible sources of commonality together and a pragmatic one of building the capacity to manage particular changes involving these three elements.

It is, of course, understandable that so much attention should have been focused on this genericist/distinctivist debate, given top-down efforts in the 1980s to remodel public sector institutions. But in a way it is a partial and perhaps unhelpful debate, which pays insufficient attention to the development during the 1980s of a richer organization theoretic base which is itself often critical of the formalistic models which have found such favour in the public sector.

Our conclusion is that there are both differences and similarities evident between the two sectors which need to be disaggregated in finer detail than has been possible in this chapter. Up to the mid 1980s, the dominant problem was that of parochialism and isolation within the public sector; since the mid 1980s the problem has been the overmechanistic transfer of concepts from the private to the public sectors. There are, however, sufficient similarities to make the application of a broader range of approaches to organizational analysis within the public sector potentially fruitful, and indeed some of them originated in public (frequently hospitals) as well as private sector settings. The public sector may also provide learning for the private sector, certainly as far as handling politicians and powerful professionals is concerned.

Some Other Perspectives

We now review a number of different streams of literature which have been developed within organization theory as descriptive models of patterns of organizational decision making. Most of them question in some way the formalistic and rationalistic assumptions made in neo-Taylorian models, and are more alert to questions of organizational process. Interestingly, all of them have been applied across sectors, and frequently public sector settings have spawned as much work as private sector settings. Public agencies are to a much lesser extent than in the neo-Taylorian perspective classified within these streams of literature as residual, anomalous or as laggards. Additionally, although there are now some powerful private sector results, these have proved more difficult to transfer across. The danger is one of public sector fantasies about private sector management models which are not borne out by empirical evidence.

A Presumption of Incrementalism: Change within Professionalized Bureaucracies

Our starting point is that health care organizations have classically been seen as professionalized bureaucracies (Mintzberg, 1990) where there can be strong resistance to innovation and radical change, given that organizational structures are designed to deliver given programmes in stable environments, rather than to create problem solving structures or to create new programmes for unanticipated needs. Under these conditions, it would be expected that the pattern of decision making in health care organizations would be highly incremental in nature (Lindblom, 1959), as successive negotiations take place through a process of partisan mutual adjustment and as a plurality of interest groups operate in decision making arenas. Some work on strategy making in private sector settings (Quinn, 1980, 1982) has used this incrementalist perspective to argue that strategic change should best be seen as 'muddling through with a purpose', through a continuous, evolving and consensus building approach. The received wisdom therefore is that change will take place through successive, limited and negotiated shifts; were we to find a pattern of radical strategic change then this might indicate that important new developments had taken place within health care organizations.

The question then arises: when does this presumption of incrementalism not hold? Certainly there is some evidence from private sector work that organizations go through periods of strategic change as well as continuity. Mintzberg (1978) suggested that strategic changes tended to come in brief spurts as received paradigms changed – interspersed with long periods of continuity – a perspective which was broadly confirmed by Pettigrew's (1985a) study of strategic change processes in ICI, which found periods of incremental adjustment, interspersed with periodic revolutionary change.

The incrementalist perspective has historically been well represented, perhaps even dominant, in studies of decision making in health care settings. Hunter's analysis (1980) of the allocation of development funds found policy maintenance to be more important than policy change, as challenges to the powerful acute sector specialities were rarely successful and the rhetoric of change did not translate into shifts in the allocation of resources. Such change as did occur was rare, of short duration, and the product of a set of political relationships which operated against radical change through norms of 'fair shares' and the allocation of more to those that already had most. Some have even argued that central policies for change are not always implemented precisely because policy makers do not intend such commitments to be taken at face value, but rather as politically and socially approved tokens of concern:

> the reasons why some policies are not implemented is that no one ever expected them to be. Acts are passed or ministerial speeches made to satisfy some party pressure or some awkward interest group, but civil servants know that they need not strain themselves too hard to achieve results. The policy is symbolic. (Korman and Glennerster, 1985, p. 7)

Central government thus responds to transient political pressure by devising policies with impossible implementation requirements for the field, but although political pressure may be enough to raise an issue up the agenda, it may be insufficient to keep it there, so that issue succession quickly develops (Downs, 1972; Hogwood, 1987).

The advantage claimed for incrementalism lay in its realism and descriptive validity: this is how organizations really did behave in spite of the formal and rationalistic rhetoric. However, recent work has questioned whether the descriptive validity of incrementalism is as strong in the new conditions of the 1980s. Between the 1940s and the 1970s, in retrospect, there was a long but unusual period of continuing growth in public agencies, but the 1980s have witnessed increasing attempts – not always successful – at cost compression which, over time, may force a move beyond 'decrementalism' or untargeted across-the-board cuts towards more radical reconfigurations.

For example, changes to the rate support grant – the source of central government financial support to local authorities – have been used by central government as a means of increasing cost pressures on local authorities. Crispin and Marslen-Wilson's study (1986) of the impact of such financial changes on the education service found significant changes in the cast of decision makers, with treasurers and central senior local politicians increasing their influence over service departments. Within the NHS, Haywood and Ranade's study (1986) of two Regional Health Authorities found an increased tendency, in the light of sustained financial pressure, to look at the reallocation of base budgets. The New York fiscal crisis of the late 1970s represents an extreme case, yet not only were decision makers able to vary the degree of retrenchment between programmes but also to accelerate 'efficiency improvement' measures (Brecher and Horton, 1985). We may need, therefore, to go beyond incrementalist perspectives in order to understand the behaviour apparent in health care organizations of the 1980s.

Diffusion-based Models of Change

In the 1960s, some key works on diffusion processes in both industrial and health care settings assumed great influence (Rogers, 1962, Coleman et al., 1966). The key problems within this perspective are to distinguish the characteristics of adopters of innovations from non-adopters, and to explain different rates of diffusion in different groups or markets. The perspective sprang from early work on the innovation adoption decisions of farmers, and then transferred to the decisions of doctors. Much of the original work was highly ahistorical and acontextual in perspective, being narrowly focused on the decision to adopt a particular innovation, although there has subsequently been a significant broadening of perspective (Rogers, 1983). There is now much greater attention to the way in which the prehistory could influence the adoption decision, and a readiness to see the communication process less as a linear and unidirectional activity and more as a convergent process, and a recognition that organizational innovation processes could take very different forms from individual innovation adoption decisions.

So diffusion-based research has been rapidly evolving: a good way of illustrating this point is to compare three sequential works produced by the same author on private sector innovation processes (Walton, 1975, 1980, 1987). In 1975 Walton had highlighted the social and organizational dimension to diffusion, examining the fates of early work efforts to spread work innovations throughout a dozen companies which had pioneered them, and finding an extraordinarily high failure rate. While pilot experiments were often successful within their own sites, they also often generated tension across the wider organization which would then resist the spread of the innovation. One implication might even be that successful, radical innovations could paradoxically generate the most resistance. This early work also highlighted the importance of the choices made by diffusion agents and potential adopters in determining the rate of spread of the innovation out from the original site. Walton's later analysis (1980) of the success and failure of innovative work structures in four plants emphasized the role of choice and of process. Yet Walton's latest work (1987) – a cross-national study of differential innovation rates in the shipping industry – could explain differences almost without reference to skill in managing the process. There was rather a rediscovery of the role of institutions in the innovation process, especially in their ability to shape learning mechanisms and to create cohesion or fragmentation among a variety of stakeholders.

Health care settings have also provided a major field for diffusion research. Coleman et al.'s (1966) classic study on the decision among doctors to adopt a new drug uncovered the interpersonal networks at work through which subjective evaluations of an innovation are transmitted, and suggested the role that 'opinion formers' could play in take off. Many other studies have examined the factors associated with the hospital adoption of medical technologies. Studies have often been inconclusive: Becker (1970b) found, for instance, that the public health officials taking the lead in the adoption of measles immunization were young, urban, liberal and cosmopolitan, while the pioneers in the adoption of diabetes screening were old, rural, conservative and parochial. Such cumulative findings as do exist suggest that early adoption by hospitals is associated with large size, the existence of teaching and research facilities, hospital ownership of the technology and urban location (Renshaw et al., 1990).

While diffusion research continued into the 1980s, it perhaps fell away as interest switched to top-down restructuring as the dominant motor of institutional change. Indeed Renshaw et al.'s (1990) criticism of the diffusion perspective was that it assumed a relatively stable set of environmental and organizational conditions. Stocking (1985), however, used the concept of 'product champions' to explain why some health care innovations were adopted, although not in a fully processual manner.

Institutional theory is multi-faceted, complex and rapidly developing (Zucker, 1983, 1988), but one strand of argument is closely related to a diffusion model and suggests that organizational structures change for normative or memetic reasons as decision makers feel impelled to move closer to received institutional norms or fashions, as certain structural arrangements come to be seen as more modern, professional or accredited. Hinings and Greenwood (1988) use this institutionalist perspective to analyse the rise of corporate organizational forms in British local government in the late 1960s through the support of 'authoritative bodies' such as professional associations or 'leading edge' authorities. Under these circumstances new ideas can 'landslide', so that the speedy adoption of new organizational forms across an organizational population is possible.

While the 1980s were dominated by an interest in top-down strategic change processes, diffusion-based models may re-emerge in the 1990s. Diffusion-based models of change are considered in greater depth in the next chapter. Current policy initiatives in the NHS, such as the roll-out of the Resource Management Initiative, the Localities Project where 'leading edge' DHAs are to experience a faster pace of change, and the evolutionary approach to NHS Trusts, imply a return to diffusion-based models of change where the construction of effective diffusion networks is critical for success. The selection of such sites may depend on 'soft' as well as quantitative data. The initial RMI evaluation (Buxton et al., 1989) clearly pointed to the need to consider the capacity for change management, and successful introduction of RMI was found to be associated both with the presence of powerful 'local champions' and also more diffuse changes to organizational structure and information systems.

Contingency Theoretic Approaches and Organizational Form

Contingency theoretic approaches flourished in the late 1960s and early 1970s, essentially based on the comparative analysis of formal organizational structures in both industrial settings (Pugh, 1973) and such public sector settings as local government (Greenwood et al., 1980) and the relationship of such organizations with external environments. Similar approaches were also applied to the study of hospitals. In America, the Cornell hospital study examined the extent to which variation in the rate of adoption of innovations in medical technology could be accounted for by variations in the organizational structure of American hospitals (Gordon and Fisher, 1975). The frequent recourse to a global 'score' which then became the dependent variable to be explained has been roundly criticized (Downs and Mohr, 1976) for lumping together incommensurable apples and oranges.

Positivistically based, and often using modelling techniques such as multiple regression, contingency theoretic studies sought to establish general associations between the characteristics of organizations (in particular the propensity to innovate), their structures and the environments in which they operated. Apart from a more consistent finding that size was positively related to the rate of innovation (the meaning of which was difficult to interpret as size could be a proxy variable for many other factors), the failure to secure robust findings eroded the value of these studies. Increasingly, contingency theorists retreated from purely structural perspectives and adopted a broader viewpoint. Aiken and Hage (1971) found the rate of innovation in human service organizations to be associated with such non-structural factors as prehistory, the rate of financial growth and the strength of the interorganizational network. Hage and Dewar's study of innovation in American health and welfare agencies (1973) found value-based predictors to have greater power than measures of structure, in particular the values of the 'behavioural elite' of strategic decision makers.

The critique of contingency theory highlights its failure to consider the social and cultural settings of organizations. For example, even formal measures of hospital structure were found to be very difficult to transfer from American settings to France in an attempt to replicate the Cornell study there (Kervasdoue, 1981). Nor does this perspective always take sufficient account of the meanings which actors attach to their actions despite the argument that decision makers retain some ability to screen out environmental signals, to define their own environments and to exert strategic choice (Child, 1972). However, it does force a consideration of the ways in which environmental pressures and opportunities could affect organizational responses, and hence acts as a counterweight to purely subjective interpretations. Finally, a great advantage of contingency theory lies in its argument that there is no one best way, but rather that the functional organizational structure is associated with the nature of the task being undertaken. While bureaucratic styles of management may indeed be appropriate under conditions of stable mass production, the processing of highly uncertain workflows calls for different kinds of organizations with stronger lateral communication mechanisms, developmental and learning capacity (this argument has obvious resonance for the discussion of HIV/AIDS provision in Chapter 5). This attempt to define different organizational models for conditions of certainty and uncertainty has been a recurrent theme in the literature from Burns and Stalker's (1961) classic distinction between organic and mechanistic organizational forms, through to Rosa Moss Kanter's (1985) analogous divide between segmented and integrated forms.

Management of Strategic Change

There is increasing interest in the public sector in moving from a focus on 'policy' to one of 'strategy' (implying a greater concern with securing action around the espoused policies). But what do we mean by 'strategy'? Often 'strategy' is seen in highly top-down, rational and formal terms, but other writers, such as Mintzberg (1990), have been trying to extend the intellectual vocabulary of the strategy literature in a process direction. Mintzberg develops the concept, by contrast, of an 'emergent strategy' (rather than the standard idea of a deliberate strategy) whereby a series of actions converge into patterns. They may become deliberate if the pattern is recognized and then legitimized by senior management, but that is *post hoc* rationalization of what has emerged organically ('a pattern in a stream of decisions'). Other forms of strategy fall between these two extremes, and combine deliberation and control with flexibility and organizational learning. For example, in an umbrella strategy senior management may set out some broad guidelines, leaving specifics to others lower down in the organization. In a process strategy, management may control the process of strategy formation – concerning itself with the design of the structure, staffing, development of procedures – while leaving the content to others. Mintzberg argues that distinct periods of stability and of change can be identified in organizations, and that major shifts in strategic reorientation happen rarely and in quantum leaps, particularly in large, established, mass-production organizations. In more creative organizations a somewhat different and more balanced pattern of change and stability may be apparent through cycles of convergence and divergence.

Clearly then there are different perspectives on what strategy really is. Johnson (1987) has distinguished between different views of the strategic management process which reflect more general distinctions in social science: (i) a rationalistic view of strategic management in which strategy is seen as the outcome of a sequential, planned, search for optimal solutions to defined problems, with implementation following on from the decisions made about such problems; (ii) an adaptive or incremental view of strategic management which evolves in an additive pattern; and (iii) an interpretive view in which strategy is seen as the product of individual or collective sense making. The emphasis within this interpretive perspective is on the cognitive and symbolic bases of interpretation.

We need also to consider the growing body of more empirical literature on the ability of organizations to manage strategic change. For example, Pettigrew and Whipp's (1991) study of private sector firms found that in order to achieve competitive success, the higher performing firms (drawn across a number of sectors) were characterized by a number of key features. In addition to the linkage between strategic and operational change and the nature of human resources as assets and liabilities, perhaps three of the factors identified can be thought to have most prima facie relevance for health care work.

1 Environmental Assessment　It seemed insufficient for companies to regard this task as a purely technical exercise, but rather the need was for organizations to become open learning systems so that environmental assessment did not remain the preserve of a sole function or a single manager. Nor did such assessment occur via isolated acts, but rather strategy creation emerged from the way in which an organization, at various levels, acquired, interpreted and processed information about its environment.

2 Leading Change　There seemed no universal rules as to who emerged as leader, but rather the reverse, as leadership was found to be highly context-sensitive, clearly relating to the circumstances facing the firm. The critical leadership tasks in managing change were more fragmentary and incremental than the popular images of 'business heroism' allow, and could involve action by people at every level of the business. Moving directly to bold action could be costly, and instead the prior need was found to be building a climate for change.

3 Coherence in the Management of Change　This last factor in managing change for competitive success was found to be at once the most abstract and wide-ranging of the central features, given that the requirements for coherence arose from the implications of the others. There has to be coherence of purpose and belief among the senior management team, even though individual styles and methods differ. Human Resource Management initiatives, for example, should produce apposite knowledge bases which match the requirements of strategy. Given the scope of the actions implied by the preceding factors, the ability to manage a series of interrelated and emergent changes (often in parallel and in sequence) is vital.

Within the public sector, there has historically been a greater emphasis on 'policy' (content) than 'strategy' (content plus process), but there is now increasing interest in the application of the strategy literature to health care settings. A perception of NHS general managers as potential 'strategists' was developed in Parston (1986), and is closely associated with the writings of Tom Evans (Stocking, 1987). Perhaps in a reaction against the policy overload and lack of organizational capacity apparent in the NHS of the 1970s, the centrepiece of this argument (Evans, 1987a, b) is that in order to achieve a high rate of service change (particularly retrenchment-based change) policy development is by itself insufficient but must be combined with systems innovations which equip the organization to handle an accelerated pace of change. The role of senior management, therefore, is to develop a coherent style which can lead to strategies for change across the organization.

Organizational Cultures and Cultural Change

Alongside the introduction of hardnosed and measurement-orientated management styles in the 1980s arose a very different – but less immediately visible – focus on organizational culture and cultural change. The perceived failure of recurrent structural reorganizations in the NHS drew attention to the deeper question of organizational culture as a background shaper of belief systems. The belief system of the Civil Service for example, according to Metcalfe and Richards (1987), operated to deprecate the possibility that any politically imposed change would stick.

Cultural models of organizational change are of long standing (Pettigrew, 1979) but became increasingly influential in the 1980s in analyses of both private and public sector change processes. Such analyses implied a return to such topics as language systems, beliefs, rituals, symbols and organizational 'sagas'. Sometimes this perspective was joined to the performance orientation also characteristic of the 1980s: so organizations which were 'value-driven' (Peters and Waterman, 1982) were seen as more likely to be successful, and those which shared strong and cohesive cultures were more likely to be flexible and cooperative (Deal and Kennedy, 1982). Transformational leadership was invoked as a source of 'culture busting', as in the case of British Airways. Similar culture building initiatives were launched in the NHS, with general managers being cast as change agents ('the Health Service Managers of today are in a new and important sense leaders of the organization and custodians of its values and standards', NHSTA, 1986). Programmatic change strategies (such as the Total Quality Management wave) represent one attempt to switch cultures in the direction of quality based values.

A key question therefore is the extent to which organizational cultures are in any sense manageable (Pettigrew, 1990). Schein (1985) for instance has taken a plastic view of culture:

> the further I got into the topic of organizational culture, the more I realized that culture was the result of entrepreneurial activities by company founders, leaders of movements, institution builders and social architects.

But while the values of a still emergent grouping (such as general management) may retain fluidity, the values of established and defensive professional groups are more deeply rooted, shaped by socialization processes outside the control of managers, and likely to survive attempts at top-down restructuring even if driven underground.

Whipp et al.'s (1989) study illustrated the importance of corporate culture and traced changes in dominant belief systems in case study firms, yet was sceptical about the construction of instant 'designer cultures':

> While the elusiveness of corporate culture makes it so hard to direct, at the same time its ubiquity across an organization makes it vital for effecting strategic change. In short, if the capacity to carry out the changes which a given strategy implies hinges on the ability to manage the process involved within which it must occur, then corporate culture can make or break that capacity.

Initial scepticism about the impact of culture change programmes in the NHS may now be tempered by an appreciation of the intensity and the continuity of the top-down pressure which has been evident. Careers have been launched which post date the old era, and a new general managerial grouping has been created which has been privileged by restructuring, and knowledge bases not accredited in the old order (such as marketing) have emerged around those roles. The new language (business management, customer care, quality assurance, market segmentation) of the internal market (now recoded as managed competition) clearly mimics that of the private sector, and may herald much deeper shifts in values and assumptions.

More analytic and less action-orientated than culture change programmes, the cultural perspective on organizational change (Pettigrew, 1979, 1985c) flags up a set of issues to do with symbolism, language, belief and ritual. Shifting language systems are themselves interesting objects of study as they provide order and coherence, describe cause-effect relationships (rationales) in times of confusion and transition, and because there may be competing language systems trying to define the same situation in different terms. For example, there is clear evidence of language shifts around the post-1989 agenda for change in the NHS, first signalled in the White Paper *Working for Patients* (Cm 555, 1989) which attempted to move the NHS in a 'more businesslike' direction. 'Boards of Directors' became 'new NHS authorities' and 'opting out' becomes 'applying for self-governing trust status' (who could object to a trust?). Metaphors and myths help to simplify – and to give meaning to – complex issues that evoke concern and may be mobilized around a symbolically charged account of past events (or 'organizational saga', Clark, 1972) which supports or undermines proposals for change. Within the NHS, certain decision arenas – visible and politically charged fora such as DHA meetings – have produced highly ritualized forms of behaviour in which the use of 'hot button language' which can placate pressure groups, arouse constituents, ensure media coverage and maximize political support is more important than the quality of the internal decision making process.

The Organizational Life Cycle and Organization Transition Perspectives

While a contextualist methodology perhaps naturally points towards the adoption of an intensive, longitudinal, case study based form of analysis, it does not by itself supply an adequate theoretic underpinning. One perspective which developed particularly in the American literature throughout the 1980s is that of the 'organizational life cycle' (Kimberly and Miles, 1980), which argued that diminishing returns were now evident from cross-sectional comparative and quantitative research and that researchers should develop a more dynamic and historically informed model of organizations.

In the most schematic form of the model, birth, early development, maturity, decline and death can all be seen as distinct organizational stages which may be characterized by different organizational processes. For example, the early stages of an organization's life may be profoundly shaped by a 'founder' who imprints certain ideas on an organization, but top decision makers who come in later on in an organization's life cycle will be likely to find it difficult to recapture such an influential role. For innovative organizations, a transition from infant to mature status may prove difficult for the original generation of entrepreneurs as a requirement for creativity gives way to a requirement for institutionalization: 'entrepreneurs may have to concede to administrators, professionals to technicians, artists to replicators' (Miles and Randolph, 1980).

Early representations of the life cycle theory were themselves sometimes attacked for their temporal determinism – the assumption that there was a fixed sequence which could not be arrested or reversed (the whole turnaround literature, for example, made the contrary assumption that organizational decline could indeed be reversed).

Even if movement between these 'stages' is not automatic, organizational transition processes themselves emerge as an important topic of study. As has been hinted above, a particularly interesting transition is from a young and flexible organization to a more mature and formal one. This formalization transition represents a frequent crisis for young organizations, with a fall-off of performance and prolonged conflict (Quinn and Anderson, 1984), which poses a particular set of challenges to managers. On the basis of his study of the rapid routinization of an originally innovative medical school, Kimberly (1980) suggests that the birth and early development of an organization on the one hand and its institutionalization on the other represent two relatively distinct chapters in the history of an organization. When an organization is both new and different, then the transition between the two stages may be problematic, as those factors that lead to an organization's success as an innovation are not the same as those that lead to longer-run success.

Where such clear-cut transitions do take place, a second scenario is that a difficult period of drift may also be apparent, where there is a gap between founders' ideals and intentions and the organization as enacted (Lodahl and Mitchell, 1980). While most organizations may go through a limited number of relatively predictable stages in their early years, it has also been argued (Kimberly, 1987) that the remainder of their life course is much less predictable. So maybe the concept of 'transition' would fit better in the tracing of an organizational biography than that of the life cycle:

> Central to the development of organizational biographies is the identification of major transitions in an organization's life and an effort to understand both their causes and their implications. Unlike the imagery of life cycles, then, the notion of organizational biography makes no assumption about temporally ordered stages or about the inevitability of death. (Kimberly, 1987, p. 234)

One approach to the formation of such organizational biographies is to see them as shaped by a series of strategic decisions that unfold. A few basic decisions are made early, are rarely changed and 'imprint' the new organization, setting important limitations on subsequent choices (Kimberly and Rottman, 1987). The great strength of this biographical perspective is that it does open up the question of the evolution of the individual organization through time, thus dealing with the question of the historical and social meaning which actors attribute to their actions. Such a perspective came under attack for overestimating the ability of organizations to effect internal change (this critique was apparent as early as Hannan and Freeman, 1977): too much emphasis was placed on adaptation, too little on selection.

Population Ecology

Partly in reaction to this emphasis on internally generated processes of development, a new 'population ecology' perspective has also been emerging within the American literature which takes a much more sceptical view of the ability of organizations to effect change:

> for wide classes of organizations there are very strong inertial pressures on structure arising from both internal arrangements (for example, internal politics) and from the environment (for example, public legitimation of organizational activity). To claim otherwise is to ignore the most obvious feature of organizational life. (Hannan and Freeman, 1977, p. 957)

There have clearly been important restatements of position, as Hannan and Freeman (1984) saw structural inertia as a consequence of selection processes rather than a precursor and also elaborated the nature of inertia in relative terms – when the environment is changing more rapidly than organizations.

In its more aggressive manifestations, population ecology represents a competing rather than a complementary perspective (Hurley and Kaluzny, 1987) and can be seen as a paradigm shift in how organizations are conceptualized. The model is seen as especially appropriate where there is a volatile environment, a large number of small firms and a high degree of competition (as in the American health care sector). Ecologists are unimpressed by the possibility that managers can turn their organizations round, and instead stress organizational inertia. Some of these inertial factors are internal (such as sunk costs); others are external (such as legal and other barriers to entry) (Hannan and Freeman, 1984). Inert organizations may even face higher chances of survival than innovative ones as new organizations without routines or stable bases of external support seem to experience higher death rates than established organizations. The perspective initially emerged in private sector organizational populations where there was high turnover (such as restaurants), but has also been applied to health care settings.

There is particular interest in the emergence of new organizational forms such as preferred or exclusive provider organizations. However, the possibility that an old style institution can transform itself to conform with newer models is dismissed: innovation is seen as a risky business. So Zucker's (1987) study of the 'hazard' of change in hospital organizations between 1959 and 1979 found that the adoption of institutionalized 'normal' innovation tended to reduce the possibility of organizational death, whereas the adoption of non-routine innovation actually decreased performance, although not enough to alter survival rates. A further implication of the population ecology argument was that change would take place at a population rather than individual level, as new organizational forms emerged. Scott's (1986) review of changes in the American mental health field argues that the dominant feature has been the replacement (or supplementation) of one type of organization – state mental hospitals – by another (community mental health centres, for example). Only gradually and partially were traditional organizations such as state mental homes being restructured to participate in the newer forms of care.

Health care settings have provided an important source of empirical studies which have informed or indeed qualified the population ecology perspective. Shortell (1988), for instance, modelled the evolution of American hospital systems through a strategic adaptation rather than a selection perspective.

Alexander et al. (1986) explicitly used a population ecology approach to examine drastic structural changes in the American health care sector as the traditional independent, free-standing hospitals came under increasing pressure and as new organizational forms based on mergers, divestiture and investor-owned hospital chains rose to prominence. In this argument, health service organizations could be distinguished according to whether they exhibited specialist versus generalist traits. With respect to environmental selection, specialist organizations are favourably selected in highly specialist environmental states, while generalist organizations may not perform so well in a narrow range of environmental states, but perform better over a broad spectrum of environmental conditions. It was found that increased environmental turbulence and instability had been associated with important changes to organizational forms in that hospitals and multi-hospital systems were diversifying and merging into larger systems.

Organizational ecology has not been without qualifiers or its critics. Some qualifications came from Singh et al. (1986), who studied the impact of organizational change in a population of voluntary social services organizations over time. They concluded:

> The extreme ecological position that all organizational changes are accompanied by increases in the death rate is not supported by the data. Equally clearly, the extreme adaptation argument that all organizational changes are adaptive with respect to survival is also not supported by the data. (Singh et al., 1986)

In order to distinguish between adaptive and disruptive changes, a distinction was made between core and peripheral changes. Core organizational changes were best described by an ecological view, and were more disruptive, whereas peripheral organizational changes were described best by an adaptation view and corresponded to a lowered mortality risk. There was thus a plea for theoretical pluralism given the need to consider both adaptation and selection processes simultaneously without assuming that either one alone explained organizational change. Singh's later work (1990) has tried to specify some of the areas where convergence between adaptation- and selection-based models might occur. One would be the effects of institutional changes (particularly in relation to the role of the state) on birth and death rates in organizational populations. A second would be the role of legitimacy in population dynamics, and how the acquisition of institutional supports reduces selection pressures on organizations. Thirdly, work on community ecology could add significantly to organizational evolution research, by studying the effects of an increasing or declining population mass on internal dynamics within organizations.

More outright criticism of the ecology model was apparent in the study by Renshaw et al. (1990), which attempted to use ecological analysis in a study of the diffusion of innovations in medical technology. For example, a distinguishing feature of the diffusion of magnetic resonance imaging has been the formation of organizations for the specific purpose of owning and operating the technology. The question of interest therefore became whether common patterns of ownership and density of units characterized similar market areas. To what extent, in other words, did the principle of isomorphism operate in that similar conditions acted to create similar organizational configurations? However, the early evidence suggested that similar diffusion patterns could be detected in dissimilar market areas and dissimilar diffusion patterns in similar market areas.

The initial conclusion was that local environmental conditions did not have so great an impact as predicted by ecology theory, and that variation remained important alongside selection. In short, important factors apart from local environmental conditions could account for entry of free-standing imaging organizations into markets or adoption decisions by hospitals. Meyer (1990), too, is sceptical about a global shift towards such a determinist perspective, and argues that we need to understand more about when an ecological perspective applies and when an evolutionary perspective.

In the next section, our own preferred research framework will be outlined. Here it is sufficient to note that there is now a wide variety of literature which crosses, in the British case, the private and public sectors and, in the American case, profit and not-for-profit settings. Much of this literature has not been apparent in the discourse surrounding British health care management and there remains – in our view – an important task in broadening the debate out from the interesting but limited question of the importance of the sectoral divide.

A Research Framework

Much of the existing literature on change processes in the NHS is weakened because of its failure to take account of some of the newer literatures reviewed above, reflecting the historic intellectual isolation of much health care research. This is in spite of the fact that much of the basic social science literature on organizational change was developed in, or applied to, health care settings: all seven of the perspectives reviewed above have important health care components. Specifically, the existing NHS literature base is weakened because it is insufficiently processual (an emphasis on action as well as structure), comparative (a range of comparative case studies as well as a single case), pluralist (a description and analysis of the often competing versions of reality seen by actors in change processes), contextual (operating at a variety of different levels with specification of the linkages between them) and historical (taking into account the historical evolution of ideas and stimuli for change as well as the constraints within which decision makers operate) (Pettigrew, McKee and Ferlie, 1988).

Choosing the Theoretical Framework

This contextualist perspective pushes us towards certain choices in selecting an organizing theoretical framework. In terms of choosing between the perspectives reviewed above, we adopted an organizational transition and adaptation perspective, although this is no more than an initial structuring device as in this kind of holistic analysis the search for a simple and grand theory of change is unlikely to bear fruit. Often a mélange of different perspectives will be evident in a case, as rational components combine with process components or indeed historical accident.

Nevertheless, it did seem that the organizational transition approach represented a fruitful vehicle for those interested in the development of a contextualist analysis of the changes apparent in health care in the 1980s. This framework is focused on processes of adaptation but recognizes that these are complex and may include jointly rational, political, cultural and learning components. While incrementalism has perhaps been the dominant approach to the study of decision making in health care systems, it is doubtful whether it is an adequate explanation of the discontinuities now evident. Nor could a diffusion-based model of change effectively model the top-down pressure for restructuring apparent in the 1980s, although it may fit the new conditions of the 1990s rather better, as diffusion-based models of change re-emerge. Contingency theory failed to offer an adequate account of the social, cultural and historical settings of organizations, although the argument that there was no one 'best way', but rather that the functional organizational structure was associated with the nature of the task undertaken was important. The degree of uncertainty may be a powerful shaper of the requisite organizational structure and process. The strategy literature was certainly interesting but ahistorical and insufficient by itself to organize the selection of sites and issues. The developing work on organizational culture added an important new concern with symbolism, language, belief and ritual, but was still underdeveloped historically and less directly concerned with the nature of issues or how organizations evolve through time. The population ecology model seemed to fit best when a particular set of conditions was present, namely a volatile environment, a large number of small firms and a high degree of competition. While the first condition is certainly present in the NHS, the second two are not so applicable in a planned service, and may not even be fulfilled in the brave new world of the internal market if the degree of central guidance and regulation remains strong. The more extreme versions of the population ecology perspective were dismissive of the potential for adaptive action within organizations and were hence unlikely to develop an interest in process (although more eclectic and pluralist versions were also apparent). Schematic organizational life cycle models were rejected as too fatalist (stage-ridden), determinist and less able to handle action within organizations. An organizational transition approach was potentially much better able to explore idiosyncratic patterns of development through time.

So the organizational transition model was used to guide the selection of topics for study. In particular we consider:

- The creation and early development of new organizations and services. Such organizations may either be new and different (services for HIV/AIDS), or new but allegedly containing a greater element of standardization (such as new District General Hospitals).
- The transition between birth and early development, where much innovation and learning may be lost.

- The management of organizational decline in Districts facing long-term pressure on resources.
- Organizational death, or the closure of hospitals both in the acute and priority group sectors.

Of course, these themes are also very relevant for many private sector organizations.

Defining the Methodology

We now turn from theory to methodology. Case study methodology is as much abused as used, and only now are some of the methodological issues implied by the adoption of a more qualitative and historical approach emerging. We need to be clear about the differences between case studies and quasi-experimental methods drawn from natural science (George and McKeown, 1985). Conventionally, case study analysis has been used for hypothesis generation, quasi-experimental methods for hypothesis testing. Thus in the final chapter we will tentatively advance some more general propositions which emerge from the detailed case study analysis. However, we rely less on within-case analysis than is conventional in much case study research and more on cross-case analysis.

Even within qualitative approaches (Van de Ven and Huber, 1990) there are choices to be made between a range of techniques: ethnographic methods, longitudinal and comparative case studies and the real time tracking through of organizations. There are also a number of difficult design and craft problems to consider: does the researcher influence as well as observe events? Within longitudinal analysis, what are the biases which emerge from the selective deposit or weeding of archives? How do the more historical skills of archival analysis sit with the more ethnographic methods such as observation?

Our own methodology is one of comparative, longitudinal and issue-based case studies. The time frame implied is of course strongly related to the characteristics of the health care issue under consideration, which involves (at its shortest) a period of about ten years for the HIV/AIDS issue, to a long time frame of about 150 years for the psychiatric care issue. Such a methodology is seen as the best placed to provide an opportunity to examine continuous processes in context, to draw in the significance of various interconnected levels of analysis and to start theory building across as well as within cases (Eisenhardt, 1989). At its best, the comparative case study method may produce powerful information as: 'Two cases may appear very similar, yet experience different outcomes. Here the goal is to identify the difference that is responsible for contradictory outcomes in at least relatively similar circumstances.'

While a natural scientist would often seek to compare an experimental and a control group, this is not really possible in organizational analysis. One objection might be: are we comparing apples and apples or apples and oranges? While comparative case studies offer an exciting way forward, there is a need to be aware of the extent to which matched or even comparable pairs can be assembled, or whether many of the supposed similarities turn out on closer scrutiny to be illusory. George and McKeown (1985) argue that the power of such case study analysis is increased when the method of 'structured, focused, comparison is used'. A comparison is 'focused' in so far as the researcher deals selectively with only those aspects of the case believed to be relevant to the study. Similarly, 'controlled' comparison is achieved when the research design defines and standardizes the data requirements through the formulation of theoretically relevant general questions which guide the examination of the case. In particular, Chapter 4 on acute sector rationalization will address this issue of inter-District comparability.

There is a spread within the study not only across different sites but across different strategic change issues within those sites: the closure of acute and priority group hospitals; the construction and early history of new District General Hospitals (DGHs); the development of community-based services for mentally ill and mentally handicapped people; the creation and early development of services for HIV/AIDS. Not only does this bring very different theoretical literature into play in each setting (at the most basic level the management of growth may pose very different issues from the management of retrenchment), but it also gives the opportunity to see whether managers in the same localities react differently to different issues. What, in other words, is the relative importance of the issue effect vis-à-vis the system effect?

A final decision rule has been to go for extreme situations, critical incidents and social dramas (Pettigrew, 1990) in site selection. The study of the response to the HIV/AIDS epidemic is an example of this approach. Perceptions and behaviours which are often hidden can emerge in critical incidents: observation at a DHA 'cuts' meeting could reveal the politics of the whole District in a powerful and condensed form. Actors are forced to consider their relationships with each other and to debate in a public forum. Such dramas provide a valuable point of data collection to supplement interview material, but set in a more extended stream of time which may be more dominated by routines. If the phenomena to be observed have to be contained within a small number of sites, then cases should be chosen where the critical processes are observable. All of the case studies studied also relate to societally important questions, such as the closure of psychiatric institutions. They are thus of strategic significance: of course many change processes proceed at a more operational level and may take different forms.

We now move on to consider one aspect of the context in which District Health Authorities operate which was seen as exercising a major influence on organizational behaviour in the NHS of the 1980s: to what extent have the changes apparent in the NHS been driven by top-down changes in the national political economy?

3

Top-down Restructuring

NHS General Management as an Institutional Reform

In the previous chapter, one of the conclusions from a review of recent organizational theoretic literature was that a fruitful avenue of research now lay in the development of a contextualist type of analysis, using comparative and longitudinal case study methodology. A further implication was that such contextualist research would be multi-layered in nature, trying to relate particular changes taking place in the localities to wider societal or political developments. Perhaps a key contextual feature of the NHS in the 1980s which must be taken into account in more micro-empirical analyses lies in the dominance of top-down chance processes, which have to be understood with reference to the changing national political economy.

No student of the British public sector in the 1980s can ignore the potential impact of the Thatcherite political economy, and of successive top-down restructurings of public institutions deemed to have failed, in a manner which would have been scarcely credible in the late 1970s when all the talk was of 'ungovernability', or 'governmental overload' and of the power of the periphery. Is such restructuring mere froth or does it represent serious and sustained pressure for institutional change? While perhaps the impact of privatization, deregulation and the retreat of government was felt first in the industrial public sector, increasingly restructuring has been felt in the Welfare State. Marquand (1988) has produced one of the most sophisticated treatments of the rise of British neo-liberalism from the mid 1970s, but even his conclusion that 'the NHS is the sole legacy of the welfare strand of Keynesian social democracy which survives in approximately its original form' (p. 41) is looking increasingly contestable.

The introduction of general management has been only one of a number of politically driven institutional reforms apparent in the NHS in the 1980s, but has perhaps acted as the keystone of the arch. The proposals contained within the White Paper (Cm 555, 1989) and now carried forward into legislation for the introduction of NHS self-governing trusts, for example, would have been much more difficult without the prior introduction of general management. Nor – unlike previous reorganizations – was the introduction of general management supposed only to effect structural change, but more ambitiously it was to change roles, 'ways of doing things', create a new cadre of 'leaders' who could energize decision making, and even to produce 'a new culture'.

There are a number of important questions which arise from these initial observations: why has so much top-level political effort been invested in the restructuring of the machinery of government rather than what used to be seen as substantive 'policy'? How have roles been renegotiated locally as well as nationally? One view might be that such top-down pressures have produced similar shifts in the balance of power across all localities and issues; another that such power shifts are much more locality- and issue-sensitive. Some would be sceptical of the ability of top-down reorganizations to produce significant changes in the localities at all. These are in large measure empirical questions: how was the new general managerial agenda defined in the localities and to what extent have initial hopes or indeed fears of radical change been realized?

Historically such ambitious attempts at administrative reorganization have been seen as doomed to fail, with the likelihood of rapid regression as soon as top-down pressure diminishes, yet such institutional reform was very much part of the political economy of the 1980s and as the decade wore on commentators increasingly noticed signs of real as well as surface change. This was perhaps linked to the much greater degree of political stability apparent in the 1980s than the 1970s, with a radical right regime in power steadily after 1979. The public sector institutions were seen from this political perspective as part of the problem, rather than the solution, and similar processes of top-down restructuring were evident across large chunks of those functions which remained within the public sector (the comparison with change processes in the higher Civil Service is instructive). In some ways, the rapid introduction of general management within the NHS represented the vanguard of restructuring within 'Welfare State' institutions, was seen by the centre as having been 'successful', and later in the decade similar processes of managerialization were being exported to sister human service organizations such as Family Practitioner Committees and Social Services Departments. Within the private sector, too, industry was rapidly reorganizing (Pettigrew and Whipp, 1991), and there was particular interest in those groups of firms which appeared to have achieved marked and sustained improvements in performance (see Grinyer et al.'s analysis of 'Sharpbenders', 1988a, b).

This chapter will explore these processes of managerial restructuring and relate them to the theoretic work which does exist on processes of institutional reform, much of which strikes a sceptical note. But first we outline the historical process of restructuring itself in some detail.

The Introduction of General Management

Historically the managerial problem in the NHS has often been framed in terms of excessive cost by auditing bodies such as the Public Accounts Committee: the cutting of apparently spiralling administrative costs was a concern of both the 1974–9 Labour government and of early Thatcherism (as seen in the abolition of the Area tier in 1982). Yet the mid 1980s witnessed a new and quite different concern with improving managerial performance, even though the salary levels of the new general managers were to rise considerably. Cost was now seen as less important than value. The perception of NHS management by politicians, in other words, had undergone an important shift.

In February 1983 the then Secretary of State (Norman Fowler) asked Roy Griffiths (of the food retail chain Sainsbury's) to give advice on the effective use and management of manpower in the NHS. His report was made available in October 1983 and accepted by Fowler, who asked for views by January 1984 but with expectation of early implementation. General management was speedily introduced on a national basis, as it did not require primary legislation, without piloting and with little research. Here was a new and distinctive pattern of policy making which can be usefully compared with the 1979 Royal Commission on the NHS: scepticism about the capacity of the NHS to effect internal reform; the use of businessmen as advisers; the decision not to commission research (although Griffiths's findings were consistent with much prior research); depriviledging of the public sector professions; and an action orientation. Although the localities were to be given more freedom over organizational structures, they were not free *not* to appoint general managers.

Sceptics included the Royal College of Nursing, which greeted the Griffiths Report 'with incredulity'. The British Medical Association wanted careful consultation and a trial, and wanted to retain the District Management Team. The Social Services Committee (1984) was sceptical of the proposed general managerial function and weary at yet another reorganization. They noted that the proposed Chief Executive role had been rejected by the government in its 1979 policy statement:

> In a few pages, without supporting evidence or argument, an idea was resurrected by Mr Griffiths which many in the Health Service had long since rejected.

and again:

> The NHS is simply not an organization susceptible to general management theories or practices.

In evidence to the Committee, Norman Fowler presented the scope of the Griffiths reorganization in deceptively modest terms:

> We set up the Griffiths Inquiry for two reasons. First of all, we wanted to check with professional managers on the initiatives we have taken, for example, the regional review system which we introduced and secondly to look at the management of the Health Service in a way that has not been done before. I think it is another way of saying that we have all been rather too preoccupied with the debate about whether there should be the Regions, whether the Districts and all that, and not enough about the management of the Health Service itself.

Although Fowler was trying to import more private sector experience into the NHS, he denied that this was a fundamental change (which may disconcert those who argue that the introduction of general management was the most significant reorganization in the NHS). In fact, this was the first reorganization to aim at process, rather than structure which had so beset reorganizations in the past and was last seen in the abolition of the Area tier as recently as 1982.

General management was introduced at District and Unit level rapidly in 1985 and 1986, with many of the new general managers being drawn from the younger administrators still in their 30s. There was then a significant generational clear-out and a new, younger cadre with a presumed attachment to a rising ideology was created (Feuer, 1975). Nurses often lost out from the reorganization (Glennerster et al., 1986). This generational shift was unexpectedly to prove more significant in the long term than the attempt to import more private sector personnel, military officers and doctors into general management. Fewer than expected were appointed, and they were disproportionately likely to leave or not have their contract renewed (Alleway, 1987), including the first Chairman of the Management Board (Victor Paige). Perhaps the culture shock, in particular the degree of politicization in management and the continuing power of the professionals, had proved just too much. The result was that the field was left all the more to the ex-administrators who, although they were the same individuals as had been in post before the reorganization, were nevertheless developing in role.

What are we to conclude from this history? Certainly previous experiences that politicians would quickly lose interest in institutional reform were not fulfilled in the 1980s:

> What is striking about the reforms of the Thatcher years is how, for all their neo-Taylorian crudeness, their momentum has been sustained for a decade. The political clout behind them has, if anything, become more confident and synoptic with the passing of time. (Pollitt, 1990, p. 62)

There are perhaps three competing views. One is that restructuring has consolidated and that a new 'entrepreneurial' management style has indeed been created. A more sceptical view (Harrison et al., 1989a) is that superficial change hides underlying continuity as the same people largely remained in post, relabelling themselves as necessary to survive. A third argument was that subtle and mixed processes of change were emerging, as a public management culture (Gunn, 1989) – which contained some differences from as well as some similarities to private sector general management – slowly took root as the ex-administrators survived but went on to develop in role. As this group of survivors was privileged in successive reorganizations and went on to 'walk the talk', so – perhaps unexpectedly – some real changes in self-image, power position and pattern of behaviour emerged.

Reforms as Administrative Rhetoric: Some Historical Evidence

Were the introduction of general management to have generated significant change within health care settings, then this would be an unexpected finding in the light of historical evidence. Previous reorganizations within health care settings have been found to have achieved only modest change: Elcock's study (1978) of the 1974 NHS reorganization at Regional level, for instance, concluded that continuity was much more important than change and that less than one-quarter of the post-reorganization membership was new to the NHS.

There is within a broader literature also profound scepticism about the substantive effects of reorganizing public sector institutions. The experience before the 1980s, after all, had been one of continuing but often incremental expansion of bureaucratic functions since the 1940s, with little attempt at radical challenge. For example, March and Olsen's review (1983) of the history of 12 twentieth-century efforts at comprehensive administrative reform in the United States found little evidence of success. Neither Presidents nor Congresses were found often to succeed in these major reorganization projects, which were typically diluted in the course of political trading within a pluralist political system. There was always a danger within these reorganizations that political attention would soon be lost given the emergence of new priorities (although the study also hinted that persistence both increased the likelihood that a proposal would be current at an opportune time and that it was embedded in a diffuse climate of legitimacy). Nor were there found to be many substantive effects as a result of all this activity, and indeed often control seemed as elusive after reorganization as before. Reorganization could be seen as much a domain of rhetoric (given the value placed on 'modernity' in Western society), of trading (interest groups will negotiate around early proposals for reform to bend them to their purposes), and of symbolic action (the appearance rather than the reality of governmental problem solving) as of purposeful activity.

In Britain, too, there has been a well-developed scepticism about the substantive impact of administrative reform in the public sector (Fry, 1981). The perceived failures of previous institutional reform programmes (Metcalfe and Richards, 1987) have included the inability of the post-Plowden Report (1961) long range financial planning system, the Public Expenditure Survey Committee (PESC), to cope with the turbulent economic environment of the 1970s; the gutting of the Fulton Report's (1968) recommendation of a shift inside the higher Civil Service away from the cult of the generalist towards the greater use of specialists; the disappearance of Heathite innovations such as effective Policy Analysis and Review; and the marginalization and subsequent demise of the grit in the Whitehall machine in the shape of the Central Policy Review Staff (CPRS) or 'think tank'.

The early 1970s had seen an earlier attempt to introduce managerial ideas from the corporate private sector into the public sector (including the McKinsey-led reorganization of the NHS), yet the impact of this restructuring was seen as relatively superficial. Why did the radical reorganization of central government promised in the early days of the Heath administration fade so quickly? Clues can be found in Heclo and Wildavsky's classic – almost anthropological – study of the process of allocating public expenditure in the early 1970s which indicated both the lack of ministerial interest in institutional reform and the domination at that time of the expansionist imperative within bureaux: 'inside his department, the spending minister who is uninterested in increased spending is likely to be viewed, if not with distaste, at least with despair' (1974, p. 130). Their conclusion was, however: 'the problem is not that the Civil Service is too strong and creative in devising public policy, but that politicians are too weak and not creative enough' (p. 378). Indeed, by the late 1970s, there was increasing concern about the overload facing public institutions, and the widening gap between the extensive range of formal functions ostensibly possessed and the capacity of those agencies to deliver them. A pessimism was detectable about the limits to government, which highlighted the capacity of the periphery to renegotiate top-down 'policy' (see Barrett and Fudge, 1981). Within the practitioners of public administration, there was also evident a scepticism about 1979 electoral commitments to administrative reform – getting Big Government off taxpayers' backs – that was not in the end borne out by events: 'past experience and their well-developed sense of déjà vu misled senior civil servants into discounting electoral commitments to administrative reform and spending cuts' (Metcalfe and Richards, 1987). Administrative reform remained an option open to the new political regime, given that in the UK responsible authority is located in the Cabinet (Arnold, 1988).

British local government illustrates the cyclical theory of reorganization nicely. This sector displayed a major movement away from traditional departmental and professionally led structures and towards 'corporate planning', management teams and Chief Executives in the late 1960s and early 1970s, heavily influenced by the Heathite managerial political economy in central government, professional and managerial fashions in local government and national level reports such as that of Bains (1972) which saw the adoption of a new matrix form of organization as a way of creating much more lateral communication and coherence. In the late 1970s, however (Greenwood et al., 1980), there was an increasing feeling that these 'reforms' had been oversold, and a move back to more traditional structures. Politically inspired retreats tended to follow from the victories of local Conservative Parties in 1976 and 1977 who were targeting value-for-money and keen to cut back top-heavy administration and return to tried and tested systems. Chief Executive roles sometimes reverted to those of the clerk. Managerial retreats were also evident, influenced by changes in the professional debate, and perhaps led by strong Departments (such as Education) whose commitment to corporate management had perhaps been skin deep in the first place:

It is impossible to ignore the ideas to which local government officers are subject from a variety of sources such as their professional associations, local government journals and conferences. During the past eighteen months there has been an increasing wave of criticism of corporate management. Whereas in 1972/3, when the new structures of local government were being designed, there were no voices raised against the prevailing orthodoxy of corporate management, this acceptance was certainly not the case in 1977/78. What was conventional wisdom three or four years ago has become subject to increasing criticism. Thus, the environment of ideas for each authority is much less supportive of the structural entities introduced under the banner of Bains. (Greenwood et al., 1980, p. 55)

Much of this wider debate about the limits to reorganization can also be seen (perhaps in a particularly dramatic form) in the health care sector. The repeated failure of attempts at structural reform in an American health care system (New York City) was explored by Alford (1975), who stressed the immobiliste nature of interest group politics in the health care sector. Alford distinguished between three different blocs: the (dominant) professional monopoly, the (challenging) administrative lobby and the (invisible) community health lobby. The scope for any consensus-based reform – he argued – was severely limited given the cleavage between the dominant professional monopoly and the challenge from the administrative lobby ('corporate rationalizers'). The community health lobby found it impossible even to get items on formal agendas. Proposals for reorganization were on the one hand legion:

over twenty investigations of the New York City health system were conducted between 1950 and 1971. The reports of them reached a peak in 1965–68, when the municipal hospitals were under almost constant surveillance by city, state and private agencies. (Alford, 1975, p. 22)

but on the other hand they were also a political tool being utilized by the corporate rationalizer lobby who were often first in the field in defining problems as 'crises', and the reports' recommendations frequently stressed administrative reshuffling or 'improved coordination' as a solution to the perceived crisis. These reports could be seen as symbolic rather than tangible responses, given that there was no analysis of the lack of impact of previous recommendations, or any diagnosis of implementation failure as a serious organizational problem. As the corporate rationalizers were unable or perhaps even unwilling (given similar social backgrounds and locations) to confront professional monopolists, these proposals for change became fatally diluted and caught in a system of bounded pluralism:

over and over again, we see even in biting critiques a contradiction between the description of barriers to change in the past and simultaneous optimism for the future . . . every reform proposal becomes trapped in the pluralist political process which safeguards all existing professional and organizational interests. (Alford, 1975, pp. 260–1)

Similar early reactions greeted the proposed introduction of general management in the UK health care system (Griffiths Report, 1983) given that improvement in the NHS management capacity had been a long-standing theme. Hunter (1984) pointed out that many of the proposed reforms echoed the 1972 'Grey Book' on management arrangements for the NHS, and had perhaps an even longer pre-history. Such earlier restructuring was seen as sinking without trace:

> The only certainty is that Griffiths is unlikely to be the last attempt to open up the NHS in order to peer inside and make recommendations on the latest management fad. If this seems unduly cynical it is not meant to be, but it would be remarkable indeed if the Griffiths Report were to attain the status of the last organizational quick fix. (Hunter, 1984, p. 94)

Administrative Reforms as Rhetoric: Some Theoretical Considerations

The clear historical evidence which exists about the limits to top-down institutional reform efforts perhaps explains the early sceptical reaction to Griffiths. There was also perhaps a more theoretic stream of literature on the limits of organizational change, but one which is increasingly coming under challenge.

The behavioural critique in the 1960s and 1970s of the old and highly formalistic public administration school of analysis led to a loss of interest in institutions as formal, rule-bound, organizations and a switch to approaches which stressed local negotiation. There was the rise of the 'garbage can' model of organization (Cohen et al., 1972) where the organization was seen as 'a meeting place for issues and feelings looking for decision situations in which they may be aired, solutions looking for issues to which they may be an answer, and participants looking for problems or pleasure (p. 25). It is interesting to see how these authors have themselves developed their position.

While such approaches were valuable in moving beyond an obsession with formal structure, there was also the danger that their micro perspective left out broader constraints on action. Within such behavioural models, organizational and indeed government structures were at best seen as dependent variables; at worst, meaningless (Peters, 1988):

> from a behavioural point of view, formally organized social institutions have come to be portrayed simply as arenas within which political behaviour, driven by more fundamental factors, occurs. (March and Olsen, 1984)

The implications of the garbage can model were clear: top-down pressures were likely to be too weak to change locally negotiated rules of the game; 'policy' was constantly being renegotiated at the periphery; innovation was likely to be bottom-up and professionally driven; human service organizations were likely to be 'frontline' agencies where professionals exercised substantial discretion irrespective of formal 'policy'.

Brunsson (1989) offers a good example of this perspective. While reforms within organizations are often presented as a dramatic change, reform itself should be better seen as a standard and repetitive activity ('reforms are routines rather than breaks in organizational life') which may be easy to start, but difficult to finish. Reforms may be oversold, or lead to the perception of fresh problems for which ever newer reforms are required: 'reforms may trigger a constant flow of problems and consequently the continuous need for reform, so that reforming becomes a stable state'. Reforms initially promise simplicity and consistency, although in later stages of implementation the ability to live up to early promises may be questioned. Strong fashions in the stock of managerial knowledge guarantee that the practices of organizations will periodically appear old-fashioned and in need of 'reform'. Reforms will often come in cycles, aided by the fact that most organizations are often forgetting rather than learning organizations:

> So reforms are facilitated not by learning but by forgetfulness, by mechanisms that cause the organization to forget previous reforms, or at least those with a similar content. Reformers need a high degree of forgetfulness to avoid uncertainty about whether the reform that they are promoting is a good one, and forgetfulness also helps people to accept reforms. (Brunsson, 1989, pp. 224–5)

More recent literature ('the new institutionalism') has by contrast suggested a more autonomous role for political institutions than suggested in garbage can theory: the state affected society as well as being affected by it and itself can be seen as a structured institutionalized order with its own standard operating procedures, values and distribution of power. While such institutions may display much inertia, March and Olsen (1989) have discussed ways in which they may undergo transformation. One scenario would consist of intentional transformation through processes of radical shock, where it is hinted that the Thatcher experiment may represent an exemplar:

> Where historical processes are inefficient, it is possible to imagine moving the political system from one (relatively) stable equilibrium to another one that is quite different. This is the sense in which political institutions are essential elements of political change. They are instruments for the branching of history. The Thatcher Government's attempts to reform the British Civil Service may turn out to be an example of such a process. (March and Olsen, 1989, p. 64)

The mechanism for such rapid transitions are now, however, spelt out, and such an argument might initially seem difficult to develop given their stress elsewhere on the ability of institutions to withstand pressures for change. But March and Olsen (1989) do suggest that such radical shock treatment could unleash forces impossible to control: 'it is easier to produce change through shock than it is to control what new combination of institutions and practices will evolve from the shock'. The implication of this statement is that the immediate post-revolutionary period may be worthy of close attention, as possibly unpredicted developments take shape.

This institutional literature may shed light on health care reorganizations. Scott (1987) has argued that the state and professional bodies may represent two powerful forces in the shaping of institutions, but that these two social blocs may seek to reorganize institutions in very different ways. While higher state officials may seek to create bureaucratic arrangements which reduce discretion, and rely on formal hierarchies, professions will typically prefer decentralizing reorganizations, relying on normative control mechanisms, and seek to maximize frontline discretion. Political and legal structures may help shape these institutional frameworks within which reorganization projects compete for time, attention and effort.

A political science perspective is also apparent in the work of Peters (1988), who points out that reorganization in the public sector may not just be a managerial but also a politically driven process, where reorganization expresses political power and realigns the relative ease with which interest groups can lobby public agencies.

Is there evidence available from other countries which could shed light on processes of institutional change? One comparison point could be change processes in other European Welfare States. Olsen's (1988) case study of the Norwegian Welfare State outlined the historic growth of a corporate-pluralist state in which a number of processes were evident: functions were transferred to non-departmental agencies; civil servants became key players in public policy making; and organized interests claimed – and achieved – direct, integrated participation in policy formulation. There was in addition a stable policy process characterized by a declining political role given to parliaments, ideological parties and the public; the delegation of authority to a network of boards and committees where bureaucrats and organized interests are the main participants; the absence of broad ideological issues; a political agenda dominated by technical issues; a low level of conflict and an emphasis on compromise.

Nevertheless, such an institutional framework was currently under challenge from a radical right government which was trying to move away from a corporate-pluralist state:

> The administrative reform programme of the conservative-centre government reveals a strong belief in the relevance of organizational design. It assumes that the organization of the administrative apparatus has a significant impact upon the content of the decisions made; that an administrative policy is important; and that government has the right and the ability to design the administrative apparatus in order to facilitate the implementation of political goals. (Olsen, 1988, p. 244)

Thus the corporate-pluralist state was seen by the radical right now in political control of the centre as too expansive and expensive, as too rigid, and as overdominated by special interests. The case study suggests that in some circumstances the centre may have a considerable range of power resources in securing the top-down restructuring of political institutions.

A second point of comparison could be the American experience. We now have useful recent insight from the American health care system where the 1980s saw a similar growth of the neo-conservative critique of liberal public spending programmes. Kimberly (1989) addressed the theme of whether Alford's earlier conclusion (1975) that little really changes as a result of successive reorganization was valid in the new era of health care management in the 1980s. Clearly this period witnessed the rise in influence of neo-conservative economists (such as Enthoven, whose advocacy of an 'internal market' was to prove as influential in the British context) who were armed with a number of key ideas. In order to promote cost consciousness (and cost containment was seen as a major objective), it was necessary to ensure that decision makers operated with the 'right incentives'. The best way to ensure that there were incentives was in turn seen as the promotion of competition between institutions and individuals. The basis of payment also needed to be shifted from retrospective, charge-based, reimbursement systems to a prospective, cost-based system where there would be greater incentives for cost consciousness. Where possible (within this account) the market should operate, with hospitals behaving more like firms, but where this was not possible, market-like mechanisms should be introduced instead.

Kimberly's own view was that there had been significant changes in American health care management in the 1980s along a number of dimensions: the environment had moved from being cooperative to competitive; the role of Chief Executive Officers had shifted from that of caretaker to that of manager; the role of the Board had moved from that of a traditional philanthropic orientation to setting corporate direction; the doctor's role had moved from that of an autonomous professional to an employee; the institutional posture was more proactive; the institutional orientation had changed from effectiveness to efficiency; the culture was less service-orientated and more bottom-line-orientated; the locus of decision making was somewhat clearer; the 'customer' was less likely to be defined as the doctor and more as the purchasers of care; and the nature of the customer was more independent.

Some of these themes have also been explored by Shortell (1988), who has also commented on the rapid pace of change in the structure of the American health care system with what was once a cottage industry populated by many individual, freestanding not-for-profit hospitals becoming a crazy quilt of systems, alliances and networks ('systems' in a loose sense of the word) in response to a number of pressures including cost containment initiatives and the drive coming from CEOs. Shortell's own view was that these new systems had not as yet demonstrated a competitive advantage: indeed their track record was rather one of unfulfilled promises.

Of course, there is also much interest within private sector settings in the nature and effectiveness of top-down restructuring processes. Most recently there have been criticisms of top-down programmatic change strategies (such as Total Quality Management) as false paths to renewal (Beer et al., 1990).

This review of the literature and of experiences in other countries highlights a number of potential themes for analysing the UK experience:

- Under what circumstances do proposals for administrative reform attract sustained, top-down, political interest, and what difference does this make to the outcome of the implementation process?
- What form does the proposed restructuring take and who defines the agenda (bottom-up from the field; driven through by higher tiers; diffusion out from demonstration sites)?
- Can deep-seated 'institutional orders' be renegotiated over time or is government commitment to reform rhetorical? Does Britain in the 1980s represent a special case where radical shock treatment has produced lasting change?

A New Order: Has the British Political Economy been Turned Upside Down?

When compared to the United States, the British history is one of much closer links between politics and administrative reorganization, as the traditional focus has been the Cabinet (Arnold, 1988) rather than expert Commissions. While the UK literature has historically been pessimistic about the ability of political leaders to restructure the institutions within which they operate, by the late 1980s a reassessment was emerging, both in central government as a whole and in the health care sector in particular, as the rate of change seemed to gather pace throughout the decade. Predictions of a U-turn were not borne out by events, and indeed the 'clouting' of public sector administration was sustained (Fry, 1984).

Many of the managerial reforms evident even in those agencies which remain in the public sector (broadly speaking, human service rather than industrial functions) have often been seen as springing out of the new Thatcherite political economy of the 1980s. Young (1989) notes that some of the implications of the radical right's diagnosis of relative British economic decline in terms of the construction of the Civil Service (and public sector administration more globally) as a political problem from 1979 onwards. The Civil Service was to be 'deprivileged':

> No government has been elected whose leader was as deeply seized as this one of the need to overturn the power and presumption of the continuing govern- ment of the Civil Service; to challenge its orthodoxies; cut down its size; reject its assumptions; which were seen as corrosively infected by social democracy, and teach it a lesson in political control. (Young, 1989, p. 153)

In a search for the reasons underlying the Thatcherite distrust of the Civil Service, Fry (1984) notes in addition to the dominance of neo- Keynesianism at the Treasury, its scepticism towards the Thatcherite project at higher levels, the heavy degree of unionization at lower levels, the lack of interest in management as opposed to policy work, and what were seen by Thatcherites as 'cosy' pay and promotion systems with automatic increments, routine career expectations and security of tenure. The correction of this perceived institutional failure remained as a leit-motif across the Thatcherite governments where the long-term momentum offered as a result of subsequent electoral victories and of continuing top-level political interest in public sector restructuring opened the way to securing real change, despite the recurrent failures of the past.

Within the Thatcherite lexicon 'reform' was used more often as a term than the more neutral 'change', springing from this clear diagnosis of the perceived reasons for Britain's relative decline. Indeed the span of reform efforts broadened considerably in the 1980s from the traditional concern with formal structure to simultaneous attempts to change financial and control systems, culture, governance, human resource strategies, the creation of new leadership groups and service strategy. The 1980s notion of 'reform' is thus far more inclusive.

As Hennessy argues (1988), reforms of central government are vulnerable to loss of prime ministerial interest. Wilson lost interest in many of the recommendations of the Fulton Report (1968) on the Civil Service as the 1970 election approached, and the three components of the Heathite strategy for institutional reform ('Superdepartments' to reduce the flow of business up to Cabinet; the Policy Analysis and Review technique; the Central Policy Review Staff) had all disappeared by 1983.

Metcalfe and Richards (1987) offer a fascinating account of a much more complex and sustained process of management reform within central government in the 1980s, with substantial retrenchment (100,000 jobs lost between 1979 and 1984), a shift in language and favoured role models from policy to management, and the moving on from small-scale scrutinies of particular areas of expenditure, which demonstrated early gains, to the emergence of a much more global efficiency strategy:

> Thus the evolution of the efficiency strategy is forcing a reexamination of basic assumptions about the organization and management of the business of government. Traditional concepts of public administration are being called into question and there is wider interest in the application of management concepts to government. (Metcalfe and Richards, 1987, p. 3)

The next question is precisely which management concepts are being applied? Hunter's review (1986) of research into NHS management argued that while research in the late 1970s was beginning to move beyond a focus on formal structure to political and organizational behavioural studies of decision making (with metaphors such as 'garbage cans', 'core groups' and 'ad hocracies' emerging in the literature), the top-down agenda of the 1980s was re-emphasizing the importance of structural clarity in public sector management. Thus the Financial Management

Initiative (Cmnd 8616, 1982) set out three basic principles within which the Departmental 'managers' should work:

1 A clear view of objectives, and means to assess, and if possible, measure outputs and performance in relation to those objectives.
2 Well-defined responsibility for making the best use of resources, including a critical scrutiny of output and value for money.
3 The provision of information (especially cost information) and access to the expert advice needed.

So the tools indicated by the FMI (Flynn et al., 1989) included increased emphasis on information systems, Performance Indicators, the delegation of budgets and responsibilities to line managers, and the development within Departments of top management systems. Pollitt (1990) argues that the dominant managerial ideology which grew up in the 1980s could be termed 'neo-Taylorian' in nature. While this focus was on clarifying line management and formulating individual objectives, combined with an interest in cost compression, alternative questions of strategic management or organizational development (Metcalfe and Richards, 1987) which could build an institution able to cope with a high rate of change seemed less evident.

In terms of process, Metcalfe and Richards (1987) do not see the FMI – while clearly an exercise in strategic institutional change – as fitting into a 'blueprint' mode, but rather as marrying top-down pressure and bottom-up action. The emphasis was on action: Departments were given a strict timetable, but only general instructions to work to. There was a strong emphasis on a bottom-up approach to the development of new forms of organization within each Department, combined with the requirements from the top that Departments should initiate change. Much change had clearly taken place (more than sceptics originally thought), although deep-seated 'cultural' resistance to (for example) decentralization remained.

An assessment of the existing strategy was carried out by the Efficiency Unit (1988) 'Next Steps' initiative which argued that FMI-related work (the clarification of objectives, the introduction of information systems and the development of Performance Indicators) had so far had less effect than staff cuts or budgeting. Further mechanisms were needed to secure a 'release of managerial energy. We want to see managers at all levels in the public service who are eager to maximize results, no longer frustrated or absolved from responsibility by central constraints, working with a sense of urgency to improve their service' (1988, p. 16). As Flynn et al. (1989) argue, the Next Steps initiative reflected not only concern about value for money but also about effecting 'cultural change' so that individual civil servants accept personal responsibility for improving performance: 'largely based on a belief that the public sector is slow to respond to new demands, excessively centralized and rule bound, a major element has been the devolution of responsibility down the management line and the establishment of identifiable units of management or departments'. The mechanism identified for further improving performance was agency status in which agencies would be headed by a Chief Executive who would have considerable delegated power over pay, grading, recruitment and structure. Such changes call for alteration in the behaviour of ministers as well as civil servants, and early candidates for agency status were mostly relatively small-scale operations. Since then the situation has changed, and the giant Social Security benefit system employing 87,000 staff is now a candidate (Flynn et al., 1989).

Although the Efficiency Strategy has clearly achieved more change than early sceptics predicted, we still do not know what would happen if the top-down pressure were removed. Have new role models been established and a new culture set, or would there be rapid regression to the old institutional patterns?

Understanding Change in the NHS

Many of these themes recur in the narrower case of NHS reorganization. Some writers have commented on what they see as a historic underestimate of the ability of the centre to achieve restructuring in the NHS. For example, Davies (1987) critiqued Klein's argument (1984) that in the NHS of the 1980s Thatcherite ideology retreated before enduring political realities. Klein had cited the switch from early decentralist rhetoric to later centralization, the failure to curb spending and the very modest expansion of the private sector in health care as evidence of continuity. In his critique of this evolutionary argument, Davies (1987) pointed instead to important changes in the powers and responsibilities of DHAs, 'attacks' on professions and supply industries, experiments in intersectoral collaboration and the importing of new personnel without a tradition of service within the NHS, helping to create a quite new public sector rhetoric:

> in this context, a restructuring could consolidate quickly. New managers, on short term contracts, are likely to want to move fast in developing innovative care packages. Interest in these at the centre is intense, and the new and more personal style of accountability should help make the innovation known. A few new programmes would then be held up as exemplars. The pressure to adopt similar approaches would be considerable, particularly if financial penalties began to loom. (Davies, 1987)

While the received literature had been profoundly sceptical about the possibility of engineering change within the public sector, a Thatcherite interpretation, by contrast, would see 1979 as a key turning point after which the rules of the game changed, especially given NUPE's leading role in the industrial action taken in the winter of 1978/9. Rising unemployment and changes in the framework of industrial law also could be seen as tilting the balance of power inside the NHS in favour of management, reducing the need to win consent from hostile public sector trade unions and diminishing the importance of the industrial relations agenda which had soaked up management time in the 1970s (Hardy, 1985). The ending of long-standing disputes about paybeds, the retreat from formal incomes policy, the introduction of more rigorous financial control through cost improvement targets and privatization of non-clinical services to squeeze out 'slack' were also seen as offering distinctively new and Thatcherite lines of policy, already apparent in the early 1980s.

A third interpretation evident in some other areas of policy would see 'Thatcherism' as offering more continuity and achieving change more patchily than its rhetoric suggests (Pettigrew and Whipp, 1991). The world was moving that way in any case. So, in economic policy, 'Healyism' predated 'Thatcherism', with money supply controls, targets for reduced government borrowing and attempts to stabilize the share of public spending in GNP all dating from 1975–6. As Britain moves into the post-Thatcherite era, the old problems of high inflation and balance of payment deficits also seem to be reasserting themselves.

How radical was the break within social policy? Flynn (1989) argues that while overall there has been a radical change towards 'new right' ideas, developments have happened at different speeds in the various areas. Looking both at expenditure levels and at overall models of policy, the fastest changes took place in housing, and the slowest in health care. The percentage of public expenditure devoted to health, for example, rose from 11.9 per cent in 1978–9 to a projected 14.1 per cent in 1990–1. So health care was seen as a 'laggard' in the Thatcherite restructuring of social policy.

What view should we take of the balance between continuity and change when the much narrower question of health care management is examined? This question in turn breaks down as follows:

- What were the diagnoses and proposals for change which were being discussed under late Callaghan?
- How did the transition to early Thatcher change this agenda?
- Are the old structures reasserting themselves under late and post-Thatcherism?

Restructuring Health Care Organizations: Continuity or Change?

Stasis in the 1970s

As a consequence of the 1974 NHS reorganization, traditionally separate health services were formally unified within Area Health Authorities on the basis of consensus management teams which included an Administrator. As hospitals lost their independent identity, the old Hospital Secretary posts were transformed into Unit Administrator roles, but this was often seen as leading to a weakening of administrative input at hospital level. While these posts often attracted able and committed people, such administrators had frequently been recruited as new graduates, been trained in specialist institutes, spent their careers entirely within health care systems, performed roles which emphasized due process and individual equity and often had been given little exposure to wider theories or experiences of the nature of the management process.

The traditional tension in party political approaches to health care management has been in the presumed choice between managerial effectiveness and democratic accountability, with Conservative governments inclining to the former, and Labour governments to the latter. As part of the post-1974 Castle reforms to the 1972 reorganization, therefore, the number of local authority representatives on AHAs was increased to a third, and there was a proposal for a directly elected staff representative, reflecting the contemporary movement for industrial democracy.

The NHS in the 1970s could be characterized by a highly developed 'corporate pluralism' with the following features: consensus management (where there could be a temptation for teams of officers to present members with a unified view rather than options for decision); a symbolic commitment to democracy (combined with administrative 'secret gardens' as a result of the lack of member representation at District); continuing negotiation between the centre and the periphery; and an emphasis on representation from various political, professional and social interests, especially with the growth of blue-collar unions alongside the traditionally powerfully placed professional associations which made it difficult to effect strategic change (acute sector rationalization in Inner London was a frequently cited example). Klein (1983) concluded that 'reorganization had, however, increased the costs of such adaptation by institutionalizing the right to oppose change. The ability to veto change – or, at the very least, to resist it by imposing delays – had been diffused' (p. 131).

Concern about poor performance was picked up by the Royal Commission on the NHS and in other research studies in the late 1970s. For example, Brown's (1979) case study of one AHA highlighted a number of fundamental weaknesses: a continuing lack of internal drive; the erosion of the quality of administration at Unit level; and the difficulties with consensus management ('it was only at District level that most of the threads came together and the emphasis on interprofessional consensus meant that DMTs had to deal with matters that could have been settled more quickly lower down', p. 147). The dominant tone was one of inertia within a pluralist yet collusive system:

It is difficult to find anybody . . . with any motive for challenging base expenditure on ongoing services. The members are local people, interested merely in the improvement of local services. The administrators are conditioned to ignore policy statements unless there is new money to go with them. The professionals are committed to their own services. All have some commitment to the inherited pattern and to colleagues whose careers are tied up with it. (Brown, 1979, p. 210)

Within the policy world, increasing dissatisfaction with the standard of decision making in the post-1974 system was also evident in terms of concern about 'waste', 'delay' or 'duplication'. This was reflected in the creation of the Royal Commission on the NHS in 1976 which itself operated in a pre-Thatcherite mode and can be seen as a useful barometer of 'informed opinion' on the verge of the Thatcher era (Klein's view (1983) was that a new consensus was beginning to emerge in the late 1970s around decentralization and simplification).

The Royal Commission was chaired by the Vice Chancellor of Bristol University; it took three years to report (Merrison Report, 1979); it commissioned extensive (often good quality) research which was much more radical than its own preference for broadly incremental change, in part perhaps reflecting its own need to engineer internal consensus (Taylor, 1981) and to avoid a weakening minority report. Apart from its suggestion that there was one tier too many, it was cautious on the question of management. As far as consensus management was concerned, it noted that there could be problems, but also that consensus management could work with the right approach. It suggested organic change: it highlighted a need for a more clearly identified responsibility to implement team decisions and the retention of clear individual roles within consensus management; it drew attention to the coordinating role of the Administrator and recommended the strengthening of management at unit level. It merely urged the Department to offer further guidance on consensus management.

However, some of the research reports commissioned painted a far bleaker picture of the standard of decision making. A Research Report from a team headed by Kogan concluded:

> The overwhelming impression of both participants and the research team is that of a top heavy and over elaborate management system. There are too many levels of administration and too much duplication of functions at the different levels . . . the consultative process should be streamlined to that decision making can be made more speedily and effectively. The process of involving everybody is in the end harmful to everybody. The balance between efficiency and acceptability is weighted too much against efficiency. The balance must be restored . . . (Kogan et al., 1978, pp. 230–1)

And again Kogan et al. found:

> a great deal of anger and frustration at what many regarded as a seriously over elaborate system of government, administration and decision making. The multiplicity of levels, the over elaboration of consultative machinery, the inability to get decision making completed nearer the point of delivery of services, and what some describe as unacceptably wasteful use of manpower resources were recurrent themes in most of the areas where we worked. (1978, p. 231)

From a financial point of view, a Research Paper for the Royal Commission by Perrin et al. (1978) also defined a number of important areas where capacity needed to be upgraded. These were: skilling up finance personnel; the introduction of specialty costings and then budgeting; a move to workload and then on to output measurement; greater budgetary delegation to units and a more integrated hospital information system.

The disjunction between the analysis of some of the commissioned research and the recommendations of the Commission have been explored by Taylor (1981) with respect to differences over such issues as: professional influence, the calibre of members ('not only a case of ducking an issue but also of misconstructing the evidence', Taylor, 1981, p. 540), and joint planning.

So while radical criticism was available in its own research papers, the policy response from the Royal Commission was much more muted. 'Informed opinion' in the policy world on the verge of the Thatcher era can best be seen as cautious, rather than anticipating what was about to emerge.

Early Thatcherism: Continuity as Well as Change

With the change of government in 1979, there was certainly a rapid switch of interest away from such issues as the control of paybeds towards new questions of financial control and value for money through the imposition of cost improvement targets and contracting out. However, at this stage change in management structures (and the focus was structural at this stage) was more organic, centred on decentralization and simplification.

Maxwell's conclusion (1988) was as follows:

> Writing in 1987, the introduction of general management appears central to the thrust of government policy towards the NHS in the Thatcher years. But it does not seem to have been premeditated in 1979. There was little hint of that line of thinking under Mrs Thatcher's first administration when, with Patrick Jenkin as Secretary of State, AHAs were abolished and the accent – characteristic of the Government's policy statement 'Patients First' – was on decentralization.

In *Patients First* the DHSS (1979) carried forward – perhaps in a crisper form – the lines of development foreshadowed in the Royal Commission. The emphasis was on slimming down and decentralization: the area and sector tiers were abolished with the District emerging as the strategic planning tier and the Unit as the frontline service provider. There was to be a strengthening of administrative capacity at Unit level as in each major hospital: 'there should be an administrator and nurse of appropriate seniority to discharge an individual responsibility in conjunction with the medical staff' and in addition 'wherever possible, staff working within hospitals in non clinical support functions should be accountable to the hospital administrator, rather than to district level managers'.

In retrospect, perhaps the most interesting conclusion was the continuing emphasis on limited, structural reform. For example, DHSS (1979) rejected the more radical proposal floated (but not supported) by the Royal Commission to appoint Chief Executives within the NHS and approved the preservation of consensus management at District level:

> The Government has rejected the proposition that each authority should appoint a chief executive responsible for all the authority's staff. It believes that such an appointment would not be compatible with the professional independence required by the wide range of staff employed in the service. Instead, each authority should appoint a team to coordinate all the health service activities. (DHSS, 1979)

But 'decentralization' had its limits as a policy, and soon ran up against competing pressures for ensuring financial control and for achieving an acceleration of longstanding strategic change agendas. The switch could be seen first of all in the introduction of regional reviews and performance indicators in the early 80s, which was cited by Klein (1984) as evidence of a retreat from early doctrine. DHSS (1982) outlined the purpose of ministerial review, which was to put top-down pressure on regions to 'perform'.

> to examine the progress made by the region in implementing the Government's policies . . . and so far as possible the RHA's effectiveness, including the relative performance of DHAs within the region.

General Management – what Is It For?

As the mid-Thatcherite government began to move on from 'decentralization' as the leitmotif for its policy towards health care management, it was not yet clear what its overall agenda was for the NHS. The care group-based planning characteristic of the Castle/Ennals era had gone, the old paybeds, income policies and industrial relations disputes were fading, yet radical privatization did not seem a politically feasible option.

The Griffiths Report (1983) represents a key document. Short, action-orientated and written by a single adviser drawn from a retail background (Sainsbury's), it was far removed from the consensus building process associated with the Royal Commission. It did not commission and wait for research, although many of its recommendations were consistent with contemporary research findings. For example, Schultz and Harrison (1983) had found that most NHS consensus management teams had made no attempt to influence the efficiency or effectiveness of services, while Stewart et al.'s study (1980) of the ways in which Administrators defined their brief found few of them to be innovators.

Griffiths clearly grasped the 'means' nettle, and the report's advocacy of change was not only structural but cultural. The old ways of doing things in the NHS were seen as having failed and outside thinking needed to be brought in:

> To the outsider, it appears that when change of any kind is required, the NHS is so structured so as to resemble a 'mobile': designed to move with any breath of air, but which in fact never changes its position and gives no clear indication of direction. (Griffiths Report, 1983)

Here was embryonic system change which with time and action could potentially become real system change. It was operating at various levels of the system from Whitehall down to the manager/clinician relationship. It was focusing on processes and roles much more than the traditional concern with formal structure. It also operated with a much greater variety of levers than had traditionally been the case in reorganizations: the creation of a centrally appointed cadre of general managers; an extension of accountability reviews; a more active concern with Human Resource Management; the recognition of the management of change and of implementation gaps as problems; a concern with strategy.

While there was within Griffiths a new language of 'drive' and 'leadership', what were the ends to which these means were to be applied, and how can the degree of 'success' be assessed? Hunter and Williamson (1989) discuss some of the difficulties involved in assessing the impact of the Griffiths reorganization. One related to the short cut-off point, as the reorganization itself is still relatively youthful, and Sir Roy Griffiths himself has been said to think that at least a decade is needed before the reorganization will come to fruition. Secondly, it was not always clear what criteria of success might be, as the ends of reorganization were not always specified.

So how do we locate the Griffiths Report? Within the document itself, three alternative managerial agendas could be glimpsed.

Financial Control and Value for Money

Certainly there was now greater interest in financial control. Political commitment to rolling back Big Government and ensuring value for money entailed a number of consequences for the NHS – underfunded pay awards, successive cost improvement programmes, the contracting out of support services, and revenue generation schemes. Parston (1988) indeed argues that the Griffiths Report sprang from the concern of the then Secretary of State (Norman Fowler) about variations in cost structures across Districts.

Thus Griffiths argues that:

> Major cost improvements can and should be initiated from within the NHS, aiming at much higher levels of efficiency to be sustained over much longer periods of time than at present . . . it is almost a denial of the management process to argue that the modest levels of cost improvement at present required of the NHS are unachievable without impacting seriously on the level of services. (1983, para. 9)

Griffiths made a number of specific recommendations on budgeting and cost control, which included:

- There should be major cost improvement programmes for implementation by general managers.
- District Chairmen should involve clinicians more closely in the management process.

- District Chairmen should see that each unit has a 'total budget' for maximum cost consciousness at unit level, and encourage interest in seeking out economies.

Initially Clinical Management Budgeting was to be tested out in four sites.

Strategic Change: Closing the Gap

Concern about possible strategic drift was also apparent as a second theme in the Griffiths Report (1983):

> Absence of this general management support means that there is no driving force seeking and accepting direct and personal responsibility for developing management plans, securing their implementation and monitoring actual achievement . . . lack of the general managerial responsibility also means that certain major initiatives are difficult to implement.

What was the strategic change agenda which was now apparent? By the early 1980s there was from the centre's perspective evidence of drift in at least three key policy areas. The long-standing policy for the acute sector based on the building of District General Hospitals implied considerable redevelopment and rationalization yet few strategic change exercises had been launched. Nowhere were the problems of acute sector change more apparent than in London, where long-standing pressure to rationalize medical education had failed to secure real change, given the dense and often hostile political environment (Flowers Report, 1980).

The Nodder Report (1980) also diagnosed implementation failure in what had been other bipartisan policies (for better or for worse) such as the rundown and closure of mental illness hospitals and thereby defined a need for enhancing strategic management. Nodder suggested that shortage of resources was only part of the problem, and that fundamental change would only be realized when central direction was given to Regions and Areas, through the setting of objectives, standards and targets, and the restructuring and strengthening of local management. In mental handicap services, too, DHSS (1980) found failure in progressing long-standing objectives for change. The document mentioned the difficulties of running down large, conservative institutions, and pointed out the confusion and layers of overlap between agencies.

Building an Organization: OD and HRM

Gunn's account (1989) of the Thatcherite approach to public sector management outlined what were seen as the five 'Es': economy, efficiency, enterprise, effectiveness and perhaps most interesting of all, 'excellence'. This perhaps reflected the wider excellence literature fashionable at the time (Peters and Waterman, 1982) in the private sector, which was now crossing into the public sector, with a greater interest in organizational culture rather than the structural reforms which had characterized change in the NHS in the past.

There was also the beginnings of a new emphasis within Griffiths on the OD/HRM capacity which was needed to support an 'excellence culture', moving on from the industrial relations agenda of the 1970s (Hardy, 1985) as changes in the national political economy eroded the base of public sector unions. In part this impacted on salary structures as meritocratic arguments for greater rewards for high 'performers' replaced the old equity basis of nationally agreed wage structures. There were also wider changes envisaged as Griffiths supported the personnel function as it attempted to move up from its traditionally lowly status (acquiring the new 'human resource' label in the process):

> Line managers need to accept their responsibility for their staff and will require better training in personnel matters. This is only part of the general upgrading of the quality of management which the NHS requires. As in any process of change, there will be a need to take staff along in a positive sense, by top class communication and training. There must be incentives for staff, through proper reward for performance and career prospects. The sanction of removing the inefficient performer must also be more easily available than at present, though always as a last resort. (Griffiths Report, 1983, para. 25)

While pluralist in the sense of hedging its bets about what the managerial agenda could be, Griffiths was clearly a managerial charter and was opposed not only by the professional associations, but also the Social Services Select Committee of the House of Commons (1984). Nevertheless, implementation was rapid, with ministerial attempts to ensure that private sector outsiders were brought into the system to break up the old culture and that a new breed of clinician managers were appointed.

Our data suggest that in this the centre largely failed, as our own sample of general managers was predominantly recruited from the old Administrators, with a few clinicians (community medicine in particular could sometimes cross from 'policy' to management) and nurse managers, and even fewer businessmen. Moreover, the clinicians and ex-private-sector businessmen seemed more likely to quit general managerial roles than the ex-Administrators. By and large, the general managers in 1988 had the same sort of primary professional background as the Administrators in 1983, but this does not mean that they had not redefined their roles, sometimes quite radically, in that time period.

Assessing the Impact of the Griffiths Report

Pleas for the introduction of general management through pilot programmes were not successful, nor was a nationally coordinated research programme commissioned into the Griffiths reforms which were more action-based in orientation. However, a number of different studies did take place, using different methodologies, and from different sponsors (most intensive empirical work does, of course, require special funding).

It seems fair to state that a consensus has not yet emerged in the literature. Initially Hunter (1984) was sceptical about the potential for change given the failure of past restructurings: 'it would be remarkable indeed if the Griffiths Report were to attain the status of the last organizational quick fix'; while Best (1987) on the other hand claims: 'whatever else may be true about the introduction of general management, its impact on the service has been *immense*'. However, the criteria against which the impact of general management is to be measured and the empirical basis for assessments of this sort surely need to be greatly clarified and strengthened.

How are we to assess the literature which has emerged? One should remember that Griffiths was not tackling completely new issues, and that there was already an established literature on consensus management. Commentators would sometimes have in the past defended multi-disciplinary teams, seeing the charges against them as 'not proven', and the product of an inevitable trade-off between a variety of different interest groups. Harrison's review of the literature on consensus decision making in the NHS for example concluded:

> The pluralistic perspective (and its corresponding rationale for the introduction of consensus decision making) is the realistic way of viewing the NHS. Many of the criticisms of consensus seem to spring from a denial of this reality: thus, there is a dislike of treating as important any issue which is important to an influential actor, a dislike of the necessity to use teamwork to enhance implementability of decisions, a dislike of the need to trade speed for commitment and of the need to compromise. (1982, pp. 387–8)

The new literature which was in the end generated by Griffiths can perhaps be divided into three groups. The first can be seen as speculative argument, as an initial reaction to the report, not requiring empirical research. Day and Klein's fascinating article (1983) for instance, spotted the change in language from the mobilization of consent to the management of conflict, but argued that change might be possible, if not easy:

> if the health service is to move from a system that is based on the mobilization of consent to one based on the management of conflict – from one that has conceded the right of a variety of interest groups to veto change to one that gives the managers the right to override objections – then the process is going to mean radical and perhaps painful change.

Hunter (1984), on the basis of the experience of previous reorganizations, was rather more sceptical that the NHS might embrace the surface but not the reality of change, given that a fundamental feature of the NHS was a delicately balanced relationship between professional groups.

A second group of writers firmly located the Griffiths Report within the context of the changing national political economy. An interesting example of this genre is Petchey (1986) who, writing within a critical but not explicitly Marxist analysis, saw Griffiths as an essentially alien document, transferring in an uncritical way managerial concepts from the private sector (where management was seen as less problematic) to the NHS:

> Griffiths's prescription is a liberal application of private sector management techniques. What he overlooks entirely is the possibility that such techniques operate successfully in the private sector only because there exists consensus about *both* the ultimate objective of the organisation (to make profits) *and* the criteria for evaluating alternative means of achieving that objective. (Petchey, 1986, p. 92)

Here the public/private sector controversy discussed in Chapter 2 re-emerges. In our opinion, Petchey's view of the nature of management in the private sector fails to capture the demands made on managers in certain sectors (such as oil or pharmaceuticals) where the political environment is also extremely important, and the complex bargaining that can go on within the firm around defining objectives and even bases of performance (Pettigrew, 1973b; Pettigrew and Whipp, 1991).

A third set of studies have been empirically based, examining changes in role following the implementation of Griffiths and often single or comparative case study methodology has been used. A major area of interest has been the renegotiation of the frontier between management and the weaker of the health care professions (such as nursing). Glennerster et al. (1986) looked at the implementation post-Griffiths of structural changes affecting the nursing profession in one Region with the break-up of traditional professional lines of accountability, finding that the CNO post had disappeared in most Districts, being transformed into a Nursing Advisory post usually combined with an operational role. The Nurse Adviser in some structures was found to have an anomalous role, and it was not always clearly understood by the encumbents of the NA post, or by unit staff, what level of involvement was appropriate. Looking at appointments to DGM and UGM posts in the Region, most senior general managers appointed were male, young (in their 30s), had first degrees and were mainly from NHS administrative backgrounds. Senior nurses tended to be older than this new cadre, and their primary education was professional rather than academic. Nurses accounted for only 20 per cent of UGM appointments. As Glennerster et al. conclude:

> The problem associated with the age profile of the new general management structure in NW Thames is that it builds a kind of compression chamber at the top. In spite of the three year contracts the turnover of UGMs predictably will not be high. Some UGMs could be in post for 20 years or more; or, as in industry, they could be facing early retirement if they do not make the grade. (1986, p. 77)

Strong and Robinson's (1988, 1990) ethnography examined the introduction of general management in a sample of Districts. Their broad conclusion was that continuity was as evident as change, as the new general management was still trapped inside the NHS hierarchy, with its political sensitivity and control over funding. Pay determination was still largely national, devolution halting and doctors continued to enjoy a

special syndicalist status. Moreover, there were special local factors which
affected the nature of the transition between old and new: the way that
previous structures had sometimes foreshadowed the new regime; how far
the old DMT still existed and moulded events; and the influence of the
new DGM's background and preferred style of working. These locality
effects were investigated further and theoretically interrogated in our
study.

An ESRC funded study (Hunter, 1989) into the introduction of general
management similarly attempted to distinguish between the form and the
substance of management, using comparative case study methodology to
consider issues around attempts to involve clinicians in management in
terms of negotiation of the respective roles of managers and clinicians.
Harrison et al. (1989a, b) report early results from their study of general
management in nine Districts with respect to the issue of 'clinical
freedom', as seen in the negotiated relations between managers and clinicians in the localities. With the exception of the enhanced influence which
resulted from resource restrictions (potentially of course a powerful lever),
this study found that it was difficult to detect a marked post-Griffiths
reduction of the ability of doctors to obstruct management action.
Previous work on pre-Griffiths NHS management (Harrison, 1988) had
characterized the manager's role as a 'diplomat', 'an actor concerned with
facilitation, provision of resources and the smoothing out of conflict,
rather than controlling professionals or changing the direction of the
service. All districts in the present study have provided evidence that this
is still how the managerial role is predominantly seen' (Harrison et al.,
1989a, p. 43). Later analysis suggested that while Districts had achieved
greater freedom to adapt their own organizational structures, while there
was a widespread (though not universal) feeling that personal responsibility had been sharpened at least at the top, and while there was greater
cost consciousness, in other areas change was less clear cut (Harrison et
al., 1989b). There was perceived to be patchy or superficial progress on
resource management and on consumerism, which remained marginal to
many respondents. Our own study will be able to investigate a subgroup
of cases where an acceleration of the rate and pace of strategic change was
seen as associated with general management, and explore why this should
be the case.

Further studies have looked at the construction of the general
managerial role within DHAs. Thompson (1987), for instance, looked on
the basis of case study work in DHAs at the extent to which 'dominant
coalitions' were renegotiated following the introduction of general
management. Were general managers found to identify with an existing
coalition (most were still in service appointments), or were they attempting to negotiate a distinctive general managerial coalition which could
pave the way for a more radical transformation? Thompson concluded:
'already there are signs that new DGMs have responded to this challenge:
they have been distancing themselves from their professional roots. Some

former District Administrators have made it clear that they can no longer be seen as the chief administrator'. It was also thought that the emerging beliefs of the general manager coalition may be more explicit and dominant than those belief systems prevalent in the consensus era. But what might a distinctive general managerial agenda look like in view of the commitments inherited from the past (many of them long term in nature)? In particular, Thompson argued that general managers might be able to balance traditional professional dominance in decision making with greater consumer involvement.

Stewart et al.'s tracer study (1987a, b) of 20 DGMs also examined how general managerial roles were being negotiated within DHAs. It was clear that DGMs had a great deal of discretion in the negotiation of such roles, with sample DGMs varying in the size and nature of their domain. Stewart et al. then took the major Griffiths recommendations and compared them with what the sample DGMs felt to be the achievements of general management:

- *'Bias for action'* Most (and possibly all) the DGMs saw this as an achievement of general management, especially at the more senior levels – accountable individuals, a reduction in the amount of paper, a tighter agenda, more informal communication and ensuring that unit level issues were dealt with at unit were all seen as associated with faster decision making, as was the introduction of Individual Performance Review by most (but not all) the DGMs.
- *Breaking down professional tribalism* A key aim of many of the new structure documents was 'detribalization'. Most of the DGMs cited this as one of the achievements of general management; most of the District directors now combine professional and functional roles and so have wider responsibilities.
- *Involve doctors in management and influence clinical practice* This was one of the major disappointments for the sample, although in some Districts DGMs said that there was an increasing managerial awareness and involvement among some doctors, and that there had been some change in the ability of managers to question doctors about their work and to negotiate changes.
- *Improvement in the measurement of health output* None of the DGMs cited this as an achievement because of the difficulties in quantifying health care interventions and health outcomes, although improving information systems was an active aim of some of the DGMs.
- *Devolution* The DGMs in general felt that there had been devolution from District to Unit, although this differed between functions and Districts. Some DGMs were also critical of what they saw as increasing intervention from the centre.
- *Improving the sensitivity of the service to the views of the consumer.*

Many DGMs in the tracer study said that the Griffiths Report oversimplified the difficulties of involving consumers, particularly at a time of financial constraint and in the absence of reliable information. None pointed to this as an areas of achievement.

Implications for Research into the Management of Change

We now review our conclusions from the chapters presented so far before we go on in the chapters that follow to present detailed empirical data. While the initial starting point for the project could be seen in terms of examining the impact of general management, this perspective can be elaborated in a number of important ways. The conclusions of the study may indeed have generic implications.

A Contextualist Approach

The methodological conclusion from the review conducted in Chapter 2 was that much promise lay in conducting a contextualist analysis through a relatively small number of highly intensive case studies. The case study technique was as much abused as used, and these case studies should be processual, multi-layered, pluralist and historical in character. We could be dealing with strategic change processes of long duration. While a sound empirical basis for this work was crucial, it was also important to have an awareness of theory both in terms of establishing an initial field and inductively as theory began to emerge from the data.

A number of implications flowed from this choice of perspective. It should not be assumed that general management would automatically lead these processes of strategic change, but this question would be settled empirically in complex and pluralist systems where there could be a wide variety of levers for change. We needed to link DHAs to their wider setting: top-down pressure from the Department and Regions; social movements and social movement organizations; and inter-organizational networks could all be important sources of change. It could not be assumed that a blanket general managerial culture would emerge, but rather the analysis needed to consider how general managerial behaviour varied both by locality and by issue. In the negotiation of new orders, the researchers needed to be alert to potential break points and moments of critical drama where normally hidden tensions (briefly) stood out in sharp relief. While there are already some high-quality single case studies of strategic change in health care settings (Korman and Glennerster, 1985), the choice of a comparative case study perspective could be justified in terms of engaging the question of 'performance', forcing compare and contrast analysis, and building up a larger number of case studies which could be used as a basis for theory building.

In terms of theoretical perspective, a number of different streams of literature were reviewed. While we needed to be alert to the implications of all this work, the model chosen to organize the material was the organizational transition perspective which was sensitive to the way in which organizational form evolved through time.

Strategic Service Change: the Unit of Analysis

But what is general management for? There are a number of answers to that question, but one we identified as latent within the Griffiths Report itself was the progression of strategic service change. Could the District formulate and implement a strategy for change? By the early 1980s, the centre was diagnosing implementation gaps in a number of fields, although other challenges (such as HIV/AIDS) emerged unexpectedly. In other words, we saw the introduction of general management as a means to an end, rather than an end itself. Of course we do not know whether the strategies adopted were in any final sense 'good', as that would have required a different kind of project with much more emphasis on the assessment of final patient outcome. There are of course many such more micro-level studies proceeding anyway (for example, Renshaw et al., 1988), but we know much less about how these systems of care acquired their characteristics or how they can be changed.

The Testing and Development of Institutional Theory

In this chapter the literature on institutional change has been reviewed. One clear theme identified has been the debate about the potential for top-down change processes – so characteristic of the UK public sector in the 1980s – to secure real change in the localities. Apart from Metcalfe and Richards's study of the Civil Service (1987), there was as yet little empirical evidence to inform this rather skeletal debate. Is commitment to institutional reform rhetorical or does it here (perhaps unusually) signify a radical break with the past? Has general management made a difference to the ways that key decisions are made in Districts and if so, how? The case studies will provide an opportunity to test some of these arguments across different localities and issues. At one extreme (if bottom-up or 'garbage can' perspectives are correct), the impact of top-down reforms can be expected to be muted, as informal or chaotic organizational life reasserts itself. If a top-down 'radical shock' perspective holds, by contrast, we can expect to see similar significant processes of general managerial role creation and shifts in the balance of power across Districts and issues. A middle course might be one in which substantial variability was found, with general management making a big impact in certain sets of circumstances, but much less in others.

Interrogating the Case Studies

It has been previously argued that case study work should seek to integrate a sound empirical base with an awareness of theory. However, such theoretical work may often take a middle-range, descriptive form rather than being highly normative or macro in nature. While a number of analytic themes were established before we went into the field, many others emerged inductively from the data. Some of these analytic themes may be highly specific to localities and issues, while others may have more general resonance. For example, the chapter on HIV/AIDS will consider questions of crisis management, clinical product champions and the role of social movements and social movement organizations as potential motors of change, as well as outline an empirical history. The potential role of social movements is also apparent in the chapters on mental handicap and mental illness, which can act as further points of comparison.

In the final chapter we seek to bring together the case study material and move towards the development of a new theory. In particular we believe that the distinction developed between receptive and non-receptive contexts for change represents a novel, distinctive and fruitful concept which needs to be confirmed, modified or indeed refuted in the light of additional evidence.

We now move to present a series of comparative case study chapters, each focusing on a major strategic change issue and chosen to cover a wide range of topics. This represents a rich data base which enables us to make an assessment of the impact of general management on these processes of strategic service change.

4
Managing Retrenchment
Rationalization and Redevelopment in the Acute Sector

The inheritance in 1948 of a patchwork quilt of antiquated Victorian estate created a double-edged change agenda for NHS administrators and successor general managers. Not only had there been from 1962 a long-standing national policy of creating a network of DGHs (and some of the issues posed by the management of such massive and complex growth will be discussed in Chapter 8), but there was also (at least implicitly) a parallel policy of rationalizing old plant: closing down Victorian acute hospitals.

Perhaps surprisingly these closure processes were not initially seen as problematic, but evidence began to emerge from the late 1960s of local resistance to closure as a corollary of the construction of new DGHs – Ham's history of the Yorkshire Region (1981) takes the example of Kirkbymoorside Hospital.

The introduction of the Resource Allocation Working Party (RAWP) funding formula in 1976 gave additional urgency to retrenchment pressures in inner city areas as it increasingly challenged the historic basis of funding, and shifted resources out from the inner cities to the suburbs and the shires where the population levels were increasing, and where the new DGHs were being built up. Through the 1980s the squeeze on funding further added to the pressure on inner city DHAs in particular to scale down the size of the acute sector which delivered medical and surgical services to their populations.

Yet health care managers attempting to develop retrenchment strategies faced formidable obstacles:

● Political hostility or ambivalence about the consequences of retrenchment.
● Negotiation with the higher Regional tiers.
● Inability to control the size or the activity of the consultant workforce.
● A fragmented, decentralized and professionalized pattern of decision making.

This policy problem can also be usefully explored through various more theoretic literatures. First, we discuss 'organizational decline' as a highly generic theme which emerged in the 1980s. Then we consider a more explicitly managerial perspective on retrenchment processes; examples are cited from private sector settings as well as a comparable public sector setting (universities). Then we examine the literature on organizational crisis and its management, which can be contrasted with a much more 'decrementalist' approach to budgeting processes within declining organizations. The 'organizational death' metaphor is discussed in relation to hospital closure processes. Finally, questions of 'non-decision making' and 'the management of meaning' are explored in relation to organizational politics and internal power relations.

Literature Review: Organizational Decline, Death and Cutback Management

Organizations may decline, die or be scaled back. These may, however, be represented in very different organizational processes: retrenchment can be seen as one proactive way of attempting to manage a decline process. Decline may also take a much more 'unplanned' form as well.

Organizational Decline: a Theme of the 1980s

First we consider 'decline' in the broadest sense. The fiscal crisis of the mid and late 1970s increasingly challenged organization theories which had been based on the problems of managing growth, as a new interest in 'cutback management', 'downsizing' and managing organizational closure emerged in both the private and public sectors. Even blue chip private sector firms such as ICI (Pettigrew, 1985a) fell off the top of a cliff in the recession of the early 1980s, as rapid decline had to be managed in a short period and a new corporate strategy assembled. In the public sector, too, a deteriorating financial environment could lead to fiscal crisis (emerging in New York City government as early as 1973–4, Levine et al., 1982). Initially, the reaction was one of disorientation within the public administration literature (Levine, 1978) as many of its traditional assumptions about incremental growth were no longer applicable and indeed had to be stood on their head. The problem was no longer one of inclusionary mechanisms to prevent 'free riders' from enjoying public goods; but one of exclusionary devices to prevent 'free exiters' from public bads.

The 1980s have been characterized by an explosion of the decline literature, in the reorientation towards 'the central organizational phenomena of the past decade – growing scarcity, downsizing, and doing better, or at least not much worse, with less' (Golembiewski, 1990). In the public sector, decline is often associated with increased fiscal stress. Of course, in the private sector, competitive pressure and technological change may also produce decline in organizations (or sub-divisions) which cannot effectively compete or change.

Decline Typologies and Organizing Metaphors As well as detailed

empirical work, there has been a search for a decline typology and for guiding metaphors. Whetten (1980), for example, distinguishes between different definitions of the decline problem: decline as stagnation (as in mature industries) and decline as cutback. Each of these categories may have implications for decline management. Decline processes could also be examined within a population of organizations (all cigarette factories, for instance, could be facing pressures to retrench) or within individual organizations.

The organizational life cycle metaphor (Kimberly and Miles, 1980), with its notion of organizational stages, provided another organization device. However, its fatalistic conceptualization of organizational 'stages' was sometimes seen as according too little space to the possibility of internal strategic choice, revitalization and turnaround. This chapter explores whether similar 'stages' occur across the two case studies, or whether there is substantially greater variability.

Sometimes 'stage' models of decline have been developed, only to be refined in the light of comparative case study evidence. Levine et al.'s initial expectation on the basis of their first New York case study was that continuing budgetary reductions would first of all produce a stage of denial and delay; then a period of across-the-board cuts and resource stretching; and finally a move to selectivity, after a reconfiguration of the power structure. In fact further case studies provided very different responses, and it seemed that the response to fiscal stress was not only determined by the extent of revenue reduction but by the nature of the authority system in each locality. Thus the strong executives in Oakland and Baltimore both adopted and implemented focused retrenchment strategies, while the less centralized Cincinnati and Prince George's County both formulated plans along the lines of a managerial model but could not implement them (Levine et al., 1982).

Jick and Murray's (1982) organizing framework related to decision theory, outlining possible alternative decision paradigms (rational, political, interpretive, and contingency theoretic) each of which would structure processes of decision making in a different way. They argued that a political paradigm would be likely to dominate decline management, indicating (for example) strategies of coalition forming or negotiation with the funding source in an attempt to win respite. The Regional Health Authority may act as banker of last resort within the NHS. Jick and Murray also point to the potential importance of the organizational crisis literature in the analysis of retrenchment and the importance of the internal distribution of power relations in determining how cutbacks are made.

Organizational Impact of Decline   Jick and Murray (1982) also speculate that perceptions of powerlessness and irrationality are likely to increase under conditions of decline and that crisis syndrome behaviours (resignations, poor morale, poor communication, less planning, more centralization) are likely to emerge.

So, organizations in decline may find it difficult to perform the unpleasant task of retrenchment. Rather they may exhibit a range of pathological behaviours which make effective management difficult (Whetten, 1988) such as conflict, secrecy, rigidity and centralization scapegoating, and low morale. Innovativeness, participation, leader influence and long-range planning may decrease as short-term pressure escalates. Conflict intensifies as groups lobby to protect turf, leading to further politicization and fixed interest group behaviour.

Approaches to Managing Decline We have not so far explicitly considered the extent to which decline can be managed (although Levine et al.'s (1982) evidence suggests that the strength of managerial resources is critical), rather than unfold inevitably. These will be explored later on in the chapter, so here it is sufficient to note that a variety of perspectives is evident.

Managing Retrenchment in Private and Public Sector Settings

'Cutback management' has emerged as an important theme of the managerial literature of the 1980s in both the private and public sector. Normative argument has been developed by authors such as Behn (1988): managers *should* decide what to cut; they should maintain staff morale yet create opportunities for innovation. The role of managerial strategic choice in the face of decline in the private sector was also highlighted by Harrigan (1988). A good public sector comparator is the management of retrenchment in universities.

Hardy (1987) argues that models of retrenchment drawn from the private sector have only limited applicability in the university setting: management cannot fire faculty; power is decentralized in the hands of the professors; and many internal and external interest groups seek to influence decision making. Nor is the balance sheet seen as unambiguously sovereign as excellence was not necessarily to be found in the healthiest balance sheet or in the introduction of new cost control methods, but was associated with the ability to recruit and retain talented and productive individuals.

A comparison of retrenchment processes at two Canadian universities (McGill and the University of Montreal) indicated important differences in the way in which they were perceived, with greater selectivity being resisted at the University of Montreal:

> Those at McGill were less critical of both the process of cutback and the general management of the institution. This can be explained by the differences in context and process. At McGill the collegial context created a situation which was conducive to the successful management of cutbacks – the faculty are loyal and nonunionized, and the leadership has high credibility. The process used to implement the cutbacks – decentralized and ostensibly 'fair' – reinforced the collegial culture. At the University of Montreal, decision making has been more centralized and technocratic, and central administration suffered from

credibility problems. The cutback process did little to improve the situation. (Hardy, 1987, p. 77)

Many of the models so far reviewed have been general, even deterministic, perhaps finding it difficult to incorporate the role of subjectivity and locality in retrenchment processes. The crisis literature, however, suggested that local variability was in part explained by the possession of managerial and political resources. This further leads to such concepts as 'turnaround management' and agency revitalization:

> Turnaround management involves taking an organization that has been buffeted by the vagaries of diminished resources and setting it on a new course. With rare exception, organizations are turned round only after the internal and organizational consequences of decline are so pervasive and severe that a consensus on the need for drastic action has grudgingly emerged. (Whetten, 1988)

The transition to new management is sometimes seen as providing an opportunity for turnaround strategies, although Whetten argues that it is important to go beyond efficiency (resource-stretching) measures to make more fundamental judgements about effectiveness. It is important for leaders to seize the initiative, creating a clear future vision which shifts the focus from survival to excellence and hence an overarching goal which can break through interest group behaviour. The provision of incentives which can work to recast the retrenchment process in a positive light seems to emerge as particularly important, and can be seen in some of the case studies presented in this book.

Private sector data can be derived from Grinyer et al.'s (1988b) study of a sample of 'sharpbending' firms which exhibited a marked and sustained improvement of performance. This study found that they were likely to have taken a series of interrelated steps ('good management', effective financial and other controls, quality orientation) rather than just one. 'Good management' could be decomposed in turn into a number of features: action-orientated; values people; good internal communications; the board and key executives having financial incentives. Grinyer et al. (1988b) conclude:

> The major distinguishing feature of the sharpbenders is that a sharpbend is not a one-off set of measures which somehow enables the company to do better indefinitely. It is a change to a new form of behaviour. The characteristics of the company in the longer run after the bend are different from those beforehand.

Within the public sector, Levine et al.'s (1981, 1982) exploration of retrenchment processes in American cities also identified a rather different constellation of political or managerial resources which were seen as important but which were often lacking in public sector settings:

- formal authority centralized within a unified and secure management team;

- continuity in top management;
- rapid and accurate feedback;
- the budgetary flexibility to recreate some sources of organizational slack;
- incentives for the management of retrenchment;
- the capacity to target cuts.

Later work (Levine, 1988) on retrenchment processes in the police service argued that agencies that adapted best to fiscal stress had the strategic capacity to undertake such tasks as:

- formulate and stick to a three to five year plan;
- develop a political and administrative climate conducive to experimentation;
- be clear about the functional components of strategy (such as budgetary flexibility);
- be able to target cuts.

Crisis, Crisis Management and its Aftermath

Crisis management represents another analytic theme which can be used to mine the case study material. Dutton (1987) argues that the managerial processing of strategic issues will be different in crisis and non-crisis situations. Much of the existing literature on organizational crisis (Hermann, 1963; Jick and Murray, 1982) stresses the pathological consequences of crisis-as-threat: namely, increased centralization and formalization, with a breakdown of integrating structures; the erosion of information channels; the exiting of key human resources; a loss of trust and loyalty as a low commitment organization emerges; denial and scapegoating (Turner, 1976); and groupthink (Smart and Vertinsky, 1977). Crisis is seen here as leading to an organizational mechanistic shift in which the creativity and flexibility needed is even less likely to occur.

There is, however, a less considered counter-scenario of crisis-as-opportunity (Starbuck et al., 1978). Major change can perhaps only take place when the perception of a crisis forces an awkward issue up crowded agendas, especially when it is associated with the presence of new leadership. The construction of crisis-as-opportunity by a band of early learners may lead to very different patterns of behaviour and a reconfiguration of power relations with the appearance of high energy and commitment levels and strong integrating mechanisms. Even in this more optimistic scenario, there remains the potential problem of how to manage the post-crisis aftermath, perhaps as disillusion or burn-out sets in.

Some empirical material on the management of retrenchment-based crises within human service organizations is now emerging. While there seems to be much local variability, this literature indicates that an effective response to crisis is possible. Warren (1984) takes as a case study one American university where the failure of the institution to meet its payroll brought a rapid top-down restructuring led in a very personal way by its President, suggesting that individuals may exert transformatory leadership even in such a complex and professionalized higher education setting.

Meyer's (1982) study of the behaviour of hospital management during an 'environmental jolt' (in this case an expected strike of doctors) is also worth citing. This work suggested that a jolt from the environment could evoke different organizational perceptions and reactions. It also indicated that a given organization's behaviour during a jolt could diverge substantially from its prior self-image and behaviour during more tranquil periods: an efficient hospital eschewed cost cutting; an anarchistic hospital acted decisively and a large, complex hospital adjusted effortlessly. The degree of forewarning was best explained by market strategy as the potential for a strike was detected earlier by those hospitals that marketed their services more innovatively, spanned their boundaries more intensively and whose administrators devoted more attention to their environments. There were some interesting examples of adaptive behaviour and Meyer (1982) concluded:

> By plunging organizations into unfamiliar circumstances, jolts can legitimate unorthodox experiments that revitalize them, teach lessons that reacquaint them with their environments, and inspire drama celebrating their ideologies.

Decremental Management

This stream of literature – essentially derived from the study of budgetary processes – often revolves around the dominance or otherwise of 'decrementalism' as a form of cutback management. It thus contrasts with the strategic management perspective on organizational decline. It relates to a wider attack on the historic hegemony of bottom-up 'incrementalism' as a descriptive theory of budgeting, in the light of its inability to theorize about top-down budgetary processes (Bozeman and Straussman, 1982) or retrenchment management. There is now a move within budget theory away from describing the budget process as a set of fixed rules and uniform repeated procedures to exploring the sources of variability in budgeting:

> recent budget theory has expanded in scope from an exclusive focus on appropriations to one that includes the politics of revenues; the organization of the decision making process; attempts to balance and rebalance the budget; and the implementation of budgets once they are passed. (Rubin, 1989)

Within the private sector, 'maintenance strategies' might be the analogous concept, but it is in the public sector that the decrementalist argument has been most developed.

The key question for the management of budgetary retrenchment is: are such decisions 'decremental' (across the board reductions which do not seek to reconfigure services in any significant way) or do they take the form of quantum reductions? While Stewart (1980) argued that retrenchment in local government was likely to lead to an increase in the degree of scrutiny and search, Ferlie and Judge (1981) found, on the contrary, that sudden demands for big cuts in Social Services were likely to erode the quality of decision making. Later work modified these early statements. For instance, later Social Services data (Davies and Ferlie, 1984) indicated that sustained and moderate fiscal pressure could in the long term lead to efficiency promoting innovation. Greenwood (1984) offered a more sophisticated reformulation of Stewart's position. Changing the budgeting system away from incremental procedures was now seen as dependent on wider changes in organizational ideologies and systems of power relations. Such shifts were more likely to take place when there was an organizational crisis in which existing procedures were inadequate, when there was commitment to change from managerial personnel who possess authority and energy, and when there was a coherent alternative ideology.

This literature was applied by Haywood and Ranade (1986) in their study of changing budgetary procedures under conditions of retrenchment in two RHAs and their associated Districts. The financial strategies of both regions were found to exhibit a discontinuity, explained most plausibly by financial stringency and the development of an alternative resource switching ideology by people with authority. However, the Districts with the bleakest financial prospects did not seem more likely to redeploy base budget resources, highlighting the key mediating role of the general managerial value system.

So change may sometimes come in bundles. On the basis of changing expenditure profiles, Kelly's review (1989) of retrenchment strategies in Social Services Departments in a slightly later period (up to 1986) concluded: 'prolonged restraint leads to some non-incremental allocations in the most restrained SSDs. These non-incremental shifts in expenditure can be clearly linked to the pursuit of the community care strategy within state-provided services for children and the elderly.' A different argument has been developed by Petrie and Alpert's discussion (1984) of retrenchment strategies in a research university. They distinguish between efficiency-based responses (such as value for money measures or efficiency savings) and effectiveness-based responses (radical reconfiguration), and suggest that often efficiency-based responses are too dominant because the real problems remain undiscussable. Although these problems are often seen in their most concentrated form in the public sector, they may also feature in private sector settings where, for example, plant closures may arouse fierce opposition.

This decrementalist controversy suggests that the case study evidence should be examined for the driving role of financial flows and budgetary procedures. Financial assumptions and routines are here seen as crucial determinants of strategy. Are 'across the board' cuts preferred to selective targets? What are the 'no go' areas? Do decision making routines adapt in the face of continuing retrenchment or do the Districts move ever deeper into crisis?

Organizational Death

Plant closure represents a highly visible but relatively discrete form of retrenchment in the public and private sectors alike. Its limited focus might make it more amenable to study, yet there is surprisingly little academic work on the management of closure in the acute sector despite the social and political significance of such processes. Clearly hospital closures might be thought to be more difficult to manage in areas of strong unionization and political resistance, but Hardy's (1985) comparative analysis of hospital closures which went through without resistance against one that met resistance also highlighted the importance of political skills and of managerial strategy in setting conditions for local action, for example in their ability to win over or lose the support of medical professionals. Sutton's (1989) analysis of the processes of organizational 'death' models the complex social psychological process by which dying organizations make the transition to death, although this is often ignored by population ecologists. First, there may be attempts to avert organizational demise. Secondly, there is a phase of uncertainty among staff in which rumour abounds. In Sutton's case study of a hospital closure these rumours included that the doors were going to be padlocked so that patients could not get in; that the building was going to be destroyed next week; and that it was going to become a large restaurant.

Then there is an announcement from leaders that organizational death will happen, providing an antidote to denial, with the emergence of anger and sadness as dominant feelings. Finally, parting ceremonies ('the discharge of the last patients') help reinforce the collective perception that the organization has died. Again organizational 'death' represents a metaphor, perhaps an imperfect one, but one which captures feelings of grieving and loss of a beloved institution.

Many of the acute hospitals considered in this chapter are large, well-known Victorian hospitals with strong institutional loyalties and proud self-images, long histories and protective buffer institutions, closed recruitment and intergenerational employment. Albeit to a lesser extent than the large psychiatric hospitals (McKee, 1988), they should be understood as a particular historical, cultural and institutional form which will help determine receptivity to, and experience of, change. Teaching hospitals, in particular, have in the past often been characterized by weak administration and the dominance of shifting but autonomous professional segments (Bucher and Stelling, 1977) which has often led to a history of incremental and professionally dominated growth rather than radical and managerially led retrenchment.

We may need, therefore, to pay particular attention to the periods in which decline threatens to lead to institutional death; to analyse managerial strategies for retrenchment in their context; to consider the particular nature, the power position of the institutions under threat and of the counter-strategies adopted; and of the transition from decline to death.

Power, Politics and Non-decision Making

Conventionally, studies of decision making within health care organizations identify and analyse 'decision points' where organizational actors made choices, but decisional processes may also result in a decision to do nothing. Organizational power can be used not only to defeat demands, but to prevent demands from appearing on agendas, or even being formulated at all. Early literature from the study of community politics identified a broader definition of the concept of 'power' which led to the use of 'non-decision making' as a term defined as:

> a means by which the demands for change in the existing allocation of benefits and privileges in the community can be suffocated before they are even voiced, or kept covert, or killed before they gain access to the relevant decision making arena, or failing all these things, maimed or destroyed in the decision implementing stage of the policy process. (Bachrach and Baratz, 1970, p. 44)

Similar logic underpinned Alford's analysis (1975) of three competing constituencies which could potentially shape health care policy. Institutional paralysis arose from the inability of the challenging managerial constituency to restructure hospitals dominated by professional groups, yet from this perspective what is particularly interesting is the inability of the more radical community health lobby to get its demands on the agenda at all.

While the non-decision making literature originated in the field of community politics, there have been attempts to apply it to health care management. For example, Marsh analysed resistance within one locality in the late 1970s to a national move to reduce management costs:

> The result of consideration by the policy makers in the health authority of the issues of structural change and management cost reductions was that decisions were not made. Initially there were efforts to prevent the issues reaching the formal policy making bodies of the authority. When these efforts appeared to be failing, the issues were referred to a specialist group constructed from among the chief officers of the authority. Ostensibly the role of the group was to produce solutions to the problems created by the presence of the issues. Within the analysis which follows, it is argued that the real purpose of the group was to remove the issues from formal policy arenas. (1983, p. 4)

Within private sector settings notions of 'the management of meaning' introduce similar sorts of arguments. Symbolic acts here help legitimize managerial behaviour and provide an organizational language (Johnson, 1990).

Can the non-decisional concept be used in the analysis of this case study material? Clearly it would be necessary to identify those proposals for retrenchment which would potentially hurt the interests of the dominant coalition, to see whether they were ruled out as 'unacceptable', whether they were suffocated in committee or whether – linked with wider changes to the distribution of power relations – they succeeded. We can here distinguish between the stopping of issues reaching formal agendas (either consciously or through the mobilization or organizational bias), and the encapsulation and neutralization of issues should attempts to prevent them reaching the agenda fail.

Conflict Without Change: Some Particular Problems in Inner London

These case studies refer to processes of acute sector retrenchment and redevelopment in two neighbouring teaching Inner London District Health Authorities: Paddington (now Parkside), which was centred on St Mary's W2 (see Figure 4.1) and Bloomsbury, which contained two teaching hospitals (the Middlesex and University College Hospital, UCH).

Context

As we have argued, understanding strategic change processes requires an understanding also of the contexts in which they occur – history, locality, patterns of intra- and inter-organizational relations, as well as the broader political, social and economic contexts in which the organization is embedded. In addition to the wider framework for change within the NHS which we have already discussed, there are some particular features of the Inner London location that are important to consider in these cases. These include: the political visibility and power position of the hospitals concerned; the role of the University of London as an integral component of the teaching hospitals; the presence of elite consultants, and their access to the media and the national political process; and high historic expectations of provision from the population. The environment of local politics and government was dense, well organized and often hostile to retrenchment. The agenda for retrenchment could – given cross-District and cross-Regional flows – only be progressed in its whole on a pan-London basis, but the lack of a pan-London strategic authority meant instead that change had to proceed through a collection of different Districts and Regions, each of which had different and often hidden agendas, and an incentive to bounce retrenchment on to the others.

In Inner London the pace of retrenchment was, throughout the 1960s and 1970s, slow and highly incremental. During this period the pressure to inject greater urgency ebbed and flowed, frequently meeting with resistance from those who might lose from retrenchment. Korman and Simons's (1979) case study of delays in progressing the closure of the old East End hospital at Poplar illustrated the impact of the complex and difficult political environment, the role of rumour in creating a downward spiral within the hospital and the lack of a clear managerial focus as the closure issue passed up and down between tiers. More generally, Smith (1981) coined the phrase 'conflict without change' to describe attempts to restructure health care in Inner London, pointing out that 'London's problems – too many acute beds, poor primary care, underfunded long stay care, fragmented specialist units and too few patients for students to learn from – have long been recognized'. Thus the Todd Report (1968) argued for a series of mergers across medical schools (first mooted in the Goodenough Report in 1944). However, objectives were redefined in the localities: St Mary's, W2's own agenda, as we shall see, was to use rebuilding as a means of heading off the merger projected for it in Todd.

Systemic change was also difficult while independent-minded Boards of Governors held responsibility for teaching hospitals, thus undergraduate hospitals were not moved into Districts until 1974, with the postgraduates not following until 1982. While the new post-1974 Districts could paint on a somewhat wider canvas (and engage in trading within their localities), they still pursued particularist objectives. By the late 1970s further pressure came from the introduction of RAWP in 1977 which can be seen as a central government mechanism for financial redistribution away from the historically well provided inner cities and operating in favour of the shires and suburbs where population levels were growing. In addition, the shift indicated in the Department of Health's 1976 priorities documents towards priority group services again raised the issue of acute bed cuts across London.

In 1979 and 1980, the London Health Planning Consortium, with members drawn from DHSS, Regions and the University, tried to develop a pan-London approach to services so as to prevent piecemeal reductions. They presented a projection of the cuts in local acute beds needed (2,300) across the teaching Districts. While the thinking was to inform the development of the new round of Regional strategic plans (1984) in the Thames Regions with their ambitious financial targets for Inner London Districts, this pan-London tier proved too weak to prevent Districts developing their own strategies, without interdistrict coordination (King's Fund, 1987).

Published simultaneously was Flowers's Report in 1980. This was a bold attempt to review the academic side of the equation, taking the issue on to a wider stage than the Conference of Deans (interestingly enough, Flowers was himself Rector of Imperial College rather than a Dean of a medical school). In the 1970s London University was also coming under financially based pressure to rationalize, as medical schools were now consuming 36 per cent of its budget, leading to the freezing of two large medical capital projects in the late 1970s. Smith (1981) argues that here was an early and bottom-up exercise in selectivity.

The Flowers Report was an unexpectedly radical document: teaching hospitals were to develop links with DGHs in adjacent districts (thus St Mary's, W2, could link to the Central Middlesex in Brent, and UCH to the Whittington in Islington). Flowers noted the rebuilding of St Mary's, W2 (which thus escaped merger and was now emerging as a focus for

Inner West London) and instead recommended a larger grouping on the UCH site which would incorporate the Middlesex and the Royal Free Hospitals, which emerged (along with the Westminster) as the clear losers from a tough review process:

> The University of London now has a painful choice: either to accept the recommendations we have made, or something approximating to them, with all their attendant problems of implementation, or to let economic and demographic forces take their inexorable and indiscriminate toll. (Flowers Report 1980, para 11.6)

These far reaching proposals had still to be got through the University Senate, and the initial proposals for consortia were narrowly defeated. Nevertheless revised proposals were later put forward (1981), and in December 1981 Senate eventually accepted final proposals recommending that the Middlesex and UCH should form a joint medical school (the Royal Free having escaped), and that St Mary's, W2, should continue as a separate medical school, developing academic links with the Central Middlesex Hospital. That Senate decision was the beginning of the huge and complex District of Bloomsbury with all that entailed in terms of management difficulties.

This section has indicated the special difficulties in management retrenchment in Inner London. While there were a series of attempts to apply pan-London top-down pressure on to the system, these instruments often had brief lives. Nevertheless there were forces emerging from the mid 1970s onwards which placed the issue of retrenchment increasingly and unavoidably 'on the agenda': the Department clearly kept a London brief; the capital sum available for rebuilding across London was likely to be constrained; and District boundaries were redrawn (and the drawing of boundaries was in many ways the crucial decision out of which strategy was likely to emerge). The construction of the retrenchment agenda in the Regions and in the localities was therefore to emerge as of major importance.

The issue for Districts was how best to address this and construct strategy in order to maximize the chance of survival. Were the early movers taking excessive risks or would the risk/return trade-off mean that laggards would find it increasingly difficult to secure political support or scarce capital investment?

Paddington and North Kensington: an Early Mover

This case study relates to North West District of Kensington and Chelsea Area Health Authority (1974–82) which subsequently became Paddington and North Kensington (PNK) District Health Authority (1982–8) (now Parkside DHA, following a merger with Brent DHA in 1988). In particular in this case we examine the moves towards the closure of the St Mary's Hospital Group's Harrow Road site in W9 alongside the

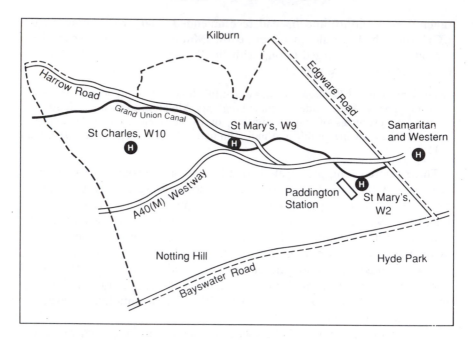

Figure 4.1   *Paddington and North Kensington District Health Authority*

redevelopment of its Praed Street site in W2 (see Figure 4.1). A notable feature in this case is the early date at which the process of acute sector rationalization began to take its course, and the continuing momentum that was obtained as a 'virtuous cycle' emerged.

North West District covered a small but densely populated area of Inner West London, and centred on its teaching hospital and associated medical school at St Mary's, Praed Street, W2, although it had a second District General Hospital at St Charles, W10 and, until 1986, a third at St Mary's, Harrow Road. There were distinct North Westminster and North Kensington patches to the District, and the North Kensington community (which includes the middle class area of Holland Park) is alert to any real or perceived threat to the viability of St Charles.

St Mary's, W2 was founded in 1854 and has been a school of medicine of the University of London since 1900. The fabric of much of the Praed Street site is poor, and there have been long-standing attempts to secure redevelopment. Retrenchment indeed was seen as the necessary price for redevelopment. In 1968 W2 merged fully with the old Paddington General, Harrow Road, W9 to form the St Mary's Group. Built as the Paddington Workhouse, the W9 site was completed in 1847 on the banks of the Grand Union Canal. The District was losing population heavily in the 1970s, and was down to 123,000 by 1983, and there were a substantial number of empty acute beds.

Post-war Bids for Redevelopment: a Legacy of Failure

Between 1948 and 1974 the key players in the locality could be seen as the Board of Governors at St Mary's, W2 and its long-standing House Governor (an integrated District was not, of course, created until 1974). Their agenda was narrowly defined and capital planning-led (the redevelopment of W2), and a long series of capital bids had been prepared which had failed. In part this was because of the 'stop–go' nature of public sector capital investment under Keynesian macro-economic policies:

> There had been plans on three separate occasions, most of which had come to grief on capital programme cuts nationally. Twice we thought that we were going to get into starts and have actually been cancelled. So that we have got wonderful pictures of the Queen Mother in 1945 inspecting the first model of the new building which we are having blown up to lifesize to present it to her when she opens it 45 years later. (District General Manager)

In such a dense urban setting, the acquisition of land was another major variable and in part failure also reflected an approach from the Board of Governors based on 'head-on attacks', involving compulsory purchase or even building over Paddington Basin which foundered in public enquiries. Thus the last set of proposals failed in 1975 when the then Labour Minister of State for Health (Dr David Owen) decided not to make a compulsory purchase order for land surrounding Paddington Basin.

'Three into Two Will Go', from 1974

From 1974 a number of key elements came together to accelerate the pace of change.

District Reorganization: Scope for Rationalization   The creation of the North West District (Kensington, Chelsea and Westminster AHA) in 1974 provided a potential opportunity to paint on a much broader canvas, and to link redevelopment with retrenchment. In this tiny District (only four square miles), there were three DGHs and ten acute hospitals: here if anywhere there was scope for considerable rationalization which could provide savings to help finance redevelopment.

The Impact of Community Medicine   There were in addition, after 1974, substantial changes in thinking, led by Dr William Kearns the new District Community Physician (who had never been on the Board of Governors), supported (and the title was significant given the legacy of capital planning) by a new Service Planning Post.

Community medicine was a relatively new specialty (Bennett and Pettigrew, 1990). The Hunter Report (1972) considering the role of community medicine after NHS restructuring, concluded that there should be a new title of 'community medicine specialist' which would have a key role as part of health service administration, rather than just an advisory role. So the DCP was to be part of the consensus management teams to be set up in the new Districts. The outcome was extremely patchy nationally, as the Acheson Report's assessment indicated:

> In some parts of the country community physicians seized the opportunity which was presented to them in 1974 and created vigorous departments which continue to make important contributions to the planning and development of health services for the populations they serve. In other places, some simply failed to make the transition. (1988, p. 6)

In NWD, however, community medicine was to play a pivotal role in redefining the problem through its developing service planning role. The DCP managed to secure attendance at the Acute Services Working Party which continued to meet, but which was in danger of becoming bogged down in very detailed issues. A counterproposal emerged from community medicine in the form of an unpublished concept paper ('Three into Two Will Go', 1976) which, on the basis of solid data, argued that the same level of service could be provided from two hospitals, and refused to specify at that stage which peripheral hospital (St Mary's, W9, or St Charles, W10) should be closed (Tables 4.1 and 4.2).

While nothing specific immediately came of the scheme, the new thinking was fed into the Acute Sector Working Party, and started to shift attitudes:

> There are two reasons to believe that the Three into Two scheme – the fact that it already existed – was a reason why we were able to move so quickly on the very tentative possibility as it was at first of rebuilding (yet again). (District Community Physician)

More Proactive Management Style   By the mid 1970s a new goal- and action-orientated style of behaviour began to emerge with new appointments from outside, quite unlike received accounts of consensus management. RAWP was taken seriously as a pressure from the mid 1970s ('we just faced the reality – we were losing money'). The first ward closures from St Charles were as early as the mid 1970s. Throughout the 1980s, the District was implementing its closure commitments. Continuity was maintained by the then DGM (1985–91) who had been General Administrator in the District and represented a link between Phases 1 and 2 of the acute sector strategy. Thus although strategic planning was not formally delegated to Districts until 1982, a strong strategic sense was coming up from NWD from the mid 1970s, with Area playing a generally reactive role. There was also a vacuum at Region, which had failed to develop a strategic plan in 1979 (one was not to emerge until 1984). As the then Area Chairman put it: 'The impetus and the drive was at District level – the Area involvement was not that great.'

In addition to focused energy on the need for change, a particular feature of the new management style was recognition of the importance of mobilizing political support. Here, a second crucial appointment was

Table 4.1   *North West District population levels*

1961	205,000
1971	182,000
1981 (estimated)	140,000
1986 (estimated)	131,000

Source: St Mary's Redevelopment: Phase 1 Feasibility Study

Table 4.2   *Acute beds in St Mary's, W2, St Mary's, W10 and St Charles*

Date	Population	Bed complement	Bed occupancy	Deaths and discharges
1962	205,000	1,443	1,224	28,572
1966	199,000	1,444	1,221	30,343
1971	182,000	1,376	1,082	29,396
1976	161,000	1,267	928	28,593

Source: St Mary's Redevelopment: Phase 1 Feasibility Study

that in the mid 1970s of Terry Hunt, the new DA, who was recruited from Area (and with no previous connection with the Board of Governors), and who was to use his existing network skilfully both to ensure a sympathetic hearing at Area level and to keep members at a distance ('you could count on the fingers of one hand the number of times members came into the District'). The DA had indeed been selected by the Chairman in order to complement the skills of the DCP. On appointment the DA (who was also Secretary to the Special Trustees) was given a clear agenda not from the AHA Chairman but from the Chairman of the Special Trustees at W2 that he was 'to do something' about Praed Street.

Overall there was now a resolve to negotiate around problems, using a pleasant style to influence external groups. Internally, the style involved working with small groups, to tight deadlines, and finding ways round cumbersome NHS procedures. One big advantage was that there were in the District potentially many more clinical gainers than losers from change – even those clinicians working from the peripheral hospitals could expect to have the opportunity to transfer to a more prestigious teaching hospital environment.

A Window of Opportunity 1976–1978

During this period various actions were taken which were to prove particularly significant in moving the change agenda forward, and which eventually unlocked the key to change, i.e. combining retrenchment with redevelopment.

In 1976 a joint Region/Area/medical school working party was set up which concluded with an approach to the Minister (1977) that it was still necessary to plan for the first phase of a new building. The lobbying for political support started immediately. People were encouraged to make site visits, which was made easier by the prestige that St Mary's could lend to the occasion: there was personal and political goodwill to being associated with the redevelopment of a visible teaching hospital in a marginal parliamentary constituency, and the hospital had friends at court. The Minister was persuaded to come on site and make a statement committing Departmental support (July 1977). Momentum began to build up as the team formed 'clubs' to win commitment, dining with those that could influence the outcome, and getting key actors to identify with the project.

With lines to the Department cleared, a small joint study group was set up (September 1977) with District (including the DA and DCP), Regional and medical school representatives. There was no clinical representative on it ('which was in part its saviour') because trust had been established, and the team was prepared to keep the functional content vague. The group worked fast to produce its major report by March 1978. There was no chairman, and the group was held together by a shared sense of mission rather than formal lines of accountability:

> We deliberately did not have a chairman, it was small, almost all the members contributed very well, very informal, we would eat and drink together as well . . . (Study group member)

The next stage was to address the acquisition of land, so crucial to the whole project as DHSS policy was only to construct new buildings on freehold land. To reduce the probability of the occurrence of town planning objections, the team decided to abandon compulsory purchase and protect public access to the canal. Informal consultation had already begun with the two key local landowners: Westminster City Council, who owned land north of the basin and had to give planning permission, and British Waterways Board who owned much of the land along the south side of the canal. WCC strongly favoured development of the south, and indicated that this view might well affect the ease with which town planning agreement might be sought. The British Waterways Board were not able to sell land, but would consider swapping canal side land at W2 for land of equivalent value at W9.

In addition, the District Administrator, as Secretary to the Special Trustees, set about buying out the individuals who occupied other bits of land, and acquiring tenancy of the site in the name of the trustees. The outcome was that a viable parcel of land was assembled and current opinion in the District regards the land deal as offering 'stupendous' good value.

The study group also considered where beds should be taken out of the system to achieve lower bed targets. There was some initial feeling that St Charles was the most vulnerable candidate, as it was outside the old St Mary's Group. But in fact St Mary's, W9 was selected for closure, along with the Paddington Children's Hospital.

Commitment to Closure, 1978

There was now a public commitment to closure at W9 by 1986 as part of the overall strategy: an unequivocal commitment to closure. W9 had been outgunned, and felt powerless against much mightier institutions. The joint study group recommended construction on site beginning in 1981 and completion in 1986 (in fact the timetable was to slip by 18 months).

The formal arguments ran as follows: closure of other hospitals (such as the Samaritan and the Western Ophthalmic) would not generate sufficient savings. St Charles should be retained because it maintained a better geographical distribution within the District, because Region had already funded psychiatric developments there, and because the fabric was better. On the other hand the closure of St Mary's, W9 would enable the District to 'swap' canal side land with the British Waterways Board, unlocking redevelopment at W2. This land argument, although important, was also played up as an 'ace card' (there were other options such as setting up a trust to rent the land) in order to prevent interminable negotiations amongst clinicians.

Table 4.3 *Beds in North West District*

	1977 bed complement	Long stay	1986 projected bed complement
Local acute	1,191	42	916
Specialties	418	0	510
Grand total	1,609	42	1,426

Source: St Mary's Redevelopment: Phase 1 Feasibility Study

There were also hidden factors. The informal power position of St Mary's, W9 was weak: it lacked the stronger institutional identity of St Charles, W10 (staff there had instituted a 'smile in' to win public support) and its middle class supporters in Holland Park. W9 was also seen as the hospital with the highest degree of unionization and restrictive practices (perhaps built up as a defence against low basic pay rates), and the failure of industrial action there in the winter of 1978/9 was seen by some as strengthening the management's hand.

In June 1978 the AHA sanctioned the project report and a draft consultation document on rebuilding and associated service changes. Later that month the RHA resolved that on the understanding that (a) a 35 per cent contribution to the capital cost was available from the DHSS and (b) that the recommended rationalization of NWD hospital services take place, that a regionally managed Phase 1 project team be set up but which effectively received from the earlier study group an agreed strategy. The formal consultation document which linked redevelopment and contraction as one package was issued in the District just three days later, effectively tying both the District and the Regional Project Team still further.

Why Did the Proposal Run?

Why should this proposal have succeeded whereas others failed? The process was not about the achievement of precise technical planning (which was delegated to successor expert groups), but the generation of commitment. This is not to say that formal documentation was unimportant, and indeed the sophistication of the argument helped convince sceptics and make the project look like a 'winner'. In particular, the following features stand out:

- The combining of retrenchment and redevelopment (capital investment in return for revenue cutbacks), which was crucial to the whole process. The broader canvas after 1974 provided the first opportunity to engage in this sort of trading which had been first floated in the concept paper.
- Learning from previous errors: the abandonment of head-on attacks and the use of consultation, negotiation and a 'more pleasant approach' as a means of solving problems; securing sound central political commitment.
- The development of a broad vision based on common core values ('you had to love it') within the District; a willingness to make concessions to permit other groups to buy into the strategy.
- The formation of a dominant coalition between administrators and W2 clinicians and the marginalization of the victims of change.
- The reduction of complexity through the use of ad hoc groups and winning the trust of those in the District to pave the way for delegation; clubbable behaviour which enriched external political networks; and circumventing the system through the use of special trustees, outside architects and utilizing remoteness from the Area to get on with the District's own agenda.

Run-down of St Mary's, W9, 1978–1985

Perhaps some of those who supported W9 closure as a means of financing redevelopment at W2 thought it would never happen: in fact the run-down process started almost immediately and during the period 1977 to June 1985 the number of beds at W9 declined from 385 to 156.

As early as 1978/9 the underfunding of the Clegg pay awards and the hike in VAT had led to a projected Area overspend of £2m, £1.25m in North West District. Members – just – decided to stay within the cash limit allocated to the District by the Department of Health and not to invite an overspend. Any loss of financial control would have been viewed with great disfavour by the centre and possibly the senior management team or the Health Authority members could have been asked to resign. The NWD DMT could use the 'VAT disaster' as a means of accelerating change and they brought forward proposals for retrenchment consistent with the new strategy, including the scaling down of beds at W9. The proposal was to close a third of the beds at W9 to save £500,000.

The 1979 proposals were pursued, even given remission in the financial situation, in order – it was now said – to finance backlog maintenance and new developments. They were broadly acceptable to most clinicians, and were consistent with long-term strategy. Major closures at W9 thus took place in October 1981, with the loss of obstetrics and gynaecology in the face of staff resistance, intensive picketing, political meetings (one addressed by Tony Benn), an occupation and an injunction.

By the early 1980s, major retrenchment was already taking place in St Mary's, W9 fuelled by what managers saw as a more vigorous and trade unionists as a more aggressive management style ('hatchet men'), introduced at the hospital with a remit to reduce restrictive practices; privatize ancillary services; and deliver substantial cost improvements. Resistance had failed and there were signs that the hospital was beginning to close itself as nursing shortages began to emerge. One consultant's view was that W9 was running down from 1984, despite some attempts to keep up morale.

Early Closure of St Mary's, W9, 1985–1986

While it was initially planned that W9 could close as the new block at W2 opened (1987), in the end W9 was closed a year early. This was because the District was once more plunging into financial crisis, and by autumn 1985 senior managers had resolved amongst themselves that early closure of W9 was the best option for substantial revenue savings which would keep the District on strategic course. The implementation process then moved into fast gear.

Given the emergent overspend in autumn 1985, the task was to find a major source of savings which would not erode the long-term strategy. The DGM was personally committed to early closure ('the only sensible thing was to shut early') and energetically led it through the DMT, where other members were seen as more reluctant. Soundings took place with members and the DHMC, and a consultation document was quickly prepared (January 1986) which accentuated both the positive and the negative: 'We strengthened that paper to paint the blackest picture. The concern was that we could have had a very weak paper, and then the members voted to keep it open and then we could have had a very serious incident'. The outcome was then a heated and protracted debate between the DMT and the various groups in opposition to the document.

External Opposition Most external comments were negative: the Paddington and North Kensington Health Emergency Campaign declared 'total opposition' to early closure, which it saw as the product of an arbitrary cash limit. In reality the only external group with power even to delay the proposal was the Community Health Council which declared its opposition and asked for more time to prepare a counterproposal. This request was rejected, given a managerial perception that the CHC's real objective was to slow the process down.

The Clinicians   A decision on whether to support early closure was made at the April 1986 DHMC meeting. Although a couple of clinicians spoke out against early closure, the Chairman gave a strong lead, and the DHMC agreed reluctantly to support early closure while noting particular concerns, such as bed management. The balance of incentives clearly pointed in this direction: no junior medical posts were to be lost; nurses would be released for other sites; piecemeal ward closures on other sites would be avoided; and most W9 clinicians would shift on to the W2 site. There were indeed very few clinical victims of change.

The Members   Paddington and North Kensington DHA was seen as unpredictable, containing both left and right blocs, but with the balance being held by 'floating voters' such as the professionals and generalists. The earlier capturing of the support of clinician 'crossbenchers' on the DHA was an important step forward for management. At the May 1986 DHA meeting, the outcome of the consultation exercise was presented in such a way as to win over the middle ground further. The document was carefully drafted, and stressed the non-financial reasons for closure (nurse staffing shortfall and a risk that the hospital might cease to be viable) and the need to avoid unplanned ward closures elsewhere. The document talked up the planning gains associated with early closure, such as the transfer of scarce nursing staff to other sites and a number of concessions were made in response to points which had emerged during the consultation process (such as strengthening of the A and E services at St Charles). In addition, a letter from Region refusing to grant financial relief was laid on the table.

Clearly this was a crucial meeting and both management and leaders of the left caucus were energetically lobbying members up to the night before, doing their own head counts. In an intense meeting during which a critical amendment was moved by members of the 'hard left', the DHMC Chairman spoke in favour of early closure. The Treasurer reminded the authority of their legal obligation to live within their cash allocation and the DGM advised members that unless a decision was made soon to close the W9 site at Harrow Road, she regretted she could not take responsibility for patient safety. The amendment was lost by an unexpectedly large margin (ten to five): the DHA had decided to close Harrow Road early.

Speedy Implementation

For the District, time was of the essence as it lost £200,000 savings for every month that the closure was delayed. So the District had to 'manage up', to ensure speedy turnround at Regional and national levels. Local MPs had to be lobbied to gain their support, or failing that, their silence. Although District saw Region as a potential block which needed to be bypassed, Region itself argued that it had worked hard to reduce the turnover time of closures by ensuring speedy processing through the RHA, sending working papers up to Regional liaison, and making an early approach to government ministers. Their private office also emerged as an important target for the DGM:

> The Department has never actually processed a closure in under three months before in terms of writing documentation for ministers and we got them to do it in about six weeks, but for the last few days, it was just hell. I just spent most of my time on the telephone . . . 'people will die in the street, we can't keep this hospital going, we are spending £400,000 of taxpayers' money a month'.

Formal ministerial approval for closure was announced on 11 August 1986, subject to a comment on A and E services which were generally recognized as the weakest area of the proposal. The formal closure mechanism was the Implementation Group, a task force which met regularly to consider operational issues within a network analysis as about 30 or 40 capital schemes had to be brought on stream on the W10 and W2 sites. In practice, much of the burden fell on the newly appointed UGMs who chaired implementation groups within their Units. The W10 implementation group was also working fast, employing outside architects and engineers to get the schemes written up quickly and using single tender action.

In the end St Mary's, W9 closed in October 1986 with patients being moved a day early to foil expected protests, which took place but were low key. It had closed not with a bang but with a whimper. Historically W9 had represented a cohesive occupational community (a substantial employer in a deprived area), with strong blue-collar unionization. Hospital work represented an important source of employment for women and ethnic minorities. Yet unlike 1981, there were now no occupations at Harrow Road, with staff accepting the 'inevitable'. The change in national political climate, the bitter legacy of local defeat, the prospect of some capital lump sums, the knowledge that the hospital was planned to close in any case, and the experience of the hospital already closing itself all eroded staff resistance. Some staff were glad to take early redundancy, and the chance to acquire at least some capital, perhaps for the first time in their lives. Others were less happy, especially if they were not given redundancy, but asked to transfer to another hospital. All staff were personally interviewed, but there were very different perceptions of the redundancy process. Management felt that there had been union representation and that broad agreement had been reached in most cases. The trade union side, however, felt that insufficient attention had been paid to staff welfare, and that too many disputes developed about the redundancy payments to be made, and indeed their actual payment.

Even after closure, however, the management of the Harrow Road site took up considerable managerial time. Gypsies came on to the site and had to be got off. There were prolonged negotiations about the sale of the site – with Labour local councillors resisting the 'yuppification' of Harrow Road – to ensure major planning gains for the District (such as a nurses' home, a health centre, and new mental handicap and disabled units) as well as a substantial upmarket property development (the name of the site was promptly changed by the developer). The closure was used nationally by the Labour Party as an example of 'cuts' in the NHS.

Rolling Forward

The merger with Brent in 1988 to form Parkside District could have led to a hiatus, while the new organization was being built. Yet by 1989 a further radical acute sector strategy for the 1990s had been assembled (this is represented in Figure 4.2), essentially involving the closure and sale of the Samaritan and Western Ophthalmic sites, the withdrawal of acute facilities from St Charles, and the rebuilding of St Mary's, W2 (Phase 2) and the Central Middlesex Hospital in Brent. Critical continuity was supplied by the DGM, who had been a General Administrator in Paddington and North Kensington in the late 1970s when the original exercise was taking place. The proposal was led through an 'Acute Sector Vision Group', which again tried to concentrate on the big picture, indicating that some of the learning from the late 1970s had been captured and was being deployed again, although the final outcome of this process is not yet clear.

The proposal went through the District and at time of writing was with the Department of Health. The Central Middlesex Hospital, meanwhile, had successfully become a first-wave NHS Trust, although that process warrants another chapter in its own right. St Mary's, W2, applied for Trust status but was put on ice until a report on the provision of health care across London was available. Two of the key London-wide strategic problems to be addressed in this report were the need or otherwise for Phase 2 at St Mary's and for a new hospital in Bloomsbury.

Bloomsbury: a Laggard

Bloomsbury DHA was only created in 1982 (eight years later than North West District), bordering Paddington and North Kensington DHA to the east (see Figure 4.3). As a result of developing links with the Whittington Hospital, there has recently (1990) been a merger with Islington DHA, effectively pushing the District further into North London. Bloomsbury has found difficulty in formulating and implementing a core strategy for its acute sector, and the pace of change has been slower not only than that of neighbouring authorities such as Parkside (which had eight years' head start) but also in Riverside DHA which was formed later (1985) but formulated and implemented its core strategy much faster (Battle, 1989).

A number of factors could account for this organizational and operational complexity. One contextual explanation for this could be the

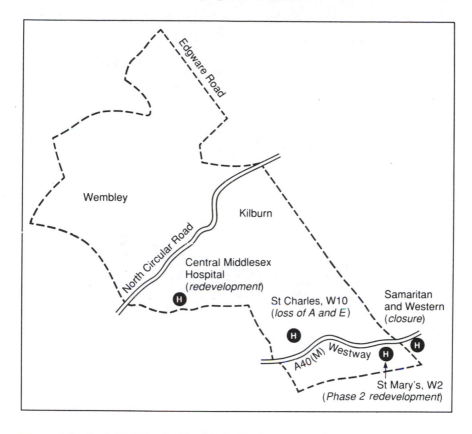

Figure 4.2 *Parkside District Health Authority: proposed acute sector strategy, 1989*

greater degree of structural complexity in Bloomsbury even than in Parkside or Riverside. The authority delivers a vast array of specialist services (see Tables 4.4 and 4.5), inheriting 19 hospital sites in 1982 which could be loosely grouped as follows. First of all there was what was seen as the 'core campus' which consisted of two major teaching hospitals (the Middlesex and UCH). These were elite hospitals with a long history of rivalry and cultural differences between them. Historically, both had operated in an unthreatening environment with little pressure for retrenchment. Clinically, UCH had a higher proportion of general work; the Middlesex a higher proportion of specialist work. It would always have been difficult to merge these two proud institutions, but centralization on to the UCH site and the closure of the Middlesex – the post-Flowers agenda – was going to be even trickier.

In addition, there were the peripheral acute sector hospitals (such as St Pancras or the National Temperance) which were also prime candidates for rationalization. Then there were the 'politically sensitive' hospitals (such as the women's services provided by the Elizabeth Garrett Anderson

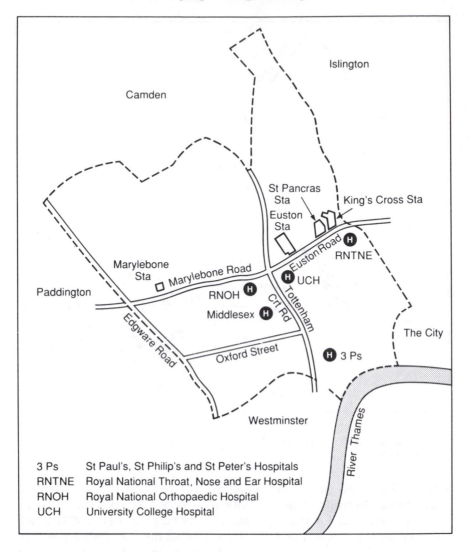

Figure 4.3 *Bloomsbury District Health Authority (1982)*

and the homeopathic services provided by the London Homeopathic) which were difficult to touch. Fourthly, there were the three postgraduate groups which until 1982 had enjoyed direct access to the Department of Health but which were at that point delegated (with certain safeguards such as the retention of Special Committees as successors to Boards of Governors) to the new District of Bloomsbury. These were in an anomalous position. There were guarantees of protected funding, too vague to serve as guides to financial allocation, but required constant referral upwards. Were the postgraduates really part of Bloomsbury or was the District an artificial creation? Two of the three postgraduate

Table 4.4 *Hospital-based services in Bloomsbury DHA, 1982*

Hospital	Available beds
St Pancras Hospital	262.4
National Temperance Hospital	128.0
Elizabeth Garrett Anderson	—
Royal National Throat, Nose and Ear Hospital (Gray's Inn Road)	106.3
Royal National Throat, Nose and Ear Hospital (Golden Square)	
University College Hospital	616.3
Royal National Orthopaedic Hospital (Great Portland Street)	85.4
Royal London Homeopathic Hospital	70.2
Middlesex Hospital	644.5
Hospital for Women (Soho)	43.7
Shaftesbury Hospital	36.4
St Paul's Hospital	37.5
St Philip's Hospital	15.6
St Peter's Hospital	37.5
London Foot Hospital	—
Marlborough Day Hospital	—
Royal National Orthopaedic Hospital (Stanmore)	245.1
Athlone House	94.0
St Luke's Hospital	69.0

Source: Bloomsbury DHA (1983)

Table 4.5 *Bloomsbury DHA bed utilization figures, 1982*

	Average available beds	Average occupied beds	Deaths/ discharges
Local acute	939.2	753.1	31,752
Regional specialties	292.1	245.7	7,443
Multi-district	73.7	48.0	3,377
Miscellaneous	136.7	76.8	5,137
Maternity	126.1	86.5	4,860
Priority services	379.3	339.7	1,921
Postgraduates	566.0	405.0	18,461
Grand total	2,513.1	1,954.8	73,451

Source: Bloomsbury DHA (1983)

groups, for instance, went on to become first-wave NHS Trusts in 1991. The Royal National Throat, Nose and Ear Hospital (RNTNE) was in the best condition, but there was a major problem of redevelopment at the country branch of the Royal National Orthopaedic at Stanmore and there had been 20 years of planning blight which had blocked the redevelopment of the St Peter's Group of Hospitals for Urology, scattered around Covent Garden.

Political Control Politically the District relates to, and draws DHA membership from, not only the Conservative-controlled City of Westminster, but the Labour-controlled Borough of Camden, whose representatives would often oppose cutbacks in local health services. The DHA could be seen as significantly to the left of those in Parkside and Riverside, although the role of the crossbenchers was still crucial. The DHA Chairman (1982–90) – a general practitioner and previously a Labour MP – was highly experienced, and had been the Area Chairman previously. Managers could, and did, lose strategic control, should the professional members and generalists vote with the left.

Management Problems   The unhappy experience of acute sector change in Bloomsbury has perhaps influenced perceptions of management style. The Regional view was that Bloomsbury was a highly conservative organization pursuing a 'cautious and incremental' approach to change. 'Bloomsbury disease' from this viewpoint entailed: failing to meet deadlines; underdeveloped basic managerial systems (such as personnel or information); an alliance between left members and professionals to put the lid on retrenchment; an inability or even a secret unwillingness of managers to control strategy; and a lack of performance in achieving objectives. Bloomsbury even had to be cajoled into competitive tendering. District's view, by contrast, was that the Region had unrealistic expectations about the pace of change (the 1984 Regional Strategic Plan had for instance dedicated a £14m budgetary reduction in Bloomsbury over the strategic period) and had often failed to exert positive leadership by providing strategic guidance or the capital needed to unlock revenue savings.

There were clearly difficulties in the District. Manpower and financial information systems were poor, and the District throughout the 1980s was recurrently trying to reduce overspends (and was a poor performer even when compared with other Inner London teaching districts) which represented a major diversion for senior managerial time and attention. There was rapid senior management turnover and hence loss of organizational memory: the four most senior managers in the authority in 1987 had all left by 1989 and this picture was also apparent at middle management level. Relations with 'strategic clinicians' were often poor, and they had sometimes been alienated by the failure to manage effectively even basic systems (such as medical records). While each of the three DA/DGMs had a different style, all were confronted with the same underlying problem of how to scale the District down. By the mid 1980s, the District Management Board had developed a cautious and pessimistic style as a vicious circle began to emerge. When asked about DMB style, one member replied:

> I mean, if there is one it is endless introspection, but seriously the Management Board does not make decisions as far as I can tell, it endlessly agonizes about how to get issues through the Health Authority . . .

And again:

> There was not any strategy really. It was fire fighting. But also the Management

Board really hated each other, I think. That became quite clear. I don't mean on a deeply personal level or anything like that but at a professional level.

Dependence on the Academic Sphere The District was highly dependent on developments in the academic sphere for success in its own service planning given its location at the core of the University of London. Yet perhaps surprisingly there was a relatively rapid transition (perhaps given pressure from the University Grants Committee) on the academic side from 'informal cooperation' (1981–3) between the two schools, to a joint and then a single school. The Unification Committee reported in 1985, tackling some of the difficult academic issues. As one clinical academic put it:

> So a lot of the problems, the tricky issues, were trying to bring together groups who had different backgrounds and mould them into one. Of course they had different curricula. There was a medical course in the Middlesex Hospital School, there was one at University College, so we had to bring those together.

However, coming down on beds was to prove a more difficult issue for the University given the school's requirements for teaching. Deans were represented on the DMB until the introduction of general management, at which point they were removed.

Lack of Common Identity There was little common identity and history. Bloomsbury as a corporate entity was only created in 1982 as a merger between five predecessor bodies: the South Camden District – centred on University College Hospital – of the Camden and Islington AHA (in North East Thames Region); the old North East District – centred on the Middlesex Hospital – of Kensington, Chelsea and Westminster AHA (in North West Thames Region); and the three postgraduate groups (Orthopaedics, Urology, and Ear, Nose and Throat) which had never before been in an 'ordinary' DHA, having lost their special links with the Department of Health.

Some Facilitating Factors Yet there were also facilitating factors. This was a new DHA with a mandate for restructuring. In addition the somewhat later timing in Bloomsbury potentially gave management certain advantages which Paddington and North Kensington had not enjoyed: changes in the national political economy were shifting the balance of power away from trade unions and Labour local councillors; there were previous examples of plans for radical retrenchment on which to draw (such as the Flowers Report); and the new authority had the advantage of scale.

'Finding the Frame' and the Two-site Solution, 1983

The case study will concentrate on what was only one but perhaps the central strategic problem facing the District: the rationalization of the

central UCH/Middlesex campus. For the purpose of analysis, the position
of the postgraduates will not be considered in detail, although of course
they further complicated the situation. In contrast to Paddington, severe
difficulty was experienced in building a consensus around a core strategy,
and a series of strategic flip-flops took place.

The RHA 1982 Operational Planning guidelines for Bloomsbury set the
following task for the DMT:

> with Regional officers beginning to prepare an acute service strategy, rationaliz-
> ing and reducing the current level of service.

The hidden top-down expectation was that the new District would close
the Middlesex which had emerged as a major loser out of Flowers. In its
turn, the District was by now aware of the likelihood of big reductions
in Regional finance and verbally at least was moving towards a more
strategic approach to retrenchment:

> we shall have to make big changes in the Health Services in Bloomsbury. We
> shall need to decide what services we are going to provide and to concentrate
> on them. That means we shall be doing more of some things and less of others
> than we are doing now. We may have to stop providing some services
> altogether. We shall have many fewer hospital beds and fewer hospitals.
> (Bloomsbury DHA, 1983, para. 1.5)

Two main decremental tactics were evident rather than strategic reconfiguration. The first was to take advantage of opportunities (such as the
expiry of leases) that presented themselves. The second tactic was to
progress single specialty rationalizations, some of which were successful,
such as the centralization of obstetrics at UCH. But such negotiations had
to take place specialty by specialty, and did not always result in a satisfactory outcome (as in the abortive plans to centralize genito-urinary
medicine, the failure of which was later to complicate the response to HIV
in the district). Moreover, members favoured the development of priority
group services for local residents, and were unwilling to invest time and
energy into the much less pleasant task of acute sector rationalization.

The formal process of strategic planning was indeed sophisticated in the
District: members were involved in a Services Committee to which officers
were encouraged to submit speculative papers in an attempt to identify
options. But anti-risky shift took place in this group as thought moved
away from radical retrenchment towards a double-site core campus, with
UCH providing a generalist core and the Middlesex retained in order to
fulfil a specialist role.

The thinking was developed in the option appraisal document 'Finding
the Frame' (Bloomsbury DHA, 1983). The document was heavily
criticized, however, by the Joint School for its neglect of research and
teaching requirements. The emphasis was on priority group, primary care
and health promotion proposals and the acute sector proposals were less
ambitious, even though only 1,950 of the 2,800 beds in the District were
on average occupied. Closure of the Middlesex was not even mentioned

as an option, and the document cautiously outlined capital-led rationalization on a UCH/Middlesex 'core campus', combined with a proposal to develop the relatively small site of the former Odeon Cinema car park next to UCH to increase beds. Indeed, complementary roles were envisaged for the two hospitals with UCH taking a more general role (with A and E being centralized there), while the Middlesex developed in a more specialist direction.

Such evolutionary proposals however sat alongside sharp reductions in finance: the District Financial Strategy had already committed the District to achieving 6 per cent savings between 1983 and 1986, and Region was likely to turn the screw tighter. A key problem related to acquiring the capital needed to unlock revenue reductions, either through internal revenue to capital transfer, or by securing more capital from Region for large-scale redevelopment.

Already by late 1983 an overspend was building up within the Middlesex/UCH Unit where the UMT was being asked to plan for retrenchment assuming that financial strategy should be consistent with present strategic aims and that there should be no significant contraction of acute services or clinical workload. Single specialty rationalization exercises were already seen to be faltering.

Despite this, 'Towards a Strategy' (February 1984) reaffirmed the intention to develop priority group services and to proceed with the 'double-site' core campus strategy with the closure of peripheral acute hospitals:

> Although the proposals for the rationalization of acute hospital services in 'Finding the Frame' are ambitious, nobody would pretend that a hospital divided between two complementary wings with a main road dividing the campus is ideal. However, the Authority believes that it is important to plan for what is achievable. There is always a danger in planning that the best will become the enemy of the good. (para. 1.14)

Clinical workload was envisaged as being retained at the same broad level, but a target level of 6 per cent savings was set for revenue budgets between 1983 and 1986.

The Strategy Falters, 1983–1985

This early strategy did indeed provide some guidance for later action: thus acute services were moved off the peripheral National Temperance and St Pancras sites, and there was a successful concentration of Accident and Emergency facilities at UCH which substantially changed the identity of the Middlesex. But in other respects the strategy began to falter as the Regional reduction in finance was to prove steeper than expected, retrenchment targets were not met, and the Odeon site redevelopment, which was crucial to the process of change in the core campus, did not happen.

In 1984, the Region adopted a 'worst case' £14m target for revenue reduction in Bloomsbury over the strategic period. As an overspend built up, Alasdair Liddle, the new District Administrator (subsequently to become the first District General Manager) increasingly tried to persuade members to 'bite the bullet' of more radical retrenchment.

Yet the District was finding it difficult to cope even with a modest level of retrenchment: the efficiency savings strategy was failing; far from capital budgets being protected, reserves were being used up; infrastructure was deteriorating further; and the District was moving into escalating overspends. Nor did the Odeon site scheme offer a way out ('it failed because it was crazy' – Region), as the District was unable to demonstrate how this relatively modest development could cut the Gordian knot.

As early as late 1983, it was becoming clear to the joint Middlesex/UCH Unit Management Team that the use of medically dominated, single specialty working parties to progress rationalization was flawed and usually resulted in 'bidding up'; that it was difficult to make substantial savings without coming down on workload; and that the parameters of budgetary review needed to be widened. There had been no real initiative on getting support costs down (there was member opposition to contracting out) or developing manpower measures which could reduce the number of consultants who were driving the workload. Some felt that the District failed to perceive the gravity of the situation, especially in 1982–5. As a Regional officer put it:

> The idea of the merger was to force rationalization and I think that it has gone at a symbolic pace. They have done things to show that they were doing things, but it has only been at a pace that was conducive to keeping people off their backs.

Into a Crisis, 1985

The introduction of general management in 1985 was associated with important changes to structure and also attempts to shift the balance of power. The DMB was less of a group forum than the DMT; Deans lost their places and powerful Divisional General Managers emerged with a clear interest in developing more aggressive cost improvement programmes. There were two acute divisions set up (a UCH Group and a Middlesex Group, both of which included the postgraduate hospitals), and while this facilitated the integration of the postgraduates, the downside was an accentuation of the UCH/Middlesex split.

The District General Manager's important April 1985 strategy paper ('Financial Service Strategy, 1985–88') noted that a £3.5m deficit was now projected for 1985–6, and that strategy needed to be rethought. The document argued that the District should now review whether current levels of clinical activity could be sustained, and identify specific rather than across-the-board targets for retrenchment. An initial management proposal was to reduce 155 District acute beds in the UCH/Middlesex core campus, later scaled down to 97 beds which was the level of reduction above which the Joint Medical Committee and the medical school were not prepared to go. Meanwhile the DGM was negotiating with the RGM, winning some limited flexibility on capital, but no change in fundamental Regional strategy.

The May 1985 DHA meeting agreed by six votes to four to support the closure under emergency powers of these 97 beds, but a tougher recommendation to instruct the DMT to continue consultation within the District to identify savings which would eliminate the deficit was lost by four votes to six. The implication was that the overspending would not be eliminated in the acute sector, and the problem was made worse when it became apparent that this package was not going to reduce expenditure as much as anticipated, as the bed closures had not led to a proportionate decline in the number of cases treated as clinical practice quickly found ways around the closures.

By autumn 1985 the District was lurching into financial crisis, with some projections showing an £11m gap between resources and commitments. It was in this context that management was beginning to see some of the new money coming in for AIDS as raidable. Management was caught in a dilemma. There was top-down pressure from Region which was increasingly alarmed by the failure (as it saw it) of Bloomsbury to deliver, while on the other hand attempts by management to achieve financial control and more radical rationalization led to major conflicts with oppositionist members and clinicians.

Thus the DGM also saw the need to regain financial control within the District as a prelude to strategic control. Within the District, the introduction of general management was also leading to a more aggressive approach to cost improvement within the divisions, if less across divisional boundaries. However, the shift from the consensual and incremental decision making processes of 1982–5 to a finance-led and management-led model (with unplanned bed cuts in the core campus – for the first time) led to a further deterioration in relations with oppositionist members ('awful. It was an absolute nightmare') and clinicians. A further package of savings went to a special DHA meeting in November 1985 with bitter debate. The CHC protested against lack of formal consultation; one member noted that the DHA had been presented with a series of savings proposals detached from any consideration of targets or objectives. The package was agreed on the Chairman's casting vote: it entailed the temporary closure of four acute wards, extended Christmas closures, a 25 per cent reduction in surgical theatre time and a freeze on recruitment.

For members, the feeling that they were being 'bounced' into unplanned cuts reinforced their determination to be given choices, and to reassert strategic control next time. For some strategically minded clinicians, these events – and a determined, hectoring, management style – proved a severe shock which led to disengagement from the planning process, especially as the UCH/Middlesex split re-emerged in discussions over where the cuts should fall. Furthermore, the introduction of general management was associated in some clinicians' minds with deterioration of vital support services (such as medical records systems), which themselves were sometimes targets for savings.

Also in September 1985 another nail was driven into the coffin of the Odeon proposal as the local authority (Camden) refused to grant planning approval, regarding it as a loss of residential stock.

'Meeting the Challenge', 1986–1987

The preparation of the District's strategic plan in 1986 once again mobilized these conflicting interest groups. As always the basic strategic debate was between the double-siters (who favoured a continuation of incremental change) and the more radical single-siters.

In March 1986, the managerial awareness of increasing financial constraints led to a draft document ('Facing the Future') which sought to reconcile service levels with finance, referring to possible developments on the Odeon site, and again floating a single-site solution. This draft was thrown out by members at a special seminar as being too finance-led.

The whole debate within the core group progressing the strategy was based on assumption of restricted capital: that there would be enough capital to build on the Odeon site, perhaps enough to rebuild the Middlesex outpatients' department, but no more. Negotiations with Region to increase the flow of capital in the end proved the key in unlocking the process of change.

In June 1987 the DHA-inspired District strategy, 'Meeting the Challenge' (Bloomsbury DHA, 1987) rejected the single-site solution on the basis of current land and capital assumptions. The proposal now was for no movement downwards on local acute beds or Regional specialties, and modest downward movement on the postgraduates (Table 4.6).

Table 4.6 *Proposed acute hospital service level*

Specialty	1986 level		Proposed 1993 level	
	Cases	Beds	Cases	Beds
Local acute	23,370	537	23,370	537
Maternity	4,810	86	4,810	82
Orthopaedics	6,970	309	6,470	253
Urology/nephrology	7,640	152	7,420	143
Ear, nose and throat	7,350	97	7,000	81
Regional specialties	9,020	292	9,020	292
Elderly	1,770	130	1,770	127
Mental health	810	129	810	111
Miscellaneous	62,280	1,754	61,210	1,648

Source: Bloomsbury DHA, 1987

The initial response from Region was extremely frosty. A regional perception was that District management was only paying lip service to financial control, and was colluding with other power blocs in the District.

Yet the oppositionists on the DHA saw themselves fighting off managerial demands from District as well as Region for retrenchment. As one influential clinician put it:

> There is no doubt in my mind, and in many minds, Region were determined to get us all on one site as a result of very drastic reduction in service in all sectors. There is no doubt in my mind and in the mind of many others that the District General Manager and managers here wished to do that too.

The oppositionist bloc fought line by line, specialty by specialty ('endless meetings, endless paperwork, producing our own tables'), examining detailed requirements by specialty, so that the broad issues did not emerge until the end of the process. As one member recalled:

> The reality was that the double site option did not get discussed right until the very end, and I mean the very end. Most of the debate inside the core group was about detailed content issues.

Three subgroups could be discerned within the oppositionist dominant coalition, although each was running its own agenda. Clinicians had a presumption in favour of retaining beds and workloads, sometimes thought parochially, and those 'strategic clinicians' that did exist had gone into opposition, often over what was seen as a hectoring management style or narrower questions such as medical records, or the distribution of cuts between UCH and the Middlesex. Members were keen to protect services for local residents in particular, and were excited by the prospect of an election in which the NHS would be a major issue, only having to come to terms after June 1987 with a continuation of the same broad policies. The medical school was concerned to retain sufficient beds (especially in local acute services) for teaching, and although it was prepared to consider teaching outside the District, it took a more conservative line as regards other proposals. The school had been turned off by what it saw as management's failure to consult, and its panic closures.

Was District management playing a waiting game? To speculate – and the evidence is still opaque – was management using this failure to unfreeze assumptions? Did things have to get worse before they could begin to get better? As a result of the impasse, what appears to have happened in the summer of 1987 was the beginnings of a personal dialogue between the DGM and the RGM about major new capital investment (some of which could be financed by the sale of land in Covent Garden), broadening out to include a senior member of the school, and other senior officers being gradually brought in, it was hoped, as in Paddington (and the RGM had previously been DGM there) that an increase in the flow of capital might in the end unlock the process of change.

In October 1987 a letter from the RGM to the DGM went to the DHA which noted two major points of concern about the DHA's document 'Meeting the Challenge'. First, the envisaged acute sector service levels were too high and unaffordable. Secondly, the approach to change was 'cautious and incremental', and a clear-cut answer was needed. The letter continued:

> I think you should look in much more detail at the possibility of developing a completely new acute hospital of about 900 beds on one or other of your central sites. Our preference would be the University College site, with the hospital in effect forming part of the University College campus, thus facilitating the important working links between the related disciplines of the hospital and the multi-faculty college.

This represented the prospect of massive new investment (a 1989 estimate was £150m new money over and above the proceeds of the sale of land), in return for reducing the number of beds in the District by about a third. It was of course both an offer and a threat: was there any alternative? The attachment of a senior Regional officer to work with the District also helped clarify lines of communication.

Attempts to Accelerate the Pace of Change, 1987–1991

The prospect of massive new capital investment provided a real incentive for change for perhaps the first time. Some of the previous plans (such as for the relocation of the St Peter's Group into the Middlesex) were also by 1990 being operationalized, the political appeal procedure finally having been exhausted. There were also some more subjective changes in role which helped change the mood. Bryan Harrison, the new District General Manager (the previous DGM had been appointed to a Regional post) had developed an interactive style which stressed interpersonal communication, and which was used to encourage some of the younger 'strategic' clinicians to come out of the woodwork and engage in the strategic management process. The DHA and the DMB started to meet less often, and more work was being done out of the formal Committee structure.

The mechanism used to progress the Approval in Principle submission (1988) was dense and complex, with a Service Planning Group taking advice from a clinical advisory structure with a myriad of clinically based groups: 'you really have to take people with you' (District). Yet in the end this dense machinery managed to come up with agreed proposals, and even to scale down its bid from 900 to 770 beds (in part by coming down on the number of designated HIV/AIDS beds).

The single-site nettle was grasped as District went out to consultation in November 1989 on a proposal to build the 770 bedded new hospital on the UCH complex, and to close the Middlesex, requiring some £150m after proceeds from land sales in Bloomsbury. This was a massive capital sum, especially as the recession was increasingly to erode the value of these planned land sales. The opportunity was taken to advocate changes in the pattern of care:

> The Authority is planning to make greater use of different types of hospital care. In future a greater proportion of patients will be treated on a day basis,

with hostel/hotel accommodation available for those unable to return home during treatment. The length of time people stay in hospital is expected to fall, in line with Regional and national trends. (Acute Services Strategy, November 1989)

At that stage, Region put the bid at the top of its capital programme. Nearly all the land involved was owned by the NHS, University College, or the UCH Special Trustees, simplifying land requirements. The proposal also outlined a number of changes to clinical practice and organization. There would be a reduction in routine planned admissions from distant Districts, which should reduce acute admissions by one-sixth. There would be a closer working relationship with the Whittington, Islington, as a sister hospital. Acute services should be less expensive to run, with a current estimate that running costs should fall by around a quarter, compared with the one-sixth reduction in caseload.

However, while there were attempts to accelerate the pace of change, other issues remained intractable. Insulation of the core agenda proved impossible as once again change followed change (the two White Papers, boundary changes with Parkside and then merger with Islington). There was a continuing high turnover in management posts. Communication systems remained rudimentary and the District contained deep divisions. The year 1990 was dominated by a drive for solvency (once again) as the District sought to eliminate a projected £7m deficit by April 1991 which could entail major ward closures in the core campus. Above all, the falling receipts from land sales because of the slowdown in economic growth in 1990 put the Region's capital programme in jeopardy, and by late 1990 it was becoming clear that direct ministerial support would be needed if the proposal were to run. As at the time of writing, the single hospital proposal was still with the Department and an inquiry (the Tomlinson Committee) has been announced which has been asked to consider the UCH/Middlesex problem as one of its core strategic issues. The Royal National Orthopaedic Hospital and the Royal National Throat, Nose and Ear Hospital were both successful first-wave candidates for NHS Trust status. UCH and the Middlesex are still on separate sites.

Cutback Management: Conclusions

Comparing and Contrasting: Receptive and Non-receptive Contexts

Certainly Smith's (1981) notion of 'conflict without change' as characterizing the rationalization of acute services in London fitted much of the history in Bloomsbury given the difficulties in resolving the key strategic question of the core campus, yet the Paddington case also showed the potential for early and sustained movement downwards on bed numbers with concentration on to one redeveloped site. There is then substantial variability even within neighbouring Inner London Districts in the rate and pace of acute sector retrenchment.

Why should this be the case? In chapter 9 we develop the metaphor of 'receptive' and 'non-receptive' contexts. We mean by 'receptive context' that there are features of context (and also action) that seem to be favourably associated with forward movement. On the other hand, there is in non-receptive contexts a configuration of features which may be associated with blocks on change. A number of these figures are apparent in these two case studies.

1 The Quality and Coherence of 'Policy': Analytical and Process Elements In looking at organizational change, it seems that a facilitating factor is the existence of a 'quality' policy, well founded, able to achieve support and also capable of being implemented.

Doing one's homework could be important in reframing arguments. In Paddington the collection of data on, for example, patient flows and empty beds (almost a subversive act in the mid 1970s) played an important part in substantiating a solid case, especially in relation to clinicians who were used to positivistic argument. However, such data collection exercises were later visible in Bloomsbury. But the District Community Physician in Paddington was also pioneering service planning in addition to traditional capital planning, and ordering such data into an interpretation of the future ('Three into Two Will Go') which eventually won clinical support. No such clear interpretation emerged in Bloomsbury, nor was service strategy effectively integrated with financial strategy. In general, therefore, the argument for 'paralysis by analysis' (Peters and Waterman, 1982) needs qualification, at least where data is used to build a substantial model of the future.

Visioning and securing political support Attention to processes of negotiation and change around 'policy' was also important. The starting point in Paddington was a 'broad vision' which could be supported by administrators and the dominant clinical grouping. Nevertheless the vision was initially extremely imprecise, which allowed concessions to be made to important interest groups (such as the surgeons) to allow them to become committed to the strategy. In Paddington one saw:

- The development of a consensual rather than a radical broad vision for change based on common core values ('you had to love it'), made easier by the fact there was only one teaching hospital.
- The formation of a coalition between administrators and W2 clinicians and the marginalization of the victims of change.
- A keen attention to negotiating with external agencies which could potentially block change.
- Use of ad hoc groups; clubbable behaviour; celebration of early progress; circumventing the formal system.

Winning support for change was here a highly complex and political process (Mumford and Pettigrew, 1975). But this was combined with shifting of attitudes and low expectations through an action-orientated small group.

Linking strategic and operational change Pettigrew and Whipp's study (1991) of performance in private sector settings argues that high performers were characterized by a greater ability to link strategic and operational change. This is confirmed in these two case studies.

There were stronger links between strategic and operational change in Paddington: the 1980s were dominated by the implementation of the strategy agreed in 1976–8. The District closed the hospitals it agreed to close, and indeed St Mary's, W9 was even closed a year early. Perhaps this was because the centre was stronger in Paddington; the divisions more of a focus in Bloomsbury. The danger there was that the centre could agree a strategy but not secure operational change in the Divisions (as seen in the failure of the efficiency strategy, 1982–5). This is a recurrent problem in highly divisionalized companies as well. The initial argument for divisionalizing stressed this would allow HQ to concentrate on strategy and strengthen incentives facing middle management, but a major problem concerns internal transfer pricing as a division may seek to maximize its own profits at the expense of lower profits for the company as a whole. So centre/division relations seem as important in the NHS as in other settings.

2 Availability of Key People Leading Change As noted earlier, the case studies also illustrate the importance of key people in critical posts leading change. Leadership in Paddington was exercised by a small group of 'outsiders' (but with substantial NHS experience), selected by the Area Chairman, coming into the District in the mid and late 1970s and in a way benefiting from the legacy of failure. There was a mandate to try something new, in the light of current failure. Different actors had different skills and handled alternative aspects of the change process but worked together as a group. Change management may be more of a team than an individual process, despite the 'transformatory leadership' literature of the 1980s. The key group which in the end achieved change was not part of the mainstream planning machinery but a rather odd and informal 'study group' with no chairman and no clinical representative. Continuity was important and the team which emerged in Paddington was kept together for a considerable time, and crucially the District General Manager who was leading Phase 2 of the acute sector strategy in the late 1980s had been part of this team as General Administrator in the late 1970s. Bloomsbury found much greater difficulty in creating and sustaining a team, indeed the rapid rate of senior managerial turnover and lack of organizational memory was an important inhibitor of change. The role of the team seemed crucial (as in Pettigrew and Whipp's study, 1991) of the private sector, and so the construction and maintenance of such teams must be an important issue.

3 Long-term Environmental Pressure: Intensity and Scale In the private sector, studies such as Pettigrew (1985a) highlight the role of financial pressure in forcing strategic redirection. The picture in these case studies is more complex.

Severe long-term financial pressure was important but was not found to exert a consistent effect, and indeed responses to similar sources of budgetary pressure varied significantly even in these two neighbouring authorities. In Paddington the DMT accepted that retrenchment was a reality from a very early date ('we just faced the reality'), using sources of pressure (such as the 1979 'VAT disaster') to legitimate a strategy which they wished to undertake anyway. In Bloomsbury financial pressure drained energy out of the system, as management seemed to be always firefighting in the face of continuing financial crises and was unable to take strategic control. Far from producing radical change, severe financial pressure here produced paralysis and loss of control. Severe, unpredictable, financial pressure, in the absence of an agreed long-term strategy for retrenchment, eroded still further the District's ability to make effective cutback decisions. Whether a financial crisis was labelled as a threat or as an opportunity also depended on the existing local configuration of features. Subjectivity was important, and a simple pressure/response model far too crude.

4 Organizational and Managerial Culture It is of course difficult to talk of 'culture' in such a pluralist organization as the NHS where there is in reality a collection of very different subcultures. Yet as far as the administrative/managerial subculture is concerned, significant differences were apparent between Paddington and Bloomsbury in terms of self-image, value base, self-confidence and patterns of behaviour.

In Paddington a cohesive DMT was emerging by the late 1970s, characterized by the allocation of different roles to individuals and clear goal- and action-orientated behaviour. It is unclear why this was the case. Perhaps it was as a result of chemistry between individuals. Perhaps it was because of the clear mandate for change. Perhaps it was because of good selection decisions. There was now a willingness and self-confidence to develop strategy inside the District, to find ways round conventional procedures, to take risks and to work with ad hoc and informal structures rather than formal bureaucracies. These findings reinforce the classic distinction drawn by Burns and Stalker (1961) between organic and mechanistic organizations, and also Kanter's (1985) more recent typology of integrative and segmented organizations. There was also a strong value base to the redevelopment project. The strong organizational memory allowed important learning to occur in the late 1980s.

The formal decision making structure was much more complex in Bloomsbury, and there was less willingness to short circuit it: the two Districts generated their plans for their new hospitals in quite different ways. This is both because there were more groups involved in

Bloomsbury and because the level of trust between these groups was much lower. The DMT/DMB was unable to develop a coherent lead, lost control of strategy at DHA level, and increasingly a defeatist atmosphere built up. It proved impossible to reduce complexity in the absence of trust and common values, and this greatly increased the difficulties in securing change.

5 The Pattern of Managerial Clinical Relations Although we are here dealing specifically with the question of the balance of power between general managers and clinicians, this is in fact only a particular example of problems which arise in a highly professional organization. Studies of law (often a private sector service) and of universities would perhaps represent good comparators (Hardy, 1987; Hocking, 1991). Indeed Mintzberg's (1990) ideal type of the professional organization implies that strategy making here should proceed in a more decentralized and shared way than in other forms of organization. Work by Bucher and Stelling (1977) highlights the way in which 'professional segments' form in an organic and unplanned way, while Strauss (1978) stresses the way in which negotiations between occupational groups proceed in hospital settings. In such a complex, highly differentiated and decentralized form of organization, one would expect that institutional orders would normally be negotiated rather than imposed.

This is not to say that these orders are not renegotiated over time, and this may also produce periods of conflict. The general management role was in many ways an expansion of the old administrative role, and this could result in an uncertain period in which new occupational identities become established (Pettigrew, 1973a).

It is interesting that even within these two neighbouring Districts, wide variability was apparent in the pattern of clinical/managerial relations. The clinicians in Paddington were much more linked into the strategic management process than in Bloomsbury. The origin of this was the coalition between administrators and W2 clinicians in the 1976–8 exercise: in the end the DMT helped these clinicians secure a great prize which had eluded them for 30 years. Great attention was paid to bargaining and negotiating with clinicians but in the end management's ability to secure capital investment was the key to getting redevelopment and revenue reductions. This lesson was learned and clinicians from both ends of the new Parkside District were also intensively involved in formulating Phase 2 in the late 1980s. In Bloomsbury no such clear alliance existed and some of the key 'strategic' clinicians had gone into opposition, depriving management of key votes on the DHA. Some of them even argued that they had been driven into opposition by an inability of management to keep basic operational systems (such as medical records) going, or a hectoring style. Nor was there a prospect of substantial capital investment from Region until much later on in the process. A clear task for the new DGM in Bloomsbury was to encourage this key subgroup of clinicians to

come forward, and to begin to work with management in a more collaborative way. This required paying attention to the poor morale
apparent in key groups of clinicians.

6   The Fit with the Locale   It could be argued that it was always going
to be more difficult to secure acute sector change in Bloomsbury than in
Paddington. The former District was much more complex: it had a
greater proportion of specialty beds, a greater proportion of cross-
Regional referrals, three postgraduate groups and, above all, two teaching
hospitals. This service complexity in turn generated much more organizational complexity. The University of London also played a more central
role. Merging two elite institutions and – even more problematically –
moving on to the UCH site was always going to prove a tricky task. The
political terrain was also more difficult, given the left turn apparent in
Inner London Labour parties in the early 1980s, which was reflected in
nominations made by the London Borough of Camden and the Inner
London Education Authority.

There is clearly something in this argument, yet it should not be
overstated. The 1976–8 change process in Paddington, if analysed
historically, might be thought to be more difficult than the experience of
the 1980s in Bloomsbury as there were few prior models, a very different
industrial relations framework and more assertive general managerial
roles had not yet been sanctioned nationally.

General Reflections

We now return briefly to some of the theoretical literature identified at
the beginning of this chapter and consider the implications of the two case
studies presented.

The change processes studied in this chapter are, of course, of long
duration: 60 years is likely to elapse between the first plans for redevelopment at St Mary's, W2 and completion of Phase 2. These are indeed
strategic change episodes, and snapshot analyses are highly unlikely to
capture these historic dynamics. The process is more important than the
episode and any analysis of operational changes in Paddington in the
1980s would be thin without an understanding of the crucial strategic
decisions taken between 1976 and 1978.

The case material provides good examples of Levine's alternative
categories of denial, decrementalism and strategic management as
responses to prolonged fiscal stress, and illustrates the importance of prior
strategy in guiding the organizational response to fiscal pressure.
Paddington's response to fiscal pressures of the 1980s was to accelerate
the closure of hospitals it wanted to close in any case. A financial crisis
could be seen as threat or as an opportunity, and in the latter case pseudo
pressures could even be constructed as a crisis. Underlying the history in
both localities were very similar long-term processes of redistribution out

of Inner London, yet the responses were very different. Levine's three-stage model of denial, decrementalism and strategic management did not apply in Paddington which went into the strategic management of retrenchment very early. Bloomsbury fitted the model better, as certainly initially the dominant response was denial, and then cost improvement programmes, but this was followed by a lurch into fiscal crisis in 1985. It is still too early to judge whether the attempts to resolve the strategic question of the core campus will be successful. Perhaps managing retrenchment at an operational level is less problematic if there is clear strategic guidance.

The literature on non-decision making highlighted the potential ability of elites to keep items off agendas. In Paddington it was, for example, always assumed that redevelopment would take place around W2 and that either W9 or W10 would be vulnerable. In Bloomsbury the ability of the Middlesex lobby to redefine the clear message from Flowers into a debate between a 'single-site' and a 'double-site' strategy provides another good example of the way issues can be relabelled.

The organizational life cycle metaphor seems too mechanistic to capture the relationship between retrenchment and redevelopment and the manner in which even organizations in financial decline can undergo internal revitalization. Subjectivity and the strength of managerial resources may play an important role. For example, the new leadership coming in to Paddington from the outside seized the initiative, creating a broad and positive vision of the future which combined retrenchment and redevelopment. Revenue reductions required capital investment; this was one way of buying change and providing real incentives. Not only did this vision engage clinicians, but it created a positive precedent – well lodged in the organizational memory – which could be rolled forward to the 1990s. 'Virtuous circles' can thus build up over long periods, especially where there is continuity in key managerial personnel, although this happens more by accident than design in the NHS.

The question is does the advantage accrue to the first mover? Was St Mary's wise to act so quickly, or has it made too many concessions? The jury is still out, but the broad judgment would currently have to be that St Mary's has certainly strengthened its position vis-à-vis UCH and the Middlesex over the past 15 years.

5

Managing Uncertainty and Crisis

The Case of HIV/AIDS

Some Organizational and Managerial Aspects of the HIV/AIDS Epidemic

For the newly appointed general managers, above all in Inner London DHAs, the response to a major new health care issue of the 1980s – HIV/AIDS – was with the benefit of hindsight to set a stern test in terms of the organizational ability to sense new and unusual problems and to process an issue characterized by an exceptionally high degree of fluidity, complexity and uncertainty and in conditions of crisis. There was also a requirement to achieve continuing rather than episodic organizational change. These of course are all organizational and managerial themes which occur in many private sector organizations as well as the NHS. Here indeed was a major change issue which required flexibility, speed, responsiveness and creativity and can be used to exemplify interesting concerns within the strategic management literature (Ferlie and Bennett, 1992) such as crisis management, product championing and processes of organizational learning.

This chapter will consider a comparative case study analysis of the organizational and managerial response to HIV/AIDS in two neighbouring Inner London DHAs which were both among the first authorities in the country to build up HIV/AIDS awareness and indeed a substantial caseload, but which soon diverged in terms of the nature of the organizational and managerial response. But first we consider some analytic themes which will enable us to interrogate the empirical material. First, who leads change and how? Secondly, how is the role of 'crisis' to be understood? Thirdly, what has been the importance of organizational design and development in the response to HIV/AIDS?

Who Leads Change?

It is not obvious who could lead change in such complex and fragmented systems and four potential and alternative bases should be considered, namely: social movements and social movement organizations; DHA members; general managers; and clinical product champions.

Social Movement Organizations: a Possible Catalyst for Change Social movements and their organizational expression (social movement organizations, SMOs) (Ferlie and Bennett, 1992) may act as important catalysts for change, sometimes bringing new values and high levels of personal commitment into formal organizational settings. In the private sector, the 'quality of life' or 'industrial democracy' movements of the 1970s may approximate to the experience that it is also evident in health care settings.

SMOs are often value-laden organizations concerned about life styles, often translating what has hitherto been seen as the personal into the political through tactics of consciousness-raising and mass or group mobilization. Such social movements are often seen as replacing the traditional class-based parties as the critical source of social and political change in advanced capitalist societies. Events in Eastern Europe have shown the strength elsewhere of such weak organizations: Solidarity and Civil Forum have in the end proved stronger than the centralist parties they replaced. Moreover, some have argued (Scott, 1990) that social movement organizations may produce a distinct organizational and ideological form: they will contain a large cultural component (psycho-social techniques such as consciousness-raising or group therapy are common) as well as an instrumental component; a common goal is the creation of 'free space'; the typical organizational expression is a loose network-like structure with a distrust of hierarchies; there is emphasis on the use of direct action and the linkage of personal experience to drives for collective social change.

More specifically, Arno's 1986 case study of San Francisco indicates the important role that SMOs can play in the construction of HIV/AIDS service systems, as organizations which are well linked into the formal organizational and financial process.

How are we to understand SMOs as organizations? For Scott (1990) social movement analysis represents a major theme within contemporary sociology, neglected both by functionalists (whose equilibrium-centred models cast social movements as marginal and backward-looking resisters of social change) and Marxists (who perceived the lack of a class basis to such movements as a crippling weakness). But a key question relates to the desire and ability of SMO members to intervene in the formal political and organizational process. 'Culturalist' (Touraine, 1981) interpretations of social movements would downplay their formal political role; whereas resource mobilization theory (McCarthy and Zald, 1976), stresses universal processes of bureaucratic degeneration whereby loose organizational forms demanding high degrees of commitment give way to tighter, more formal, organizations where the organizational burden is shouldered by quasi-professionals. Scott concludes that there is a wide continuum:

> Contrary to culturalist interpretations, no categorical distinction can be drawn between social movements, pressure groups and parties. Social movements are best understood in terms of a continuum stretching from informal network-like associations to formal party-like organizations. (1990, p. 132)

So the more value-laden and exclusive the SMO, the more it may approximate to the sectarian form of organization, based on special values, where there is apartness from the wider society, and where it is difficult to apply rational criteria to the operations of the organization. Wilson (1967) here suggests that in such organizational forms there is likely to be a bias against hierarchy, a high level of lay participation, intense personal involvement, and indifference or even hostility to the secular society and the state.

The Arno study suggests, on the contrary, that there may also be SMOs which are keen to lobby the formal organizational sector and are adept in so doing. In the United Kingdom, Louw (1989) argues that social movements have also had some success in capturing the specialist HIV labour market being set up within the NHS, in effect launching a social movement from within public sector bureaucracies. These case studies will furnish further evidence of the role of social movements and social movement organizations in two of the key frontline DHAs. In particular:

- How influential are SMOs such as Terrence Higgins Trust in determining strategy within these Districts? Are 'culturalist' or 'resource mobilization' perspectives better able to explain the strategy and behaviour of actors drawn from such settings?
- How useful is the concept of organizational 'zealotry' (Downs, 1967) in explaining the rapid early growth of new agencies? Zealots contain important functional as well as dysfunctional traits in the launching of organizational innovation as they have implacable energy which they focus on promoting their sacred policies, although their vociferous attacks on the present state of affairs make it difficult to build a coalition.
- Within the organization do 'bureaucratic insurgents' (Zald and Berger, 1978) appear, challenging perceived inaction at the top through caucusing, coordinating committees or mass action?
- More modestly, are common value systems apparent which drive and energize change across conventional organizational and occupational boundaries?

DHA Members A second potential basis of leadership for change could be appointed members on DHAs who perhaps equate to the role of the non-executive director in the private sector. While there is a controversy about the extent to which such members are no more than 'rubber stamps', some writers argue that they can exert an influence either through setting boundaries and local rules of the game (Stewart et al., 1987a) or more proactively, especially through proposals coming from a small but influential subgroup of member 'strategists' (Ranade, 1985). Pettigrew, Ferlie and McKee (1990) also suggest that a small number of senior members are able to win influence, especially where they have boundary-spanning networks into (for example) Social Services or the voluntary sector.

General Management   A third potential basis of leadership could be general management, which had indeed been created in order to provide a clearer focus for driving through change. Did the agendas of the new cadre of general managers in these Districts revolve around financial control rather than the management of strategic service change or organizational development, both of which represent possible alternative constructions of their early brief (Griffiths Report, 1983)? Moreover, many of the characteristics of the HIV/AIDS issue (crisis management, uncertainty, systemic implications) seemed to indicate the development of a management style able to cope with continuing rapid change. It will be interesting to use the case material to see how general managers in these crucial Districts approached these tasks.

Clinical Product Champions   A final potential source of change was that clinicians might emerge as 'product champions', an important role which has been discerned both in studies of industrial innovation such as Project Sappho (Rothwell, 1976) and health care innovation (Stocking, 1985), although sometimes not in a fully processual manner.

A number of studies have stressed the personal characteristics of entrepreneurs as key motivators. So Boswell's 1973 analysis of the characteristics of private sector founder entrepreneurs (many of whom stayed with their firms for a long period) stressed personal traits such as drive and hard work. Schön (1973) also discusses some of the personal characteristics of the effective product champion: a risk taker; a willingness to use all informal as well as formal channels to promote the cause; drive and energy (perhaps to the point of obsessionality, as in Downs's (1967) conception of organizational zealots), perhaps also a personal history of achievement. An effective product champion (Burgelman and Sayles, 1986) is seen as being able to work effectively in a non-programmed environment, and able to deal with a variety of groups over which there is no formal control and each of which may have different or even contradictory goals, but each of which may also be crucial to the project's success. However Louis et al.'s (1989) study of academic entrepreneurs found that individual characteristics were weak and unsystematic predictors of forms of entrepreneurship, and that organizational effects were crucial.

Other writers have therefore stressed roles, power bases and organizational structures and climate as important facilitators of effective product championing as well as the personality and biographical characteristics of the product champion. As Pettigrew (1979) argues in his study of the founder of a British boarding school, the essential problem is the transformation of individual drive into collective purpose and commitment. High levels of commitment in such new organizations could derive from a number of sources: the vision of the founder which could 'consciousness-raise' within the new organization; the sacrifice needed to build exclusive new communities; or the creation and utilization of myths.

There is some empirical material on role construction by product champions: Rothwell and Zegveld (1982) found that the effective product champion not only took a vital interest in all aspects of the new product, but also had considerable power and prestige, and was able to use informal patterns of relations within the organization. Often new ideas were found to exhibit an organizational life cycle: they were generated by creative scientists, were initially promoted within the organization by a product champion, processed by a project manager (whose job it was to integrate the various functions and weld them into an integrated whole), and then passed on to a venture team which should contain a balance of different skills, and be achievement- rather than power-motivated. The orchestration of this creative process indicated a role for strategic management, yet there were sometimes found to be difficulties: 'The general picture that emerges is one of caution and lack of long-term commitment by corporate management, and of internal friction and resistance to change experienced by venture managers in their dealings with other, more conventional, corporate departments' (Rothwell and Zegveld, 1982, p. 111).

It is also interesting to note the variety of roles which have been surfaced in analyses of organizational innovation processes. So Downs (1967) distinguishes between 'zealots' who were seen as loyal to relatively narrow 'sacred' policies, possessing great energy but also finding difficulties in coalition building, and 'advocates' who, on the other hand, were loyal to a broader range of functions than zealots, more aware of the need to build a broad base of support, but perhaps exhibiting less drive. As advocacy requires great time and effort, advocates may only continue in role in relation to policies which they believe to be important and which they can influence. Burgelman and Sayles (1986) also differentiate between the product champion role and that of the 'organizational champion' who is better able to relate the particular venture to broader strategy, perhaps an upper manager willing to risk reputation on the highly visible sponsorship of an untried and radical innovation.

The case study material may furnish evidence of clinical product champions in process: their biographies, personalities and skills; their approaches to the innovation process and their power position within the organization. It is likely that unplanned and idiosyncratic processes of role creation and expansion will be evident (Miner, 1990) as money and attention started to pour into the HIV/AIDS field, given the arrival of national budgetary windfalls (Levine et al., 1981) which had the potential to promote rapid development. A fleeting opportunity was there to be seized.

The Role of Crisis: its Construction, Management and Aftermath

Crisis management represents a second analytic theme which can be used to mine the case study material. The naive view that 'necessity is the mother of invention' and that high caseload would by itself force the HIV/AIDS issue up agendas is disconfirmed by Shilts's comparison (1987) of the response in New York and San Francisco, where HIV/AIDS attracted less governmental attention in New York despite (at least initially) higher caseload: HIV/AIDS can become a problem without emerging as an issue. The balance of local political and organizational forces, and the way in which issues are received into pre-existing networks, may be important mediating factors.

Dutton (1987) argues that the managerial processing of strategic issues will be different in crisis and non-crisis situations. Certainly between 1983 and 1986/7, HIV/AIDS quickly emerged nationally in the UK as a high profile health issue to a point where it was often labelled as a 'crisis': the early epidemiology was taken as indicating that the UK was only four or so years behind America; an unparalleled national health education campaign was launched; and there was huge media interest. The HIV/AIDS issue acquired many of the characteristics of a crisis as defined by Dutton (importance; immediacy and uncertainty): indeed it was often said that there had been nothing like it in health care since the Second World War.

Here was a crisis which contained both real and constructed elements but maintenance of the issue was to prove more problematic than creation. Issue succession took place and by 1989 the focus of attention had moved on to the health care White Paper (Hogwood, 1987, even suggests that the natural history of public policy issues is from crisis to complacency).

How did the perception of crisis affect the response from health care organizations? Much of the existing literature on organizational crisis (Hermann, 1963; Jick and Murray, 1982) stresses the pathological consequences of crisis-as-threat: increased centralization and formalization, with a breakdown in integrating structures; the erosion of information channels; the exiting of key human resources; a loss of trust and loyalty as a low commitment organization emerges; groupthink and scapegoating. Crisis is here seen as leading to an organizational mechanistic shift in which the creativity and flexibility needed is even less likely to occur.

There is, however, a less considered counter scenario of crisis-as-opportunity (Starbuck et al., 1978). Major change is seen as taking place when the perception of a crisis forces an awkward issue up crowded agendas. The process of strategic change in ICI would be one example (Pettigrew, 1985a) where concern was skilfully orchestrated by the new leadership in the company. The construction of crisis-as-opportunity by a band of early learners may lead to very different patterns of behaviour from that envisaged in the crisis-as-threat argument: continuing pressure from pioneers; the formation of special groups who reach out to the rest of the organization; high energy and commitment levels; strong integration mechanisms through special coordinating machinery and a sense of shared purpose. The perception of crisis, in other words, facilitates rapid learning, consciousness-raising and mobilization. Even in this more optimistic scenario, there remains the problem of how to manage the post-crisis aftermath perhaps as disillusion or burnout sets in. In the related field of organizational decline, Sutton (1989) argues that differences in pre-existing shared cognitions and emotions shape organizational responses, and help explain why loss of environmental support leads to rigidity in some organizations, while others respond to threats in flexible and imaginative ways. Tracing through the response of DHAs to the HIV/AIDS issue provides an opportunity to develop some of the literature on the management of crisis.

Certainly there are parallels with the emerging literature on the generation of major or discontinuous change within established organizations. Inertial pressures are seen as extremely strong, yet Grinyer and McKiernan's (1990) project on 'sharpbending' firms where improved performance was achieved suggests that it may sometimes be possible to achieve change in advance of an externally generated, real crisis, as long as there is a shared perception in the higher tiers that old ways are no longer good enough and that urgent action is required. There may then be situations where it is functional for managers to 'create crises' in a proactive way in an attempt to mould a potentially difficult future. Thus Grinyer et al.'s (1988a, b) study of 'sharpbenders' highlighted the importance of triggers for radical change, which could include pseudo-crises manufactured by management as well as real crises or a change of leadership or ownership.

HIV/AIDS: an Opportunity for Organizational Development and Design

The perception that the NHS has remained in many ways a frustratingly underdeveloped organization created in some localities an alternative general managerial agenda. Indeed the creation of greater autonomy and flexibility in organizational design was one of the themes explored in the Griffiths Report (1983). Certainly this had resonance in the case study localities: in Bloomsbury the first DGM wrote:

> It was recognized from an early stage that one of the key management challenges was not just to implement change, but to develop an organization's capacity to cope with change. The aim, in a sense, was to create a different kind of organization, capable of learning, responding to and even generating change, rather than simply reacting to it. (Liddell, 1987)

Such a learning organization is likely to develop distinctive decision making processes, for instance, greater reliance on minimalistic, temporary structures such as problem solving groups (Hedberg et al., 1976). Such an approach might seem very different from the densely organized formal consultative machinery often adopted in the past, but the correlation in terms of timing between the introduction of general management and the construction of HIV/AIDS as an issue provided an interesting and naturally occurring opportunity for organizational development (OD) and design. Action can be used to generate higher order learning rules which can be transferred to other situations. As Lant and Mezias (1990) put it: 'Entrepreneurship can be conceived of not only as product or technological innovation; it also includes innovation in organizational structures and processes'. So acting entrepreneurially may come to be seen more favourably – more valued and supported as an activity – in some localities than others. It should also be remembered, however, that the history of OD efforts in the NHS has not always been encouraging, and too often work has remained at the micro level and it has been difficult to move on to more macro issues of organizational design (Edmonstone, 1982). Early promise has not always been followed through, and organizational design issues have often remained low on NHS managers' agendas.

Nowhere were these general arguments for organizational design and development more applicable than in the rapidly emerging HIV/AIDS issue where there was a requirement for speedy action, where strategic planning was taking place under conditions of gross uncertainty and where there was a premium on lateral communication as a host of very different specialties which had historically never had contact found themselves unexpectedly going to the same meetings (for example sexually transmitted diseases and dentistry). Moreover, the emergence of ear-marked resources provided a windfall which could be used to accelerate such processes of service development. But as Levine et al. (1981) argue, while windfall growth can promote the politics of extraordinary change, new interest groups may quickly emerge into a dominant coalition to capture the new resources, excluding constituencies which emerged just that little bit later. This points to the critical importance of very early choices in designing machinery to process the new HIV/AIDS issue and of retaining control over the new resources. Key organizational development themes may be: the development of lateral forms of communication and integrating devices within a matrix approach; the use of facilitators to develop capacity; the construction of benign organizational niches in which innovators can shelter; and the importance of strong organizational cultures which reward risk takers. Are there examples of such special machinery and have theories of innovation been used to guide action? Have human resource or organizational development departments seized the opportunity to use the HIV/AIDS issue as a containable test bed for a wider agenda? Have particular norms or subcultures arisen which drive action?

The case study material can also be used to investigate how strategy is made under conditions of gross uncertainty. With the erosion of the more mechanistic forms of corporate planning dominant in the 1970s (McKee and Ferlie, 1988), there has been increasing interest in the development of strategic planning methodologies which script uncertainty in, rather than attempt to script it out. The focus on the capacity of organizations to retain strategic flexibility is a key concern of the 'excellence' literature.

Such flexibility is seen as related to such techniques as: proactive environmental scanning; the creation and use of organizational slack in responding to the unexpected; keeping options open and resisting specialization; empowering multiple perspectives and pursuing several options at once (Starkey and Wright, 1990).

We also need to explore the pattern of organizational strategy and change exhibited by these two DHAs to explore two other themes about strategy. Mintzberg (1978) used retrospective analysis of the step-wise escalation of the Vietnamese war and patterns of strategic change in Volkswagen to identify two main patterns. The first was the tendency of a strategy to have a life cycle from conception to decay and death, and secondly a tendency for strategies to change not in a continuous incremental fashion, but rather for change – even incremental change – 'to take place in spurts, each followed by a period of continuity' (1978, p. 943). Yet can such occasional paradigm shifts produce a capacity for continuing change, which an issue such as HIV/AIDS would seem to indicate?

The nature of strategy under such conditions of uncertainty may also take on special and interesting characteristics. Given the role of clinicians and other professionals as early learners and product champions, a large degree of bottom-up, professionally driven innovation can be expected. Behaviour in the field may often precede formal strategy, and indeed formal strategy may serve mainly to 'bless' actions which have already been undertaken. It will be interesting to explore whether the strategic planning process is top-down or bottom-up in nature, what is the role of the centre, and whether there is effective dialogue between the two forms of planning.

Paddington/Parkside: a Flying Start Falters

By 1990 a huge HIV caseload had built up in the District (492 AIDS cases and 1,354 HIV seropositive cases were known to the District by March 1990) and the special AIDS allocation to the District rose to almost £10m. A commonly heard phrase in the District was: 'if it was going to happen anywhere, it was going to happen here', with the largest Sexually Transmitted Disease (STD) Clinic in the country and a big Drug Dependency Unit (DDU), both acting as important and open access filters into the system. This combined with a tradition of research within the medical school into microbiology and virology, with an earlier research group forming around hepatitis B.

Clinical awareness that a major problem could break arose very early on in St Mary's, partly through their location in international research networks (a November 1981 Conference in Puerto Rico was mentioned as a significant information-sharing event with American clinicians). A balanced team was quietly built up (a key immunology appointment was made at this time) and 'soft money' obtained from the Wellcome Trust to start in 1982 the first UK cohort study of homosexual patients

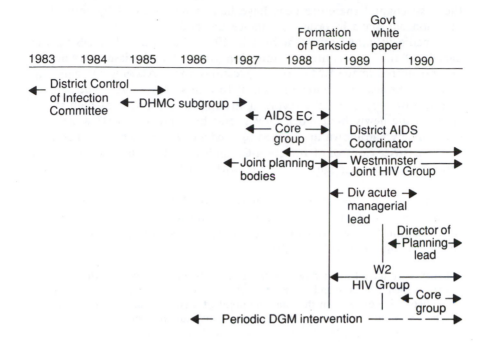

Figure 5.1 *Paddington/Parkside: key decision making arenas, 1983–9*

providing important early evidence within sharply accelerated research timetables (Pinching et al., 1983) to back clinical insight that a problem could be about to break. The study also facilitated the employment of contract research staff who were increasingly to shoulder a service load thus devising a way round regional manpower guidelines which were trying to restrict the number of junior medical staff. All these early developments were not 'managed' but arose from the bottom-up initiatives of clinicians anxious and able to find their way around constraints on action.

Figure 5.1 summarizes the complex history of changes to lead role in the District over the 1980s, indicating that initially clinical ownership of the problem was to prove dominant, with less administrative input.

Infection Control: the Crisis Explodes

Working in a teaching district in a cosmopolitan area, clinicians at St Mary's had already responded to earlier cases of smallpox and Lassa fever, and had also developed a policy to control infection from hepatitis B which was seen as a partial model for an AIDS policy. This emphasis on infection control was also strengthened by the physical lay-out of the hospital. Because of the lack of side rooms, control of infection cases were managed in an infectious diseases ward as a common resource for the District, and therefore beds have had to be allocated by control of infection clinicians in order to balance demands.

A media inflamed crisis emerged in 1983 which pushed AIDS up the agenda of this core control of infection group, but the issue was not as yet transferred to the DMT arena. Questions about AIDS were beginning to be mentioned in minutes of clinical fora in summer 1983, but debates seemed low key, essentially revolving around the allocation of high status space in the newly built block at W2. But by September 1983 a crisis of staff anxiety had blown up, fanned by media coverage, which was tackled by the District Control of Infection Committee (DCIC) (a clinically based group) through arranging meetings with staff to discuss fears about safety.

More precisely, over the 1983 August Bank Holiday weekend growth in the number of patients and an escalation of media interest led the Control of Infection Officer to call an emergency meeting with two clinical academic colleagues. She recalls:

> [They were made] to sit down on the evening before they were both due to go off on their holidays and we wrote a sheet of paper . . . closely modelled on the hepatitis policy from the handling point of view . . . and a fairly firm idea that if you did not have sexual contact or blood handling contact then you were reasonably safe, and we tried to maintain that line very strongly from the beginning . . . this caused a lot of tension and pressure because we could not get other people to take it seriously. We knew that we were going to have real patients and real problems, and people seemed to flip between not being bothered and not caring, and it was something very minor and peripheral to being something that was so serious that it was untouchable.

Initial leadership was provided by an existing small group of clinical academics, linked more by personal friendships and common interests than lines on an organization chart. This group initially championed the issue in a climate where there could be rapid mood swings between cynicism and panic, shouldering much of the initial firefighting work, as each time a story hit the headlines, there was a wave of staff concern which had to be resolved through lunchtime meetings. One of the key clinicians commented:

> We had to do a lot of firefighting, we had to go and talk to people over and over again to try and allay fears . . . we were all under very considerable stress at that period because the other clinical staff to begin with were not prone to worry about AIDS.

The DCIC went on successfully to develop a range of control of infection policies, on a complex, clinically political basis, taking account of the realities of inter-consultant diplomacy. Of course, safety policy was legitimately a DCIC 'core' issue. However, because of the organizational vacuum, the DCIC was by the end of 1984 again being drawn in to consider resource issues such as the level of nursing staff or projected bed requirements. While the safety crisis had been well handled, it was to prove more difficult to use the perception of crisis to change resource flows within the hospital.

Special Funding: the First Bid to Region, 1984

Clinicians from the major London centres soon emerged as powerful national product champions on the HIV/AIDS issue, with good access to the media, the Department of Health and other national fora such as the Select Committee on Social Services which could be used to press a case and mobilize around the crisis. For example, Dr Anthony Pinching, a key consultant at St Mary's, W2 told the Committee it was 'absolutely incredible' that the Chief Medical Officer had told the Committee that he was unaware of plans to change restrictions on medical manpower in the light of demands made by HIV/AIDS (Social Services Select Committee, 1987, para. 120). Another respondent recalled a W2 clinician who appeared on television with the then Minister for Health in 1983 or 1984:

> Now at that time about 14 or 15 people had been diagnosed or had died with AIDS, and he was saying 'well, how many corpses do you need, do you need 20, 100, 200, when is it enough? You can see what is happening in the States.

But although such clinicians were involved in lobbying at national level, and were getting messages that monies would be released centrally, they were also finding it difficult to secure early action in the locality where the 'crisis' label was resisted, where management was not yet fully engaged and where 'enthusiasm' from the clinical 'AIDS lobby' also increased the danger of a backlash from other clinicians, especially if clinical coalition-building did not take place.

The District's response to the issue perhaps lost momentum in 1984. For the DMT, AIDS remained a secondary issue delegated to the W2 Unit which had been asked to compile the first bid for resources. Furthermore, the introduction of general management in 1985 destabilized management across the whole District: the well-established team of Chief Officers (including the DMO) broke up, the new DGM arrived in early 1985, other roles were clipped back and expertise was lost. At hospital level there were still difficulties relating to the lack of administrative continuity and a confused split between the Unit and the DMO.

Initial approaches to Region in spring 1984 for funding foundered because of the lack of a substantiated bid, and in the end the first bid was largely compiled by key clinical and nursing product champions within the hospital. This first bid (1984) of course reflected these origins, and was essentially hospital-based, although practice was to develop rapidly. The compilation of the first bid helped determine early ownership of the issue and can be regarded as a key decision point.

The DHMC Fills the Vacuum

As of early 1985, responsibility for taking an overall view on AIDS across the District was still unclear. The District Hospital Medical Committee (DHMC) filled the vacuum, pulling the issue back to the main body of W2 clinicians. Any teaching hospital will be concerned to maintain a balance between specialties, and a sudden growth in any one specialty could set up a disequilibrium within the whole hospital. A DHMC AIDS working party was set up in February 1985, including surgeons who were anxious to discuss workload and safety implications, with the brief 'to advise on a general District response to the problem and to suggest specific procedures to be used in dealing with these patients.' Differing accounts were received on the nature of this group. For some there was a clear need to ensure that balance within the hospital was maintained: 'I felt it was a very important job to make sure that whatever happened with this new epidemic, it did not stop the rest of the District working.' Others were more critical, seeing it as motivated by a negative desire to 'keep the lid on AIDS', and unable to engage in positive strategic planning. Some saw it as a DHMC-led rather than AIDS-led, with a hidden agenda to lower the hospital's profile: 'At one time the subgroup circulated a letter saying that people were not to mention St Mary's in the context of AIDS which was clearly ludicrous and was widely ignored.'

Its first action was to cap the use of beds in the infectious diseases ward at eight, combined with a policy ('cloud cuckoo' in the view of one respondent) that patients should be referred back to their District of origin. The DHMC subgroup also handled the question of relations between clinicians. There was pressure from AIDS patients with dementia and a difficult interface with the psychiatry division. But from late 1985, the DHMC subgroup also administered the special allocations which were being unlocked at the centre. Although the DGM and the DMO were both on the subgroup, most members were acute sector consultants, and the DMT did not usually interfere, seeing the resource implications as 'small fry'. Essentially, the group collated and prioritized bids from the W2 divisions within a special annual funding cycle on a highly visible yet incremental basis, and did not engage in strategic planning or the development of community care.

Managerial Intervention, 1986

There was some feeling that the District as a whole continued to lose ground in 1985 and 1986, with uncertainty about overall direction or leadership, and general management was now to make an appearance. The new DGM, Barbara Young, had been keeping a watching brief:

> The funny thing was that AIDS had not impinged on my consciousness at all until I got the job here . . . I became aware that (a) there was such a thing as AIDS and (b) Paddington and North Kensington was in the thick of it. And then I got here, it went wroom!, from that moment on, more and more time was taken up. I sat on the DHMC AIDS subgroup just to get the hang of it, and it was clear that it was getting bigger and very swiftly a District ethic that AIDS is important takes over.

Alarm bells began to ring with signs of a major escalation of demand for inpatient beds, at a time when the District as a whole was under pressure to reduce its acute bed numbers. In December 1986, the DHMC subgroup put forward a £3m bid for 28 beds. Some of the costing work had been badly prepared and the DGM was dragged into detailed reworking of the bid. The political profile of the AIDS issue was by now taking off centrally and in any case more space was appearing on managerial agendas with the successfully completed early closure of St Mary's, W9 in October 1986.

Until late 1986, therefore, there had been little managerial involvement in the AIDS issue other than to support clinically derived bids for resources. Action had been clinically driven and preceded 'policy', the momentum of service development was coming up from the field, resource allocation had been handled within clinically dominated forums in an ad hoc manner, and little strategic work had been undertaken. There was now a prospect of a hospital-based system gathering momentum and soaking up more and more beds.

How are we to make sense of the crucial decision point in late 1986 which started the transfer of the AIDS issue from clinical to managerial fora? There was widespread consensus that the DHMC system was no longer effective. The DGM was also concerned that there should be greater role clarity and responsibility to set up a strategy, although it was unclear precisely who was to become the AIDS strategist as issue leadership could have gone either to the St Mary's UGM or the new Head of Community Medicine. In the end the issue went to the latter: Dr Deirdre Cunningham, the new Head of Community Medicine, was proactive and had positive proposals, had been a UGM in mental illness services where joint working was a key skill, and had an incentive to attract new issues with resources attached. And no one else wanted to do it.

Towards a District Strategy, 1987–1988

Consequent to this change in leadership, there were now – in formal terms at least – radical changes to the policy stance that had been associated with the DHMC borrowing from priority group models. A commitment to community care, to collaboration with primary and social care agencies and the further development of drugs services were important signs of new thinking.

Embedding these new strategies in behaviour and turning round resource flows was to prove a more complex task. A key managerial assumption was that a new structure was required to support the new strategy, reflecting the view that strategy determines structure (Chandler, 1962). So a new and large AIDS Executive Committee was formed which now reported to a managerial rather than a clinical forum. There were also a number of iterations designed to produce new formal joint care planning mechanisms. However, there were important limits to the effectiveness of formal structural change as informal organizational life often reasserted itself. The key group of consultants still dominated discussions: they sat together, held their own arguments in public and were difficult to challenge. The strategy document was slowly being written, but in a top-down way as the lead role was increasingly being played by the Head of Community Medicine and also a senior planner (both of whom lacked direct control over resources).

Strong financial pressure arose with a disappointing financial allocation. The first meeting of the new AIDS EC determined – despite the new strategy – that the first priority should be to protect new beds, even if this meant that community care or health developments could not be funded. It was at this point that the DGM firmly moved to bounce the bid back for revision. The final strategy document was written in spring 1988, and while there were some gaps (drugs strategy was not really developed) nevertheless this was the first attempt to generate a coherent framework. Yet it was to become apparent that an implementation deficit would soon emerge.

Organizationally, a new notion of 'normalization' was now in evidence, and the implication was that in the future services should be drawn into and from existing systems, without the need for superimposed ad hoc committees (which were not seen as having executive authority) (Roderick and Stevens, 1989).

An Implementation Deficit and a Switch to General Management, 1988

> We never really implemented the strategy. The first operational plan that we did as a result of the strategy was what blew the whistle, it was dire. (Management respondent)

As Roderick and Stevens (1989) write:

> At the same time, an operational plan was written quite separately, but it became swamped with financial rather than strategic issues, dominated by the District's overspending. Individuals expended considerable energy at the AIDS Executive complaining that AIDS money was not spent on AIDS facilities.
>
> An operational group was set up to evaluate the numerous bids. Once the operational plan was submitted, it was realized that the Executive could not exert an executive function, despite its title, and that the DGM was having the final say on AIDS resource allocation. Moreover, although Unit Managers had been coopted on to the AIDS Executive, many of the decisions taken by the committee were not implemented by them.

Why should this implementation gap have arisen? Of course the transition from Paddington to Parkside in 1988 was likely to complicate all strategic change exercises, but there also appear to be some special factors at work in the HIV/AIDS issue. The epidemiology suddenly changed in 1988, with a noticeable plateauing of caseload. Perhaps lack of ownership was important, as the strategy – however well thought out – had in the end been developed by Community Medicine in isolation from line management or the service innovators in the field. Secondly, there was a perceived lack of managerial focus as Community Medicine did not relish the task of facing down colleagues in the bidding process, given norms of clinical collegiality. Thirdly, management was still playing a secondary role as the UGMs did not yet have access to the support and advice needed within the Units despite the presumption of normalization, as decision making revolved around direct negotiations between the AIDS EC as funders and the specialties as bidders. Fourthly, the management capacity to handle the rapidly escalating resource flows was still rudimentary – especially given the marginal role played by the UGMs – and the first designated AIDS Coordinator did not arrive in post until July 1988. Nor was there much organizational learning or a theory of how to manage under conditions of uncertainty which could have been used to guide future action – indeed, increasingly the emphasis was now to be on 'normalization' and the transfer back to more conventional forms of decision making.

Top management's perception was that the AIDS EC had in essence failed, and in late 1988 the AIDS issue was pointedly general managerialized, with the new post of Divisional Acute Services Manager taking a lead role. But alongside this switch of focus at the top, and a move to the hegemony of line management, a less visible process of organizational development was being launched by the newly appointed AIDS Coordinator. If the UGMs were to undertake more of a role, as advocated by the 'normalizers', then they needed access to more advice and support within their Units than had hitherto been the case. While St Mary's, W2 had been dealing with AIDS patients since 1983, it was not until early 1989 that a formal Unit level group was set up (chaired by the UGM), following pressure from (and indeed lunch with) the AIDS Coordinator. The merger with Brent to form Parkside had also raised questions for drugs services, given the different histories at either end of the new District, and a small group was formed (again with input from the AIDS Coordinator) to move on from the ad hoc innovation previously evident in drugs services which had so far remained comparatively remote from the development of HIV strategies.

The transition to general management was associated with new doctrines of 'unitization', 'normalization', damping down the noise level which had grown up around HIV/AIDS and strengthening the role of line management. The role of the centre of the District was eroded and there was soon (autumn 1989) to be a further change of lead in the shape of the Planning Directorate. A new team of committed staff was recruited, a central Policy Advisory Group set up and the centre of the District re-established itself, leading (for example) thought on the implications of the post-White Paper stress apparent on the internal market (Cm 555, 1989) for the still emerging HIV/AIDS services. But the dominant impression must be a sense of disappointment as the District seemed to face difficulties in translating its early – often clinically driven – energy and activity into sustained progress. The contrast with the rapid pace and early date of change in the District's acute sector strategy is an interesting one.

Analysis and Discussion

Returning to the three analytic themes identified in the first section of this chapter, what can be learnt from the case study?

The first theme related to the leadership of change, where four different potential bases were identified. This case study suggests first of all that DHA members on the whole have had only marginal impact on local strategy (perhaps with the exception of one generalist), perhaps because DHA interest was concentrated on those issues which could more readily be defined as 'political' (such as hospital and bed closures). The role of social movement organizations was also less evident than might have initially been thought. While such social movements were perhaps surprisingly influential at national level (with good access to the Department) and at ward and service level (especially over non-resource-based issues such as regime), they were less visible in the middle of the pyramid. Liaison between the District and the voluntary sector remain undeveloped throughout the early period, except where voluntary organizations could provide a discrete resource (such as London Lighthouse). There was little evidence of assertive lobbying, nor was it possible to detect bureaucratic insurgency within the District. Although there was self-selection by generally liberal professionals, a cohesive caucus was not really formed.

A third potential basis of leadership identified was general management. General management was on the whole slow to engage with the issue in the District, with the interesting and important exception of the DGM who was involved from an early date and maintained awareness, perhaps because of a lateral and wide-ranging interest in health care issues. Nor was there a conceptual interest in devising a new form of management which could process such a rapidly changing and uncertain issue. The key push for service development came instead from service providers, where a number of talented and lively staff (not only consultants but also others) developed services in an ad hoc, informal and bottom-up way. Professional segments formed in an unpredictable way around particular client groups or issues, and these shifting and multi-disciplinary groupings were a major source of 'strategy'.

In particular, the concept of the clinical product champion was found to have great resonance in the case study. This can be a demanding and uncomfortable role to adopt: in this case study it required constant drive and energy over a long period of time; fighting a corner could lead to difficult arguments with others in the District; and building a media and political profile perhaps aroused the suspicion of other clinicians. The key consultant – who had been a 'backroom' lab scientist – found his role transformed by the HIV issue, as he came out of the lab and into the policy process propelled by his contact with both the early science and the first patients. Moreover, this was a decision with long-term (perhaps even career-long) implications as there was to be no switching of issues or jumping off bandwagons should they begin to falter:

> I did not go into it because I had any wish to have a public profile: I hate committees, I absolutely hate them because I have to deal with such incompetence when the issue is perfectly obvious. I am very impatient really, that's my problem. If I see the solution I can't see why we just don't get on and do it, and I think that is an aspect of 'product champions', somebody who wants to learn but can also see their way through the morass and see a direction. (W2 clinical product champion)

Here was someone who saw the challenge, and who was keen to work in a non-programmed way, reflecting perhaps academic self-confidence. But HIV also represented a distinct biographical discontinuity, radically redefining roles and tasks. Alongside the drive and energy perhaps went the frustration of having to operate in an intensely political environment where deals had to be done and coalitions built. While the product champion was able to step into the initial vacuum and thus win an initial lead role, greater difficulties were experienced in maintaining this lead role within the District as more actors became engaged in the issue.

The second analytic theme identified earlier related to crisis construction and management. There was a paradox that W2 product champions found it initially easier to secure movement nationally than locally, and some local groups (such as the DHMC subgroup) resisted the crisis label. Nevertheless, an inflated bed projection (592 beds!) coming out of the Strategic Plan exercise was seen as helping unfreeze attitudes. There seem to have been three separate phases to the AIDS 'crisis' in the District. Initially, the crisis was one of staff anxiety which resulted in a range of pathological organizational behaviours (rumour, scapegoating, stigmatization, panic) and which was 'managed' by clinicians. Strong (1990) has analysed just this 'epidemic psychology'. In the second phase, however, the perception of crisis was used much more creatively to buttress a sense of mission and fuel high energy levels as groups mobilized around the issue. In the third and subsequent phase, the pace of development was threatened as burn-out, disillusionment and withdrawal set in. One W2 early innovator commented:

> For the last three or four years, we have had a relentless task with trying to manage not only a frightening new disease, which is escalating in patient numbers every six months, but which takes a very severe personal toll and because we have a very dedicated staff who are very concerned to optimize management, we are finding people in our clinic, for example, are working 12 hour days for five days a week.

Clearly the crisis label affected organizational responses but in a complex and phased mixture of functional and dysfunctional ways. While this reinforces the argument that crisis issues do differ in important ways from non-crisis issues, it also suggests that these effects may be multi-faceted and differ over the time period under study.

The third analytic theme identified related to organizational development and design, where it was argued that the arrival of HIV/AIDS as an issue might be linked to attempts to build a different kind of organization. While ad hoc machinery was devised, there seemed to be little organizational theory available in the early days to guide action, and the new issue was routed to a succession of different bodies, sometimes with a short life and difficult internal dynamics. The peripheral role for general management perhaps accentuated this isolation from questions of organizational development and design. The picture began to change in late 1988 as management capacity started to build up and (despite the frustrations) the potential role for an AIDS Coordinator in such tasks as constructing lateral networks, creating and supporting Unit level capacity and marrying bottom-up pressure with top-down concern was already beginning to emerge.

The case study also provides some evidence about strategy making under conditions of uncertainty. The retention of strategic flexibility was seen as important and was pursued in this locale through an increasing policy of 'normalization', based on generic rather than specialist services, so preventing over-reliance on presumably rigid specialist services. However, premature delegation to unsupported line managers could result in an erosion of effort.

A further observation is that the process of change seemed continuous in nature, combining both periodic radical change (the internally generated reorientation of 1987; the implications of the externally generated White Paper in 1989) and continuous incremental change. *Contra* Mintzberg, there seemed very little evidence of periods of continuity in between episodes of change.

Bloomsbury: a Benign Micro Climate Emerges and Is in Part Created

In Bloomsbury, too, HIV/AIDS was to emerge as a major organizational and managerial issue, as well as a clinical one. By 1989 a total of 1,045 patients had tested HIV-positive in Bloomsbury DHA, and the special allocation for the financial year 1990 had risen to £5.2m, which although less than that in Paddington, still represented a major budget to manage. Bloomsbury, like Paddington, could be seen as one of the Central London Districts hit hardest by the epidemic, although its response was to diverge in some interesting ways, which was perhaps the more remarkable given the general difficulties that the District faced (as explored in the previous chapter's analysis of acute sector strategy).

Some Antecedent Conditions

The Double-site Problem in Miniature: Two STD Clinics   The general problem within Bloomsbury of building one organization was apparent in STD services as well as in the acute sector strategy as a whole. HIV emerged as an issue in 1983, just after the formation of Bloomsbury in 1982, and there were between 1982 and 1989 two largely independent STD Clinics in the district, one sited at University College Hospital and one (James Pringle House) at the Middlesex Hospital. While there had been early clinically based attempts to rationalize on to a single site in 1983–4, these had come to nothing, and it was James Pringle House that captured the HIV/AIDS issue within the District. This reflected its distinctive character as the second largest genito-urinary medicine department in England, its large gay caseload (seeing about 5,500 homosexual men annually), and its reputation as a centre of research excellence (with Professor Michael Adler as the first Professor of Genito-Urinary Medicine in the country) with good academic, policy and ultimately political links. As in St Mary's in Paddington DHA, initial issue leadership went to academically orientated clinicians outside the powerful acute specialties. While by no means outsiders, they were not always fully insiders either in terms of mainstream clinical politics.

Drugs Services: a Difficult Transition   Not only is there a big drugs scene in the District centred on Piccadilly and Soho, but the Drug Dependency Unit at UCH operates as a sub-Regional specialty for much of North London. The DDU had historically built up an active research profile in the drugs field under a respected consultant, and was in the early 1980s trying to extend multi-disciplinary work, day care and family therapy even before the advent of HIV. But the long-standing consultant retired in the early 1980s, and the DDU was left without a consultant at a crucial moment. The prevailing ideology within the DDU of collective leadership could sometimes be difficult to reconcile with some of the assumptions of the NHS. A third problem was that many of the long-standing staff who had grown up with the abstinence-orientated models of the 1970s ('you have to get them through the detox') would increasingly be confronted by the very different post-HIV emphasis on harm reduction.

General Management and Organization Development   Management and indeed some senior DHA members were developing an intellectually sophisticated approach to strategy and OD: this was a cerebral District where organization theory was taken seriously. The general managerial manifesto for the District highlighted the need to develop the capacity of the District to cope with change and to operate as a learning organization (Liddell, 1987).

Problem Anticipation: Clinical Lessons from Abroad

Just as in Paddington, the very early response in the District was shaped by clinicians' international colleague networks. The first American material on AIDS came out in June 1981 and soon found its ways into James Pringle House (JPH) consciousness. Visits to America from clinicians both in JPH and the DDU convinced them that HIV/AIDS was likely to become a major issue in London. HIV/AIDS was now bubbling up in a number of clinical and research arenas: virologists remember discussing the phenomenon 'on the grapevine' in 1981–2. The launching in 1982 of the St Mary's Cohort Study reinforced pressure on JPH to set up its own cohort study, very early on (1983), before the identification of the virus. As in Paddington, much of the drive and energy was coming out of the field where incipient service systems were developing on the basis of soft money and the employment of contract research staff (although the lead in Paddington was from Immunology; the lead in Bloomsbury from STD/Public Health). Some staff at the DDU were also into the HIV field extremely early (perhaps reflecting nurse-led innovation), and by mid 1984 were working with voluntary organizations producing a pamphlet on drug use and AIDS.

JPH as a Motor of Change

JPH was to emerge as a powerhouse behind many of the early developments both clinically and academically. Staff there interpreted their academic brief widely, moving beyond STD and epidemiology into such areas as the basic science, drug use and HIV infection (raising potential interface issues with the DDU) (Adler, 1986), cost estimates (Johnson et al., 1986) and medical sociology (Hart, 1989). It was also to provide a powerful focus for early policy and planning within the District and epidemiology was to retain strong links with the policy process.

Clinically, JPH was also the initial channel for inpatient admissions to the Middlesex, still at a modest level in 1984. Nevertheless a number of clinical problems were soon emerging: the earliest cases were treated in the Intensive Care Unit which made it difficult for other clinicians to get their cases in; AIDS patients were taking up scarce side wards and clinical practice needed to be developed rapidly. JPH had experienced early problems in referring on to a number of clinicians, but an important change in the clinical coalition took place in 1984 when the Professor of Medicine (a general physician with an interest in thoracic medicine) declared an interest in the AIDS work, previously undertaken by a senior registrar. A clinically appropriate (in view of the frequent presentation of patients with pneumonia) focus had emerged, and while such diversification also helped protect bed state which might otherwise be under threat, the presence of a powerful and highly respected friend within the mainstream acute specialties certainly helped the traditionally more marginal genito-urinary medicine physicians to argue their case ('it began to make the whole thing a lot easier for all of us').

JPH was indeed lobbying to put the AIDS issue on agendas nationally as well as in the District. The key professor had a community medicine background together with an interest in policy and had emerged as a product champion within the District and indeed nationally. He was writing for *The Times* as well as lobbying the Department through the community medicine network. The Social Services Select Committee of the House of Commons was another important national target for mobilization, where he took advantage of a platform as an expert witness to argue: 'we are in a situation where we do have a public health crisis – in fact the greatest public health crisis that any of us in our professional lives have ever seen' (Social Services Select Committee, 1987, p. 161). Within the District he was approaching the DMO ('he was on my door-step, saying for God's sake, this thing is here, we have got to do something about it, we cannot sit on our hands'). The DMO's acceptance of this hunch (the first formally published British evidence assessing the prevalence of htlv-iii antibody did not emerge until September 1984) reflected both his personal credibility and personal friendship (both had grown up in the District and both shared a community medicine background).

Given that a number of pressures were bubbling (such as pressure on side wards), it was decided apparently on the basis of this informal alliance that a joint appointment of a senior registrar/lecturer should be made of a community physician (again through soft research money) within JPH to pick up many of the planning and policy issues now emerging in relation to AIDS. This was a key appointment which considerably energized and broadened the District's subsequent response, offering the key product champion support from a professional 'Young Turk'. Thus, much of the early policy work in the District was undertaken by community physicians, most notably within JPH but supported at District, allied from 1984 to a powerful acute sector professor within the Middlesex. The fact that early planning (particularly the first bid) had community medicine fingerprints helps explain why the District's response was from the beginning not simply bed-based but considered broader issues such as prevention.

The 1985 Bid and Allocation

While a clinical and public health focus had emerged by 1984, administration was slower to come on stream and at this point the DMO was still seen informally as the key coordinator within the District. The stimulus for change was the arrival of financial incentives in the form of a letter from the Regional Treasurer in March 1985 calling for bids, which was routed down to the new community medicine appointment in JPH. Together with Middlesex Finance, a bid was compiled ('a finger in the wind exercise') grounded in the first results from the Middlesex cohort study among gay men showing an alarming increase in the percentage showing htlv-iii antibody-positive from 3.7 per cent in 1982 to 21 per cent in 1984 ('it was much easier once we had got the evidence there, quite clearly').

But the bid was also an exercise in coalition-building, containing requests for the development of inpatient care, outpatient care, pathology services and also dedicated dental facilities. An early emphasis on preventive work was also detectable within JPH and indeed other settings in the District such as the DDU (Johnson and Miller, 1988): for example, liaison with Terrence Higgins Trust about safer sex, talking to the District Health Education Officer in early 1985, and encouraging outreach work which subsequently developed into a special outreach project. The process by which such bottom-up initiatives got formally scripted into District policy often reflected reassessments about fundability in an increasingly benign financial climate.

Subsequent revisions to the bid (September 1985) sought to develop the community care component further. In October 1985, Region announced an AIDS allocation to the District of £275,000. How this money was to be spent, and who was to do the spending of it, now became important decision points which brought in the new general managerial function for the first time. A substantial overspend had been built up in the Middlesex Division and while it was argued by the AIDS lobby that this money should be earmarked for new AIDS services, others felt that the Middlesex was incurring costs (nursing time, drugs) within its base budget. The new Divisional General Manager inclined to the latter position, perhaps reflecting pressure from senior clinicians from within the hospital with the DMB now discussing AIDS for the first time. The proposal that the money should be used to reduce the overspend led to keen lobbying of sympathetic members to raise AIDS at DHA level and pre-empt managerial diversion of funds. As one member recalled, AIDS could be used as a mechanism for more general discussions about control over strategy:

> It had almost never come up. I do not recall it coming up at a DHA meeting before, to my surprise . . . I had asked behind the scenes when is it ever going to come up to the DHA as an issue. It took quite a while before it did. In fact I used that issue as a means of getting more open discussion at the health authority.

In the end, DHSS Regional Liaison was asked for a ruling, coming down in favour of confining expenditure from the allocation to new developments. While this was an inauspicious debut for management, a managerial focus now quickly emerged around the Divisional General Manager and despite initial scepticism ('managers are much more switched on by money than by the tag that money attaches to' one respondent cynically remarked) genuine managerial ownership of the issue was evident ('there was a complete volte-face'). Until that point, the DMO had been informally acting as coordinator, but in November 1985 the

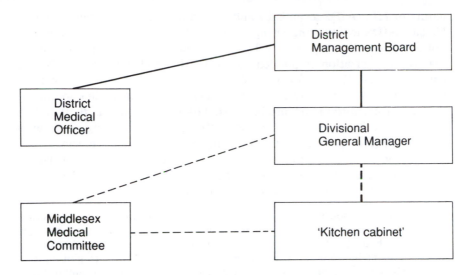

Figure 5.2　*Organizational structures within Bloomsbury DHA, 1985–6*

DGM formally made the Divisional General Manager lead officer across the District on AIDS. This switch was regarded – perhaps surprisingly – as largely consensual by respondents.

Why was this decision made? The then DGM, Alasdair Liddell, was clear that the overall approach to general management entailed that AIDS should be handled in this way:

> It is a management issue. The whole way in which we try and run the District is to devolve service and operational planning issues, individual strategy issues, to devolve them to the general managers who run the divisions . . . The other point I think is this one. I see it as a management issue and therefore it being more appropriate for general managers to take the lead, they may need support from community physicians and others in the way that they approach it . . . but the questions that it raises for us are issues which are the core of management. How we use our resources, how we respond to an expressed demand for service from patients. Absolutely general management issues.

Tim Matthews, the Divisional General Manager, was seen personally as having the skills needed to handle the AIDS issue well. Words like 'trust', 'respect' and 'confidence' were used by a number of clinical respondents, and relations between managers and clinicians were better in AIDS than many other issues facing the District.

General Management and HIV/AIDS

In this District the introduction of general management did make a difference to the way in which the HIV/AIDS issue was tackled. The new Divisional General Manager shared the more cerebral and conceptual approach to management evident at District, giving outside talks on the nature of HIV/AIDS as an issue and indeed test for general management. He saw AIDS as requiring change in the delivery of service, training and policies where there was a critical role for general management in ensuring that the organization responded to the need for change coherently and collectively. AIDS was also pervasive both in terms of staff implications and services, with few areas of activity being untouched, thus indicating the need for coordination mechanisms. His conclusion was that: 'AIDS presents a critical test of management's capacity to bring together a diverse range of policies and services to respond to the problem.'

This indicated the creation of ad hoc groups and strong lateral communications rather than line managerial hierarchies or the use of mainstream professional advisory machinery:

> It was quite a good illustration of the way a problem can be now more effec-
> tively handled as a planning and management issue. Under general manage-
> ment, I had the facility without any formal sanction from the District
> Management Board other than 'you have got a brief – AIDS', to pull together
> the right sort of people to carry forward that particular task, and pull in where
> I felt I could get the right financial help and right service help.

Given that the allocation was substantially less than the bid, choices had to be made and the DGM took advice from a 'kitchen cabinet' of key actors who had already emerged within the District. This was a small group of well-informed people with different skills, who would try to take a corporate view (although those outside the magic circle could be more critical, with those in GUM at UCH bitter about the way money was 'pouring into' James Pringle House). As long as this group was able to demonstrate effective decision making, it was left to get on with it. The Divisional General Manager reported bids upwards to the District Management Board and then the DHA, but this was essentially for ratification.

Getting the Ward, 1986

Securing a ward now emerged as a top priority for the group but at this stage (early 1986) plans for converting the ward involved minor works only ('a new coat of paint') in order to get the facility up and running as quickly as possible. However, this objective was rapidly to be redefined.

By 1985 a severe overspend had arisen in the acute sector in Bloomsbury which resulted in the shock of major and virtually unplanned retrench-ment at the Middlesex. There was the permanent closure of two wards, additional temporary ward closures and an acceleration of the closure of the Accident and Emergency Department, the substantive and symbolic heart of a hospital. The self-image of the hospital began to change: it had known better days; it was being absorbed into UCH; it was slowly crumbl-ing. Given that it was seen as impossible to divert AIDS money into the base budget, the use of this special money to reopen a closed ward contained a number of attractive features as well as dangers for the hospital.

The AIDS lobby was pressing for a ward, and the Rubicon was crossed when the Professor of Medicine accepted the need for a dedicated in-patient facility because of concerns about fragmentation within the hospital. Others were resisting such proposals, especially surgeons who were losing a ward. The argument was then taken to a clinical forum (the Medical Committee) where in spite of some coded resistance, the go-ahead for the ward was given. The political skills of the Professor of Genito-Urinary Medicine were seen as crucial in steering the proposal through a difficult committee, particularly as the Professor of Medicine 'did not want to be seen to be making a grab for extra beds'. Management, although supportive, was seen as being one step back from the battle: 'what management tend to do is stand aside from it, and let the clinicians fight it out between them, so they do not actually get involved in confron-tation.'

In the end, substantial refurbishment took place, and in April 1987, following informal approaches made by the District which was con-sciously in the game of image management, the new ward was officially opened by the Princess of Wales ('it boosted morale right through the hospital, and was seen as a very genuine visit, and I think people felt honoured by it') in a gesture which helped improve the image of AIDS in the hospital and helped put it 'back on the map'. As one respondent remarked:

> People have seen AIDS as far as the Middlesex is concerned as actually a good thing, quite coincidentally it came along at a time when the hospital was at a fairly low level of morale, battered by a series of service reductions, ward closures, uncertainty, during 85–86, this was in a sense the first new thing which happened which started to put in back on the map in clinical terms . . . and the Royal opening was quite important in that regard.

As the managerial workload produced by AIDS grew, so did the need to formalize the ad hoc arrangements which had previously existed. The 'kitchen cabinet' had been invoked to process bids, rather than to consider formal strategy (although a sense of informal strategy existed in the core group). But the management of AIDS services now not only revolved around processing bids for expansion but increasingly also managing the special teams that were springing up. A large steering committee was formed which included representatives of Social Services Departments. It was, however, essentially an information exchange forum, too large for effective decision making, and tended to ratify deci-sions which were still made in the 'kitchen cabinet'.

An important focus for lateral coordination was the AIDS Coordinator post, set up in late 1986, reporting directly to the Divisional General Manager. The post holder had worked previously in the District and, although lacking formal line managerial power, was able to win influence and expand her role into acting as a focal point for planning and resource allocation until her departure on promotion in 1990.

Moving out of the Hospital, late 1980s

What was the District's emergent strategy? Clearly there was a global, if often informal, sense of where the District should be going at least in terms of its expenditure profile. The report to the DMB (9 May 1986) defined expenditure plans in the following terms: the provision of additional staffing and accommodation in JPH to meet the increasing outpatient load; the development of a counselling service at JPH; meeting the costs of pathology; the development of a dedicated inpatient area and the provision of special dental facilities. While this was by no means a wholly bed-centred bid, it did not yet fully reflect developments in preventive and community care which had been bubbling in the District for some time but which were empowered by Department of Health Circular HC(86)2 which emphasized preventive activity and suggested Regional resources might be available.

Some respondents had been aware from the start of the need to move activity out of hospital settings:

> We have been quite clear from the word go that yes, we certainly have a clinical problem, but that we had to put all our effort into prevention . . . there is no point in piling up beds, beds and beds, bronchoscopes, and all that sort of stuff, you have to be putting such energy as you can into prevention.

These changing signals were picked up by the Divisional General Manager, who wrote back to Region in August 1986 to revise the original bid:

> The pace of change in this service is very rapid given the growing numbers, and our requirements are being kept regularly under review. The District is conscious of the need to invest resources in education and prevention as well as in inpatient and outpatient services and we are currently examining the possibility of funding this year a community outreach programme.

It is here important to explore some background material to what was to emerge as an important – and generally seen as successful – transfer of lead, even though succession planning has not generally been seen as NHS management's strongest point. Louis Smidt, the Unit General Manager for Local Services, had been building up awareness of AIDS as an issue in late 1986 through personal and professional links ('Sunday lunchtime conversations about where the hell is this all going to stop'), and already had a good cross-unit working relationship with the Divisional General Manager (Middlesex) over other issues such as rehabilitation services. AIDS started to gather momentum as an issue within his Unit, moving up from concern about isolated 'incidents' which had characterized its status up to that point. Interest centred not so much on the community nursing service (which had only nursed nine cases by 1987) as the launching of small-scale innovations.

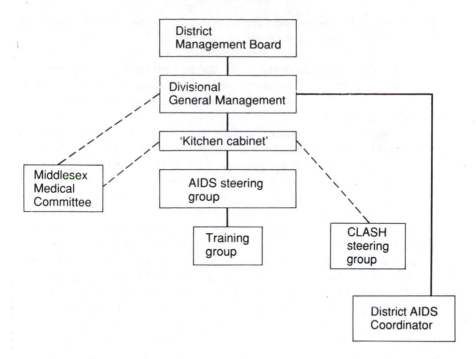

Figure 5.3 *Organizational structures within Bloomsbury DHA, 1987*

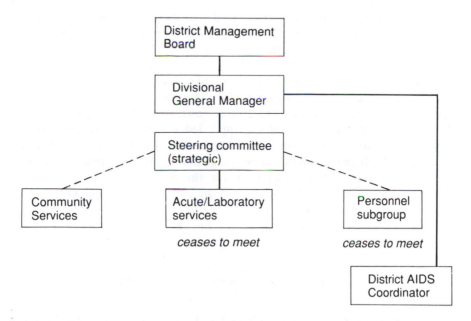

Figure 5.4 *Organizational structures within Bloomsbury DHA, 1988*

This UGM had been on the steering committee from the start and was asked to join the 'kitchen cabinet' as community issues assumed higher prominence: changes in managerial leadership could be seen as loosely associated with changes in strategy. By the end of 1987 not only was the need for development of community services recognized corporately, but important coordination issues were emerging in new but fragmented community services.

In 1988 the District suddenly faced an important point of transition as the Divisional General Manager was promoted out of the District. How would the succession be managed? In fact a well-positioned potential successor was available in the UGM (Local Services) who was by now socialized into the style of operations and was nominated to take on the lead role across the District, a position reinforced on his promotion to a Divisional General Manager role. Perhaps the impression of success reinforced the arguments for continuity. There were still interface issues with some of the powerful UGMs in the acute sector who represented alternative successors, but nevertheless the special AIDS steering committee retained a much more important role over the allocation of the special money than was evident in Paddington. The second lead manager's style was certainly different from the first (perhaps less likely to commit thoughts to paper; a sharp awareness of tactics) but there were also substantial continuities: the 'kitchen cabinet' still met, the inherited organizational structure was retained, and the AIDS Coordinator developed in role.

So had the group successfully effected a Weberian transition from the charismatic to the institutional, and from the personal to the impersonal given the emergence of special offices? Clearly there was a substantial degree of continuity now established within the group at the centre of the District. However, it proved difficult to replicate the initial response either in care groups coming on stream slightly later (such as drugs or services for women and children) or to cascade it down from the steering committee to its subcommittees, most of which led a desultory existence. Nor were links into the mainstream power centres of the District always strong: in the balloon debate taking place among all the clinicians in the District to scale down bed demands for the new hospital it was HIV/AIDS that in the end was thrown out of the balloon. One argument might be that with the removal or disengagement of two or three key actors there would be rapid regression to the norms of the organization as a whole.

Drugs Services – ad hoc Innovation without Strategic Change, 1985–1989

Within the Drug Dependency Unit in UCH there had been a developing interest in HIV as early as mid 1984. An AIDS working party was set up (late 1985) within the clinic to develop a multi-disciplinary approach to control of infection and health education, but it found it difficult to get issues on agendas. What were the nature of these obstacles which were emerging?

It was proving difficult to move from ad hoc innovation (a number of special teams) to strategic change. Morale among staff in the DDU seemed poor and there was a high turnover: there was a self-perception of isolation, powerlessness and an inability to effect change internally let alone externally ('The DDU is not a happy place, it is not a place which is happy for staff or patients'). The introduction of general management within the Mental Health Unit had been unsettling, with rapid turnover, and no real managerial focus had emerged in the Unit at strategic or at operational level until 1988/9. The newly created Dependencies Care Planning Team had been charged in 1986 with developing strategy and retaining a managerial perspective in monitoring and evaluation, but in practice adopted an increasingly operational emphasis. Indeed as far as HIV/AIDS was concerned: 'it was considered that AIDS be regarded as a general medical problem and not an issue which the DCPT should address' (DCPT minutes, 28 April 1986). Nor were these the only obstacles. Alongside multi-disciplinary working sat an operational management vacuum within the DDU. Links with external agencies were also surprisingly rudimentary, with existing mechanisms for access and outreach inadequate for the new tasks. Drugs services had traditionally been a dark corner of the NHS, and did not appear on senior management's agendas.

Moreover the DDU did not fit into the emerging division of labour around AIDS:

Certainly at that time JPH was seen as being the centre of expertise as regards AIDS so there was not really any awareness that we should be taking on AIDS at all. When we discussed for example the health care needs of drugs users, it was felt that was beyond the remit of the Mental Health Unit. (DDU respondent)

A senior nurse within the DDU, together with a Senior Lecturer in Psychiatry, sensed in late 1985 a change in the funding weather and began to put up proposals:

At that time, late 1985, when a number of us heard that money was going to become available for AIDS, we decided to write the proposals ourselves. So we went ahead and did it, and then submitted them to the AIDS working party without any help or consultation really with the general management. And that created problems.

Innovators in drugs services were finding it more difficult to get their voices heard than the key product champions in STD, reflecting both their weaker power position and their historic isolation from the AIDS machinery that was springing up within the Middlesex (the DDU was, of course, attached to the UCH Division). It was not until 1989 that a concerted attempt was made – combining top-down pressure from the

AIDS steering committee and bottom-up concern from the field – to develop a Drugs/AIDS Strategy which would enable strategic change to take place. Indeed the number of strategic bodies operating in drugs policy suddenly went from famine to feast: a District Drugs Advisory Committee was set up to link into local external agencies such as the police; and the DCPT adopted new terms of reference (November 1989) which now included a brief for HIV/AIDS.

Postscript

While HIV/AIDS was widely seen as one of Bloomsbury's successes, one concern was that management was too much focused on the annual spending round, and that strategic thinking could slip. So a small Strategy Group was set up to review services in early 1990 to report to the AIDS steering committee, continuing the utilization of informal, focused, problem solving machinery but incorporating personnel who had by now built up considerable experience in the field. While a drugs strategy was identified as a major gap, this group also drew attention to the implications of the White Paper (Cm 555, 1989) as a new top-down initiative which would change the language of HIV/AIDS services as all other services as the NHS moved in a more market-like direction.

The presence in the group of a Public Health senior registrar was once again to prove helpful. The first senior registrar, who had been intensely involved in policy work in the District in the early days, had by now been appointed to a consultant post, but her successor was looking for new issues with which to make a mark. Indeed his task was to produce a paper on the implications of contracting (Bentley, 1990) for HIV/AIDS services. The result of this early preparation was that HIV/AIDS was able to nominate itself as a pilot for business planning and go into that process with clear ideas about how the plan should be structured. This is not to say that there were not tensions within the group: both on the management and clinical sides there were struggles for leadership. But these tensions did not prevent the group from achieving a rapid learning curve. For example, a District respondent was asked to rank the performance of HIV/AIDS as one of the pilots for business planning:

> HIV would, I think, come towards the end of being more prepared and enthusiastic, not because they are enthusiastic about business planning, but because they are enthusiastic about themselves and their services, so they are always thinking about them and how they will get next year's national money and all the rest of it.

So, the reaction to the White Paper indicates that at least some of the self-confident, conceptually based yet action-orientated style evident in 1985 had been rolled forward to 1990, and had not totally evaporated. The danger may be that it proves impossible to sustain the very unusual form of decision making apparent in the case study, and that the overall norms of the host organization will reassert themselves, perhaps if a few key actors are pulled out. This raises the question of sustaining and institutionalizing organizational change (Goodman and Dean, 1982).

Analysis and Discussion

We here revisit the three analytic themes identified at the beginning of the chapter. As far as the leadership of change is concerned, the Bloomsbury case suggests that DHA members generally have a marginal impact, although a generalist did act to protect the allocation at a crucial early moment. Otherwise the DHA did not display a great interest in the issue – despite the escalating allocations – concentrating instead on retrenchment in the acute sector. Social movements and social movement organizations seemed influential in certain settings in the District (notably James Pringle House), but found it more difficult to influence the higher tiers or more mainstream specialties in the teaching hospitals directly. Some of the frontline workers such as Health Education Officers or Health Advisers shared many of the values expressed by these social movements, but on the whole were not organized enough to act as effective insurgents within formal organizations, although the formation of a Workers' Forum in 1989 offered a potential platform. A group of elite and on the whole liberal professionals – often drawn from public health medicine and from clinical academia – dug themselves in and influenced the management process within the District, and although this group was committed to broadly liberal value systems, they were much less radical than some social movement organizations.

A third potential basis of leadership identified earlier was general management, and general management did indeed play an important role in this District. Two senior general managers in particular helped shape service development, but both of them displayed idiosyncratic features: the first had a conceptual interest in AIDS as a management issue; the second was an ex-clinician, and therefore particularly keen to have a chance to develop services rather than cut them back, which was the usual agenda in Bloomsbury. Middle management was slow to develop and hence there was little other support available. Perhaps Bloomsbury has been lucky, as elsewhere managers would often take little interest in HIV/AIDS, or develop interest only in so far as new resources became available ('managers are not turned on by AIDS, but by the tag that attaches to AIDS' remarked one clinician). The managerial thinness and instability of the Mental Health Unit was one important factor in retarding the development of an effective strategy for drug users, who could be seen as the second wave of the epidemic.

But once again a clinical product champion was identified who had a major role in leading change, requiring a high level of drive and commitment over a number of years. But the role was constructed in rather a different way from that in Paddington. The role in Bloomsbury was not so individualistic but rather embedded in a large public health-oriented academic department, which meant both that 'Young Turks' were periodically available as senior registrars to beef up the planning process, and that argument could be supported by a large and distinguished research group. There was also a major research management task in building up and keeping together these key staff in the face of obstacles such as inadequate and cramped accommodation, rigid manpower and promotion controls and poaching by other institutions. There was an emphasis within Bloomsbury as well on the steady accretion of political support, both internally and externally:

> I think probably I am the only physician in Bloomsbury who has actually made a point of developing as good a relationship as quickly as one can with new ministers, because I think that is the leverage that you need for the specialties, STD, but for AIDS locally because if there is any nonsense – it's terribly important to have a line to ministers. (Clinical product champion, Bloomsbury)

It is interesting to note that the early clinical product champion who emerged in 1984–5 retained and indeed consolidated his initial lead position in the organization: for example, leading the AIDS/GUM business planning exercise in 1990. This perhaps points to the critical importance of very early responses in 'birthmarking' roles in new organizations and decisions made back in 1983–4 may have very long-term consequences.

The second analytic theme identified above was crisis construction and management. Clearly a major task for product champions was to use the perception of crisis in a positive way to raise consciousness around the issue and legitimize early action both locally and nationally. The House of Commons Social Services Select Committee was one such national target for lobbying and consciousness-raising. Again the complex pattern of a short-term pathological crisis of staff anxiety, a medium-term crisis of opportunity which released energy and commitment and a long-term problem of burn-out was evident. Managing the transition into a post-crisis phase is likely to pose some tricky issues, as some of the initial innovators withdraw from the fray and others need to search for new angles on the problem in order to keep interest alive.

The third analytic theme related to organizational development and design, where it would be interesting to explore (in this District above all, given public statements of intent) whether the arrival of HIV/AIDS as an issue would be linked to organization-building. Indeed conscious attempts to build a different type of decision making were apparent, which survived one change of lead and were still recognizably in place in 1990. Perhaps surprisingly, such organization-building was initiated by line general management rather than staff functions such as personnel. However, questions emerge as to whether the style has been institutionalized, or whether it remains vulnerable to turnover. Certainly difficult interface issues (with UCH or District Finance) were sometimes dodged; it proved impossible to cascade the style down into subcommittees; and the experience of developing a drugs/HIV strategy proved a major disappointment. The style has survived; its institutionalization will be much more difficult.

'Strategic flexibility' proved too abstract an issue to address through the annual planning round, and there were few innovations in terms of planning methodology. The experience in terms of strategy making was less that of internally generated radical change (although the White Paper was to prove an important external source of paradigm shift) but rather of continuous incremental pressures for change which could sometimes run into resistance. Indeed exactly the same issues – and many of the same people – were apparent in drugs services in 1990 as in 1985.

An interesting theme is the relation between small specialist groups and the wider organization. A small elite group emerged in Bloomsbury to steer the AIDS issue organizationally which was often value-based (liberal rather than radical) and given control over special resources. While this separated out the AIDS issue from a largely unfavourable macro environment and thus facilitated self-directed change, the major problem which arose was the management of boundaries with a largely unchanging host organization. There were recurrent disputes with District Finance on the spending of the allocation (for example what was to be done with any underspend on the drugs budget?). Nor was it clear how much influence this group really carried with mainstream power centres.

Comparative Case Analysis

There are, of course, both similarities and differences between the two case studies, but it is the latter which are rather more interesting than the former. Given that the same HIV virus was impacting on neighbouring Districts at the same time through the same exposure categories and gateways into service, it is this chapter above all others that might be expected to show broadly similar responses. But once the analysis gets beyond declarations of formal strategy to more historical and processual accounts, important differences start to emerge between the two Districts. Moreover, much of the history of the development appears to be District-led, with higher tiers such as Regional and the Department of Health able to advise, encourage and warn, but certainly either unwilling or unable to act more prescriptively in shaping service systems. The early frontline Districts were largely shaping their own strategies, with less guidance from the higher tiers than might have been expected. As Regions develop their own strategies and offices, this freedom of manoeuvre may well diminish in the 1990s. The acute sector study (Chapter 4) suggested Paddington enjoyed a higher performance ranking than Bloomsbury; analysing the two Districts' response to HIV/AIDS, perhaps the rank order was reversed.

Issue Leadership

First, let us consider some similarities and differences between the two Districts in relation to the question of issue leadership. Both cases suggested that DHA members generally played a marginal role, although in both cases a generalist maintained a watching brief. Perhaps any further work on the role of members in HIV/AIDS should concentrate on that small subgroup of members classified by Ranade (1985) as 'strategists', and examine how they construct their roles and ensure a flow of information.

The influence of social movements was found in both cases to be weaker than might have been expected at strategic management level. While there were close links at field level between, say, JPH and some of the gay voluntary organizations over such issues as counselling, the strategic decision making machinery remained predominantly closed to social movement organizations in both Districts, except when discrete resources were being bought in. Nor was there much evidence of active insurgency within formal health care organizations (with the important and interesting exception of the health outreach CLASH team in Bloomsbury which had close links with radical voluntary sector organizations). Certainly many frontline workers were close to social movement organizations, but their demands tended to remain at frontline level and not to filter up the hierarchy.

What were the main differences in the leadership pattern evident in the two case studies? The Paddington case indicated that general management was slow to take a lead, with the exception of the DGM who maintained a watching brief. The dynamics in Bloomsbury were rather different, driven by a more conceptual interest in the management implications of HIV/AIDS. Initially the lead came from the newly appointed Divisional General Manager (with District much more in the background) who saw in HIV/AIDS an opportunity to develop some managerial themes, while the successor UGM had himself come from a clinical background, had been socialized into the HIV/AIDS machinery and relished the task of developing services in a system otherwise geared to contraction. Both these managers provided – in slightly different ways – important impetus behind the process of service development.

Clinical product champions emerged as crucial in the Bloomsbury case, as in the Paddington case, but the roles were constructed differently and the STD product champion displayed ability in retaining a leading role in the organization. There was perhaps rather more concern in Bloomsbury with 'advocacy', coalition-building, committee work and compromise, as seen in the alliance with acute sector physicians. Yet the Bloomsbury product champions in drugs services found much greater difficulty than Bloomsbury STD product champions, reflecting both their more marginal power position and the turbulence of the Unit in which they were operating.

Different specialties were also involved in the two Districts: GUM emerged as a key base for product championing in Bloomsbury rather than Immunology, as in Paddington. Moreover this was a department with a record of academic achievement, a high profile ('you have to put the subject on the map, not just for Bloomsbury, but for the rest of the country'), and well linked into planning and policy: HIV/AIDS accentuated these traits, but it did not mark so sharp a discontinuity as for Immunology in Paddington.

Other actors were active in proposing service developments, but the example of drugs services indicated how important organizational power base was in determining outcome. The Bloomsbury case also suggests that a clinical product champion may be more effective when supported by a second tier post (here a senior registrar) operating at a less macro level. In both Districts clinical academics emerged as production champions; in neither District was the process of development in drugs services free of problems.

It is finally worth commenting on the critical importance of some of the very early choices made by the Districts: many of the differences which were evident in the Districts in 1989–90 had their roots in long-term implications of decisions made in the very early days of the epidemic. In both Districts, for example, the clinical product champions who emerged in 1983–4 were still active in the strategic management process in 1990. A self-image quickly built up as to whether the District had done 'well' or 'badly' on HIV/AIDS which influenced collective self-confidence and ability to tackle new challenges.

Crisis Management

The second theme was that of crisis construction and management where the Paddington case indicated a pathological short-term phase of crisis-as-panic; a second medium-term phase of crisis-as-energizer and a third phase of crisis aftermath leading to withdrawal and burn-out. Broadly speaking the Bloomsbury case confirms the model, but perhaps two qualifications can be made. The first is that there was not only an initial short-term crisis but that further short-term crises could flare up periodically, perhaps as a result of a government campaign. For example, during the government's big campaign of 1986–7, the workload on the Bloomsbury GUM clinics suddenly escalated:

> the people who felt the stress most were people who had never been stressed before, the medical staff probably coped alright, the nursing staff coped OK, the people who cracked were the health advisers who have never had to work at that pace before, some of them were young girls who tended to take their worries home with them, they stopped taking coffee breaks, they stopped taking lunch breaks, they were working well over hours. (JPH respondent)

How did individuals cope with the transition to a post-crisis phase where the dangers were those of exhaustion, burn-out and disengagement? Certainly a number of actors who had been important in mobilizing consciousness in these two Districts in the mid 1980s were getting out by 1989–90. But there were stayers as well as quitters, who faced the problem of retaining interest perhaps by constructing mini crises which would maintain the profile of the HIV/AIDS issue for a time (such as heterosexual spread). But individuals could also adjust or broaden their workload so as to engage with interesting new tasks, such as the implications of the White Paper (Cm 555, 1989) for HIV/AIDS services. Paradoxically the agenda for the 1990s may be even more difficult than the 1980s unless actors are able to re-engage with the problem and create new sources of momentum, under criticism from sceptics and cynics that they have been crying wolf all along. Perhaps such tasks will call for a second generation of product champions, who have not been so scarred by the campaigns of the 1980s.

Organizational Development

It is in the organizational development and design theme that perhaps the clearest contrasts emerge between the early experiences of the two Districts. It is interesting to note that the crucial managerial input was made in both Districts by line management rather than specialist staff functions (such as Personnel or Organizational Development) which retained a more peripheral involvement.

The early managerial response in Bloomsbury was clearer and more theoretically driven, reflected in the design of special organizational arrangements deemed to be able to manage change more effectively. This special style persisted into 1990, although attempts to cascade it down into subcommittees were less successful and it is too early to say whether it has been effectively institutionalized. A mixed core group was formed in Bloomsbury as the focus of the District's decision making machinery (involving management, clinicians, finance and public health) and was kept together, but the experience in Paddington was more difficult. In both Districts important struggles went on to control the special allocation, but the power position of the core group in Bloomsbury seemed stronger. Perhaps the public health ownership of the initial strategy in Paddington both reflected and further contributed to lack of involvement by line management. However, in both Districts the important role of an AIDS Coordinator in building lateral networks and encouraging strategic thinking was evident.

Managing Crisis, Uncertainty and Growth: Conclusions

This final section will seek to speculate more broadly about some of the wider theoretical implications which seem to follow from this comparative empirical material. Clearly the organizational and managerial response to

HIV/AIDS posed a number of complex issues to do with the management of rapid growth in systems traditionally geared to contraction. But the process of growth was very different from that involved in the construction of new DGHs (explored in Chapter 8): here high commitment service systems were being built up which were not only new but different, less based on physical fabric and more on models of care, and less geared to standardized design and more suffused with values.

An Organizational Transition

The concept of an 'issue attention cycle' (Downs, 1967) has sometimes been invoked to explain how issues get on and off political agendas. Using this analogy, the period between 1983 and 1989 perhaps represented a period of early growth, when resources quickly escalated and service systems were rapidly built up. From 1988/9 not only did political attention wane as other issues such as health care restructuring once again shot up central agendas, but the special allocation ceased to grow, and 'climbers' (Downs, 1967) started to clamber off the faltering AIDS band-wagon. There was therefore a difficult period of transition, as increasingly pressure was felt to 'normalize' AIDS services.

In organizations which are both new and different, the transition between birth and early development on the one hand and institutionalization on the other may be difficult, especially for policy entrepreneurs and clinical product champions (Kimberly, 1980) because the institutionalization stage reduces their scope for autonomous action. Alexander (1974) studied such a process of formalization in a new and initially informal organization (the Peace Corps). For a while, the philosophy of non-routinization prevailed, because it was feared that routinization would drive out its ability to innovate. But routinization crept in in spite of this formally espoused ideology, and this process accelerated after the first head of the organization left. So organizations become more conservative as they age: statuses and roles are assigned; patterns of behaviour stabilize; individuals settle into characteristic parts; and standard operating procedures are established. Eventually, the new organization becomes a bureaucracy (Starbuck, 1965).

But there are a second and deeper set of transition difficulties in the case of HIV/AIDS. If it is correct to expect a second wave of infection in the 1990s among drug users, perhaps followed by a slow 'silent' epidemic among heterosexuals, then those long-term pressures for continuing change in HIV/AIDS services suggest a need to resist routinization. Often organizations become more routinized as they age – which can happen surprisingly quickly: Kimberly's (1980) case study of an innovative medical school suggested substantial routinization over as short a time scale as four years. But while bureaucratization may indeed be adaptive where organizations face increasingly stable environments and learn how to structure their relationships, it may also be dysfunctional for organizations relating to environments that continue to display gross turbulence.

Organizations facing such conditions may need to achieve continuing change, rather than seeing change in terms of the radical but periodic paradigm shift. Analysts of social movement organizations, for example (Zald and Ash, 1966), argue that not all organizations become more conservative as they age, although the downside is that this may be related to the establishment of sectarian exclusivity. Jelinek and Schoonhoven's (1990) study of continuing innovation processes in high technology firms concludes: 'innovation can be maintained in large firms – but not by traditional bureaucratic management methods' (pp. 417–18). They suggest that the achievement of continuing change in products, process and technology is linked not only with repeated structural change but is combined with a strong organizational culture which acts as a normative glue (which takes the analysis back to the potentially positive role that social movements can play as one means of providing this normative glue). A potentially fruitful way of providing this strong culture is through the emergence (possibly even the creation) of an 'organizational saga' which celebrates earlier innovatory exploits, setting precedents and raising confidence levels. Glimpses of such a mythology could be found in the Bloomsbury case study. Clark's (1972) exploration of such sagas, defined as a collective understanding of a unique accomplishment in a formal group, explicitly considers their essentially value-laden nature: 'the participants have added affect, an emotional loading, which places their conception between the coolness of rational purpose and the warmth of sentiment found in religion and magic.' While Weberian bureaucracies have often regarded 'strong cultures' with suspicion ('too involved'), this analysis indicates that they may also contain some important functional elements in innovation processes.

The Dilemma of Specialist Groups

Yet while social movements and their organizational products such as bureaucratic insurgents and exclusive in-groups may provide a powerful means of generating the strong culture which enables organizations to cope with rapid change, there are also important dysfunctional aspects to their appearance within formal organizations. The dilemma is that the greater the degree of value cohesion within the specialist group, the greater the internal energy for change, but also the higher the probability of difficulties in external relationships with the large out group.

The more general question in the creation of new specialist groups – such as the specialist HIV labour market – is how organizational relations shift over time (Pettigrew, 1973a) to accommodate such greater specialization in the division of labour. There are some broad themes such as how the new specialist group defines its task; how it protects its identity by the development of a system of values; and how it links itself with the activities of interdependent specialties. In new settings such as HIV/ AIDS many of these negotiation processes will be especially complex because of their controversial nature (Strauss, 1978) where there are few precedents and there will be a period of role crystallization as occupational identities form. There will be pressures for, and blocks on, expansion in the emergent specialty (as clearly seen in the counter-reaction observable in the Paddington case), within a context of boundary testing and stereotype-building.

Pettigrew (1975) suggests that such specialist activity within organizations may evolve through a variety of emotionally distinct phases: in particular from conception to an initial pioneering stage, followed by drift into a self-doubt phase. The emergence of burn-out in a number of early innovators in the HIV field, together with the end of the period of rapid escalation of budget, and the switch of attention by the NHS power structure to White Paper issues may herald such a transition into self-doubt. If this is the case, then the way in which HIV groups cope with this self-doubt phase may be critical for their continuing existence. A maladaptive response may lead to demise or absorption; an adaptive response to a continued use of the Unit's expertise in the short run, and to a more effective response capability for dealing with periods of self-doubt in the future.

Organizational Learning

The case material also sheds interesting light on how organizations learn when confronted with new and difficult situations. Much learning was individual and experiential: clinicians learned from experience how to develop practice. While individuals, particularly if motivated, may learn quickly, the diffusion of that learning to groups takes longer, and to organizations longer still. As Hedberg (1981) argues:

> organizations do quite frequently know less than their members. Problems in communication, such as filtering, distortion, and insufficient channel capacity, make it normal for the whole to be less than the sum of the parts. This appears to be particularly prevalent when organizations face crises or when rapid changes in an environment overload communication networks.

Organizational ability to learn may be linked to the emergence of a theory of action at a higher level of generality which can be used in a series of different learning situations (in drugs services, for example, as well as STD). Yet organizations seem to have great difficulty in establishing such metalogics, and general theories of action, which often remain largely inaccessible to managerial intervention. Such evidence as we have in HIV/AIDS suggests (Bennett et al., 1990) that much of the early learning that has taken place came initially from dedicated clinical product champions, disseminated from them to their immediate reference groups, and thence more widely throughout the organization. This process has been facilitated by individual professional autonomy, by the provision of rewards in the form of resources, and by the emergence (or even the creation) of organizational climates in which people could learn informally as well as formally. However, entrenched attitudes and beliefs have been more resistant to change than more superficial behaviour patterns, and such processes of change that have occurred have taken considerable time and effort.

But given that much of the early learning was driven by high status clinical product champions, how has management learnt from the experience? The most negative scenario is that it has not: theories of action have not been developed; the bubbles of specialist expertise which have emerged have been insulated from other management of growth issues; and the high turnover of personnel in the HIV labour market means that Districts will experience process without memory. In the NHS, the urgent often displaces the important and the 'culture of panic' may mean that active reflection or the building of longer-term layers of organizational capability does not take place. The NHS still has a way to go before it can be seen as a 'learning organization'.

6

Managing Major Change

Psychiatric Services

Analytical Themes and Organizational Framework

Some changes arise suddenly by force of circumstance or through the burgeoning of a new idea or the surprise breakdown of old practices. The way health care organizations can respond to such crises and 'new' problems is well rehearsed in the previous chapters on managing AIDS and acute sector strategy. In the psychiatric sector, however, change is not characterized by emergencies, condensed time-scales nor indeed by any singular 'crunch' point. Instead it evolves from a protracted historical movement away from custodial care towards a diffuse range of community-based services and results from a complex interaction of changing state policies, social movements, economic imperatives and medical practices and values (Busfield, 1986; McKee, 1988).

This chapter reports the experiences of two DHAs (St Helens and Knowsley, and Preston) confronting the long-standing implementation problem of closing a large Victorian asylum (respectively, Rainhill and Whittingham) while simultaneously reproviding alternative, non-institutional facilities for mentally ill people. Although the similarities of the management task and indeed organizational legacy will be shown to be dominant, the comparison provides insights about how a common change agenda can be modified, and reshaped to accommodate the subtleties of local culture, context and managerial process. The common themes that emerge and the apparent repetition of the problems across the Districts add to our understanding both of the type of context susceptible to change – 'receptive' (Pettigrew, McKee and Ferlie, 1989) – and of the importance of the timing and sequencing of change (Pettigrew, 1985b).

The first section outlines four analytical themes emerging from the data which serve as an organizing framework for case comparison. Particular attention will be given to the nature of the change issue itself and the change cycle. The peculiar characteristics of psychiatric service change and its historical and sociological significance will be briefly discussed. The analysis signals that it is a lengthy change process spanning governments and administrative forms, embracing multiple organizations and professional groupings, crossing organizational boundaries, and involving radical changes in beliefs, knowledge and values as well as technical change.

The way service problems are defined and perceived, the language and symbols used to convey meanings and the strategies that consequently evolve form a second strand of analysis. This issue of 'problem definition' has been well rehearsed in organizational literature and the data here add useful insights and points of comparison.

In human service organizations the professional–managerial interface is a strong determinant of organizational form, culture and operation. In health care organizations, the clinician–management interface is especially central and influential. The role of clinicians in the change process and the texture of clinician–management relations in each case study represents the third analytical theme. The complexity of the inter-organizational network and, indeed, the important 'centre–local' (intra-organizational) relationships, deeply affect the process of change in psychiatric services. The two case studies provide an opportunity to examine the differential role and significance of such multiple players and agencies.

The following case summaries will highlight unique elements of each change chronology before synthesizing the management issues raised. By integrating and comparing the experiences of the two Districts it will be possible, in the fourth section, to comment on the conceptual issues of change cycle, definition of the problem, clinician–management interface and inter/intra-organizational relations. Management process will also be interrogated with an evaluation of management style, language and approach across the Districts.

The Nature of Psychiatric Service Change and the Change Cycle

Evolutionary and Revolutionary Change   Organizational theorists have usefully directed attention to the history of strategic change, suggesting that it is crucial to take a long view of organizations (Mintzberg, 1978; Quinn, 1980; Miller, 1982; Pettigrew, 1985c). In particular, attention has been drawn to the fact that large-scale change in major organizations may be prolonged and protracted, defeating the energies and attention of a single administration or group of change leaders (Quinn, 1980). Quinn sums up this continuous process:

> Significant strategic shifts in large enterprises take years if not decades to accomplish. Consequently, it is rare for a single person to mastermind a complete change in a major organization's total strategy . . . What one sees in the short-run as an important strategic shift very often turns out to be part of a much large continuity that has been building for some years and later will gently mutate and evolve into a quite different form than it now possesses. (1980, p. 146)

Change in psychiatric services may simply represent an extreme form of this evolutionary incremental process; and as the potted history which follows shows, spans not just decades but centuries.

Interestingly, the lengthy process of strategic change has been found not to roll forward steadily and evenly but rather to display periods of high and low energy for change (Mintzberg, 1978; Miller, 1982; Miller and Friesen, 1982). Pettigrew (1985a) discusses the 'ebb and flow of strategic concentrations', showing how these movements may be connected with crises, both real and constructed, ideological shifts, changes in leadership and power, and environmental conditions. In the study of strategic change in ICI it was found that change occurred in 'radical packages interspersed with longish periods of both absorbing the impact of revolutionary action, and then coming to terms with the fact that further changes are eventually necessary' (Pettigrew, 1985a, p. 447). Mintzberg (1978) identified two patterns in the waxing and waning of strategic changes, finding that a life cycle analogy fitted much change – from organizational conception to decline – and that again there were energetic 'spurts' of change followed by periods of continuity. As will be suggested, the notions of revolutionary and evolutionary change, high tides of change followed by a lull, can be usefully applied to the history of psychiatric change. The concept of life cycle helps to focus in the case examples on the status and stage of the changes witnessed in the 1980s, which as will be shown was (in the early period) one of high energy, concerted action and considerable movement, in contrast to the previous decade of seeming inertia and indifference.

The History of Service Change   Histories of the discovery and management of mental illness show that from the seventeenth century onwards, the dominant trend was towards confinement and isolation of mentally ill people (Foucault, 1967; Scull, 1979). The process by which the insane were singled out from other confined categories is well documented, as is the 'colonization' of madness by medicine, with the invention of 'mad doctors' and the emergence of the specialism of psychiatry (Foucault, 1967; Scull, 1979; Busfield, 1986). Busfield (1986) usefully identifies three historical phases: 'the period of commercial and charitable healing' of the seventeenth and eighteenth centuries; the period of public asylums with heavy state sponsorship and legislative powers typical of the nineteenth century, dominated by medicine; and the present day thrust towards community care and non-institutional therapies.

Both Rainhill and Whittingham are classic examples of large nineteenth-century state mental institutions and represent the second phase of care with emphasis on the separation and medical treatment of the mentally ill. Explanations for the evolution of this particular form of care range from materialist to functionalist or humanitarian accounts (Foucault, 1967; Scull, 1979; Busfield, 1986). Importantly, the growth of asylums and the classification and treatment of mental illness by medical specialists did not represent a rapid social change but evolved slowly and unevenly. Both the first and second phases of care, the charitable and the public, demonstrate halting progress spanning over one hundred years and non-linear change with advances and retreats occurring simultaneously.

The movement from the charitable phase to the public phase was marked by a mixture of economic, social and political changes as well as medical developments.

Contemporary psychiatric change can only be appreciated in the light of earlier change, giving the 'change issue' its shape and texture. Reviewing the move from the first phase of care to the second provides lessons about the shift to the third phase as well. Thus pressure for change can be attributed to early nineteenth-century social concern about poor standards of care, leading to increasing parliamentary intervention and the introduction of bureaucratic structures to oversee developments.

A blend of state and clinical change is also a strong and relevant theme: psychiatry emerged as a separate specialism within medicine in the mid nineteenth century and the first professional associations and journals were set up. Many of the clinical innovations of this period revolved around patient and disease classifications, diagnosis, novel patient care regimes and control of infection, with some developments in neuro-physiology (Busfield, 1986).

Busfield (1986) regards the 1930 Mental Treatment Act as the critical break with the second phase of care: laying the foundation stone for the 'care in the community' policies of the third phase. It focused on voluntary admission, strengthened the concept of 'patients', and introduced the term 'hospital'. The legitimacy of the nineteenth-century institutions was seriously challenged by the new approach. The relevance of many former custodial practices was replaced by therapeutic and rehabilitative ones, requiring a substantial organizational shift in terms of staff training, values, attitudes, admission procedures, patient care, hospital administration and managerial control (Busfield, 1986). Arguably, many of these radical changes were never undertaken in full and remain on the current change agenda, illustrating the duration of the change task. The move from phase two to phase three was a radical upheaval from previous care regimes and protocols and not simply an add-on innovation. Despite restructuring vestiges of the old asylums remain. The organizational change at both hospitals considered here is centrally driven by the desire to divorce the services both symbolically and in reality from a nineteenth-century approach and institution.

New psychotropic drugs, the open door movement, growth of patients' rights in the 1959 and 1983 Mental Health Acts, developments in social psychiatry and psychiatric rehabilitation, the 'anti-psychiatry' lobby and the post-war establishment of general hospital psychiatric units are all influential in the gradual movement to replace the large mental illness hospitals. Busfield (1986) stresses the importance of psychiatrists wanting to align themselves with other medical practitioners in physical medicine and the enhanced status that practising in general hospitals brings. The concept of care in the community (CITC) gained in status in the 1960s and its potential was heightened as more and more patients could be maintained or treated at home with the new drugs. More able patients were either not admitted or often moved out of hospital during this period and the 1960s spirit of optimism is encapsulated in the *Hospital Plan* White Paper (Cmnd 1604, 1962), predicting a halving of psychiatric beds and large numbers of hospital closures in 15 years.

Problematic Change Some 30 years later it has been recognized that the anticipated speed of a radical restructuring of the psychiatric services was over-optimistic, if not unrealistic and that the momentum of moving patients out could not be sustained. Change in service patterns and in alternative provision has been observed to be uniformly protracted and uneven (McKee, 1988; Tomlinson, 1988; Korman and Glennerster, 1990). Just as it took decades to invest in the physical plant of the asylums and for their value to be publicly embraced, the decommissioning of such extensive resources and symbols has not been automatic. Similarly, it has been recognized that not only have new services not been replacing the old mental hospitals but that they themselves represent a structural anomaly in a modern, unified health service. Resettlement of patients was also recognized as involving different degrees of difficulty dependent on the patient's well-being and history.

The pressure for change and the expectation for change have thus grown, often outstripping the economic, political, or managerial capacity for change. 'County' catchment areas and the 'District' boundaries of modern DHAs are not normally coterminous, the hospitals themselves are frequently distant from population centres and inaccessible, the estate is often in poor repair, and internal medical arrangements into 'divisions' can complicate liaison and thwart the integration of comprehensive service planning. Several public enquiries and scandals about the quality of patient care have further brought management and organization of these large hospitals under scrutiny in the past decade.

Concern mounted in the 1970s with repeated government White Papers and HAS Reports exhorting DHAs and local authorities to make mental illness a priority (the White Paper *Better Services for the Mentally Ill*, 1975; the Nodder Report (1980); *Care in Action* (DHSS, 1981a) and the Social Services Select Committee Report on *Care in the Community* (DHSS, 1981b)). Although patient numbers in mental illness hospitals had declined significantly, the momentum and pace of change was flagging. It was becoming obvious that the old asylums would not easily self-liquidate nor would a new network of community services naturally or comprehensively emerge. Despite exceptions the overall picture was bleak. Instead of DHAs and local authorities advancing towards some unitary ideal there were marked intra-Britain differences in interpreting and implementing national policy (Hunter and Wistow, 1987a, b). Many accounts for this have been advanced emphasizing the structural, financial and organizational barriers to achieving new forms of service provision (Audit Commission, 1986).

The Nodder Report (1980) advanced an analysis of the problem which went beyond problem-sensing and diagnosis, commenting that shortage of resources was only part of the problem and that fundamental change depended on giving central direction to Regions and Areas through setting objectives, standards and targets; restructuring and strengthening local management; and coordinating social services' and health services' planning and approach. This is a portent for the managerial response to the issue developing in the 1980s and illustrated so clearly by our case material. The evidence from the two Districts on the quality of the hospital closure and CITC policy shows national policy itself to be vague and lacking a robust financial basis. The cases also highlight deficiencies in strategy formation at a Regional and local basis as well as shaky implementation or audit mechanisms typifying the 1970s.

Problem Definition   The creative potential of strategy makers is a strong theme emanating from recent work of organizational theorists (Kanter, 1985; Pettigrew, 1985a). Strategies are not inert, unambiguous prescriptions, but are socially constructed through the cultural and political processes of organizational life. The ways meanings and realities are shaped and managed – problem definition – is a crucial element in strategy construction. Through the process of legitimation, ideas are promoted or defeated, sponsors won or lost, actions applauded or ignored (Pettigrew, 1973b). The content of a strategy is no neutral, rational, analytical artifact but a blend of political and cultural factors produced through legitimizing actions, symbols, words and images (Pettigrew, 1985c).

   Kanter (1985) itemizes steps needed for an innovative strategy to take shape, and although not intended as a 'formula' for strategic success her analysis is helpful in drawing attention to the active, processual features of strategy formation and problem definition. In her view, very few innovations or changes are self-started; more typically they are fuelled by a climate of opinion, listening to organizational cues, information gathering and researching conflicting perspectives. Reading the politics of the organization, preparing a convincing case for change, interviewing stakeholders, are some of the tasks she describes as essential at the 'problem definition' stage. The implication is that for a strategy to 'stick', for it to be 'saleable', these steps cannot be skipped. The process of 'problem definition' refers not just to drawing boundaries around what needs to be done, moulding ideas, but also conscripting a critical mass of support for the belief that something needs to be done (Schön, 1973). The development of concern about the status quo, raising of tension in the organization and highlighting organizational contradictions and performance gaps are all part of problem-finding (Pettigrew, 1985a).

   The nature of the environment will also crucially determine results, with 'integrative' organizations being more compatible with such approaches, allowing free flow of information and ideas. In the NHS the dominant impression is of major strategies being decreed, as unproblematic, from above: top-down circulars; review procedures; government-inspired policies bearing down on Regions and Districts. Failure of such centralist dictates to be translated into local reality has frequently been lamented (Nodder Report, 1980; Griffiths Report, 1983; Audit Commission, 1986). However, it may be more useful here not to ask why centre-led strategies have failed, but to look instead at how assignments have been locally constructed, interpreted and activated. The two case studies selected shift attention away from the overarching issue of an 'implementation gap' to the local processes of strategy formation. How top-down strategies are perceived and received, 'talked up', 'sold', the language and symbols used, the process of coalition-building – all can be interrogated in both Preston, and St Helens and Knowsley.

This is not to decry the importance of structural barriers to change highlighted elsewhere (e.g., Audit Commission, 1986), but to complement our understanding of modes of problem solving in the NHS. The issue of NHS culture (as discussed in Chapter 7 on mental handicap services) has a bearing here too. If the NHS as a whole is segmentalist in character, then success with top-driven change could be more likely with the bringing in of outsiders, who could defy conventions, or as a consequence of 'holes in the system', windows of unplanned opportunity (Kanter, 1985). If integrative cultures are created in the NHS system conditions for change strategies would be more favourable (see again Chapter 7 for elaboration). In the ICI study (Pettigrew, 1985a), it was concluded that change occurred when leaders turned segmentalist structures and cultures around and introduced more integrative *modus operandi*, allowing novel ideas and actions to flourish.

Clinician–Management Interface   The tension between medical and managerial constituencies is part of the architecture of the NHS. As Strong and Robinson note (1988), vested medical interests have created controversy and acquiescence among politicians and public alike from the beginning of the Service. In their words: 'The absence until very recently of a chief executive officer at every tier of organization has meant the ideological as well as the practical domination of the NHS by a single clinical trade – the doctors.' They write, 'doctors have ruled the roost' and 'obstructed . . . the creation of an effectively organized service'. The power of doctors to control resources, determine priorities and veto change has been a strong organizational echo, with successive reorganizations failing to shift the balance of power or the clinical bases for decision making.

The Griffiths reorganization of 1983 was perceived as the first serious attempt since 1948 to empower NHS management, to change the 'hand-maiden' role of administrators (Bidwell and Vreeland, 1977; Ferlie, 1990), introducing a different value base to decision making (Carrier and Kendall, 1986; Strong and Robinson, 1988; Harrison et al., 1989a). How far that change has succeeded in moving the power bases of various clinical groups, agendas and operational practice has been found to be equivocal. In the Strong and Robinson (1988) study of health authorities for example, managers interviewed were much exercised by their efforts to contain medical expenditure, encourage resource-consciousness among doctors, rationalize expensive treatments and new technologies, introduce concepts such as value for money and quality control, and entice doctors to think managerially. The Griffiths changes also initiated the clinician–manager concept, and gave rise to trials of resource budgeting for clinical directors. Strong and Robinson (1988) reported also that active medical management, although 'a delicate business', was generating a feeling of 'real progress': managers, however, had to proceed cautiously and be aware of deep medical divides, the sense of autonomy, clinical hierarchies and the frequent 'disdain for management'.

The management of clinicians raises societal as well as organizational questions, with doctors bearing strong, public mandates in their exercise of clinical freedom and special expertise. Such special societal status, with its authority to decide over life and death, is deeply and historically legitimated (Freidson, 1970a, b; Johnson, 1972). The considerable national power and ready access to public attention and sympathy wielded by professional medical organizations can easily subvert managerial intervention. Loyalties are often inspired across professional reference groups rather than to the sponsoring organization (Bucher and Stelling, 1977; Scott, 1986; McKee, 1988), or to an organizational ideal ('The NHS') rather than to the local unit of organization. 'Whistle-blowing' to the press, 'shroud-waving', or talking up crises as tactical moves when medical interests are threatened, have not been uncommon, despite the new managerialism. Medical innovation or change has been tied into professional, collegial rankings and promotion rather than into local organizational best interests, or best practice.

Managers have often played a subsidiary role in administering changes, with doctors featured as the dominant change champions (Stocking, 1985; Scott, 1986; and see Chapter 5 on AIDS, where medical leadership was a strong theme in the promotion of change). On the other hand, Peters and Tseng (1983, p. 64) display scepticism as to whether doctors ever initiate strategic organizational change, being typically reactors rather than initiators.

Here there is scope to explore how medical and managerial stakeholders lined up in the face of major organizational change in the two Districts. Thus consultant psychiatrists have been described as traditionally lowly placed in any hierarchy of clinical specialties (Strauss et al., 1964) and it will be of interest to examine how their bargaining strengths shake down as the institutional base of their service is revolutionized. The case study material will reflect on the local character of management–clinician relations, the pressure for and leadership of change, and the impact of general management on this crucial interface. Were there clashes of authority and perspective? Did management win over medical backers?

Was there a clinical product champion? Did general management herald a dawn of productive relations?

Inter- and Intra-organizational Relationships   One of the hallmarks of this particular strategic change is the complex inter- and intra-organizational network implicated in the achievement of any shift from institutional to non-institutional care of the mentally ill. Along with services for mentally handicapped people, mental illness service change is about moving responsibilities across organizational boundaries, about redefining who controls, directs and delivers services, and about altering the knowledge-base concerning appropriate forms of care. The number of stakeholders is extensive and historic assumptions as to the pre-eminence of the health service and its professionals (doctors and nurses) are challenged in envisaged post-institutional services. Consequently, the context is composed of insiders (health care personnel) and outsiders (statutory and non-statutory bodies); losers and gainers; 'givers' and 'receivers'; experts/specialists and lay people. The key players include local DHAs, RHAs and, of course, local authorities at District and county levels, as well as voluntary organizations and pressure groups, politicians and the general public.

Tomlinson (1988) argues that it is useful to develop a way of assessing discretionary interpretation of centre-led policies by local authorities (including here health sector authorities). In his study of the closure of two psychiatric hospitals in North East Thames RHA he devised five ideal-type authorities, along a continuum from the tightly 'controlled', centre-determined model through to the 'Athenian' model, where the authority exercises considerable discretion in responding to local needs and implements changes accordingly. In the latter there was maximum 'action space'. He found it useful to typify and match both health and local authorities along this continuum, concluding that 'differences between types of local state' had 'profound implications for the implementation of social policy' (Tomlinson, 1988, p. 193). He cites examples where DHAs displayed considerable autonomy in formulating local community care policies, only to be thwarted by disinterest or hostility at local authority (LA) level. The problem of getting priority attached to mental illness by local authorities has also been picked up by others (DHSS, 1980; Norton and Rogers, 1981; Bromley, 1984). It has been described as 'non-decision making' and been attributed to health authorities as well as to local authorities (Haywood, 1977). Tomlinson (1988) also noted that a mismatch exists in policy and administrative autonomy within health authorities themselves. In particular, he found a number of technical issues impeding policy change: for example, 'subcontracting other agencies to provide services'.

Other blocks to 'jointness' in community care policies have been well documented (Wistow and Fuller, 1984; Audit Commission, 1986; NCVO, 1986), reflecting on structural, financial, managerial and ideological differences between the different key agencies. In the Nodder Report (1980) differences are tabulated, contrasting the dominance of clinical skills as against social work, lines of accountability to the DHSS as against elected representatives, and central as against local funding.

The role of the RHAs in stimulating and steering closure plans was also reviewed by Tomlinson (1988). He speculates about whether Region could adopt a 'vigorous promotional role', lobbying politicians, local and national, to ensure strategic change; whether it should push devolution of responsibility and insist on local 'ownership' of the policy; and whether to lend technical assistance to DHAs. Korman and Glennerster (1985) found the RHA playing a direct, enabling role in the closure of Darenth Park Mental Handicap hospital by securing a financial base for the strategy, providing specific coordination and a clear focus for leadership of the project. Ferlie (1990) found such themes of positive RHA leadership repeated in his case study of psychiatric service change in Milton Keynes.

We can extend the insights on the influence of inter- and intra-organizational factors through the cases of Preston and of St Helens and Knowsley. Common difficulties are exposed as well as differences; the management approach to establishing, sustaining, and exploiting external alliances will be compared and contrasted. The analysis is developed still further in Chapter 7 on mental handicap service change.

Rainhill Hospital: an Action Orientation is Adopted

Rainhill lies within the St Helens and Knowsley DHA, part of Mersey RHA. District population is 350,000, split between the industrial town of St Helens and a newer urban area of Knowsley, accommodating population overspill from Liverpool. There are some rural areas and some affluent suburbs. Urban renewal is taking place, although parts are characterized by very high levels of unemployment, housing problems and multiple deprivation.

The DHA budget of £54m is shared by three Units: hospital, psychiatric and community services. The District is currently 16 per cent below the financial target suggested by the Resource Allocation Working Party (RAWP) formula for funding, and moving further away. It is promoting the Regional 'flagship' change in psychiatric services, with planned closure of Rainhill by 1992. Simultaneously, there are plans to reprovide services in the community and to develop acute psychiatric facilities at DGH sites. A major restructuring of hospital services is in process, involving a complex and lengthy consultation programme. Community services are also being reorientated, particularly to develop health promotion, services for the elderly, the mentally handicapped and the younger physically disabled. Managerial and system changes are also being tackled at Unit and District levels.

Management Style and Culture

The Griffiths changes brought top-tier (DGM) change to the District (although two of three UGMs had served in the District before, while the DHA Chairman had been in post since 1983). This followed a period of rapid turnover in senior posts in the late 1970s, and senior DHA officers were steadily trying to achieve objectives by building up trust: gradualist, low key tactics were felt more appropriate than high profile, challenging behaviour.

A hallmark was emphasis on member involvement. The Chairman often displayed leadership during authority crises; members were encouraged in regular contact with officers; visits, seminars and informal meetings were the norm. There was a strongly political dimension to management and volatile, sometimes conflictual, relationships with the two local authorities. Polarization of the two urban communities – St Helens and Knowsley – was a potential threat to the integrative plans of the DHA: the tension between centralized directives and localized demands was never far from the surface.

Thus 'political sensitivity' was regarded as an essential and desirable management skill: change by education, consultation and persuasion was preferred. It was felt that radical approaches could destabilize this District, creating unnecessary opposition. It was also recognized that management were in the midst of building their own corporateness, a new managerial culture and awareness. Leadership styles and intra- or inter-organization relationships were emergent and fluid, not realized and fixed.

The element of social concern and of working from a deprived base was threaded through all the research interactions. On the one hand, the legacy of social disadvantage, ageing estate, inequity in past resource allocation, high mortality and morbidity rates resounded in all the DHA's dealings. They were central to the District's persona: being a regional 'underdog', having to be 'on the make' for correction of old wrongs. This coloured many transactions and postures, and sometimes resulted in defensive or reactive behaviour. On the other hand, there was a sense of mission, a loyalty of purpose pronounced even when means were disagreed with or ridiculed. Staff, including many clinicians, were mainly local people with a strong sense of local pride; outsiders spoke highly of their adopted area.

Key People, Events and Issues, 1851–1974

Unique characteristics of Rainhill need to be set against the history of mental illness provision above to fully appreciate the antecedents of contemporary changes at Rainhill. Rainhill Asylum opened in 1851 to accommodate 400 patients. The county appointed a Committee of Visitors but effectively day-to-day management fell to a Medical Superintendent. From 1851 to 1948 Rainhill had only seven Medical Superintendents. They had a powerful influence, remembered and associated with numerous initiatives and innovations. However, even they met implementation problems and some novel schemes failed to be adopted. The role ended at Rainhill only in 1971, long after the creation of the NHS and the introduction of Hospital Management Committees and Regional Hospital Boards. Consequently, there were still many employees at Rainhill who had worked under this particular leadership and management configuration. The introduction of team management affected their autonomy but not always their centrality, authority and power. In 1971, five catchment area-based psychiatric cog-wheel teams replaced the role of Medical Superintendent. This sectorization resulted in medically led, geographically bounded, multi-disciplinary teams – two teams serving Liverpool, one based in South Sefton at Fazakerly and Walton hospitals, a St Helens and Knowsley team. These teams form a crucial part of the change process and dynamic.

From the outset, a key theme in Rainhill's development was that of overcrowding, with increasing admission rates. By 1900 there were 2,029 inpatients; numbers peaked in 1936 at 3,000, 1,000 over the planned optimum. After the Second World War reductions did occur and these should not be underestimated. As a result of clinical developments, natural decline, changes to patients' status, altered admission practices and progressive psychiatric policies a steep drop to 1,730 by 1974 took place, yet the process was not as rapid as expected, nor was the pace sustained or easily predicted. This mirrors patterns elsewhere, reinforcing the conclusion that it was not easy to dismantle these large institutions, disinvent custodial care, or find alternatives. It was also apparent nationally that resettlement for less able patients was neither straightforward, cheap nor without controversy. Deciding on appropriate models of care for patients with severe problems continued to vex policy makers and managers alike from this time onwards.

The *Hospital Plan* White Paper (Cmnd 1604, 1962) included the first serious policy references to bed reduction, care in the community, and hospital closures, but Rainhill was displaying rising admission rates, a growing inpatient population and overcrowding – all contrary to both ministerial forecasts and guidelines. The 1960s and early 1970s reveal a sense of growing crisis at Rainhill: the erection of temporary wards to deal with overcrowding; increasing references to the need to restrict admissions from Liverpool; a letter to the Liverpool Regional Hospital Board asking for guidance on reducing ward size.

The later period was characterized by increased managerial complexity and turbulence. The 1948 NHS Act added additional decision making tiers: the Liverpool RHB and a local HMC. Psychiatric and nursing management had changed radically and staffing numbers risen and diversified. In the 1974 NHS restructuring Rainhill came under the jurisdiction of Liverpool AHA (Teaching) and the HMC was dissolved. Then, in May 1978, structure changed again, with management accountable to an Area team of officers, comprising a nurse, a doctor, a treasurer and an administrator. After 1978, there was a significant reduction in senior management resource (see Committee of Inquiry, 1979) when the hospital became administered as one of the seven sectors in Liverpool AHA (Teaching). Several senior posts were lost and management expertise was further eroded when the Sector Administrator retired after some 45 years, to be replaced by an administrator from outside the area.

These management changes were overlaid on a hospital already coping with deep-seated and complicated service shifts. Resources were increasingly limited by Area and budgetary control had tightened since the 1950s. Personnel issues demanded a lot of management time with two strong unions, themselves often at loggerheads. Communication problems were endemic (Committee of Inquiry, 1979). There were short-comings in terms of planning and implementation of promised improvements. In 1978 there was a period of intense industrial disaffection, a series of allegations were made about maladministration and malpractice, culminating in a visit from the then Minister of State for Health, Mr Roland Moyle, and finally a formal Committee of Inquiry.

The Inquiry found no malpractice but made recommendations on staff/management relations; relations between the Area and Rainhill's Management Team; the personnel function; and industrial relations training for managers. Importantly, it rejected notions dividing responsibility for Rainhill between Liverpool and St Helens and Knowsley AHAs. Also rejected was site-based division of hospital management; or any divisional structure following catchment divides. Instead, it supported the status quo, seeing the solution lying in strengthening of the management resource at Rainhill. This change was announced in the consultation period preceding the 1982 NHS restructuring which removed Area tiers and introduced District management. The rationale was that 'unless there are powerful reasons to the contrary' all Units should be managed by the DHA in whose territory they are situated.

The Pressure for Change, 1981–1984

A Confluence of Influences Consequently St Helens and Knowsley DHA came to manage Rainhill Hospital in 1982. At least three strands of influence can be identified in this volte-face by Region. First comes the policy context: indeed, it is the official rationale in the consultation document, a kind of 'territorial rationalization'. Secondly, government had increasingly put emphasis on local service provision and management. 'Localism' was replacing the practice of distant management with its recurrent problems of physical separation from operations, communications and industrial discontent. This change in emphasis was spelt out even more explicitly in the Nodder Report (1980), where RHAs were recommended to develop 'mental illness District services in place of distant mental illness hospitals'. Thirdly, in a consultation process Mersey

Region canvassed views of the 'Steering Group' (established in 1978 to coordinate regional mental illness provision).

The Copeland Report, 1981 Simultaneously, Liverpool AHA had established its own working party under the chairmanship of Professor Copeland. It met between February and June 1981 and produced a very detailed report on the way forward. Key features of the report were:

1 An emphasis on the need for overall organizational and administrative change. The report argued that 'any change at Rainhill can only be undertaken by a change in the organization as a whole' (Copeland Report, 1981, p. 51) and: 'As long as the hospital remains in its present administrative form staff will continue to identify with it and fight to preserve it. A fight which must seem to fail in the end as wards progressively empty' (p. 52). The susceptibility of Mersey RHA to these arguments is demonstrated by its readiness to pass the gauntlet of change to the newly formed St Helens and Knowsley DHA.

2 Explicit identification of a run-down exercise. In the report, run-down of the hospital was labelled as such and for the first time treated expressly as a management exercise to be both planned for and governed. The need to recover revenue savings from ward closures was argued and the report suggested that wards should be assessed to determine their long-term future regarding closure or upgrading making detailed recommendations about which wards should close, in which order of priority.

3 Attention to certain morale boosting initiatives through the transition to new forms of care. The proposals also included plans for specialized units which cut across clinical teams, directed at needs rather than at catchment areas. Although developing community provision was seen as a priority, with these specialist developments it was envisaged that Rainhill would have 'new developments within its walls'. Some six years later the issue of specialist units has long disappeared, but specialist patient groups continue to pose questions concerning future provision for clinicians.

Other key issues raised by the working party which continue to be central to the present closure programme include: commentaries on the relations between local Social Services and Health Services and the pattern of joint planning and working; ward management and staff communication and morale; the nursing shift system; the hospital laundry; overcrowding; staff training and recruitment; nurse management; and paramedical services.

Regional Intervention and a Strategy for Run-down At Regional level, the raised profile of mental illness reflected the national trend to 'priority group services' (endorsed by *Care in Action* in 1981). In the Ministerial Accountability Review of 1982, Mersey RHA was told to make dramatic improvements in its mental illness and mental handicap service.

This was a catalyst to plans and developments already being laid.

Mersey RHA had anticipated the issue by appointing a liaison officer for the priority group services (an SCM) in 1980. The profile was further heightened by revised mental illness and mental handicap proposals. This document, 'The Green Book' (Mersey RHA, 1982), affirmed the commitment to running down large mental illness hospitals. At this stage no closures were envisaged and Districts were expected to build new, comprehensive services in a 'step-wise fashion'. Primarily Region was trying to move away from a 'pedestrian, bed-orientated service', and a sluggish Care in the Community programme.

Urgent decisions had to be made about the future design of local psychiatric services including short-, medium- and long-term proposals for Rainhill Hospital. An 'Outline Strategy on the Future of Rainhill' was produced in November 1982 to form the basis for a later in-depth study. It was concluded that the hospital could be reduced to 891 beds, in 33 wards on one site, with all support services, the teaching unit, and the Regional specialisms. At this stage neither financial nor staffing implications of the change were spelt out. This was left to the projected in-depth study. However, considerable capital investment did proceed and during 1982–3 some £635,000 was spent. This was used to improve sanitary annexes, renovate medical staff residences, replace laundry equipment, upgrade laboratory facilities and cover backlog maintenance.

In 1983 the promised in-depth analysis emerged. The 'Project Team for the Development of Rainhill Hospital' was set up at the DHA Chairman's request. Made up of Rainhill's new Unit Management Team, plus District and Regional officers, it worked through expert working parties with particular tasks: demography and rate of patient decline; development of clinical services; rehabilitation; patient services and support services; estate management and development; and equipment and furnishings. Time scales were sub-divided into short (up to 2 years); medium (2–5 years) and long (more than 5 years).

Three detailed reports were produced between May 1983 and April 1984. Although more sophisticated, in quality of information and operational detail, than the Copeland Report and the outline strategy, they reproduced a similar vision in commitment to a reduction model, to upgrading part of the site (Sherdley division), to improvement of the physical environment, to establishment of more personalized support services, to rationalization of wards and to release of funds for substitute services. The unique features of these reports were that actual projected costings were included in order to realize the objectives; a detailed estate survey was completed; a patient census was conducted; and an inventory of furnishings and equipment was provided. Disposal of hospital land and property, including farm land and staff housing, was raised as a way of diverting funds to proposed developments.

Thus the management thrust begins, in 1984, at the point and with the same diagnosis as reached in the Copeland Report some three years earlier. There seems to have been much repetition of effort. The Copeland

Report itself appears to have been lost to history by temporal accident, by discontinuity in management arrangements and in managers, and perhaps because it did not translate its clinically driven plans into management terms and programmes. Although they had to be rediscovered by the new management, its findings none the less remain critical catalysts in the change history at Rainhill. With the benefit of hindsight, this example of 'lost learning' or 'reinventing the wheel' may seem to represent a waste of management time in responding to urgent strategic problems. Chiming with the observations of Kanter (1985), Pettigrew (1985a) and others on the non-linear nature of extended strategic change, it raises a general question about how organizations can archive past experience and insights, and short-circuit cumbersome and familiar investigations. Can a library of knowledge and expertise be maintained in the face of changing personnel and ideals? Can organizations build up, harness and release intellectual and experiential reserves? A point also emerges about the role and value of research in preparation for change; interrogating organizational documents and staff for 'what do we already know about the issue?', a search for 'received wisdom'.

In May 1984 the first 'Strategy for the Development of the Mentally Ill' was produced, an amalgam of existing plans of the District and of the Project Team. This consultative document was structured into two inter-related components: development of services for the mentally ill of St Helens and Knowsley, and redevelopment of Rainhill Hospital.

Reduction of the size of Rainhill Hospital from 1280 to 600 beds (excluding specialty beds) and anticipated closure of one management site (Avon Division) was restated. Fairly detailed suggestions were included concerning liaison with the 'receiving' DHAs and local social services, to ensure that there would be broad agreement on transfer of care of patients and proper coordination of plans during the run-down.

The capital developments identified at that time in the Project Team Progress Report of May 1983 totalled over £13m (including that for the Regional Secure Unit). The anticipated additional revenue to meet the new developments was estimated to be £2.8m. The two urgent tasks identified for the District at this stage were to produce an estate development plan and to find ways of progressing and accelerating service developments at Liverpool and South Sefton DHAs (see DHA Minutes, 12 June 1984). But 1984 was to prove to have an even more radical set of agenda items ahead.

From Run-down to Closure, 1984–1985

Then, between May and September 1984 the long process of deliberation about the run-down of Rainhill Hospital altered radically: the prospect of total closure emerged in official documents for the first time, in what was labelled the 'Alternative Strategy'. This was taken to the mental illness sub-committee of the DHA on 11 September for discussion.

A complex medley of factors were at work. One cannot isolate any one 'crunch' issue or influence which diverted local management away from their original strategy during this critical year: but in brief it was the viability of objectives that was brought into focus. From the detailed estate survey it was apparent that huge amounts of capital would be required. Furthermore, the District had just received an unfavourable Health Advisory Service report, indicating that the run-down of Rainhill should be accelerated and highlighting the poor quality of patient conditions and physical environment. The District had also just experienced a thorny period of industrial disruption, culminating in a strike of the hospital porters.

The Regional review laid down expectations that at least one mental handicap hospital should close. There were indications, too, that the Regional Programme Budget (the financial strategy initiated to advance Regional plans on mental illness and mental handicap services) was not working well: as wards closed this strategy would return Districts' savings to Region, to be recycled for mental illness (MI) developments, assessed through a complex bidding procedure. It was becoming apparent in 1984 that Districts were not making savings at the expected rate, making bids to upgrade existing facilities, and not developing services fast enough. By 1986 the Programme Budget was over-committed by some £3.5m, there was inequity across the Region in the speed and the type of developments, and the notion of a 'step-wise' progression of District services was becoming redundant.

There were two further dimensions: Griffiths's general management was imminent, and there was the opportunity for radical reflection upon the way forward; and the District's strategy had thrown up the issue of whether Rainhill should retain acute beds (additional to those at Whiston General Hospital), or become entirely a long-stay institution, with all its implications for staff development, training and morale. At least one account of why Rainhill had to close referred to this as the precipitating factor.

> We decided to close Rainhill – or, we decided to recommend that it be closed – because of the plan that came in from St Helens about 1983/4: something like that, 1984 it would be. We realized that, out of Rainhill, Liverpool would want to develop their own service and South Sefton, and what really threw us, and put a question mark over the whole viability of Rainhill, was St Helens' desire to develop their own acute psychiatric service off the site in Whiston and St Helens hospitals – and I thought that tolled the death knell of Rainhill.

The new strategy, with detailed implementation proposals for closure, went to consultation in October 1985, and was approved by the DHA in April 1986. This was the change with which the District was grappling at the time of this research. In the meantime new general managers are in place in all the DHAs concerned; and a radical management change is taking place alongside a radical service change.

Implementing the Closure Decision, since 1985

There has been a proliferation of activity since 1985 towards implementation of the closure decision.

Preparing for Closure In the next two years management activity was devoted to getting new management structures in place, preparing a patient census and a costed action plan, ward rationalizations, improving communications and creating joint mechanisms of planning coordination across the three Districts and with SSDs. Emphasis was also placed on developing a programme of CITC schemes and associated financial mechanisms.

The Regional Programme Budget While balancing the tasks above, the Unit started to tackle the crisis of the 'faltering' Regional Programme Budget; the District was asked to make £2m savings over the next financial year. This had a profound effect on short-term Unit priorities. By accelerating ward closures, £600,000 was recouped and returned to Region. The Regional Programme Budget had to be recast after 1987, and at the end of the research exercise the District still awaited precise details of the sums of money to be allocated under that new regime. The Unit was thus still inhibited by lack of budgetary certainty. This was imposed on an already heavy change agenda and robbed the UGM of some authority and autonomy in implementation. It highlights continuing tension between devolution and centralized control, and the uneasy way in which UGMs have acquired responsibility and accountability, not matched by budgetary control. Region still maintained the 'power of the purse' and the leverage for change.

The Impact of General Management Thus far, there has been a strong action bias in advancing closure, with strong UGM leadership in ensuring that things get done. Many have commented that since the UGM appointment in 1986 the pace has increased: having responsibility vested in a single person has sharpened up implementation. Many respondents felt that the impact of general management on service change was very noticeable in long-stay hospitals, explained by bringing in better calibre managers, auditing Units on change and vesting the task in one empowered individual.

Other explanations of the shift included the effects of devolution to Unit level, tighter consultation chains (lessening 'the dead hand of bureaucracy'), intensified emphasis on 'change', and clear definition, legitimation of the UGM's contribution to the process. Short contract arrangements were also seen as influential: 'General managers that don't up the pace of change won't be in their jobs long.'

Some Tensions Three general observations about the manner of approach to the closure task can be made. First, there is a tension between the ordering of priorities and the scarcity of management resources: where to place efforts – in ward rationalizations and accelerate closure? In continuing management of the transitional institution? In planning resettlement plans and alternative services? The dilemma could be seen in the action choices of the first year of Griffiths-style management, with ward closures prioritized. Partly owing to Regional strategy, ward closures were also used to communicate the seriousness of intentions about retraction: to signal that the UGM meant business. This lost the UGM some supporters and, some claim, damaged his credibility.

Secondly, although responsibility to effect change had been devolved to Unit level, management resource was little different to that provided for a maintained service. There was some ad hoc use of management consultancy (for example, in identifying staff training needs); and short-term secondments of Regional officers and clinicians: but several respondents thought this help 'too little and too late'. The theme was developed at Region, District, Unit and also externally, summed up in the phrase 'Rainhill is managerially very light'.

The third general observation is of a two-fold categorization of steps taken: those 'action'- or 'outcome'-driven – ward closures, demolitions, new planning forums, the patient census – and others directed to education and legitimation – revision of clinical teams, the restructured UMB. The tendency for action to dominate over legitimating and educational activities is well documented in the management of change literature (Pettigrew, 1985c), and it was detectable early in this study, with a rush to get results, to see visible change.

Thus staff were often reluctant to accept its legitimacy. There is still disbelief in parts of the organization that total closure will take place, fuelled by continuing upgrading work and by the absence of visible new alternative services. Closures has been mooted for more than 20 years, but never actualized; and there is scepticism about management's ability to deliver.

Multiple versions of where and why the decision to close arose also weaken credibility. The coincidental change in management has also dissipated communication channels and destabilized former lines of authority and accountability. There was insecurity about the implications for job security, and management assurances have not succeeded in allaying this. The new general management system has sharpened the division between clinicians, nurses and other staff; and there have been instances, particularly concerning ward closures, where there has been a direct collision of interests between clinicians and management. Nurses have described themselves as being 'piggy in the middle'. This degree of uncertainty and lack of clarity about roles and responsibilities has caused considerable turbulence and disaffection concerning the efficacy and speed of the closure programme.

Whittingham Hospital: the Search for Legitimacy

There are many parallels between Whittingham and Rainhill: both projected closures of established, large, long-stay institutions in the context of the long waves of service change in psychiatric care analysed at the beginning of this chapter. The experiences in Preston DHA reinforce the conclusions from St Helens and Knowsley: but of course there are also differences in the change context and process, the management issues and style, which require explication and analysis.

With a population of some 127,000, Preston District is dominated by the administrative 'county' town of Lancashire, historically both a major port and a centre for the county textile trade. In economic decline for several decades, Preston's major industry now is engineering and aerospace. There has been significant population movement out of the urban core into suburbs and village communities, and with Central Lancashire New Town there is substantial urban renewal. High levels of unemployment, housing problems and multiple deprivation remain. The inhabitants of the District experience more ill health than the national average and in particular rates of lung cancer and cardiovascular disease are high.

In 1982 Preston DHA was created by separating Chorley and South Ribble District (to the south) from Preston. The overall budget for the DHA is £70m with responsibility for a number of sub-Regional specialist services. The Royal Preston Hospital is a major new DGH of 723 beds; there is Ribbleton Hospital for the elderly severely mentally infirm (ESMI), Sharoe Green Hospital with gynaecology, maternity and some geriatric and orthopaedic beds, and Whittingham Hospital with 720 MI patients. Closure of Whittingham is a 'flagship' change in psychiatric services along with the necessary plans for reprovision in community and acute DGH psychiatric facilities.

In acute services, a major redistribution from Preston to Chorley is in process. An immediate issue was the reduction of an acute sector overspend involving review of activity in the new DGH. Again, these form part of a substantial list of change issues, which in Preston's case included ward closures, closure of a small charity hospital for the elderly, rationalization of maternity provision, a rationalization of the ambulance service and waiting list initiatives, plus the common factors such as Griffiths management arrangements, competitive tendering, action on the high mortality rates in preventable illness, staff development initiatives and provision of community services to priority care groups. A heavy 'change load' again emerges, following hard on a period of major change in the early 1980s, with opening of the DGH, separation of Districts, and closure of older acute hospitals (Preston Infirmary did not finally close until 1987).

Management Style and Culture

The Griffiths initiative brought major change in senior level posts, again after a prolonged period of managerial instability. At DMB level, the sole continuity lay in medical membership, with a new DGM, three new UGMs and a new District Treasurer (a post vacant for 18 months prior to 1985). The Chairman's post was itself vacant for a period before January 1985. This was a time of weak financial management, described by some as 'easy-going', by others as 'out of control'.

The new DGM inherited a number of unresolved issues: the overspend, acute sector growth, lack of trust in management. Management–clinician relationships had typically been poor, with informal decision making processes influenced by a large team of high-calibre, independent-minded clinicians. There was also a history of conflict between District and Region, with hopes that the new DGM would signal a period of improved relationships.

In the DGM's approach there was devolution of decisions, a minimum of formal meetings, and emphasis on decision making as informally as possible, at as low a level as possible. The new 'team' were described as action-orientated, an 'up-and-at-'em brigade'. At this date there was still much to achieve in middle tiers of the organization, where managers remained undeveloped: described sometimes as 'inertia'. Equally, relationships between Districts and Units were transitional and 'variable'.

The DGM was seen as dogged, 'fair but firm', attentive to detail, and prepared to take necessary, but unpopular decisions. He was seen to have emphasized better communication, but as missing some political dimensions of problems, perhaps of solving details at the expense of the wider or bigger issue. Relationships with staff have, particularly in the Whittingham context, been fraught, but were now viewed as much improved, with clear communication, consultation and negotiation.

The District Authority was characterized as well-balanced, not 'overly political', with strong commitment to priority care groups and community services. Officers and members maintained contact through seminars, visits and member panels, while the Chairman was closely involved in a non-executive stance, with a high profile locally. Local authority relationships were described as problematic, again with no coterminous LAs (Lancashire County and Preston Borough Councils). In Preston this was complicated further by inter-District tensions in respect of neighbouring Chorley and South Ribble DHA, the main partners in the restructuring necessary to achieve Whittingham's closure.

Key People and Events, 1869–1971

This section provides a brief overview of Whittingham Hospital's history: there are more detailed treatments elsewhere (e.g. Whittingham Hospital Management Committee, 1973). The asylum was sanctioned in 1869, receiving its first patients in 1872. It grew quickly until the mid twentieth century, when inmate numbers peaked at 3,533. In 1923 'mental hospital' replaced 'asylum'. There were other reforms, in line with national trends – 'open door' policies, voluntary patients, outpatient facilities, an EEG service.

Claims have been made that Whittingham was the largest mental illness hospital in Britain at this stage, and its history parallels that of Rainhill (see above) in other ways. With the establishment of the NHS the Lancashire Mental Hospital Board was dissolved and a Hospital Management Committee set up. In the early years of the HMC there were the characteristic staff shortages, recruitment difficulties and problems of cost control.

By 1961 the HMC was already planning for reduced bed numbers, working towards 'community care'. The *Hospital Plan* White Paper (Cmnd 1604, 1962) envisaged a reduction to 2,000 beds by 1975 (the number was 1,719 in 1972). As with Rainhill, there was increased attention to specialized needs, with a new unit for the psychiatrically ill deaf opened at Whittingham in 1964, for example. Patient discharges were increasingly limited by the availability of community facilities, rather than institution attitudes. The concept of the closed, custodial regime was gradually being superseded by that of a 'therapeutic community'.

As with the national pattern alluded to above, many early managerial preoccupations centred on the estate, ward size, patient intake, bed occupancy, standards of care and the containment of infection and epidemics; clinical and therapeutic changes were incorporated on an incremental and ad hoc basis. Changes began to be made in the 1950s, with formal recognition of innovation in service design and rationale, but only piecemeal changes were made. GP services in the hospital were introduced, on-site shops for patients were established, rehabilitation services were accentuated and physical upgrading begun in some wards.

Towards Recognition of Closure, 1962–1987

Paradigmatic shift in service operation was a long way off, however, and before 1960 there is little evidence of any strategic thinking. When the first serious national policy references to closures were made in the 1962 White Paper (Cm 555), Whittingham was displaying rising admission rates, a rising population and overcrowding. Cog-wheel team structures and the Salmon reorganization of nursing administration, staff specialization and diversification, the extra decision-tier of the HMC, all had increased the complexity of management.

Committee of Inquiry, 1971   During the later 1960s there was a series of escalating concerns and complaints, ranging from maladministration, staff victimization and financial irregularities, to ill-treatment of patients. Following the death of a patient and subsequent internal and police inquiries, the hospital became the subject of a Committee of Inquiry in

1971, examining 'the administration of and conditions at Whittingham Hospital'. The Inquiry marked a watershed in recognition of problems, in the urgency of change, and of the reorganization of management to effect change.

The report focused on:

1   Poor quality management. Existing management was described as 'management by labyrinth' (Committee of Inquiry, 1971, p. 18), with preoccupation with trivia, fragmented decision making, inadequate delegation, complacency and passivity, disregard for strategy formulation (particularly in respect of the hospital run-down or closure) and poor internal communication between HMC and the Manchester Regional Hospital Board.

2   Inadequate therapeutic and clinical practices. These were described as 'drifting behind the tide of progress' and resembling still a 'locked hospital' in some areas.

3   Weak community links. Links with community and voluntary sectors were found to be weak, with local authority community provision minimal: a resource of two discharges per year compared to the list of 160 eligible patients.

While there was discussion of the principle of closure in the 1960s, the Inquiry Report gives the first formal recognition of a movement to closure, seeking a clear plan, agreed by HMC and MRHB, and setting a clear management challenge. In the AHA 10-year Strategic Plan of 1979 there was a projected DGH Unit, with 169 ESMI beds at Preston, plus 120 beds (and 160 day places) for adult psychiatry. Whittingham was to run down naturally, by no new admissions. There was still, however, no strategy for community provision or resettlement: the nettle had not been grasped. This state of affairs continued through the 1970s. The immediate outcome of the Inquiry was the resignation, en bloc, of the HMC and the appointment of a new Medical Superintendent, 'a progressive man' who inspired many changes in practices. The 1970s became a period of renewed clinical managerial energy with many new staff and much new activity. However, a conscious strategic thrust towards planned closure remained absent and this was noted in an HAS report of 1980. The report commented on the continued absence of positive planning, and concluded that it was unclear whether there were a policy for maintaining or reducing services at Whittingham.

A Directive for Closure   Thus, despite the decade-long recognition of closure, Preston District came into being in 1982 with these issues still unresolved. There was no firm plan for closure, nor yet any firm understanding with Region as to strategy. This latter began only in the 1983 Regional strategic planning round, when Region affirmed adherence to national policy of closing large long-stay hospitals, assumed leadership of the issue, and linked it to community care development. Firm target dates were established, with 1996 the target for Whittingham; a financial strategy was sketched out, with a 'ring fence' on mental illness monies; a working group was established to develop guidelines; and Districts were asked for their individual strategies in line with Region's.

Preston's view, articulated in July 1984, was that the hospital would run down to 417 patients by the end of 1993, although there was still reluctance to go beyond this run-down to actual closure. Yet further momentum was added by the 1984 Ministerial Review process, with its requirement: 'the plan will set out a timetabled programme for development of District mental illness and mental handicap services showing the run-down and closure of existing large hospitals.' Preston were accordingly pressed for a revised plan to include closure, which they produced later in 1984.

Yet Further Delay As closure now became a strategic reality, the District was identifying the crucial problems: a poor – almost non-existent – data base for planning; the difficulty of propelling management from incrementalist planning to a radical restructuring model; the question of meeting externally imposed timescales and targets; and the difficulties of reconciling anomalous, unknown or unanswerable aspects of a complex policy. It might be argued, of course, that local inaction left no alternative to this imposition of a top-down policy. Certainly the pace of strategy information became precipitate from 1984 onward, under the spur of Region and central imperatives. These difficulties, neglected for over a decade, had now to be resolved in a very short space of time.

From the end of 1984 the closure plans for Whittingham were being developed and refined in iteration between Unit, District and Region: a process that was still ongoing at the time of this research. The DHA's first documented policy commitment to closure comes in February 1985, anticipating closure by 1993, but with great concern over meeting timescales, and again the doubts as to achieving the requisite conjunction of retraction and reprovision. This 'policy' was highly problem-centred, stressing areas such as the underprovision for the ESMI group and the uncertainties of providing community care schemes and of achieving provision in receiving Districts. With 1,091 occupied beds, the District was telling Region that the closure target was not realistic (Table 6.1).

Table 6.1 *Bed complement at Whittingham Hospital, 1985*

Adult acute	53
ESMI assessment	40
Long stay	283
Historic long stay	647
Interim secure	24
Psychotherapy	20
Deaf Unit	24
Total	1091

Plus: 130 Industrial Therapy Unit places

Source: District Strategic Plan for MI services

The Role of Region   Before there could be a response from Region, the Griffiths arrangement in Preston brought the new DGM (December 1985) and the appointment of the UGM (Psychiatric Services) in mid 1986. The Region's response came in the form of an interim, short-term strategy document on run-down and closure of large hospitals. Without refining Region's role, this paper – the 'Yellow Peril' as it became known – charged Districts with the tasks of producing detailed, costed contraction and resettlement plans, with Development Control Plans for site and asset disposal, and details of patient assessment schemes and resettlement arrangements. It was essentially an attempt to structure the planning framework in terms of patients' service needs, in terms of quality of life assessment, by reference to joint planning.

While Districts were being urged to construct detailed strategic plans, however, the Region's own strategy formulation was slipping. In June 1987 a further consultation document was issued, intended as an iterative part of longer-term strategy formulation; but it comprised a discussion of the values or philosophy of care rather than the Region's strategic framework, and many District-level managers and clinicians saw it as overly detailed, prescriptive and preoccupied with detail rather than structure.

With a strategy document long awaited, it was also misread, as that strategy itself. Such delays and confusion reveal Region's complex brokerage role between the Department and the Districts: trying to accelerate the strategy process while simultaneously seeking commitment from local service providers. The hiatus in creation of strategy at Regional level has proved a blockage in the planning process for District(s) and Unit(s). There was uncertainty as to the pace of change and as to crucial interlocks between Districts, between District and Region, and in financial arrangements for reprovision.

Bearing this in mind, the new UGM in 1987 developed Preston's first 'closure' plan for Whittingham in a Proposed Contraction Plan. The closure target date is presented as 1997, with patient numbers to be reduced gradually over the ten intervening years. Residual long-stay patients would be transferred to nursing home provision at the time of total closure. There was, however, a further 'option', whereby the hospital remained open until it became no longer viable: no target date is specified, but 'viability' is forecast to end in March 2009. This alternative is used to recommend the target-driven option ('Option 1') as giving a clear management direction, although it involves greater expense to District and to Region.

Implementation   The picture in Preston was one of impressive recent activity in planning formulation. From mid 1986 activity had been devoted to an agenda almost identical to that of Rainhill, with general managerial changes, operational ward closures and rationalizations, personnel and inter-organizational initiatives and policy formulation the dominating concerns.

There were also a range of informal negotiations by the Unit with other Districts and with LAs and voluntary agencies to enable planning to proceed. Internally, considerable effort was put into establishing with staff that change was indeed imminent, always a hard task when 'closure' has for long been an abstract threat. The tasks were part of a dynamic strategic process; some were further down the track than others, in a highly complex, intricate process. Not least, the Unit was being asked to make £1.1m savings (on £14m annually) in the short term. Finding such retraction money imposed further heavy strain in the crowded change agenda: as noted above in the context of Rainhill, Region still retained the financial levers, even if its financial strategy had yet to pass beyond a crude 'dowry' system of releasing funds along with resettled patients. The Regional 'ring fence' was a useful commitment, as was bridging finance for a CITC scheme start-up, but not sufficient for detailed long-term planning: the Unit span of control remained inhibited by lack of budgetary autonomy.

In effecting the changes that have occurred, the new UGM was perceived as having speeded up the pace of change, sharpening up responsibility and displaying leadership previously absent. As at Rainhill, there were many comments that general management worked well in long-stay hospitals – a return to the 'Medical Superintendent' model, perhaps. However, respondents also noted the constraints upon the UGM. They highlighted that however competent the individual and his/her team of officers, a number of crunch factors impeded the route to success:

- The quality, clarity and soundness of Regional strategy.
- The tenor and speed of build-up of inter-agency links.
- The defective database for decision making.
- Inertia at management levels below the general managers.
- Public attitudes to and acceptance of mentally ill people.
- Clinical attitudes and the absence of clinical product champions.
- The legacy of institutionalized staff and workforce, resistant to change and with a scar of the Inquiry report.
- Local and national underdevelopment of human resource policies.
- External uncertainties and bureaucratic obstacles.

It is always tempting, with such an imposing 'obstacles' list, to 'blame up', excusing management inaction by reference to external constraints. This was said to happen, Whittingham being described by some as 'the least cooperative' of the large mental illness hospitals in the Region, as 'further behind' in the acceptance of change: 'they tend to identify the third parties, whether it's Region or whatever, as the main reason why they can't do something.'

Indeed, with all these constraints and especially with the slow response by Region to the District retraction plan, managers could see few incentives for progress, and it was feared that this might lead to a culture of defeatism and erode earlier periods of high energy. This lack of incentives

Table 6.2 *Achieving change in psychiatric services: the context and content of change*

	Preston	St Helens and Knowsley
Regional strategy	All major institutions to close	Rainhill – targeted/'flagship'
Hospital size	700+ (1987)	800+ (1987)
Timescale of closure	1997/?	1992
Pressure for closure	Committee of Inquiry Ministerial Review HAS report General management	Committee of Inquiry Ministerial Review HAS reports 1982 re-organization Overcommitted RHA budget General management
Structural complexity	Five major receiving Districts but 15 in total Multiple local authorities and borough council	Three major receiving Districts Four local authorities; two metropolitan borough councils
Clinical composition	Diverse specialties	Five clinical teams Professional unit

and rewards was also a theme at Rainhill where the issue of maintaining a change momentum, even through times of apparent immobilism, similarly arose.

Management of Closure: the Two Cases Compared

The points of difference and similarity between these two Districts are summarized in Tables 6.2–6.5. Table 6.2 summarizes the context and content of the change in the two Districts. The scale and shape of the change issue is remarkably similar but key differences exist in the clarity of timescale and in the scope of the Regional strategy. The pressures for change in each instance were almost identical with a mix of internal and external forces and top-down as well as bottom-up leverage being applied at different points in the change trajectory. Tables 6.3 and 6.4 include the change chronology of each closure and the parallels are striking, with a protracted planning process and many iterations of detailed closure plans. Both cases reveal a repetition of effort and instances of lost learning spanning successive administrations. New problems were flushed out by external inquiries and HAS visits but a managerial response and strategic approach only emerged late in the day. Table 6.5 highlights some of the differences and similarities in the processing of the change.

The similarity of these items reflects the centrality of the service change as the key influence in setting the agenda: the qualitative difference in approach of the two Districts was found to be in the language and style of their efforts, with more emphasis at Rainhill on symbolic and challenging action to achieve strategic goals, whereas at Whittingham there

Table 6.3   *Changes in psychiatric services at Rainhill: key chronology*

1970	Increasing complexity and fragmentation of management
1978/9	Industrial strife and Committee of Inquiry
1981	Copeland Report (details run-down programme)
1982	Transfer of management to St Helens and Knowsley
1982	Ministerial review and production of an outline strategy (1982–92)
1983/4	Project Team for the development of the hospital
1984	Strategy for the development of MI services
1984	Alternative strategy emerges
1985/6	Regional programme budget falters. Introduction of general management closure decision
1986/7	Towards the implementation of closure

Table 6.4   *Changes in psychiatric services at Whittingham: key chronology*

1970	Increasing complexity and fragmentation of management
1971/2	The Committee of Inquiry. In post-Inquiry period injection of funds, personnel and accelerated developments
1979	Lancashire Area Health Authority Strategic Plan 1978–88
1980	HAS report
1982	Preston District Health Authority created. Abolition of Lancashire Health Authority
1983	North West HA Outline Strategic Plan 1983–93. Concept of ring-fenced budgets
1984	Ministerial review
1984	(i) Outline strategy for Preston's psychiatric services
	(ii) The development of psychiatric services in Preston and the closure of Whittingham Hospital
1985	District Strategic Plan: strategy for MI services
1986	North West HA short-term strategy for the run-down of large hospitals
1987	(i) Whittingham Hospital: proposed contraction plan
	(ii) Comprehensive psychiatric services for Preston
	(iii) Regional discussion document on MI services
1986/7	Slippage in Regional strategy formation. Steps towards implementation of closure

seemed to be less confronting action and a stress on re-educative input to legitimate such goals ('change by erosion'). Some differences were found too in the 'belief system' and attitude of the two Unit managements to the change with a 'can do' (the language of opportunity) approach being more characteristic of those at Rainhill and a 'can't do' (the language of obstacles) attitude sometimes typifying those at Whittingham. This was especially evident when the two managements reflected on their relationships and experiences with Region. Here the common, critical issues are discussed and the similarities – and contrasts – drawn out with particular reference to the analytical themes outlined at the beginning of this chapter.

Table 6.5 *Achieving change in psychiatric services: the process of change*

	Preston	St Helens and Knowsley
Management resource	Thin No external resources	Thin, plus access to Region/ consultants
Regional strategy	Not defined	In formation
Regional leadership	Low-tier in organization Not Regional MI priority	Higher profile/'flagship'
Site of change management	Unit managers 'old' and new New UGM	Unit managers 'old' and new New UGM

Unit leadership style	Emphasis on building:
	  Climate for change –
	  education and consensus
	Staff preparation/training
		Action – bias in terms of closure
		Closure – led and authoritative
		'Getting results'

Unit leadership language	Few risks Language of 'obstacles'	Risk-taking Language of 'opportunity'

Co-option of other groups in change	Efforts to build joint
	  infrastructure/strategy
	Clinician absence
		Weak joint action
		New clinician/management
		  structures

Time horizon	Longer-term approach/
	  incrementalist change
		Expediency/pace/radical
		  change

Change Cycles

In these two cases change policies ebbed and flowed over long timescales, with organic, evolutionary changes emerging to modify practice, beliefs and models of service. Pressures for change both top-down and bottom-up were shown to spring variously from economic, social and clinical concerns about models of care, the role of the state and the place and status of psychiatry in the hierarchy of skills and knowledge.

Revolutionary breaks were rare, with the 1930s epitomizing a period of high change activity and an ideological leap of faith away from the attachment to custodial values and services. The imperfect translation of this ideological transformation into action, or indeed a value base, has been revealed in the persistence of institutional care some 60 years later. As Busfield notes (1986), there has been a certain stubbornness about the second phase of care and although the ideology of community care has come into the ascendancy, the old custodial ideologies have not been fully disowned or replaced.

Brunsson's work in 1982 on the way ideologies change may be of relevance here. He contends that radical changes have to be preceded by and initiated through ideological shifts. He argues that the most stable ideologies are those which are vague and have a wide applicability. Interestingly, he suggests that when old and new ideologies are in competition, and the old ideology still provokes allegiance, there will be a poor context for action.

Thus it may not be fair to characterize the earlier decades as ones of inertia or policy failure but instead to recognize them as historically important decades in which the 'problem of change' crystallized; where the precise contours of the change task were illuminated in preparation for prescription and action; and where it was recognized that the organizational capacity for change had to be enhanced. Equally, the 1970s revealed much incremental change and modification to institutional life: evolution, not revolution.

The question of whether the few hospital closures that have been achieved represent an implementation failure typical of the NHS as a whole is important since it has become part of the wider academic discourse about strategic change in the public sector. It is also the way the 'problem' has typically been cast.

It is argued here, in the light of organization theory, that it may be useful instead to recast the problem and treat psychiatrist service change as ineluctably prolonged, in need of a long-term view and persistent approach, and because it is a radical change involving ideological as well as action-driven changes, knowledge- and value-based as well as technical change, and multiple actors and agencies, to regard it as not susceptible to a 'quick fix' (McKee, 1988). This shifts the emphasis away from why the policy has failed to be implemented towards questions about what stage in the change cycle has been reached, how to capitalize on periods of high energy for change and how to sequence the change. It also helps to focus attention on the process of change, the influence of leaders, culture, language, politics and communications, rather than on outcome alone.

Certain policy changes may have to have a realistic time frame, and in the case studies it emerges that policies cannot be naively translated into direct outcomes or even directly intended outcomes, that government policy is only one of the lubricants for change and that what might appear at one point as a policy breakdown may be seen with hindsight to be only a transitional blockage during which the change takes better shape (Quinn, 1980).

In general, some of the key characteristics of the long-term service change manifest in these cases can be summarized thus:

- long cycles of service change;
- perceived long-standing implementation problem;
- periods of evolutionary and revolutionary change;
- pressure for change: social/medical/governmental/economic/political;
- pressure from 'above' (top-down) but also grass-roots innovations;
- knowledge- and value-based change;
- spans several organizations and professional and voluntary groups;
- managerial response developed late in the day (1980s).

The Definition of the Problem

At these two sites and at all large long-stay institutions there seems to be a continued issue about framing and defining the change problem, articulating and agreeing a robust strategy.

Strategic Vagueness   This is not as unproblematic as would first appear. Securing the formal strategy was only a first step and while on paper the direction, shape and philosophy of the service change look unequivocal there remain many unanswerables, areas of uncertainty and poor definition within the official documentation (McKee, 1988). There was much evidence of equivocacy over strategy definition, even at national level, and about-turns in policy could readily be detected in these cases. Brunsson (1982) has noted that where ideological inconsistencies and vagueness exist, it is difficult to promote high levels of energy and commitment which are necessary for radical organizational change to occur.

There is clearly a balance to be struck between a broad initial strategic vision which allows for manoeuvre, negotiation and emerging consensus and sustained strategic vagueness. A number of informants from both Districts had felt the vision of the future and the problem parameters to be unclear. They also felt excluded from the strategy design stage (McKee, 1988). The comments are derived from officers and professionals alike and at different levels in the hierarchy:

> A lot of people leading this exercise are purporting to have no vision of it. They don't know what it will be like. They have no concept of how they will run a comprehensive psychiatric service or manage it.

> The mistake was in reaching the decision to shut the hospital, the Region failed to get the people on the ground floor on their side. And they have had an uphill task persuading them whether they like it or not, this place is going to close, so you can knuckle under or cooperate.

Different Perceptions   As well as there being a lack of coherence in the desired strategy, or in the District/Regional strategy process (especially accentuated in the Preston case) the point was repeatedly made that different constituent groups had different perspectives on what an ideal strategy would look like. This lack of a shared world view was felt to be a weakness in advancing the change. The absence of a clear professional lead in particular, was seen as handicapping the process. Again the experiences support Brunsson's views (1982) on the difficulties of advancing change in the absence of a critical mass of support.

The Presentation of Strategy   A recurring debate in both Districts seemed to be whether the change is presented as a hospital closure/retraction exercise, which then leads on to finding alternative forms of care, or as a shift to providing community care, with a consequential closure of a hospital. One has a positive imagery and message while the other can be seen as retrograde and politically motivated. The labels used in managing the change, the emphasis placed upon development as opposed to contraction and the language describing the change process all contribute to the symbolic reality and affect people's attachment and orientation to it (Morgan, 1986). At Rainhill and Whittingham respondents reported that the language of contraction/retraction seemed to dominate, certainly at the early stages; and there was some perceived ambiguity about whether contraction was more important than development. At Whittingham the blame was placed on the publication of the 'Yellow Peril' strategy document, which was said to set a negative tone from the outset. However, Unit management described themselves as aware of the imagery problem and were taking steps to rectify the closure emphasis with considerable effort being placed on education and training, highlighting the positive aspects of community care.

> Part of the daft business is, that the task became closing the hospital, as opposed to making a better Mental Illness service, and leads to contradictions which make people feel that the philosophy of the approach is flawed. (Unit officer)

Intractability   In the problem definition exercise there seemed to be considerable scope to attend to imponderables in the 'received' strategy. Some of the recurring areas of uncertainty in both cases included provision of services for 'new long-stay' patients; the provision of appropriate facilities for certain vulnerable groups, for example chronic schizophrenics, ESMI patients, patients with severe neurological difficulties, stateless persons (e.g. the Polish community at Whittingham), extra-Regional patients; public education or lack of it; and the role of general practitioners and other primary health care workers in the reprovided service. The development of a financial strategy which prompted resettlement and motivated both receiving and giving Districts equitably was also a central but intractable problem for both Districts.

The Clinician–Management Interface

Internally, within Rainhill, the clinician–management interface had undergone some considerable turbulence, with examples of direct conflict over ward closures and transfers of patients. Clinicians had perceived management as interfering in clinical decisions and eroding their clinical authority. Management had perceived clinicians as behaving obstructively and inhibiting rational plans (McKee, 1988). The clash between clinicians and management was also about philosophies of care and there was a sense among clinicians that decisions over quality and type of care have been wrested from them. Some clinicians felt that they led the campaign to move away from institutional-based care and that this pioneering lead had now been devalued and redefined as a management-led initiative. The clinicians felt that they had been excluded from the recent managerial decision making process:

> We've always argued that it was the consultants in this hospital who tried to get the move going; although now I think these people [managers] think that it is the consultants who are trying to block it. (Consultant respondent)

On the other hand, management characterized clinicians as reactionary, anti-change and 'bed-hungry'. The struggle was one about legitimacy, leadership and control (Hardy, 1985). Other studies on organizational change in health care settings have concluded that clinicians are 'rarely initiators of strategic organizational change' but are more likely to be 'reactors to change' (Peters and Tseng, 1983, p. 64). The managers' images of clinicians in this case study were mostly negative, ranging from at best passive to, at worst, obstructive. Some of the comments were that they were 'reactive', prone to 'stonewall' and to 'bugger things up'. One Unit officer expressed his frustration thus:

> Their attitude doesn't seem constructive and forward-looking: but then that seems to be the case with all clinical teams . . . Things are happening in spite of the clinicians, the clinicians are not lending their whole-hearted support.

A similar but less dramatic portrait of clinician–management relationships was displayed at Whittingham, summarized by one respondent as 'benign hostility'. Overt conflict was avoided, but some negative labels were applied to clinicians, ranging from 'hostile', 'unbridled', 'destructive', through to the view that they were an irrelevance to the change process. There were also analyses of the clinicians as lacking any corporate opinion, and thus presenting opposition by default. They were seen as passively powerful, but not as using their power in a support fashion vis-à-vis management. On the other hand, some clinicians held management in suspicion and feared a loss of control to management. There was some dissent over the pace of change and philosophies of care.

For managers the establishment of constructive relationships with clinicians is complicated by the fact that medical staff themselves do not always form cohesive groups, nor is there a tradition of unanimity of clinical opinion or practice. The 'federal' system of clinical teams, led by a consultant, sits uneasily with a new unified and streamlined Unit management system, in which teams can play off their 'uniqueness' and plead special cases. The histories and styles of the teams mean that they face differing change objectives and problems. Neither do consultants relate to each other on a line basis. Rather, the picture is one of professional diversity, autonomy and organizational independence.

External Relationships and Linkages of the Districts

The character of external relations was also crucial to the change processes described here. The significant factors were:

- Focused, committed energy directed towards achieving cross-boundary communication and coordination.
- The difficulties of communication and collaboration across different styles, cultures, levels of engagement with a change agenda.
- The need for clarification of respective roles, responsibilities and power in the change process.

Inter-District Liaison   Some important first steps had been taken in gaining inter-District cooperation and coordination both at Whittingham and at Rainhill. In the latter case, the communication, especially between the three UGMs, had been actively developed both on a formal and informal basis. There was much goodwill at senior officer level, although it was not clear how far this had diffused downwards in the respective Districts. Linkages across personnel and nursing functions were only just being established. Generally, trust and optimism in these tripartite relationships was expressed by respondents. In the case of Whittingham, there had been little clarification as to who should take 'lead responsibility' for ensuring that other Districts delivered their plans. It was reported that it was assumed that Region retained the initiative but there was uncertainty about what levers were being used and how this was prioritized. In both instances there was some confusion over behavioural barriers and structural barriers to change.

The UGM at Rainhill had been given 'lead responsibility' for ensuring that the other Districts delivered their plans: however, this did not extend to having any real authority (other than holding the purse strings) over the behaviours of his colleagues in the receiving Districts of South Sefton and Liverpool. In addition, it was repeatedly pointed out that the Unit structures and job remits of the three UGMs differed in the emphasis given to MI services; and for both Liverpool and South Sefton there were other, pressing priority services within their job descriptions. The management arrangements in the three Districts also varied in their maturity; and the UGMs had widely differing experience and expertise. It has been quoted that 'the giver is ready to give, but the receiver is not ready to receive'. These frustrations have long dogged the transition to new models of care.

Joint Planning and Joint Working with Local Authorities Local authority/health service joint planning and liaison continued to influence the shape of new service developments. For both Preston and St Helens and Knowsley these relationships had an unhappy past and were in a developmental phase. At Rainhill, the two Metropolitan Borough Councils had themselves been recently restructured and many new senior officers were in post in both agencies. The DHA had introduced new joint planning arrangements which were still evolving. There were differing layers of trust, or mistrust, and again the timescales and urgency of the task varied between the MBCS. These relationships were variously characterized as 'hostile', 'marked by hatred and viciousness', and 'adversarial'. The differing personal styles of health authority officers and local authority members were described as causing a lack of mutual understanding:

> this new breed of members [local authority] have been asking questions, but they've been asking them in their idiom. They've been asking 'What the bloody hell's been going on 'ere?' They haven't been asking 'Now could you let us have your forward strategy and your short-term plan?'

This pattern of acrimony was rooted in history and with the new structures and personnel at local authority level it was hoped that there might be opportunities to build bridges, to make fresh allegiances and to develop a common vision and language.

In Preston, as far back as the Inquiry, the point was made that lack of coterminosity and poor dialogue at senior levels concerning the future provision of psychiatric services could impede the closure of Whittingham. In 1980, the HAS report on MI services in Preston District commented on the patchy collaboration between Health and Social Services, highlighting poor communications and a tradition of low resourcing of MI services in Lancashire. Despite increased AHA joint planning, it was noted that there was poor information-sharing at local levels, and continued sparse LA provision. These themes were reiterated again in the course of this research in 1988. An example was given of how the local authority and health authorities had developed mental health strategies in parallel in 1987, without the full involvement of the other party. Comments from both sides referred to 'surprise documents', 'cursory consultation' and a lack of 'meaningful dialogue'.

At operational level in Preston, however, joint working relationships were positively described; and there were hints that attempts were being made to overcome the legacy of fragmented planning of service development. For example, a special task group of both health and social service personnel had been set up locally, to try to move towards a joint strategy. As in St Helens and Knowsley, such a grouping was in its infancy.

In these relations, the introduction of general management in the NHS, but not in local authorities, has meant that cultural and managerial differences have sometimes been sharpened and the collaborative process complicated. It was felt that there had been some clarification over who took responsibility for enhancing 'jointness': the UGM was seen as a focal point by the local authority, and this simplified the previous labyrinth of communications. However, there was some anxiety expressed in SSDs in both Districts that the new thrust in the NHS on performance, short horizons, time limits and performance within short contracts sits uneasily with the incremental, evolutionary approach to service change typical of local authorities. There was some distrust of motives, with local authority officers perceiving UGMs and DGMs as 'bonus-bound high flyers'. SSD officers feared that health service personnel might wish to bypass formal joint procedures and 'bounce' plans up the system. The different systems of accountability were also thought to be divisive. The accusation of health authority 'short-termism' and of circumventing the formal joint systems were perceived as endangering the change process over the longer term. These views were common currency in both Districts. The health authority management felt frustrated by the cumbersome, slow and erratic interface between the bureaucracies, and the low priority given to mental health provision.

For both Districts there was a chronic sticking point of who had influence over funding arrangements for reprovision of psychiatric services. LAs see it as difficult to plan any community services when funds are both short and tied to numbers of bed closures. The concerns about the lack of incentives and of control reflect those picked up by the Griffiths Report (1988) on community care: 'The health authority has got the whip hand. We've got to go cap in hand to the health authority in order to satisfy their needs to close the hospital; and their criteria are, that you will empty beds, and you will do it in the way we want.'

Other Agencies Although the relationships between SSDs and the DHA have assumed primary importance, relations with local authority housing departments and with the voluntary and private sector are an important future theme. St Helens and Knowsley had made some considerable headway in its liaison with Housing Associations in particular, and new consortium arrangements were being formulated during the research period. Some teething problems were arising concerning the precise configuration of the consortium, terms of reference, follow-up care and who should be the proper collaborators. It was feared that conflicts of interest could arise in these financial and managerial experiments. In Preston, the links between the voluntary and public sector were described as relatively underdeveloped, although some joint initiatives had taken place with the charity MIND. The relationships between the voluntary sector and Whittingham had not always been positive and there was reported to have been tension, both in objectives and in methodology. Some improvements were noted, with the involvement of MIND representatives in training.

District, Unit and Region: Roles and Relationships Clarification of the roles of District, Unit and Region seems vital to the success of the strategic change. In both cases District/Unit relationships were still in transition following the implementation of Griffiths. Devolution of responsibility and accountability was therefore ambiguous and at times there was an expressed lack of agreement over roles and responsibilities, with frustrations sometimes experienced over precisely who was running the show at any point, and their exact span of control. These tensions surfaced particularly in relation to planning at Rainhill, with Units feeling that District was divorced from operational reality and, consequently, providing inappropriate guidance and advice. In contrast, District officers felt that Units often took a narrow view, had poor appreciation of or experience in lateral working with other agencies, and that they displayed 'political naivety'. The DGM at Whittingham similarly commented on the distance between Unit and District operations, saying: 'relationships are amicable, although I do have to remind them fairly often that they are part of the District.' Such perceptions were reinforced in both cases by the physical isolation of the large hospitals and the historic blurring of responsibilities.

For both cases, District to Region and Unit to Region relationships were also problematical. District officers expressed some fears about Units 'declaring UDI' and bypassing the District in their dialogue with Region. At its worst this could lead to confusion, broken trust and misunderstandings within Districts. At North West Region, concern was expressed that the links to the District were not better developed, and one Regional officer felt that 'next time' there would be more attention to this rather than concentration on direct relationships with the Unit.

Mersey Region, on the other hand, emphasized the importance of direct Unit linkages, giving the Rainhill UGM 'lead responsibility', an innovative though not an executive arrangement. It defied usual management conventions and created many anomalies about the exact contours of the Unit–District line. It also legitimated more active involvement from Region at Unit level.

Both Regions were described as playing an ambivalent role throughout the change process, vacillating between a directive, interventionist stance, where Districts were told to deliver savings, and a more distant, facilitative and devolutionary stance, where Districts and Units were left to take decisions their way. Undoubtedly both Regions played an important part in stimulating Districts to think strategically about psychiatric services in the early 1980s but they took a long time to grasp the nettle about what they saw as the future of their long-stay institutions. In managing a change of this scale, Units sought direction from Regions and especially wanted a definitive view. Regions were not always able to provide this and were themselves managing in a climate of uncertainty and tension. Units' and Districts' abilities to manage the 'moving picture', the 'moving goal-posts', emerged as part of the strategic challenge.

At times Region 'interest group behaviour', detected at Unit level, was in evidence, and reports show that there was at times a potential clash of interests between the clinical, estate, finance and planning divisions. It is not the intention to exaggerate the effects of these inter-disciplinary differences, but rather to signal that there was some turbulence at this level which led to some inconsistency in the messages being transmitted to Districts and Units.

Resource allocation issues were also significant. In St Helens and Knowsley some Regional expertise and resource had been made directly available but this was described as inadequate by some and 'mismanaged' by others. These resources were perceived as not always planned in concert with the Unit or District and leading to a waste of scarce resources. The under-resourcing of the change and the heftiness of the change-load were persistent themes.

In Preston the leadership of the strategic change at North West Region was questioned and was perceived by some to be located too far down the administrative hierarchy. The responsible officer at Region did not have authority over all key decisions and was not perceived as having the power to deliver the strategy single-handed. Many saw the process of change and of District–Region relationships as having improved under his direction, but it was felt that he was operating under serious constraints of bureaucracy and professional interest group behaviour. Other criticisms levelled at North West Region by Preston District include:

- A lack of coherent policy framework and contradictions within existing policies.
- A Regional style overemphasizing monitoring, intervention and control. Words like 'paternalist', 'centralist', 'prescriptive' were used.
- A tendency to rely upon an incrementalist planning approach, and a failure to target or to prioritize.
- An inability to provide incentives to Districts or to encourage innovation.
- Underdeveloped mechanisms by which Districts could influence Regional agendas and strategies.
- The slow pace of Regional policy development and the long delays in response to District initiatives in strategy and policy.
- Inadequate Regional resourcing of the change.

Region perceived flaws in the other direction, too. Regional officers described Preston as slow in respect of MI services, failing to pick up Region's messages and signals, and sometimes failing to exploit opportunities. Some of the local planning was felt to be unrealistic, or overly ambitious. Some Regional respondents also described Preston officers as either tending to take a confrontational or defeatist position vis-à-vis Region, rather than finding ways around Regional barriers, or manipulating Regional policy for their own ends. Unit officers, on the other hand, questioned why these barriers had to exist. This was a comment about the political skills of Preston management: and reflected upon the complex process of bargaining and 'trading' that takes place between Districts and Regions. District officers wondered whether this was a function of distance from Regional HQ, complexity and size of District, or amount of change to be created in a limited time.

The experiences of these Regions and others (Tomlinson, 1988; Korman and Glennerster, 1990; see also Chapter 7 on mental handicap services) show the Region–District interface to be crucial in expediting change, as centre–division relations are in other organizations. The Regional linkages with local authorities also emerged as a critical but underdeveloped issue, especially when new services were dependent upon considered joint response (Tomlinson, 1988). The susceptibility of Regions to changing national priorities could leave Districts vulnerable. The speed with which Regions pick up national policies may influence their later success. Although the closure of psychiatric hospitals was to remain an important ministerial policy throughout the 1980s, growing demands from the acute sector caused priorities to shift from 1988 onwards, with reduced emphasis on fast-track closure.

Closing Hospitals: Conclusions

Ideological Confusion and the Legacy of the Asylum: a Poor
Context for Action

These case studies have narrowly focused on the issue of shifting care
away from large-scale psychiatric institutions towards a policy of care in
the community (CITC). The closure process and its management has been
given particular attention rather than the build-up of non-institutional
services. The historical view has shown how the policies and strategies for
change have themselves been weak and ambiguous, although the mandate
for change sharpened in the 1980s. Relying on Brunsson's thesis, such
vagueness of policy/ideology is a poor context for change, creating
difficulties in the marshalling of widespread support for action. The splits
between clinicians themselves, between District Health Authorities and
local authorities, between clinicians and management, across organizational tiers and other professional groups (nurses and social workers),
evident in these cases, highlights this ideological fragility of the proposed
change. It might be possible to suppose that the context was less than
'change receptive'.

Features of the hospitals themselves, their governance and organization,
may also predispose the change issue to stability rather than to change,
and to incremental rather than to radical change. Equally, aspects of
medical organization may make for difficulties in achieving a radical,
knowledge-based change.

For example, the asylum has been described (Goffman, 1968) as a most
particular historical and cultural form, marked by all the characteristics
of a total institution designed to provide custody, containment, isolation,
protection and, more recently, treatment. Goffman noted that such
institutions contain a majority of long-stay, chronically ill and elderly
patients; induce institutional behaviour in patients and staff; enshrine
patient–management rules which promote the 'comfort and convenience
of staff'; have a strong public mandate; and depend on occupational
communities with patterns of generational and inter-generational employment.

Asylums have also been typified as having a strong unionized workforce, sometimes internecine union struggles (viz. Rainhill), and a stable,
long-serving workforce. They are closed and close-knit, inexperienced in
change and yet used to strong leadership and managerial control.

The consultant psychiatrist and the specialism of psychiatric medicine
have come to occupy a lead role in the skill/strategy/knowledge hierarchy
and for a long period of time this was institutionalized in the role of
Medical Superintendent. Life was highly regulated for staff and patients
with the emphasis on damage limitation and the minimization of risk.
Such institutions also developed a tendency to be 'inquiry-prone' and
marked by industrial disaffection.

The shift to community care is about not just the extinction of an institution, it also implies a complete upheaval in the ranking and status of organizations and their professionals. The threat to old hierarchies is real, with medicine competing with social, non-somatic models of care, consultant psychiatrists at risk of being unseated by non-medical specialists, and the statutory bodies having perhaps to relinquish their tight grip on service and policy direction and provision (Busfield, 1986, McKee, 1988).

The place of assertive change management was fairly new, fairly 'unstable' and fairly low in credibility – emerging in the early 1980s, late in the day. How far management could turn these negative contexts for action, with their 'segmentalist' cultural features, into creative, innovation-prone contexts was just beginning to be played out in these cases.

These themes were all resonant at the two case study sites. Neither Rainhill nor Whittingham had particularly 'happy' experiences of management. Periods of distant management, mismanagement and neglect have been identified and have left scars. Organizations like asylums seem to have 'memories' and certainly, through the existence of long-serving staff, recount a strong folk-lore, where management feature as good or bad fairies.

As organizations both institutions had very strong self-images and both were closed and close-knit. Staff expressed strong organizational allegiance and protectiveness. However, they also felt beleaguered and maligned. Many of those interviewed were anxious to correct what they felt to be an unjust, damaging image. There was evidence of low organizational self-esteem and defensiveness, impacting upon morale, motivation, energy levels and creativity.

Both hospitals formed occupational communities and were characterized by generational and intra-household employment. There tended to be long tenure and little geographic mobility, at least of junior and middle grade staff. Closure was effectively 'breaking up a way of life' for many.

Both had strong traditions of unionization. Qualified psychiatric nursing staff, in particular, were a scarce and valuable resource on which the new services depended totally. This meant that a dominant preoccupation was the 'people plan'. Establishing a viable and comprehensive human resources policy emerged as a priority.

At the time of the research, personnel and manpower issues remained a source of concern, both in terms of morale and in terms of the staffing of future provision for patients in the community and within other districts. Acute shortages of trained staff had been identified or predicted; and questions were asked about whether the new services could or would be adequately staffed. At neither site had detailed conclusions about staff transfers yet been reached and there were predicted staff recruitment and retention problems. There were many unanswerables about training staff for the future and the type of staff mix required. The St Helens and Knowsley District policy of no compulsory redundancies was seen as posing problems, with more than 1,000 staff in service requiring relocation.

Environmental Pressures: Medical Practice, State Policies and Managerial Influences

The change in psychiatric services reveals, in an accentuated form, the subtle, complex and shifting interaction of state policies, medical ideas and practices, and economic realities. The different phases of care, seen in a historical perspective, show how different pressures bear down at different points in time. Confining the insane to institutions was, in the first instance, simultaneously a humanitarian idea, one which bolstered professional interests, achieved financial gains, and enabled collective social control over inmates (Busfield, 1986). Likewise, the dismantling of the large institutions supports not just the vested interests of state welfare policies but, in a complex way, the vested interests of the medical profession. While medical allegiance to the mental hospital has been shown to be strong, benefits are also to be drawn from the incorporation of psychiatry into mainstream, DGH-based medicine, with the close alignment to 'physical' medicine (Busfield, 1986: McKee, 1988).

Although the rise of managerial agendas and leadership was in evidence in advancing closure strategies of the 1980s, the historical account shows that, over time, management has occupied a secondary role. The 'new managers' exemplified in these case studies were working largely with received assignments, characterized by external biographies, timetables and scripts. The ability to personalize, to create influence from below, and to steer change upwards was heavily circumscribed. The lack of 'prime movers' for change in affiliated organizations dogged progress for even the most assertive of managers, as did the sway of shifting external priorities. Constant wrestling of ideas and ideal policies between the different constituencies and stakeholders was at a stage of causing tension and negative energy, and many of these debates lay outside managerial control.

The vulnerability of management in the face of such ideological pluralism amidst such a forceful plethora of stakeholders was striking. Whether a newly organized service and the stability of general management will, or can, strengthen the managerial lead in psychiatric service change remains to be seen. Equally, questions remain about how long 'priority services' will command state attention and preference. A landslide in priority rankings is ever possible and the period of high change may once again subside into incremental, evolutionary, step-wise progression and regression. This raises questions of how momentum can be secured, of who is attending to keeping up momentum, and how the future can thus be shaped and enacted by management.

7

Some Aspects of Success

Mental Handicap Services

Context and Concepts

The attempts to transform services for mentally handicapped people
reproduce many of the themes developed in the previous chapter on
psychiatric services. Both reflect the dominance and resilience of the large,
custodial Victorian hospital (Goffman, 1968) and the cumbersome and
protracted process of incremental change (Hunter, 1980; Quinn, 1980).
Inter-organizational and 'centre–local' complexity are accentuated (Hardy
et al., 1990) as are gaps between official policy and rhetoric and policy
and reality (Walker, 1982; Korman and Glennerster, 1985; Wistow, 1985;
Audit Commission, 1986, 1989; Hardy et al., 1990). Furthermore, health
service managers face comparable organizational change tasks with a
remit to translate top-down, centre-inspired governmental policies into
locally meaningful plans and services. Incoherence, ambiguity and inconsistency have been frequently noted in national policies (Korman and
Glennerster, 1985; Ferlie, 1990; Hardy et al., 1990). Similarly, the
resource context for such massive policy change has been volatile and
dogged by uncertainty, only sharpening up in the 1980s (Audit Commission, 1986; Griffiths Report, 1988).

Understanding the vagaries of change in mental handicap services
usually emphasizes policy failure, 'why so little change?' The starting
point for much analysis is to ask why a 'policy-implementation gap' exists
(Nodder Report, 1980; Audit Commission, 1986). Answers have usefully
concentrated on structural and financial barriers to change (Audit
Commission, 1986, Griffiths Report, 1988; Hardy et al., 1990) –
especially pointing up the way professional, medical interests have
contained change – the under-resourcing of the change, and the failure of
the 'centre' to 'structure local environments by itself providing a coherent
framework of service and resource policies compatible with the national
objectives it is seeking to achieve' (Hardy et al., 1990, p. 141).

Our case studies in Chapter 6 provided additional insights into barriers
to change, underscoring the deficiencies of community care strategy
formation at Regional and local levels and showing how the 'change'
objectives in psychiatric services had been poorly defined from the outset.
We revealed too the clash between medical and management change
paradigms and described how such differences inhibited the change

process (McKee, 1988). At a micro level, we reflected on the weakness in the early leadership of psychiatric service change; the poor communications within and without the organization about the change prospectus and the heavy, competing demands on the managers of change. Weak organizational capacity for change was also described.

While the hindrances to change are crucial, it is the aim in this chapter to deflect attention away from difficulties and shortcomings and to focus instead on *positive* outcomes and facilitators for change. Movement and 'change' goals have clearly been achieved in parts of the service, in fact unevenness and variability are part of the character of the implementation (Hunter and Wistow, 1987a). To provide a contrast and to enhance further an appreciation of the impact of local context on change processes, we draw upon two 'success' stories in the mental handicap services. This concentration on positive change examples is not new and has proved a rich source of organizational learning (Peters and Waterman, 1982; Kanter, 1985; Pettigrew, 1985a).

Some analytical themes have emerged from the case study material which help to inform the debates about why a particular change configuration occurs. The three themes chosen for development here are: the role of culture and people; the tenor of inter-organizational linkages; and the resource climate. By reducing the case study material to three analytical categories it is hoped to make the material more accessible without betraying the complexity of a multi-dimensional, dynamic change process, to allow for organizational comparisons and to heighten a conceptual appreciation of where the accounts fit vis-à-vis other organizational studies.

In order to preserve the authenticity and integrity of the cases studied (following the previous chapters) the chapter will present fairly detailed change histories of two DHAs where substantial service progress has been made and will provide a comparative analysis. No attempt will be made to judge the quality of outcomes at a clinical level and, as in other chapters, the stress will be on 'changing' and on the change process.

The Role of Culture and People

The concept of organizational culture has gained authority in organizational literature, particularly in the past two decades (Pettigrew, 1976, 1979, 1985a; Deal and Kennedy, 1982; Kanter, 1985; Schein, 1985). Morgan (1986) upholds its power as a metaphor for making sense of organizational activity. He refers to its scholarly origins in anthropology and sociology and alludes to its definitional elasticity. Quinn, Mintzberg and James take an ironic view of how the concept has been exploited and sometimes misrepresented 'on the management scene' in the 1980s, describing it as arriving 'like a typhoon blowing in from the Far East' (1988, p. 344). Indeed, this reference to the Far East is not accidental, for as Morgan (1986) notes a great burst of interest in corporate 'culture' was prompted by cross-cultural comparisons between American and Japanese performance, managements and organizations.

The words 'culture' and 'ideology' are sometimes used interchangeably in the organizational texts and generally imply something about the 'informal aspects of organizational life' (Hardy, 1985), including the beliefs, values, norms, myths, rituals, symbols and language that are the sum of an organization (Pettigrew, 1979). It is asserted that organizations draw meaning and shape from their culture or subcultures (Pettigrew, 1979; Salaman, 1979) and cannot be deciphered without an appreciation of these deeper level systems and attributes (Schein, 1985; Kilmann et al., 1986).

However, the proliferation of interest in organizational culture has not been unproblematic. As well as having an infinite number of meanings, the concept has been used for different interrogative and interpretive purposes and discrepant conclusions have been reached in organizational analysis (Schein, 1985; Alvesson and Melin, 1987). First, considerable effort has gone into decoding and typifying different kinds of organizational cultures, for example, segmented versus integrated (Kanter, 1985); missionary versus bureaucratic organizations (Mintzberg, 1990). The classification of the organization's culture is usually linked to predictions about how individuals in that organization will act and behave in given circumstances. In the 'integrative' companies described by Kanter (1985) the environment is portrayed as 'team-oriented', 'cooperative' and innovation-prone. Ideas spread across boundaries, there is flexibility, open communications and 'rancorous conflict' is minimized (1985, p. 28). For Mintzberg (1990) the 'missionary' organization will be change-resistant with members of the organization committed to protecting traditions and sloughing off interference. Action and culture are presumed to have a close and obvious symmetry (Alvesson and Melin, 1987).

Many analysts have also found a consonance between styles of leadership and broad cultural orientation, each again being a likely predictor or progenitor of the other (Kanter, 1985; Schein, 1985). Indeed, Schein asserts that 'culture and leadership are really two sides of the same coin' (1985, p. 4). In his view, an organizational leader is seen as being both formed by the organizational culture and creatively engaged in forming that culture. Such a dynamic view includes a belief that cultures can become dysfunctional, be destroyed and rebuilt by the actions of leaders.

Many critics, however, as well as pointing out the definitional confusion over the use of culture in organizational studies, have recently begun to question how manipulable cultures really are and how far leaders can intervene (Alvesson and Melin, 1987; Grieco, 1988). Equally, attention has been focused on the limitations of a view of organizational culture as homogeneous and unifying.

Questions have been raised about the persistence of conflict in organizations and some analysts emphasize the need to extend the model of culture to allow for this (Alvesson and Melin, 1987; Grieco, 1988). Alvesson and

Melin (1987) are also unhappy about the assumed symmetry of cultural beliefs and actions, suggesting that within organizations, counter-cultural and contradictory behaviour is not unusual. They similarly query the notion that the majority of an organization's members display a deep commitment to the organization's culture, claiming that this can be differentially affected by phase in employment life cycle, position in organizations and so on.

In human service organizations, the interest in culture has grown (NHSTA, 1986), often spilling over from studies and insights from the work carried out in large corporations (Hage and Dewar, 1973; Kimberly and Evanisko, 1981). In Chapter 2, we speculate about how far an appreciation of cultural issues has developed within the NHS and whether cultural change has been effected, if only precariously, through recent top-down managerial initiatives (Griffiths management, performance reviews, etc.). However, much of the existing literature on NHS culture is descriptive and takes a macro-level perspective. To date, most studies have focused on characterizing the organization as a whole, showing it to be a multi-professional, bureaucratic organization where administrative and clinical paradigms coexist and where, traditionally, medical elites have dominated (Paine, 1978; Stewart et al., 1980; Thunhurst, 1982; Stewart and Smith, 1986; Thompson, 1987). There have been useful accounts of how decisions and policies are processed (Schultz and Harrison, 1983; Haywood and Ranade, 1985; Hunter, 1986) which often depict the bureaucratic origins of managerial inertia (Pettigrew et al., 1988).

The general picture that emerges is of an organization governed by 'a large number of "street level bureaucrats" and by a shadow professional organization located within bureaucratic structures' (Pettigrew et al., 1988, p. 308). Increasingly, there is an image of a segmented organization, where deep-seated tensions exist between managers and clinicians; between groups of professionals/clinicians; between the centre and the periphery and across service sectors (Haywood, 1974; Barnard et al., 1979; Haywood and Alasweski, 1980; Hunter, 1980; Klein, 1983; Korman and Glennerster, 1985). Hardy et al. (1990) use the term 'professionalized policy network', administering medical priorities, to sum up the organizational character of the NHS.

Much is also known at a general level about the medicalization process itself. Sociologists have developed a sophisticated and coherent view of how medical knowledge has gained ascendancy and there is now an extensive literature on the way doctors influence the construction of knowledge and the organizational process (Freidson, 1970a, b; McLachlin and McKeown, 1971; Illich, 1976; Navarro, 1976). Specific case studies exist which illuminate the medicalization process even further, for example, Ann Oakley's work (1980) on childbirth and Foucault's work on mental illness (1967).

Although research on the NHS has avoided presenting a unified, harmonious, monolithic image of organizational culture and indeed a conflict

perspective has emerged, local 'micro' cultures have still been largely
neglected (despite a few notable exceptions: Korman and Glennerster,
1985; Pollitt et al., 1988; Tomlinson, 1988; Hardy et al., 1990). Still
relatively little is known as to why one Health District has a particular
character and behaves in a particular way when compared with a neighbour. The texture and shape of local or federal contexts, aspects of local
culture and its influence on outcomes has scarcely been reviewed. The
connection between culture and action and culture and change processes
is still poorly understood.

This chapter provides an opportunity to describe and dissect some
micro-cultural features, taking a District Health Authority as the unit of
analysis and not the NHS as a whole. The mental handicap service change
reveals a lot about the importance of language, values, symbols, rituals,
leadership and organizational style and image. The data will reflect on
questions such as what part did working styles and relationships play in
the change process; how did organizational values influence behaviour;
what sort of leadership emerged; how important was it that people took
risks; what was the general orientation to organizational change; and how
were innovations communicated? In short, the District's 'chemistry' and
'ways of doing things' will be revealed as a part, if not simple, explanation for outcome.

Inter-organizational Linkages

Increasingly, it has become clear that the NHS is only one organization
involved in trying to effect service changes for groups such as the mentally
ill and mentally handicapped (see Chapter 6). There is a need, as was
shown in Chapter 6, to appreciate not just internal barriers to or
facilitators of change but also to look outside the single organization to
its organizational cohort. Implementation studies have been especially
useful for revealing the structural impediments to inter-organization
cooperation and progress (Benson, 1982; Glennerster et al., 1983; Audit
Commission 1986, 1989; Hunter and Wistow, 1987a, b; Hardy et al.,
1990). Usually it becomes apparent that organizations in a 'policy
community' (Rhodes, 1981, 1986; Hardy et al., 1990) show differences in
historical evolution of services, power and information bases; financial
and resource bases, accountabilities in models of care and in human
resource practices (Wertheimer, 1986).

Wistow (1989, quoted in Hardy et al., 1990) suggests that mental
handicap services and policies have from the outset been dominated by a
medical (and nursing), professionalized network and that moving services
to a community care perspective seriously challenges the hegemony of this
professionalized network (Hardy et al., 1990). In the view of Hardy et al.,
this in part can account for the slow progress towards community care
objectives. They also, through detailed analyses of two RHAs, show how
the national/Regional interface affects outcome and their study is

especially valuable for showing how different interpretations of policy and implementation mechanisms emerge. Their conclusions suggest that the NHS took the lead in mental handicap service change and SSDs followed; that RHAs led DHAs by controlling resources; *but*, most importantly, 'local–local interactions' predominated. They state that: 'the form, direction and speed of change was, to a substantial degree, locally initiated and locally directed' (1990, p. 159).

In this chapter we are able to shed further light on the complex local networks involved in changing mental handicap services and inter-organizational patterns. We will question how communications across organizations were conducted; examine the notion of organizational 'lead' and review how deliberately inter-organizational ties were developed and managed.

Resource Context

The influence of resources on the management of change and on change results has been found to be equivocal. Pettigrew (1985a) has shown how financial stress can flush out new behaviours and jolt an organization into action, leading to rapid and productive change processes. Kanter (1985) emphasizes that the resource environment alone will not determine whether an organization is susceptible to change and she cites instances of change and innovation occurring in both 'resource-rich' and 'resource-lean' times (Kanter, 1985, p. 21). She comments that the domain for innovation simply shifts in differing resource circumstances. In Stocking's analysis of innovation in the NHS, she also remarked on the low role of finance in stimulating novel projects and schemes (Stocking, 1985). The concept of financial growth was one variable associated with innovation in the study of American human service organizations and in the analysis of British local government reorganizations (see Hage and Dewar, 1973; Greenwood et al., 1980). Davies and Ferlie (1982, 1984), using a contingency theoretic approach, also reported in their study of community care provision for the elderly that the financial climate exacted (along with other factors) important effects. They claim that growth-based innovation varied markedly from distress-based innovation.

More recently, critics of contingency theory have pointed out that while the 'objective' resource climate may be important, it is also important to understand how the financial resource climate is perceived and managed (Pettigrew et al., 1988). Organizational leaders can creatively use 'financial crises' to orchestrate change or can indeed develop a concern with predicted financial stress (Pettigrew, 1985a). The message is that financial or resource environments can be skilfully managed to promote change and financial distress does not simply equal organizational decline (see Chapter 5 on HIV/AIDS and crisis management).

In Hardy et al.'s (1990) analysis of the mental handicap sector and the slow implementation of community care policies, they point to the close interrelationship between resourcing acute sector policies and those of priority groups. The greediness of the acute sector and its heavy resource demands are directly blamed for the slow progress in achieving community care objectives. Ambiguity about availability of resources, competing demands on resources and poor financial incentives for social services to develop community care projects are all felt to be crucial.

The present study will enable us to explore the impact of the resource climate in specific contexts. Questions will be asked about levels of resource – comfort/discomfort, the efficacy of particular financial strategies in promoting change and the structure and role of reward and incentive schemes in facilitating policy implementation.

Huddersfield District: a Pragmatic Approach

Huddersfield District Health Authority is part of Yorkshire Regional Health Authority, and formerly part of Kirklees Area Health Authority, together with Dewsbury. The historic links remain important at an operational level, especially since the local authority boundaries encompass both DHAs. Huddersfield DHA has a population of 210,919 (based on OPCS projections for 1988), of whom approximately 70 per cent live in the town or its suburbs.

The area was a major industrial centre (textiles, chemicals and heavy engineering industries). Decline has occurred in the past 20 years and the industrial base has become more diversified. Unemployment has also risen in recent years and greatly exceeded the national average in some wards (in one ward reaching 50 per cent as against 12 per cent in 1983). The impression of the District is one of contrasts: spacious, owner-occupier stone houses set in rolling countryside alongside decaying, privately rented, town centre terraces with poor amenities; prosperity alongside poverty.

The DHA is a major employer, with approximately 3,650 whole time equivalent (wte) staff and a revenue allocation (based on the 1987–8 figures) of £44m. There are three main units of management – acute, non-acute and community/mental health – each with discrete management boards and a Unit General Manager. Since the early 1980s, Huddersfield DHA has been engaged in a substantial amount of organizational change. In the field of mental handicap services, the District was singled out at an early stage of the research as a site of high activity and progress, especially in strategy formulation and community developments. Historically residential mental handicap services had been provided at the Mansion Hospital, located in the grounds of Storthes Hall, a large Victorian mental illness hospital, and at Fieldhead Hospital in the neighbouring health District of Wakefield. Other specialized units were located at Huddersfield's Princess Royal Hospital site. The District provided an opportunity to study simultaneously the run-down of a small-scale mental handicap institution (the Mansion – 44 beds) and the development of community-based provision for mentally handicapped people.

Changes in the mental handicap services formed only part of a wider portfolio: management had to ration their energies across large-order changes in other sectors: the closure of Storthes Hall Hospital (within 6–8 years) was a dominant and complex change, with the concomitant establishment of a comprehensive community-based psychiatric service; in the acute unit, there was centralization of maternity services at the Huddersfield Royal Infirmary site, among rationalization of other acute services; the HRI was one of six pilot sites nationally for the development of the Resource Management Initiative, a major preoccupation for staff during the research period for this book. Managers were also attending to the relocation of the Community Unit along with the Mental Handicap Resource Unit on the Princess Royal site. There were explicit concerns to improve some levels of the District's performance.

Early Period of Inertia and Concern, 1976–1982

The first steps towards translating national guidelines for shifting services from an institutional basis to a community basis in Huddersfield can be traced back to the mid 1970s. In 1975–6 a joint venture using joint finance between the Social Services Department and the AHA was undertaken, to form a Special Care Unit (Lindley Special Care Unit), to provide day care for severely mentally handicapped people living at home. This venture was a success, was still running at the time of this study in 1989, and was the first demonstration that cooperation and collaboration between the agencies could work.

In 1976, further demonstration of concern was apparent in the inpatient census of mentally handicapped people at the Fieldhead Hospital, an attempt to define the long-term needs of Kirklees. The Area Administrator of Kirklees AHA, along with the Social Services Committee of the Kirklees Metropolitan Borough Council, invited the National Development Team to help assess the best way to provide a comprehensive service to the mentally handicapped and particularly those in residential care. The AHA also began to petition Yorkshire RHA for the appointment of a consultant in mental handicap.

Although the service at this time can be characterized as mainly institutionally based, this period reflects the growth of awareness of the need for change, with the AHA both responding to national directives and stimulating local investigations to provide the background to change. The NDT's 1977 report identified the need to reduce reliance on Fieldhead Hospital as local community provision increased, and recommended the extension of joint finance to assist this process. Recommendations also included suggestions about discharges from Fieldhead to the Mansion, and Mansion to the community, and for a Community Unit. Shortfalls in adult training places and a general under-provision of services for mentally handicapped people were also identified.

The NDT report prompted some response and action by the District, in

'Development of Services for the Mentally Handicapped: Report of the District Development Planning Team' in 1978. It identified policy issues which required resolution, but the main focus was on beds. There was very little discussion of rehabilitation, Care in the Community schemes or the role of the Community Units or Teams.

Importantly, a joint planning forum for mental handicap was developed at local level during 1978: again an early indicator of the increasing priority. Until 1978 community services, including outpatient services for Kirklees, had been provided by Wakefield (from Fieldhead Hospital); but from 1979 a local community nursing service was initiated, sowing the seeds for the development of a Community Mental Handicap Team.

Region was also showing a growing commitment to improving services in mental handicap. The Yorkshire RHA Regional Strategic Plan 1977–88 (published in May 1978) endorsed commitment to CITC. Areas were instructed to prepare their individual plans for local CITC services. The RHA Strategic Plan 1979–88 contained further emphasis on preventing the admission of children with mental handicap to hospital settings, commitment to community residential units and a shifting of responsibilities for adult services to the local authorities. Again, Areas were asked to prepare joint plans with LAs for community-orientated services.

The pace of change at this development stage was generally perceived to be fairly slow: and this was picked up by the follow-up visit by the NDT in 1981. They were concerned that more had not happened since their last visit. In a fairly critical report, they again highlighted shortfalls in local provision, little local innovation and that service was largely remote from local users. Action had usually been in response to immediate needs and crises, results were a piece-meal mix of short-term with a few longer-term solutions. Overall, there was very little sense of strategic direction or of visionary thinking. Services continued to be in the main fragmented and poorly planned and coordinated, especially across agencies. The lead for change was diffuse, although largely professionally and policy-based. There was no evidence of any strong management lead or inspiration.

The greatest omission of all in the eyes of the NDT was the failure of local managers to produce meaningful plans to ensure the specific commitment of resources to the development of services. They commented that in their five years of operation, Kirklees had devoted the lowest proportion of its joint finances to services for the mentally handicapped of any authority yet visited. A shift in priorities was felt to be crucial.

The NDT wanted to see immediate progress in: planning; establishment of community teams (three) and units (three); phasing out of the Mansion; appointment of specialist staff; extension of support services (for example psychology); and shifting of agency responsibility from the health authority to the local authority for the more able residents.

The response of the local AHA was subsumed in the larger-order change about to overtake the service. In 1982 Huddersfield DHA was created, and it is difficult to disentangle how much of the next part of the chronology was shaped by the groundwork of the NDT and how much by the new local circumstances and players. Certainly, 1982 does seem to provide a significant 'crunch-point' in the evolution of change, heralding a period of energetic planning, priority-setting and reformulation of the problem.

Towards a Strategy, 1982–1984

A number of key elements and events can be identified as significant during this period.

A Web of Pressure Devolution to a more localized management was seen to have released a greater sense of control and autonomy over local plans and priorities, nowhere better exemplified than in the design and progress of all mental handicap services. The period from 1982 shows an impressive array of activity: the firming up of concrete service plans (based on a September 1982 discussion document 'Services for the Mentally Handicapped'); the creation of a task-orientated planning forum (Mental Handicap Planning Team); the establishment of a Mental Handicap Resource Unit; and a concerted drive to get a local consultant (mental handicap) appointed.

The impetus came not just from within the newly constituted Huddersfield DHA, but was also generated by the 1982 Ministerial Review, anxious that Regions and Districts should demonstrate a commitment to CITC. Yorkshire RHA were directed to complete a review of their mental handicap services and prepare a Regional plan by the end of 1983. This subtle interplay of top-down national and bottom-up local influences was central to the plot of this change process. The NDT, the new local managers and professionals, the Yorkshire RHA, the Minister and the DHSS formed a complex web of forces all converging on the problem.

In addition, many respondents reported that by the early 1980s, users of mental handicap services and their families had stepped up the pressure for increased resources and improvements to existing facilities. The inertia of the 1970s was being challenged from within and without, and 'there was a groundswell of opinion', especially critical of the impoverishment of community services:

> My perception . . . was that [in early 1980s] most parents were very happy with the hospital arrangements and were very happy to see the provision of institutions continue, but things like day-care, respite care in particular, care assistants, all these were areas where there were a lot of deficiencies and felt there needed to be corrective action. (District officer)

Pressure from service users built up quickly. Local groups of the voluntary organization Mencap were active and assertive. The DHA provided a conduit for this pressure in its arrangements for service planning through Development Groups:

> Now when we first began, one of the things that was initiated, with encouragement from the Chairman, was to start meeting with Mencap with the planning team. That hadn't happened at all, so we opened up a forum to talk about developments and changes and to talk about deficiencies. (District officer)

With this culture of opportunism, bypassing the formal machinery and managing top-down directives with bottom-up concerns, the District achieved some early and concrete results which paved the way for acceptance of change later and provided a model:

> The breakthrough was to set up one or two Community Units, Lindley Cottage was the first, Queensway, The Gables . . . those were absolutely critical to achieving users of the service and relatives and parents, but also from our own staff, to see something on the ground, outside a hospital, was a new experience. Having a working example to take people to, and say, 'That's our community care work' was marvellous. (District officer)

Driving Change – New Energy   In 1983 the newly appointed consultant in mental handicap wrote the bid for a six-bed, domestic style children's unit, catching the spirit of Region's aspirations as well as those of users, and securing three years of funding which allowed property purchase in 1984 and opening in 1985. Respondents locate the appointment of a consultant, with a very positive community orientation – and that of the new Director of Social Services at Kirklees – as key elements in moving rapidly forward to turn the perceived problems into realized solutions. In 1983 there were moves to establish a 'half-way house' for women patients awaiting transfer to local authority care arrangements from their beds in the Mansion. Plans were initiated during this period in response to national directives, and utilizing nationally allocated monies, to promote the more rapid transfer of mentally handicapped children out of hospital.

Regional Strategy   In June 1984 fresh impetus came from the Yorkshire RHA Outline Regional Strategy. This raised explicitly the commitment to closure of large psychiatric and mental handicap hospitals; it earmarked £7.4m for joint finance CITC schemes, over the decade to 1993–4; it provided for £1m capital to be reserved by Region throughout the strategy period to enable mental handicap developments; it again exhorted Districts to push towards community-orientated service. District have available to it a resource base which could be applied to the solutions emerging from its planning processes.

These early planning steps provide some interesting insights about the career of service change. There was no immediate, rigid masterplan for future services. Instead between 1982 and 1984 many different plans rose and fell, objectives were debated deeply alongside efforts to make real progress. There was blend of action and reflection. Within a firm commitment to making mental handicap services a priority this provided a more general framework for action rather than a narrow prescription. Commitment to developing mental handicap services was not just symbolically important but also created opportunities for officers and professionals to think creatively about the problem. The 'will' to change was thus embedded in the higher tiers of the organization and then matched by devising a realizable financial strategy, that is, 'the wherewithal' was made available.

Backstage There were also more subtle and backstage change activities – 'building a climate for change'. In the local context it involved finding new ways of incorporating the views and experiences of service users and providers in the service design and plans; strengthening the clinical and professional commitment to the new direction; learning and researching about alternative service models from elsewhere; fact-finding about the extent of needs; and liaising with other concerned bodies, both statutory and voluntary. In short, the period was largely one of experimentation, consultation, education and legitimation, with key words such as 'opportunism', 'flexibility' and 'results' being used to describe the process.

Towards Implementation, 1984–1988

As we have already seen, Huddersfield DHA did not approach changing its mental handicap services by following a blueprint. Instead, some services were set in train prior to the emergence of a formal strategy and much preparatory work had been undertaken on the ground by a core of key staff, working sometimes in an ad hoc and entrepreneurial and opportunistic way. This approach was consistent with the managerial climate being fostered in the District at the time. Indeed a formal strategy only evolved in 1985 after much real progress had been achieved, in some ways consolidating the past as well as pointing the way forward.

Crucial Steps to Implementation Two key events in 1984–5 were the appointment of an Assistant Director of Social Services with special expertise in services for mentally handicapped people, and the establishment in October 1984 of a country-wide joint focus for the planning of community care – the Kirklees Partnership for Community Care – including health authorities, local authority and voluntary sector representatives. It was agreed that 'any services to be provided on a community care basis must be as good as the services they are currently receiving'.

A number of other significant steps were taken in 1984–6 which indicated that the earlier period of seeming immobilism was coming to an end: the local authority offered two houses to Mencap for use as community residential units which was seen as a vehicle for enhanced local authority/voluntary sector links; and SSD moved five patients out of a house in Storthes Hall to a residential community unit.

Real progress was marked in 1985 and 1986 by resettlements from hospital, with the opening of a Community Unit at 'The Gables', agreement for the local authority to take back 70 patients from Fieldhead and 27 from the Mansion and plans for the opening of Queensway residential home and further local authority community accommodation. Preparatory work had also begun in the development of a Mental Handicap Register to allow for better targeting of community services. The volume of voluntary sector activity also accelerated with new plans for the provision of residential homes and day care facilities. The base and the scope of the voluntary effort was broadening and deepening with Housing Associations getting involved in the process.

Embeddedness in Formal Strategy   Alongside the above, commitment to mental handicap change became part of the 'written strategic agenda'. In 1985 a five-year (1985–90) Strategy for Services for the Mentally Handicapped was prepared by the Planning Team. The spirit of the document was further reinforced through the draft Yorkshire RHA Strategic Plan 1985–94 (although never formally approved by the DHSS). Importantly, this document continued the commitment to community-based services, hospital closure and reductions. Top-level attention was further ensured through the initiation of a Regional option appraisal exercise set up to examine services for the severely mentally handicapped, behaviourally disturbed and physically disabled. The local ten-year strategy – Huddersfield DHA Strategic Plan 1985–94 – crystallized and reflected the District's aspirations. In this document the commitment to changing mental handicap services is once more underwritten and translated into firm plans for community residential units and the creation of a community-based service within the strategy period. All these formal documents signalled a coherent message and intention if only at a general level.

However, the strategic direction remained constant at both District and Unit level ensured by minimal changes to key personnel. In April 1986 the DHA faced the introduction of Griffiths general management. The new Unit structure with a UGM was not judged to have provoked a radical effect on the way the mental handicap services was being devised or delivered. Thus the approach to the issue also remained consistent and the key planning forums retained more or less the same membership, persisting with their original objectives.

Differential Responses   Some unresolved issues surfaced in 1986 with joint training of health and social services staff being initiated; shortage of short-term care being accentuated; and the needs of the severely mentally handicapped after discharge from Fieldhead and Storthes Hall being debated. The shortfall in short-term care was being addressed by the local authority but the DHA also located a bungalow which was subsequently purchased for this purpose (see Thomas, 1988).

A period of active planning for specialist needs in mental handicap services followed. Plans were submitted to the RHA for approval of a ten-bed unit for severely handicapped and emergency situations and for a 28-bed cluster unit for people with multiple handicaps, but were not approved at Region until 1988. This interface between District and Region shows up the complexity of planning and implementation in the service and reveals that blocks may occur at various tiers of the organization. In this instance, the Region expressed reservations about the model of care being proposed by the District and indeed, there was a difference of opinion even within the local ranks about the merits of the 28-bed unit. This equivocacy about the ideal design of services may again explain why some health service change is more incremental than radical. Professional opinion can be divided and in a knowledge-based change, these differences may be a serious impediment to speedy implementation (Hardy et al., 1990).

Towards the end of 1986 it was also reported that some impatience was being felt in the DHA because progress on actual patient transfers had been slow. The local authority only began to fulfil its commitments in 1987 with community placements coming on stream in February and with Housing Associations and Mencap developing concrete proposals with the release of joint finance. Generally, DHA respondents felt that the local authority were the laggards and themselves the change champions. One DHA manager comments:

> Some of the reasons we started being proactive . . . was because of the lack of activity on this by the local authority, particularly the Social Services Department. Had they been prepared to move along at the same pace at that time perhaps we wouldn't have developed all the residential developments that we have done.

Some of the variables which were reported as affecting the pattern and speed of changes across the agencies included: the availability of finance and accommodation; local reactions to community houses; bureaucratic procedures in acquiring and upgrading facilities; assessing and preparing residents for transfer; differences in agency priorities, decision making mechanisms, structures and competencies.

Sustained Momentum A number of key additive events in the change cycle were seen in 1987. At Regional level the thrust for improving priority services was maintained in the Yorkshire RHA Strategic Plan 1985/6–1992/4 (June 1987) further supporting a community-based service, it showed an increase of £9m (29 per cent) over the 1985/6 expenditure level during the planning period. At local level, the fruits of previous energetic joint working and planning materialized in a substantive document endorsed by all the key organizations. 'Services for People with a Mental Handicap: a Framework for Action', published by the Kirklees Partnership for Community Care in 1987 was welcomed both as real and symbolic evidence of the progress that had been made in inter-organizational collaboration over the planning period.

Again, the District could be seen to be delivering on its strategy and intentions were being translated into reality. The District's sense of pride in its achievements and the extent of the expansion in its services for mental handicap people was reflected in Huddersfield DHA's document 'Comprehensive Community Based Services for People with Mental Handicaps – "Huddersfield Model"' in 1988. In the foreword the consultant psychiatrist for mental handicap commented:

> Since 1985 the Huddersfield district *has made vast advances in developing community services for people with mental handicaps*. During 1985 there were 144 old long stay mentally handicapped patients residing in hospitals, including Fieldhead Hospital, Storthes Hall Hospital and the Mansion Hospital. Over the past 3 years *83 patients (57 per cent) have been discharged to community care residences in Huddersfield District*. Plans have now been made to discharge the remaining 61 patients to new community units over the next 2 years.

Interestingly, in the Chairman's introductory message in the same document he also congratulates the District on its progress but notes that there is still more to be done: 'I hope you will agree that the list of services is expanding, and that although we must never be complacent and fully satisfied there is a general improvement in provision.'

During 1988, the impression given within the District was of the strategy rolling forward more or less unproblematically but flexibly. The key remaining concerns were about realizing the plans for the unit for the behaviourally disturbed mentally handicapped; the residential unit for the severely, multiply handicapped; extra day care; relocation of the Mansion and Fieldhead patients; and the expansion of further residential houses across the District. Some anxiety was expressed about keeping to timescales and a fear was raised in the local authority about diminishing resources for services for the mentally handicapped. In this context, the growing empowerment of the voluntary agencies was seen as crucial and every encouragement was given to new voluntary ventures by the statutory bodies.

One area of concern was that of the role and functioning of the Mental Handicap Resource Unit. Initiated in 1982 following the creation of the DHA, it was part of an early response to perceived deficiencies in the service and an example of proactivity and a desire to get services quickly in place, part of the ethos of the new DHA. In 1988, it was considered timely to review the Resource Unit and a panel of members was set up for this purpose. At the time of the research, the results of this review had caused some division within the District. The controversy seemed to hinge around perceptions of how the review had been instigated and managed, as well as its conclusions. The role of community nursing, the management of the Resource Unit and its composition and purpose were all under examination.

This is an interesting point at which to end the chronology. It heralds a new phase in the change cycle, revealing how earlier solutions to a problem become subject to monitoring, review and perhaps renewal or transformation. This aspect of change is often hidden and difficult to describe. It is easier to describe successes and to assume that they are permanent or consider change outcomes as immutable. However, many schemes fall by the wayside or are modified in process as circumstances, needs or ideas change. What was happening to the MH Resource Unit, although unwelcome to some, may simply be a reflection of this dynamic.

Both Strategy and Action The four years from 1984 to 1988 can be characterized as a time of both assertive strategy formation and implementation in changing mental handicap services. There was evidence of real progress at an operational level with transfers of patients from institutional settings to the community; with the widening of responsibilities for care from the health authority to the local authority, private and voluntary sectors. Simultaneously, there was significant progress in the development of achievable and financially grounded plans and policies and the consolidation of joint mechanisms and structures to facilitate objectives.

Constructive joint working relationships and understandings had to be actively fostered and were not automatically guaranteed. At the earlier stages there was some suspicion and hostility between some of the key actors but by 1988 these relationships had improved. More positive relations had been built gradually, through small pragmatic steps and attention to trust-building among a small caucus of managers and professionals. Formalization of the relationships through planning structures and plans was of secondary rather than primary importance. New issues of staff preparation for the new service were firmly grasped and training policies and programmes developed. Equally, short-falls in existing provision were identified and plans initiated accordingly.

There was action on multiple fronts and levels, professional, managerial, operational and strategic. There was also both inter- and intra-organizational networking to communicate and secure a commitment to the general strategy across the tiers and various agencies. The articulation of the strategy in a formal document came relatively late in the day. Long after its sponsors had been won, there had been 'hard results' and a 'critical mass' of enthusiasts had been scripted into the mission. One respondent described the methodology of change as 'creating change at the margin rather than Big Bang' and expressed the notion of change becoming 'infectious' so that the threat was reduced. Pacing the change and sequencing it appropriately was felt to be of central importance to a number of informants and they described a necessary period of conservatism followed by experimentation and trial which would inform the final strategy: 'we needed to get some action before we knew where we were going'.

Mid Downs: Retaining a Sense of Priority

Located in the County of West Sussex and in South West Thames RHA, Mid Downs DHA is an expanding District based on a collection of towns (Crawley, Horsham, Burgess Hill, Hayward's Heath and East Grinstead) and a large rural area. Crawley has been growing rapidly as one of the New Towns of the 1960s designed to facilitate migration from London, and is now buoyant economically, given its proximity to Gatwick Airport. There is in Crawley, as in other New Towns, a legacy of social planning which helps liaison with the NHS. The locality is on the whole prosperous with development land at a premium (this makes estate rationalization an attractive proposition for the DHA). The District was a financial gainer, under the RAWP formula.

When the old West Sussex AHA was abolished in 1982, Mid Downs DHA succeeded the old Cuckfield and Crawley DHA. Four units of management were identified, including mental handicap (256 beds at Forest Hospital in Horsham and 24 beds at Goddard's Green Hospital). The current Chairman and DGM (originally the DA) have both built up long experience in the District, so there has been important continuity of leadership.

As well as rapidly developing acute sector hospitals, the Forest Hospital for mentally handicapped people had traditionally provided a country-wide service, together with a major psychiatric hospital (St Francis), which had historically taken many of its patients from Brighton DHA (in the South East Thames Region). In priority group services, therefore, Mid Downs was very much a 'giving' rather than a 'receiving' district.

The Mid Downs District's Strategic Plan in 1985 centred on service rather than managerial and organizational process objectives, identifying the following care groups: acute, elderly, mentally ill and mentally handicapped. Services for mental handicap were expected to experience major change during the strategic period. The key was an explicit commitment:

> to close the Forest Hospital by March 1990 and to make satisfactory alternative provision for existing residents in small community-based health units in Mid Downs, Worthing and Chichester Districts, or in Social Services, or voluntary sector accommodation, as appropriate, in the residents' best interests.

Emphasis was also placed on building up other elements of a comprehensive community service such as an expansion of Community Mental Handicap Teams.

The Forest was a Victorian medium-sized old-fashioned mental handicap hospital serving the whole of West Sussex. With 256 beds it was smaller than many mental handicap hospitals. It was in a village-like urban setting, a locality sometimes seen as being more 'caring' than the new facilities in other areas. The hospital could generate fierce loyalty (such as the Friends of Forest) as well as criticism from relatives who lived further afield. Earlier schemes for modernization had not come to fruition, and the opportunity for more radical change was now to present itself.

In the 1970s Chichester and Worthing were beginning to develop their own facilities. Some professionally led innovation was beginning to emerge, such as the creation of a Community Mental Handicap Team working from the Forest. Nevertheless, the Forest entered the 1980s with dilapidated workhouse and hutted accommodation, and only creeping improvements to the quality of service. There was only one CMHT at the Forest, covering the District for creation of new resources. The pattern of medical staffing was also unbalanced as all three of the consultants in the county were based at the Forest, despite a need to spread the service across the county.

External Pressure for Strategic Change

An abrasive 1982 National Development Team Report provided an early external stimulus for change, which was also seized upon internally. 'The overriding impression of services for the mentally handicapped in West Sussex was lack of development of locally based services, in spite of the opportunities afforded by some new buildings.' Area's development plan was criticized for only including £10,000 for mental handicap, with the largest scheme being a central 'wash up' at the Forest. Joint finance remained small scale. Nor were agency priorities aligned, with the SSD seen by the NDT as giving higher priority to the elderly and children than to mental handicap services. The NDT recommended a more community-orientated service strategy; collaborative machinery should be slimmed down and made more effective, using joint finance to level up provision.

Nationally, the environment was increasingly benign, with the DHSS (1981b) considering ways and means of accelerating the move to community care, with financial support. DHSS also announced a special scheme to get children out of mental handicap hospitals. By 1983 Region was beginning to use the new review process to press for more rapid developments within the Districts.

The Members' Working Party, 1982–1983

It is noteworthy that the new Mid Downs District went on to develop its own strategy rather than follow the NDT's normative advice on all aspects of service. The Chairman and other key members of the new Mid Downs DHA were keen to promote change in mental handicap services. The NDT Report was used as good ammunition, but the early drive for change came from members. Even before the new authority had been formed, local voluntary organizations had been putting forward arguments for the more radical development of community care. Three member working groups were set up to consider key issues (mental handicap, mental illness and estates), and it was the mental handicap group that was able to generate most momentum. It is important to note the use of time-limited working groups rather than standing committees. Even in 1982 the first steps were being taken to implement some of the NDT recommendations, with DHA agreement to the sale of land at the Forest, 'ring-fenced' for use in the first of the new community units.

The Report of the Members' Working Party (April 1983) represented a radically internally generated strategy with a firm and public date for closure of the Forest (March 1990). One respondent commented that the members had wanted an even more ambitious five-year closure programme, the officers wanted ten years, and seven years was a compromise. But closure was only one part of a much broader package and a number of policy objectives were identified:

● The development of a District-based service with minimal cross-boundary flows.
● The development of a community-based model of care.
● Greater reliance on local residential care by the Health Authorities rather than by other sectors.
● Better provision for education and training, both of patients and of staff.
● Attention to family support, including short-term care.
● The provision of specialized health care facilities needed by some mentally handicapped people.
● Appropriate early detection and health education.

The initial strategy essentially reshuffled the pack between public sector agencies. Little was said about the service provider role of voluntary organizations (although Mencap was built into joint planning machinery, the core of the negotiation process was within Health and between Health and Social Services), client advocacy, changing professional roles or the extent to which 'normalization' was or was not accepted as a care model. The strategy needed to be fleshed out further, but the gaining of inter-organizational cooperation was clearly critical even at this early stage. A major task was to start negotiating with Social Services. Effective joint planning also needed to be energized with Chichester (33 mentally handicapped patients of Chichester origin were in Mid Downs's care) and Worthing (62 patients), where the current District Plan was seen as discouraging.

The Members' Working Party Report considered a number of service issues from the 1982 NDT Report. It recommended 'smaller units in a community setting'. At the end of 1982, an officer group agreed that top priority should be given to building a 24-place unit for adults in Crawley (three eight-place bungalows). Capital would come from the sale of surplus land at Forest, but the source of revenue funding remained unclear. There could be some scope for redeploying the revenue from the Forest site, although other sections of the report seemed to anticipate a financial initiative from higher tiers.

The NDT Report had also recommended 88 'Special Hospital Provision' beds in Mid Downs, but there was dissension in the District about how best to proceed. Some staff favoured the retention of the Forest, others the provision of specialized community health units. A third view was that small numbers of those requiring specialist care should be accommodated in each of the community health units. The interim conclusion was as follows: 'The Working Party feel that thought should be given to the provision of one or more smaller specialized community health units, rather than to a large single central unit. However, this will need a good deal more research and discussion'. Nevertheless, the crux of the matter was a public commitment to closure:

> The long-term plan must be to close Forest Hospital and sell the entire site. Whatever the ultimate decision concerning a specialist centre (or centres), the use of the Forest for mental handicap should cease. The site has the disadvantage of being associated with institutional mental handicap care and even a smaller unit replacing the hospital would tend to inherit this reputation.

March 1990 was mentioned as the target date for closure, but this was to be influenced by factors outside the District's direct control: the ability of Chichester and Worthing to take back patients; capital and revenue availability for the new units; the extent of SSD provision for the less handicapped; regional bridging and the acquisition of sites. The closure was also seen as dependent on such 'process' issues as provision of retraining for nursing staff, and a public relations campaign to ensure that the exercise was seen as a 'devolution' rather than a 'closure'.

Consultation on the Members' Working Party Report,
1983–1984

The comments returned during consultation give evidence of the political complexity of the Forest exercise. The report was broadly welcomed by such key organizations as the DHSS, the Regional Health Authority, West Sussex County Council and Chichester and Worthing DHAs (although Worthing stressed the need for a joint group which should undertake more work before a firm date could be attached to the Forest closure). The voluntary sector was divided. Closure was opposed by the Friends of Forest and by the Horsham branch of Mencap as 'asset stripping', but supported by the county branch of Mencap. The Friends of Forest opposed closure but supported rebuilding Forest as a 'residential village' and they were backed by 424 signed, standard letters, all opposing the sale of Forest 'because of its enormous potential as a central specialist services complex, rebuilt in the community style, for the mentally handicapped'.

The professions took different and sometimes parochial lines without at this stage a professional 'champion of change'. Nursing was lobbying to ensure that nurse 'ownership' of the community units was retained. As far as the Mental Handicap Unit Management Team was concerned:

The medical member of the team would not commit himself or his colleagues to the policy changes, but agreed, as a basic proviso to any change, that Community Health Units should be directly controlled by the health authority and staffed by professionally trained nurses with appropriate medical and other professional input.

The move from hospital to social care was opposed by the consultant psychiatrists ('all the advances in prevention and treatment have been medical'), whereas the clinical psychologists argued the opposite: 'mental handicap itself does not require medical treatment'. The three consultants then at the Forest also had important reservations. They doubted whether the SSD could cope with mentally handicapped people who displayed problem behaviour or who went on to develop psychiatric symptoms. They stressed that the NDT had been complimentary about the standard of care at the Forest. The DHA Chair was subsequently to meet with these consultants to discuss their reservations and secure their public commitment to the community units. There was subsequently consultant succession, with all three original consultants leaving the District and a new consultant coming in who was supportive of the overall exercise and was to have a major influence in writing the District strategy.

When the DHA met to consider the outcome of consultation in August 1983, members approved the report unanimously. Closure of the Forest by March 1990 and reprovision of services on a county-wide basis was now DHA policy, and there was from the start to be emphasis on time-table setting and monitoring. So the DMT was asked to work on a nine-point action plan and to bring back a progress report by February 1984. Securing early momentum and conveying an impression that change really was going to happen were seen as important objectives.

At this early phase in the policy cycle, change had operational as well as strategic implications. DMT Minutes (21 October 1983) listed nine heads of activity 'achieved' in 1983–4. The weak point was that many were as yet small-scale or district-specific. While the Members' Working Party Report had provided a broad steer, there was no elaborated District strategy which tackled such tricky questions as transfer to other agencies or the extent to which special facilities should be retained at the Forest.

The Mid Downs Strategy Document, 1985

The complexity was reduced – and coherence increased – by entrusting the fleshing out of the strategy document to the new consultant at the Forest, who had had long experience in joint working at Area level and was also interested in policy and planning work. Endorsed by the DHA in December 1984, this was a comprehensive strategy document which thought through a number of issues broader than the Forest closure itself (such as genetic counselling and estimating the number of likely new clients) and steered many of the subsequent developments in the county. It also moved many of the NDT's targets for health care provision downwards and was incorporated more or less unchanged in the District Strategic Plan.

The document gave some indication of the number of 'profoundly handicapped' (who would remain in NHS care) and of District of origin. The scope of Mid Downs's own provision was projected to narrow to two or possibly three 24-place community units, located in different parts of the District. Three CMHTs would operate on a 'sector' basis, and respite care be developed within the community units. Provision in the other Districts and social care would expand. There was greater specification of the projected county facility, which could be retained by Mid Downs, but which required agreement from the other two Districts, now developing their own services with their own consultants.

This county unit was now seen as consisting of 12–15 places, provided on a 'joint user' basis with a high level of professional staffing. Such a proposal raised some tricky issues about model of care, access and medical cover, and the history of the Assessment and Treatment Unit, together with comparisons with another District developing a different pattern of community based services for mentally handicapped people, is considered in much greater depth in Thomas (1988).

The NDT Community Health Unit model was adopted for two (possibly three) units. It was noted in the strategy document that the devolution of services carried capital and revenue consequences and helped make the proposals self-financing. Day care was also flagged up as an issue of increasing importance. For the profoundly handicapped, day care was seen as being available on site, starting with the Bewbush Unit within the District at Crawley. But consultation with SSD needed to continue so that a fuller range of day care programmes could also be provided.

There were also personnel issues to consider. The danger was not one of staff surplus but of staff shortage. Although personnel policy was to retain all staff currently employed, devolution would also require mobility and more flexibility. The appropriate staff/resident ratio would increase as the economy of scale of a large hospital was lost. Attention needed to be paid to the retention of staff: 'failure to implement a sensitive staff redeployment policy very soon may create a situation of insufficient staff to manage the Forest Hospital before any person has been moved, and this will be avoided.'

Reassessment of Strategy, 1988

It is one thing to formulate strategy, another to ensure that it retains flexibility and undergoes periodic reassessment. There was concern, especially as new officers (such as Directors of Planning and Personnel) came into the District, that the 1985 strategy was dating. An 'away day' and a more group-based format was used to think through ideas which emerged in the 1988 Position Statement 'Further Development of Mental Handicap Strategy'. This argued that the long-term objective would be to develop ordinary group housing. So discussions were started with the local district authorities about acquiring council properties. The profile of the voluntary sector was raised as it was seen as a potential service provider (either United Response or Mencap Homes Foundation). The development of a joint day care strategy with the SSD was seen as an urgent priority, and indeed in this sector real progress towards a joint strategy was being made. A small group was set up under the Director of Personnel to review manpower strategy and consider potential recruitment problems. There was an emphasis on communication with staff and staff organizations ('staff are partners in the change process, not merely the recipients').

Increasingly ideas were being floated about developments after 1990, in particular the need to develop population-based medical services (the CMHTs had identified 600 mentally handicapped people in the District, as opposed to just over 200 beds by that time at the Forest) and health screening and promotion. The consultant-authored document 'Into the 1990s' (produced in 1988) thus suggested a more population-based perspective, based on health screening and promotion in relation to physical and psychiatric needs. Thus people with Down's syndrome have a high incidence of congenital heart disease, develop eye cataracts and are much more likely to suffer dementia in middle life.

This case study suggests that 'strategy' is an important concept in understanding the change process: many of the developments have been strategically driven rather than opportunistic or incremental. The study reveals that this strategy needed to undergo periodic reassessment; that the strategy started off broad and only subsequently became more detailed; that it made choices about alternative models of care; and that it accumulated political support from members, managers and the key clinician.

'Foreign Policy'

The 'local–local' context was highly significant and complex – both across health authorities and between Health and Social Services Departments. The nub of the inter-organizational problem was to devise a strategy that matched expectations and ensured 'binding decisions' and cooperation. This implied creating inter-agency structures and internal machinery which could deliver the strategy, foster collaboration and achieve widespread support.

Existing joint care planning machinery was unlikely to deliver the goods. It was seen as insufficiently focused or tied into power centres. Two problems therefore emerged: the first was one of structure and devising a core group; the second (more difficult) problem was one of trust building within that group, especially given the historic lack of county-level joint strategies between Health and Social Services. Such a group also had to cement political as well as officer support for the exercise.

The District was able to use the support of Region which was increasingly picking up mental handicap as an issue in its reviews as a legitimating device for the creation of a county structure. The Regional Chairman thus blessed the formation of a West Sussex Member/Officer Group, in which Mid Downs was to play the role of 'lead' agency. The County Liaison Group chaired by the Mid Downs Chair first met in November 1983. An early task was generating commitment amongst the three Chairs as well as at officer level. Mid Downs clearly supported capital and revenue transfers to Chichester and Worthing as a means of offering help to the 'receiving districts' and stressed that the Forest proceeds could be used as a county resource. However, there was evidence of some initial tensions between Chichester and Mid Downs over whether the key planning unit should be District- or County-based.

Political commitment was built up during the 1984 negotiations: 'The three DHA chairmen and chairmen of Social Services confirmed their commitment to the overall strategy as outlined, and gave agreement for their officers to proceed with the implementation of the agreed action.' The Officer Group first met in January 1984, chaired by the previous AHA Specialist in Community Medicine (Social Services), subsequently the new consultant at the Forest, and who was to play a major role in developing the Mid Downs strategy. Skills in joint working and close links with the Chairman were thus combined with a central position in the main institution in the county. The remit of the Officer Group was to engage in:

> consideration of the statement of intent, and how plans of each authority might be coordinated, so that the development of community services for the mentally handicapped would be smooth and that in the use of resources the best available capital and revenue projects be agreed.

There was a gradual change in the nature of officer negotiations towards a tighter focus. By 1986, the three DGMs and the Director of Social Services were handling much of the inter-organizational negotiations personally, representing a very small and senior group. From the Department of Health's point of view, one frustration was that such strategically important issues could be drawn away from the Social Services Department to Policy and Resources, involving another set of decision makers not involved in the original negotiations. Inter-organizational negotiations dragged on through 1985 and 1986 with an increasing emphasis on finance, centring on patient flows and devising satisfactory compensation mechanisms.

Internal Machinery

Much of the early work had been progressed outside the traditional administrative machinery but in an ad hoc way, centred on either securing political agreement through the Chairman or the process of forming strategy, where the Consultant played a major role. Both these ad hoc solutions had grown out of existing joint finance and joint working arrangements. Once a strategy for change had been agreed, the question of how it was to be operationalized assumed major importance. While the sharpening up of a general managerial focus represented one change from traditional patterns of inter-organizational negotiation, there was also the question of developing internal decision making machinery. The Mid Downs DMT had kept a watching brief on developments until the completion of the 1985 strategy, but there was now an opportunity to introduce new structures. Although there was an existing Mental Handicap UMT, and soon to be a geographically based UGM and UMT, perhaps the high profile of the mental handicap issue ensured that the focus was kept at a District as well as a Unit level. Under the Chairmanship of the DMO, a Mental Handicap Project Team was set up, with the following remit (DMT Minutes, 17 January 1985):

1 The implementation of the county-wide strategy as it affected Mid Downs.
2 The preparation of a timetable for implementation of the District strategy.
3 To ensure that the Mental Handicap UMT and other groups would be accountable to the Mental Handicap Project Team for the implementation of the various elements of strategy, including transitional arrangements at the Forest.
4 To develop the special care project.
5 To implement personnel policy, which had been identified as the first priority, including nurse training.

This group would supervise operational management, coordinating the individual project teams. An important early task was ensuring that the children from the Forest were moved out to the new development, and re-utilizing the space in the hospital. Other 'operational' issues, however, re-opened complex negotiations and proved difficult to resolve within this forum, and threatened the timetable of the devolution exercise as a whole.

While the MHPT spent much time on progressing the special care proposal at 'operational' level, this was dependent both on the outcome of attempts to develop a Regional strategy for mentally handicapped people with special needs, and gaining consent from Worthing and Chichester to the proposed operational policy for the ATU. The consultants from the three Districts met in order to come to a greater consensus about admission procedures, given that proposals for a quota system could conflict with the flexibility needed for crisis intervention. Negotiations with the planning function at Region over the ATU also dragged on, owing to reservations about the principles behind the scheme, about Regional cost allowances, as well as the Regional policy vacuum on special needs, and had still not been resolved during the period of fieldwork for this study.

By late 1987, at least certain members of the group had reservations about its effectiveness: it had completed many of its tasks; it was sometimes too deeply involved in detail; and some perceived a degree of internal conflict. It was therefore replaced by a new Mental Handicap Coordinating Group. A more senior group – still chaired by the DMO – was formed with individuals having a more specified role: the DGM was on the group, undertaking liaison with other authorities and monitoring the overall timetable, through chairmanship of the West Sussex DGMs/Director of Social Services Group; the Finance Director was to take the financial overview; the Planning Director was to look at capital developments and liaison with Region; the UGM (West) was given responsibility for commissioning and decommissioning; the consultant was to advise on clinical aspects; the DMO to examine day care strategy; and the DNA to advise on care standards, nurse training and liaison with personnel. The Chairman also attended from time to time. Its remit was as follows:

1 To coordinate all aspects of the mental handicap programme, including the work of dedicated project groups on day care and the ATU.
2 To identify the remaining major issues and to develop plans for their resolution including: (a) the additional hospital facilities at the Dene, (b) any additional residential care requirements, (c) the future management arrangements for the mental handicap service.
3 To consider the development of the service after 1990.
4 To report to the DPG/DHA every six months.

The meeting of this group observed during fieldwork indicated a high degree of common purpose and lively concern with ensuring that the timetable was met. Although the DGM played an important role and sometimes acted as 'informal' Chairman, it was not a general manager dominated group, but involved a much wider group of officers.

Finance

Securing financial agreements was to be the dominant theme for much of the rest of the change chronology. This is picked up in the later section on resource context.

Positive Change: the Two Cases Compared

Comparing the two cases of Huddersfield and Mid Downs generates some interesting insights, in particular about change processes and local contexts for change. Although the Districts were not exactly matched on major variables such as social structure and economic status/conditions, there were many general points of similarity as well as dissimilarity. Both were medium-sized NHS organizations, both were among the first Districts in their respective Regions to tackle change in services for mentally handicapped people and both faced the dissolution of a long-stay mental handicap institution. In each case, the District, rather than the

Region, was assertive in leading the change and in preparing District-based strategies to enable community care services to be developed.

Interestingly, in the two Districts the stimulus for change was a mixture of top-down concern over standards of care for the mentally handicapped (NDT reports), and internally generated pressures for improvements, both statutory and voluntary. The external climate for change, which was focused in government publications, such as *Care in the Community* (DHSS, 1981b), created opportunities for local actors in both Districts who wanted to promote new policies and directions. The period of 1982–3 was one of high energy and new thinking in Huddersfield and Mid Downs and coincided with the reorganization and formation of each health authority. New DHA Chairmen, with a strong interest in and commitment to services for the mentally handicapped were appointed with the birth of the new Authorities. Regional review procedures also sprang into being and drew attention to deficiencies in provision and plans.

Organizational Culture

In both cases attention to the impact of cultures and key people provides a powerful analytical tool for understanding the change process. Cultural factors were particularly striking in the case of Huddersfield where, despite the overall context of 'segmentalism' often seen to characterize the NHS, there existed a much more 'integrative' local culture (Kanter, 1985). This District gave an impression of being open and frank both in its communications with outsiders and its internal dealings, with stress on reflection and analysis about the change process itself. The establishment of this style was traced back to 1982, to the origins of the District and to the influence of its Chairman, who, with the newly formed DMT, was regarded as having instituted a climate of pro-activity in the new Authority.

This managerial culture which was seen to have developed over the period since 1982, was described as multi-faceted and respondents highlighted some of the following District management characteristics and values:

- A tradition of experimentation with a readiness both to make use of research and outside learning as stimuli and models of change and to challenge bureaucracy and 'received wisdom'.
- A 'bias to action', a climate of proactivity, opportunism, calculated risk-taking and an attitude of 'can do'.
- Stability in top managerial and professional posts.
- A commitment to shared goals of development in priority services.
- The emphasis on 'bottom-up' innovation including openness with users and providers in service design/delivery and their involvement in planning groups and procedures, and decentralization of responsibility for 'owning' change.
- Flexible mechanisms for planning and development to take leadership in promoting change issues.

- 'Political' management in dealing with external organizations.
- A climate of harmonious and cooperative relationships exists between doctors and management.
- A parallel climate of established, team-working amongst senior managers and professionals.
- A strong sense of pride in local achievements and a District-wide organizational confidence and high self-esteem.

Mid Downs was also seen as a self-confident, action-orientated, District though somewhat more formalistic than Huddersfield – for example, preparing an exacting strategy for change and sticking to it.

Respondents highlighted a number of cultural features in trying to sum up the District character and approach:

- It was seen as a 'busy', high change, high energy District. Major strategic change was proceeding on most of the major sites in the District: acute services, a large psychiatric hospital, and the mental handicap service. Managers had to support an ambitious service change programme and juggle resources, time and effort between a number of different and potentially competing strategic objectives. Sometimes the bias towards action was seen to push out reflection.
- There was perception of division between the two main hospital sites. Greater integration and coordination between the two hospitals had been found difficult to achieve.
- It was seen as having flat management structures: low administrative costs; a small central core; only slowly developing unit level capacity. There were only two UGMs, despite the fact that the District was complex and expanding.
- The senior management team was generally seen as cohesive and working well together with some esprit de corps.

The overall impression is of a serious and self-conscious, planned administration. There was an emphasis on analysis, control, financial audit and strategic thinking. Alongside this was a public and publicity-conscious approach, combined with initiative and a desire to 'keep your eye on the ball'.

Yet while both Districts placed considerable emphasis on team-working, good communications and bottom-up innovation, the differences in style and culture meant that they also differed in means and in ends. Huddersfield displayed (and managers characterized their approach as such) a pragmatic and opportunistic style, buying properties and putting schemes in place often in advance of a definitive strategy. There was considerable experimentation, preparedness for compromise, taking the 'less-than-ideal' solution and subjecting it to revision. In Mid Downs the approach was that of following the defined strategy. These differences led to contrasts in the nature of the ultimate services. Huddersfield services were consequently more eclectic, with, for example, some large units accommodating up to 14 people alongside small domestic homes for three to four people; purpose-built as well as converted units; and Mencap homes and Housing Association properties. Mid Downs set out to achieve purpose-built residential units organized into three bungalows each accommodating eight people. The strategy was followed carefully and when difficulties arose, care was taken to bring together the management group to produce a strategic orientation which included increased day care and voluntary agency involvement. It was not in the character of management to allow the strategy to be dismantled or eroded by chance but instead to once again subject the process to analysis and planning.

Key People

A 'figurehead' for change emerged in each District, in the role and direct involvement of the DHA Chairman. In Huddersfield the Authority Chairman was appointed in 1982. Some of the descriptions applied to him by respondents include: a 'leader of change', a 'principled man', a 'guy who makes things happen', and 'an enthusiast'. The DGM and chairman reported a relationship of mutual support, where each respected the other's distinctive expertise and role. The Chairman was described as being closely involved in the running of the Authority, and in some eyes, played an executive part. Mostly it was his talent for stimulating change and providing a catalyst for progress that was pinpointed by those interviewed.

He himself had some very clear ideas about his role and position, and stressed the importance of giving the organization confidence and daring. He felt that it was not his place to maintain the status quo, but to ask and pursue questions in a creative way, yet to support his managers fully and publicly. He believed in and promoted a climate where he, and others, could introduce ideas – 'set hares running', 'putting a stick in and stirring' – and diffuse a quest for new ideas and solutions. His commitment to shifting decisions closer to the consumer and involving the consumer in the design of services was well known; and this was reflected in the District's development of strategy for mental handicap services.

In Mid downs the DHA Chairman was also seen as exerting strong leadership, being involved in NAHA at a national level as well as serving in a senior level on West Sussex County Council on both the Social Services Committee and Policy and Resources. Links with the Chair of Social Services were thus exceptionally close, and he was in a strong position to influence the behaviour of the Director. He had a personal as well as a policy interest in mental handicap services and was willing 'to put his head above the parapet'.

Both men were deeply knowledgeable about the change issue and this degree of 'expertise' was perceived as significant in effecting the change. The close association of the Chairman with the change also gave it both a public and political platform. Consumers and politicians could be scripted into the change process from the outset. The way in which both Districts translated the change beyond the confines of management and of the single organization, is noteworthy. The two Chairmen served in a sense as 'boundary-spanners', working beyond the bureaucratic structures, influencing, persuading and keeping the profile of mental handicap services high. They were not just 'product champions' in the narrow sense of the word but had an active public relations and marketing role. Both had well-established contacts with the NDT, local voluntary groups, political parties, senior local authority personnel, other DHAs and consumer/clients. The networks were consciously maintained and they were both lateral and vertical. Both Chairmen were supported by the character of the other Authority members.

In Huddersfield, Authority members were in general seen to be a very committed and well-meaning group, although the bulk of the substantive work fell to a small caucus of seven or eight members, who could devote the most time to Authority business. Management encouraged member involvement discussion groups, seminars, a mix of formal and informal meetings, and 'think tank' sessions. In Mid Downs there were a small number of 'strategic' members who acted as opinion formers and who needed to be consulted and brought into a broad coalition, through task-focused working parties rather than standing committees. There was little division on party lines in regard to mental handicap services, and cross-party willingness to protect the mental handicap budget.

Nor, despite the highly individualistic character of each Chairman, did they operate in isolation from management or other officers. The common denominator in Huddersfield and Mid Downs was the way the *leadership of change was shared across a caucus of people.*

Thus in Huddersfield both the DGM and the UGM Mental Health played highly significant roles, both committed to bottom-up innovation, to the testing of new ideas and to experimentation. The consultant in mental handicap appointed in 1983 was seen as an energetic, pro-active individual whose commitment to community services and change was said to be one of the key ingredients in the progress made by District from 1983. There were also identifiable 'product champions' in Social Services and the voluntary sector. However, in this case there were a *large* number of individuals perceived as key actors in the processes of strategy formulation and implementation – including nurse managers, planners, finance directors, senior administrators and local authority personnel.

It was from this collectivity, this 'critical mass of enthusiasts' with shared values, that many ideas were spawned, strong planning, financial, medical and nursing expertise powerfully combined, shared 'ownership' of change generated and the strategy eventually delivered. The dominant theme in Huddersfield was the power of the 'team'.

In Mid Downs, the core of key actors was tighter, smaller, with fewer tiers and specialties and often the consultant, the DGM, the Chairman and Finance Director were held up as the power-house for change. This may in part explain the more streamlined strategy that evolved in Mid Downs, with fewer constituencies having a direct impact on service design. None the less, once again, like Huddersfield, it was the *combined* efforts of key players that led to positive results. The clinicians (especially the mental handicap consultant) and professionals, the members, the Chairman and the District Treasurers and DGM all made separate but collectively powerful contributions. Nursing innovators were seen as playing a lesser role than elsewhere but the voluntary service played a large part. Social Service personnel were also powerful actors in the change drama.

The clinical input is of particular interest across the two Districts. Both reported the need to shed 'change-resistant' clinicians who were wedded to institutional solutions. Only after the appointment of consultants with experience and commitment to community care was progress especially noted. More than that, the overall shape of the strategy and its ultimate preparation remained largely the responsibility of the clinician in each District. The nursing-lead was less apparent in Mid Downs than in Huddersfield (although the influence of nurse managers was not unproblematic in Huddersfield and some conflicts did emerge late in the day about the levels of nursing involvement and the role of the Mental Handicap Resource Unit).

It is also worth underlining the significance of the relationships between planning, finance and general management which were crucial in Huddersfield and Mid Downs. There is a strong sense in each district of a careful orchestration of these functions and actors. A strategy grounded in financial realism emerged in both cases. The structures created to develop and implement the strategies reflected this close interdependency in each District. Huddersfield was especially strong on creating ad hoc groups to process urgent decisions, and there was much informal and regular communication among key officers within the District, whose officers were in close proximity. Lunch-time meetings, chance encounters in corridors, after-work get-togethers to deal with crises were not uncommon, so information circulated easily across the top tiers and functions. This could sometimes lead to frustration at other levels in the organization with occasional criticisms arising about the District being too 'centralist' and some key actors feeling excluded from an inner 'cabal'.

Continuity of management was another salient factor. In Huddersfield the arrival of Griffiths-style general management in 1984 had only minimal impact upon the management process, because of the continuity and the established management style. The District General Manager had been in post (previously as the DA for the Health District within Kirklees AHA) for 14 years, with long experience, a network of long-established contacts both within the District and with neighbouring DHAs and the local authority Social Services Department. This continuity and stability was apparent in all tiers of the organization and there were many senior personnel with lengthy service. In Mid Downs the current Chairman and District General Manager (originally appointed as the first DA) both had built up long experience in the District. The new general managers were in-service appointments: with no recourse to businessmen or other outsiders. The two UGMs also had NHS experience as in Huddersfield, this enabled managers and external agencies alike to draw upon a 'memory' of District services, relationships and objectives. There was no major disjuncture of approach or ambition.

The Capacity for Change

The change in mental handicap services was only part of a fairly ambitious change programme in Huddersfield and Mid Downs. Huddersfield was associated with several other large-order changes, for example, in mental illness services and in clinical budgeting (as part of a national pilot). Mid Downs, likewise, was engaged with run-down of a mental illness hospital and acute sector expansion. There was therefore a climate and expectation of change in each case, coupled with reports of high self-esteem and self-confidence across the Districts. These Districts were perceived as high-performers and innovators within their Regions and externally. The Huddersfield Chairman and managers were especially self-conscious of this and reported instances of where new ways of doing things were instigated, where formal, bureaucratic obstacles were by-passed and rules bent to enable change. The overall impression gained is that of 'pro-change' environments, at least at senior levels. What was more difficult to discern was how far this orientation to change permeated the whole organization and whether it encompassed all client groups.

Inter- and Intra-organizational Linkages

'Foreign Policy' The significance of 'foreign policy' for organizational development was underscored in these cases. Both mental handicap and mental illness services straddle several organizations, both in terms of provision and responsibility. In both sites considerable attention was paid to the way in which the change issue was presented and communicated. In Huddersfield there was a key emphasis on building organizational and cross-organizational momentum behind a positive vision of change in mental health and community services. In Mid Downs the District attended to supporting service strategy with action and deliberate personnel and communication strategies. There was considerable stress on 'selling' the devolution objective. There were pockets of resistance and uncertainty about reactions of neighbours but the District put substantial effort into winning 'hearts and minds' through the production of a video and public meetings. Both areas tried to develop joint working, devising superior 'joint' schemes and solutions when compared to many Districts. Nevertheless attempts at organizational boundary spanning were really, relatively modest. Many procedures, values, decisions and ways of working were tightly organization-bounded. Partisan behaviour and thinking

was still in evidence in preferences for types of carers (nurses or care assistants, for example), labels ('clients' or 'patients') and types of accommodation. No real institutional shift (Douglas, 1987) was discernible and 'ownership' of the problem was still professionally determined.

How mental handicap services could be detached from the statutory construction/control was never really tackled in either District. Shifting decisions, policies beyond institutional boundaries may be the large-order challenge demanded on the NHS in the next decade. Certainly, as the self-governing trusts become established and contracting of services is developed the interface with a wide organizational hinterland will increase in importance. It would seem there are few guidelines or precedents to follow for most joint working remains strait-jacketed and low-key. The case studies have given a few clues as to how to begin to build external alliances but perhaps a whole new language, or paradigm, will have to evolve. It will be interesting to see if sufficient managerial attention is devoted to these extra-organizational and political issues in the reorganized service.

The Role of Region   The two case studies provide excellent examples of the confluence of top-down with bottom-up pressures in driving change, in particular here in how local District-based initiative and plans can accelerate changes, originally triggered at higher tiers. While undoubtedly the Regional review process and visits from the NDT accentuated the need for change, what is marked in respondents' accounts is the Districts' positive use of this top-down, external pressure for change; it was the energy and foresight at local tiers that translated the external pressure into local needs and positive action. In the early 1980s, Huddersfield and Mid Downs perceived their Regions as providing strong opportunities for change. Early bids were placed for available funds and Huddersfield prided itself on forging ahead of Regional expectations. The financial strategy of Yorkshire RHA was described as facilitating local plans, allowing Districts 'to personalize' plans and to use savings imaginatively for internal schemes rather than 'clawing' them back to the Region. At South West Thames RHA two key facilitating steps were described: first, the approval and commitment to local closure plans and second, the granting of 'lead' agency status to Mid Downs in progressing the closure. Both Regions claimed to prefer a 'bottom-up' or 'stand-back' approach to District change.

Frustrations were expressed in both case studies about bureaucratic impediments in Regional–District interactions, for example, delays over capital developments, and fire regulations for conversions. Equally, there were policy differences between District and Region over key client groups. In both Districts, general management was seen as enhancing the District–Region interface, by breaking up a centralist tradition at Region level. However, as the 1980s progressed fears were expressed that top-down pressures and financial control might augment and District's autonomy once again be infringed. These tensions were never far from the surface in either case. Neither Region provided specific resources for the management of change.

DHA/Local Authority Relations   The tenor of relationships between the local authority and the DHA has also been a crucial influence on the change process. Unlike many of the case study Districts, Mid Downs and Huddersfield had the good fortune to be coterminous with their respective local authority boundaries. Equally, both inherited the partnership from pre-1982 days, contributing to a common history of negotiations and relationships. The impression gained in the two Districts was of actively developed inter-agency links which started from a low base of cooperation and understanding but were increasingly becoming more productive and harmonious. This did not happen by chance and deliberate efforts were made to secure better joint relationships not just through formal joint machinery but informally as well, with key people, in key posts, in both the DHAs and the local authorities, and a will to positive action.

In Huddersfield, the linkages were multiple – Chairman to Chairman; Chairman to Chief Executive; DGM to Social Services Director and so on. There was an especially fruitful and well-developed liaison between the Assistant DGM and Assistant Director of Social Services. The hallmark of these ties was that they were both formal and informal, both embedded in structures and extra-organizational. Continuity of people in posts had allowed both objectives and trust to mature. The development of such relationships was perhaps less advanced in Mid Downs, negotiations appeared more precarious and 'jointness' a more fragile concept, with different perceptions according to location in the network. In both Worthing and Chichester, 'receiving' DHAs for Forest residents after closure, there was a positive sense of Mid Downs and commitment to change but some doubts about its 'fast' pace. There was evidence of some joint progress through the securing of the county-wide Memorandum of Agreement which locked external agencies into a public commitment – although the financial discussions were tough and dominant.

Voluntary Sector Ties   The impression of the role played by the voluntary sector (mainly Mencap) in the two case studies provides some contrasts. In Huddersfield, there were two Mencap organizations with strong, assertive membership. Members were party to NHS plans from the outset, exerting pressure for change and influencing the direction of change. A member of Mencap was included in the formal planning team and full consultation was ensured. Furthermore, Mencap were actively involved in creating new community services in full partnership with the statutory bodies. Huddersfield DHA and SSD put a high premium on this jointness.

In Mid Downs Mencap had mixed fortunes; the organization was seen as weak in Horsham but stronger county-wide. At times, the voluntary sector felt itself to be marginalized from statutory plans and services, retaining a more lobbying than policy making role. Towards the late 1980s, the emergence of Mencap Homes Foundation was proving of interest to the statutory agencies so the potential for partnership was developing, as it had in Huddersfield.

The Resource Context

The striking similarity between Huddersfield and Mid Downs District is that each kept mental handicap services as a priority despite external pressures, policy dips and financial vicissitudes. This was also in the context, in both cases, of considerable attention to financial control and the financial reality of attainable targets. The persistence of objective and continual restatement of priority was enabled partly by the fact that the acute sector was kept in check. There was avoidance of crisis, unlike some of the other case studies, and an emphasis on growth rather than decline. Neither District faced an overspend or a runaway level of acute sector demand – so there were certain 'comfort levels' either contrived or inherited. For example, Huddersfield were able to commit 'growth monies' to the exercise. Mid Downs was able to use 1982 sale of land at Forest to generate ring-fenced monies for use in new community units as well as securing joint finance support for a number of relatively small-scale mental handicap projects and providing a 'top-up' facility on capital. The determination to reform mental handicap services was grounded in financial realism as well as in genuine values and intentions, with a commitment to pragmatic, incremental change and the matching of priorities with available monies. There was no 'poaching' of priority services monies to bolster other expenses and management in both cases successfully screened out competing demands. There was evidence of strong leadership and the District Finance Officers were key players in formulating both District strategies. This financial leadership did not end internally but continued into external liaisons. The Huddersfield Director of Finance had close communication with SSD counterparts and Mid Downs showed a similar pattern. The skill in preparing a sound financial strategy was especially crucial in securing effective inter-organizational plans.

The Regional context also provided some financial incentives to initiate change. This was essential in galvanizing the process and attracting bridging monies, ring-fenced monies and capital monies. In Mid Downs, high land values enriched the process while in Huddersfield the existence of properties suitable for conversion was a definite asset.

The financial robustness of SSDs and the ability of local authorities to retain mental handicap as a priority was a strong concern for both Districts. This points up the complexity of the resource context and its perpetual interdependence and fragility. The stringencies of the external environment were ever-imminent.

'Change-Content' and the Change Process

It is important to remember that it is the integrative interplay of the themes which determines the final plot. Brief attention is drawn here to one further issue – that of the 'change content' and its effect on the change process. Two views emerged in the research suggesting, first, that it may have been easier to achieve change in services for mentally handicapped people when compared to others (for example, mentally ill people). Some of the positive features identified were that:

- Mentally handicapped people formed a measurable, discrete population, which was relatively stable in size ('countable').
- There were strong advocates for this client group.
- The client group was championed by individuals with personal interest who were highly placed in positions of control and government.
- A reasonably clear and coherent set of values had evolved concerning models of care for mentally handicapped people: for example, 'ordinary life' models, 'normalization' and deinstitutionalization. However, it is important not to overstate the case, since professional and lay equivocacy remains.
- Achieving a service development with only a small parallel run-down does not equate with closure of a large long-stay institution.

On the other hand, it is also recognized that it may be more difficult to achieve change for this priority group, because of:

- The low political purchase attached to the issue: 'there are no votes in mental handicap'.
- The persistence of public resistance and ignorance, and the continued unpopularity of CITC schemes.
- A remaining stigma associated with mental handicap, popular stereotypes and prejudice.

Mention should be made too of the size of the change task – both the Forest and Mansion hospitals were small to medium-sized, unlike some of the massive-scale closure exercises tackled elsewhere. Clinical complexity was reduced by having single-handed consultants of mental handicap in each District. Unions were not especially dominant players in either context and the pace of change was not unduly hurried. Communities were incorporated into the process gradually and opposition tackled incrementally. In Huddersfield, change 'rolled forward' rather than galloped and detractors were gradually won over. Likewise in Mid Downs, public opposition was gently wooed. There were no national scandals or public confrontations and indeed major clashes between internal staff groups/management were avoided. The overall 'mood' was therefore temperate and communications remained overt and open.

The complex and multi-faceted character of change is nicely brought together in two quotes which are final reminders of the need to retain a holistic perspective on change. They are drawn from the Huddersfield experience:

> They have had the good fortune, for a range of historic reasons to have never been financially really squeezed, which I think makes a difference. So, significant Chairman, long-serving administrative execution, representing continuity of knowledge, stability, and they believe in bringing people on . . . They did business in an effective way with a Labour Council, which then became hung, but they actually made things happen. There is a value base to what they are about. (Regional officer)

> In terms of the moving of mentally handicapped people into this District, and the closure, I think it's very multi-faceted. There has certainly been a change in philosophy to Care in the Community, and the closure of large hospitals, to develop more home-like environments. I think that philosophical change has gone through the system . . . and has come down from above. I really see it as something that has come from without the District. The other thing of course was the arrival of the Chairman. He is obviously a key person as well. (Clinician)

Creating Change in a Change-resistant Context: Conclusions

One of the interesting aspects of this chapter is the way it contradicts many firmly held assumptions about the NHS as an organization. Against the general picture of a 'segmentalist' culture (Kanter, 1985), we find examples of 'integrative' District organizations; there are examples of strategic thinking; usually seen as an organization marked by 'top-down' leadership, there were strong occasions of 'bottom-up' initiative; characterized as often working in isolation from other agencies and poor at external liaison, we have seen instances of close cross-organization planning and working; and, usually, dominated by medical or clinical perspectives, there exist here new social care models where the medical model is subsumed or at least under modification.

Theoretically, the findings add to an appreciation of the power of micro-cultures and the malleability of contexts (Pettigrew, 1985c). They strongly attest to the power of key individuals to shape and define realities (Morgan, 1986). The ideas of fostering 'cultures of pride', developing organizational self-esteem alongside individual self-esteem and 'performance stimulating pride stimulating performance' (Kanter, 1985, p. 151) were validated in the case study examples. The attachment of key people to their organizations was obvious in both cases and continuity of service fuelled trust and a common language and approach. However, the 'prime movers' for change did not just rely on loyalty or the merit of their ideas but actively communicated their intentions at every level and on every occasion. A supportive culture for change was deliberately enacted. The 'talking up' of change in mental handicap services typified the Districts and, politically, produced competent change 'figureheads' who moulded both the agenda and symbols for change – drawing in teams of supporters and activists from within and outside the organization.

The themes of the timing and sequencing of change (Pettigrew, 1985a) also loom large in these findings. It is important to note that no radical solutions were proposed, more typically the changes were conservative and aligned to national policy. Many of the problems, ideas and solutions had been bumping around for more than a decade before action was taken. The theoretically interesting finding is the way that previously inert policies became animated through a mix of local action, regional and national pressure, financial circumstance, social movement/public will, consumer lobbying and happy accident (finding suitable premises for conversion, for example). This marrying of 'right people' with 'right places' and 'right times' was beautifully illustrated, especially in the Huddersfield case (Kanter, 1985).

8

The Creation of New Organizations

Building the District General Hospital

While Chapter 4 considered some of the issues involved in the management of acute sector rationalization, this chapter will instead analyse processes of creating and maintaining new District General Hospitals (DGHs). This raises the question of the management of growth, where the organization's ability to learn rapidly under conditions of expansion may be related to certain features such as the nature of its structure and reward system (Normann, 1977). But do growth issues vary in their essential characteristics to a greater degree than this relatively homogeneous management of growth perspective implies? As a growth issue, the creation and early development of new DGHs can, for example, be usefully compared with the response to HIV/AIDS (see Chapter 5) which was also a growth issue but possessed a distinctive set of characteristics, being new, different and crisis-based. Other growth issues may be more like the national programme of DGH construction, being characterized by a longer-term timescale, a more stable technology and a greater degree of prior learning which may be potentially transferable.

There are therefore a number of key generic issues which are explored in this chapter as well as issues specific to NHS management:

- The process of founding new organizations.
- How stabilising control processes do or do not emerge in these new settings; how new organizations undergo institutionalization.
- The degree of learning transferred from one site to another; how organizational 'templates' operate to reduce uncertainty; the role of organizational development.
- The nature of the organizational culture (inherited or new) apparent in these settings; whether the culture is strong or anomic.

The construction of District General Hospitals as the core of a comprehensive and locally accessible service has been national policy since the early 1960s (Cmnd 1604, 1962), and indeed the comprehensive coverage of the NHS acute sector is now an important strength when international comparisons are made. Many Districts have had experience in constructing new acute sector settings, yet we know little about how such processes are managed. There have been powerful engineering- and economic-based arguments for securing economies of scale and the Department of Health has made continuing efforts to standardize many of the repetitive features of cost planning, design and construction work from the early 1968 'Best Buy' hospital ('two for the price of one') through the 'Harness' concept developed in the early 1970s which envisaged big cuts in hospital planning periods but was then abandoned as too expensive, and then on to the 'Nucleus' design which was seen as a flexible and easily extendible first phase development. Regions have also developed their own standard design and construction packages. The tension between standardization and uniqueness, and between the requirements of technical and social systems, will be a major theme of the chapter.

Since the late 1970s there has been a move away from a 'National Plan' perspective and programmes have been increasingly developed within Regional strategic service plans. Nevertheless the Department of Health routinely examines all Approvals in Principle above £10m, while individual cases above £15m go to the Treasury and above £50m to Ministers (February 1989 limits), so securing central political support for a proposal may be the key to its success. There are then important social and political, as well as technical, dimensions to consider.

What is the Problem? A Range of Diagnoses

It is not altogether clear initially what the central problem might be in the study of these growth processes, and unsurprisingly different constituencies and streams of literature have different versions of where the problem lies. Here we present a variety of different ways of approaching the issue.

Following Capricode Procedures

One common response in the field – faced with tasks of such complexity – has been that the problem is one of grasping and following standard procedure, and that therefore the prime need is for clear accounts of how best to implement the Capricode procedure, the standard planning mechanism outlined by the Department of Health. However, we do not subscribe to this mechanistic view and shall seek instead to explore some other potential problem definitions. All are agreed, however, that such an ambitious programme of capital investment has (unsurprisingly) not been without problems.

A Problem of Complex Work Design

From a social research perspective, too great a concern with standardization may mean the creation of new DGHs is seen as a technical, commissioning-based problem amenable to standard guidelines and 'cook books' (Millard, 1981). Thus Vann-Wye (1991) has argued that models for workplace design in new hospital settings have often been too narrowly based on essentially physical design problems: 'the planning and design of a new hospital work organization is only conceived in terms of a generalized system of intra- and inter-departmental activity flows taking place within the physical envelope'.

Sometimes 'official' accounts are highly prescriptive in tone, and have only recently begun to consider such organizational questions as the nature of the relationship within the commissioning team and the commitment of local management. The construction of a new DGH, and the closure of peripheral hospitals, may herald an important break in the pattern of work undertaken, although it is also possible that continuity is more substantial than the planners expect. Since the early 1970s sociologists have been investigating the effects of increased standardization on design activities in new DGHs, sometimes with a sceptical eye on how much design activity could really be standardized across very different settings, where even slight changes in geographical siting or the balance of specialties could lead to very different functional relationships and patterns of workflow.

Some recent work has emerged on work design in these new acute sector settings. Grieco (1991), for instance, took the example of a central treatment suite as a way of examining the impact of central direction of work organization and practice through the adoption of standard design in two new DGHs. She found, however, that the innovation could be largely suffocated by existing organizational culture and work practices. Even in 'green field' organizations, previous organizational histories and forces were found to be in play which served to produce differences between the two locations. Moreover the informal power of nursing staff – particularly ward sisters – was found to be greatly underestimated in accounts of work organization within hospital settings:

> The divergence of practice in two identical sites, subject to the same central policy direction, is, we argue, largely attributable to the carry over of practices from the old organizational structures into the new. This should not be taken to imply that the new sites and new designs have not resulted in any modifications to past practice, for indeed they have. We are merely attempting to establish the position that more care should be taken in identifying organizational pre history and culture than is currently the vogue. (Grieco, 1991)

Value for Money and Financial Control

Problems are of course likely to arise with any large-scale capital investment process, in the private as well as the public sector (the construction of the Channel Tunnel might be a good example). However Hall (1980) argues that the difficulties may be greater in the public sector as, whereas in a market the entrepreneur who makes a capital investment misjudgement faces losses and eventually bankruptcy, in supplying public goods, public entrepreneurs face no such penalty (although their careers may suffer) and have little relevant consumer feedback. Capital expenditure on NHS hospitals runs at about £700m annually, and major new hospitals are usually developed as a number of discrete phases over a number of years. The national policy system – as well as researchers – has for a considerable period been probing into some of the weaknesses associated with the programme of DGH construction.

Thus the Public Accounts Committee (1980, 1981, 1984) has taken a recurrent interest in this question from a value-for-money perspective. In particular there were concerns in the early 1980s about the inability to meet the revenue consequences of new hospitals (as in the case of the new University Hospital at Nottingham); design and construction faults; the difficulties experienced in closing old stock; and inadequate investment appraisal criteria. A recent revisiting of the problem concluded: 'we are concerned at the inordinate time it takes to plan, design and build new hospitals, and the implications this has for patient care and the delivery of improved facilities' (Public Accounts Committee, 1990). In the assessment of delay, a tricky issue is when the 'inception' of a scheme is calculated. The Public Accounts Committee considered the case of Redditch DGH, when inception was given as 1971 (its first appearance in a Regional capital programme). Yet Terry Davis MP (then the local Member of Parliament) commented:

> Now I know from personal experience that people were discussing the need for a new hospital in Bromsgrove and Redditch three years before that date, discussing it both locally and at the Region and at Westminster, so the gestation seems a little protracted before it gets to the inception . . .

In particular a common problem has been the rapid emergence of 'overspends' in DGH settings: all three of the case study hospitals in this chapter quickly went into financial deficit. The rapid escalation of clinical activity in such settings raises the question of control over clinical work, the ability of management to control or even influence such work patterns, and of concepts of 'clinical autonomy' which will be discussed as an analytical theme in its own right in a later section.

The Uptake of Central Design Solutions

There is also the question of whether standardized and centrally derived or customized and locally based design solutions are or should be utilized. The Nucleus hospital (McMorrin et al., 1990) design was developed as a cheaper option by the Department of Health in the mid 1970s. It operated by standardizing all departmental design to fit within a standard cruciform building shape called a 'template' which could be assembled on a modular basis. Continuing local resistance to standard design packages led to an attempt by the centre in 1984 to issue guidance that the Nucleus design package should always be used unless there were extremely strong arguments to the contrary. This, however, has proved difficult to enforce. While the PAC's response to the National Audit Office Report concluded:

> We regret that, despite the evidence that the Nucleus design would reduce

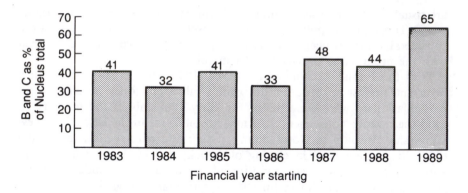

Nucleus schemes are classified according to four headings:

A1 schemes using a good proportion of Nucleus
    templates

A2 similar to A1 except the whole hospital standard
    design is not used

B   Nucleus-related

C   one-off designs using Nucleus material as a starting point

Figure 8.1   *Use of the Nucleus hospital design (McMorrin et al., 1990)*

construction and running costs, it has not been more widely applied. We expect the Department to take stronger action to promote its use nationally. (Public Accounts Committee, 1990)

It remains to be seen whether moves to a new order of 'managed competition' will erode still further the force of such top-down signals.

Stronger Project Management

Project management surfaced in other policy documents as an important target for improvement. The Griffiths Report (1983) had recommended that procedures for handling major capital schemes should be streamlined and provide maximum devolution. New guidance from the Department in 1985 sought to restrict the role of the centre to determining strategic priorities, and urged DHAs to give high priority to building major capital projects to time, to cost and (an interesting if elliptical reference) to quality.

The National Audit Office's (1989) Report gave perhaps the most comprehensive official view of the problem. It was concerned to assess the effectiveness of the recent building programme both against time (see Table 8.1) and against cost (see Table 8.2).

The NAO looked at the 16 hospital schemes costing over £5m completed in 1986–7 from 'inception' (defined by the NAO as the setting up

Table 8.1 *Time performance (schemes over £1m completed in 1983–1987)*

Year of completion	Schemes over £5m				Schemes between £1m and £5m				All schemes			
	No. of schemes	Original contract period (yr)	Overrun (yr)	Overrun (%)	No. of schemes	Original contract period (yr)	Overrun (yr)	Overrun (%)	No. of schemes	Original contract period (yr)	Overrun (yr)	Overrun (%)
1983	8	24.8	(0.2)	(0.8)	32	60.8	3.8	6.3	40	85.6	3.6	4.2
1984	4	11.8	0.9	7.6	37	68.3	2.2	3.2	41	80.1	3.1	3.9
1985	4	2.7	0.0	0.0	45	78.5	5.2	6.6	49	91.2	5.2	5.7
1986	9	27.5	2.5	9.1	35	63.8	4.8	7.5	44	91.3	7.3	8.0
1987	7	21.8	1.4	6.4	47	88.6	9.1	10.3	54	110.4	10.5	9.5
Total	32	98.6	4.6	4.7	196	360.0	25.1	7.0	228	458.6	29.7	6.5

Source: National Audit Office (1989)

Table 8.2   *Cost performance (schemes over £1m completed in 1983–1987)*

Year of completion	Schemes over £5m				Schemes between £1m and £5m				All schemes			
	No. of schemes	Original approved contract (£m)	Overrun (£m)	Overrun (%)	No. of schemes	Original approved contract (£m)	Overrun (£m)	Overrun (%)	No. of schemes	Original approved contract (£m)	Overrun (£m)	Overrun (%)
1983	8	72.79	2.28	3.1	11	27.81	(0.12)	(0.4)	19	100.60	2.16	2.1
1984	4	34.60	1.67	4.8	7	22.03	0.48	2.2	11	56.83	2.15	3.8
1985	4	34.56	0.99	2.9	8	17.25	1.82	10.6	12	51.81	2.18	5.4
1986	9	90.19	8.40	9.3	12	26.77	1.36	5.1	21	116.96	9.76	8.3
1987	7	88.57	7.63	8.6	29	71.95	2.02	2.8	36	160.52	9.65	6.0
Total	32	370.71	20.97	6.5	67	165.81	5.56	3.4	99	486.52	26.53	5.5

Source: National Audit Office (1989)

of an appraisal team) to first use. However, these indicators were contested by the DHSS which argued that the appropriate indicators were from the approval in Principle to completion of the building. Using the NAO criteria the range was from seven to fifteen years (with an average of ten years); using the DHSS criteria the corresponding figures were 4.5 and 9.5 years, with an average of seven years. As far as delivery against cost was concerned, the average cost overrun was 5 per cent, with design changes identified as the main factor. There was also the question of delivery against service needs. Were the new facilities openable or were the revenue consequences such that they were mothballed? The NAO found little evaluation, despite the fact that evaluation procedures had been built into Capricode. The NAO also examined the extent to which decisions had been delegated from Region to Districts, following on from the new 1985 DHSS guidelines. A final topic considered was the question of the impact of changes to arrangements for project management which had also been introduced by DHSS in 1985:

> Before 1985, in general, projects were run by designated project teams drawn from a variety of disciplines within the health authority. These teams included client parties operating on a consensus basis. The Department announced in 1985 that responsibility for planning and management of each capital building project should be clearly vested in an individual project manager accountable for keeping the project to time and cost. (National Audit Office, 1989)

Resistance to what may be seen as standard design advice which is inappropriate or unacceptable locally may entail delay. Grieco's (1991) analysis of the negotiations around the incorporation of a central treatment suite in local planning demonstrated the penalty which could be paid for rejecting central guidance: 'hospitals which began their planning processes at the same time but followed the standard package template have enjoyed a substantially more rapid material translation from design to bricks and mortar'.

While the policy and management system has clearly been concerned about weaknesses in the national programme of constructing new DGHs, are there also more social scientific themes which can be usefully explored? Two such themes will now be introduced: the birth and early development of new organizations and the control of clinical workload.

The Birth and Early Development of Organizations: the Literature

In this section, social scientific literature on the creation of new organizational forms is outlined and discussed in addition to the policy literature reviewed previously. One way of seeing the construction of a new facility such as a DGH is as the birth of a new organization, although professional and local contexts may also influence such developmental processes. The language is one of 'becoming', as a new organization emerges and undergoes institutionalization. But whereas the development of services for HIV/AIDS considered in Chapter 5 was found to be a highly value-laden activity, some of the new DGHs considered in this chapter were by contrast found to be anomic organizations: there were inadequate operating systems; no sense of organizational history but rather separation from the past; social and authority structures were unformed; there was little common value system or ideology and a need for a period of 'stabilization'. Sarason's (1976) subtle work on the creation of new settings within human service organizations reminds us that such growth processes can never guarantee a happy ending; new settings may abort; and in particular capital- rather than idea-led planning – typical in standardized systems – may result in the problem of 'buildings as distractions' in which service and human issues are neglected. Sarason's own experience of designing an innovative mental health centre alerted him to the danger of monumentalism, a situation in which the new building could become an end in itself and the process of its design and construction exacerbate existing inter-group tensions and conflicts.

How can this perspective be tested against what we know of the birth and early development of other new organizations? Clearly the pattern seems very different from Simon's (1953) classic case study of a federal agency (the Economic Cooperation Administration) which rapidly grew through cell splitting and assumed a coherent form, without ever being planned. The timescales are much longer, and the planning systems much more elaborate than in the picture of rapid and opportunistic growth described by Simon. Other writers (Child and Keiser, 1977) have sometimes distinguished between societal conditions and the role of 'founders' as alternative explanations for the creation of new organizations. For example, Stinchcombe (1965) analysed the societal conditions under which people could be motivated to found new organizations, when they find or learn about alternative or better ways of doing things which cannot be done within existing social arrangements. The role of social movements and their organizations in promoting value-laden social change is, for example, discussed in the chapter on HIV/AIDS, although their contribution may take the form of 'bureaucratic insurgency' within formal organizations. Other sources of 'strong culture' which can help energize change may be organizational 'sagas' (Clark, 1972) or central organizational myths. Stinchcombe also directs our attention to the special problems of new organizations in constructing an agreed division of labour and where there may be an initial dependence on social relationships between strangers (where relations of trust may be precarious) and a lack of stable ties to customers or clientele. These institutionalization processes will be considered later on in this section.

On the other hand, Boswell's (1973) analysis of the development of young firms concentrated on the characteristics of their founders, often relatively young men (in their 30s) with personal characteristics which stressed drive, hard work and ambition for growth. Such founders also displayed little need to adopt formalized approaches to planning, control or other managerial problems which were handled personally. Perhaps this analysis paid too little attention to the relationship between the entrepreneur and the context, as the key problem in institutionalizing innovation may be the transformation of individual drive into collective purpose and commitment. So, for example, Pettigrew's (1979) longitudinal study of a British boarding school explores the role of the headmaster as an entrepreneur in the sense of 'any person who takes primary responsibility for mobilizing people and other resources to initiate, give purpose to, to build and manage a new organization', which may require extraordinary amounts of time and energy.

The implication of this literature is that we need to know far more about the organizational and small group processes involved in the creation of new settings such as DGHs; consider dysfunctional as well as functional elements; and analyse sources of pressure and of leadership.

Organizational Templates

The creation of such a complex organization as a DGH is above all a strategic process. Yet it may be illusory to expect conscious strategic management, at least according to writers such as Mintzberg (1973), who have argued that contrary to rationalistic myths, managerial work is typically brief, varied and fragmented and based on time and contact management rather than analysis or strategy. What then happens to strategic, analytical or political tasks within the organization? One response may be to reduce uncertainty and base responses on existing models and experience, either central or local. So Sharifi (1988) has argued that managerial practice is embedded in the temporal and political contexts of organizations and that managers build sense making and decisional models that include past, present and anticipate future events. These are organizational templates:

> 'templates' are guiding systems, which include a set of definitions of events, decision outcomes and activities and can be used to routinize and rationalize unfamiliar situations or unexpected outcomes. (Sharifi, 1988)

> The design of a new institutional type leans heavily upon existing exemplars both in terms of physical form and work organization. New types of enterprise adapt existing design formulations developed in other circumstances to their own needs. Existing 'knowledge bases' form 'templates' which act as springboards for action. (Vann-Wye, 1991)

Sharifi's case study of the design of a new DGH found that although there were indeed formalized ways of designing, planning and commissioning hospitals, and a standard design package, past experience of local managers had also created a distinctive local template. In this situation the new Nucleus hospital was to be built on a green field site, an element which administration used to attempt to renegotiate roles (turning it into a 'Nucleoid' hospital). They therefore tried to alter the standard design package to insert new rules regarding the relationship between the medical staff and the DHA, but in the end 'the resulting outcomes seemed only to reproduce an existing equilibrium in the political system'.

Other authors also associated with the University of Aston, such as Vann-Wye (1986), studying the same DGH, further developed the idea of a 'template' which acted to produce substantial incrementalism in organizational design, despite surface appearances of radicalism. Powerful professionals (medical and nursing staff) operationalized the working of new facilities in a way which:

> denies the possibility of establishing new patterns of resource use and deployment when these patterns are not professionally approved. Incremental change and the persistence of strong organizational template forms is thus as much a consequence of professional control over the rate and direction of change as it is of 'one best way' of building hospitals and doing hospital work. (Vann-Wye, 1986)

The two key presumptions here are that of local renegotiation of central design packages and of substantial continuity despite surface radicalism, with the carrying over into new physical fabric of many of the social systems, power relationships and workflow patterns of the old institutions. This chapter will give the opportunity to test these arguments against three more case studies.

Institutionalization Processes

If social orders are formed through negotiation processes (Strauss, 1978), then these processes may be particularly difficult in new settings. Although new DGHs are less 'different' than, say, constructing entirely new services around HIV/AIDS, they nevertheless do raise important questions of role formation. They may approximate to Strauss's description of roles on experimental psychiatric wards which were found neither to be well crystallized nor disorganized, but rather characterized by evolving social forms. The more general question is raised of how new organizations are 'institutionalized' (Pettigrew, 1973a). Zucker's review (1988) of the field indicates that there may be different accounts of institutionalization processes, some arguing that once institutions are formed they are likely to be highly stable, while others see institutions as likely to erode, and hence in need of continuing institution building. How stable are roles and understandings in these new organizations or must they be consciously reproduced if they are not to erode?

Organizational Development

The Organizational Development (OD) literature has also argued that the creation of new organizations such as DGHs involves far more than capital planning, it requires global organizational change. The Trent OD

Unit has been particularly involved in the study of new DGHs within the Trent Region:

> It is clear that the major trauma for staff involved at all levels is not just due to the impact of technical nor procedural changes or physical relocation, but also due to the threat (and realization) of change in culture, roles, social and working relationships. A major part of the trauma occurs before the transfer and is based on fears, fantasies, rumours and uncertainty about the new situation rather than any real change. (Collin et al., 1981)

Edmonstone (1982) has also stressed the slightness of the organizational resource devoted to commissioning: 'relatively junior managers were members of commissioning teams and the tacit knowledge which they developed was lost as they changed jobs – commissioning was seen as a "once in the lifetime" task and the wheel was continuously being reinvented.' But the strategic development of the new organization was seen as being beyond the brief of technically orientated commissioning teams and as requiring the early and deep involvement of senior managers and clinicians in determining overall design. Perhaps a key conclusion from this stream of work was:

> The development of a DGH involves far more than planning, commissioning and opening the new building. It affects the entire locality and creates change in almost every aspect of health care; change in the role of the various existing health care facilities and change therefore in the role of local staff. The running down or change of use of existing hospitals is of great concern to both staff and the community. There is a tendency for commissioning to be a piecemeal process, each department being developed separately. In fact an entire new organization is being created and organizational change is a difficult process to manage. (Collin and Wilson, 1985)

This chapter should provide an opportunity to put some flesh on these interesting but rather abstract bones, and in particular to explore whether certain problems tend to recur in the early phases of development in DGHs.

Medicine and Management

The three case studies in this chapter offer perhaps the best illustration of a much more general tension in the NHS as significant 'overspends' emerged in all three settings – the extent to which professionally derived claims to 'clinical freedom' are sustainable in the face of resource constraints. What is the ability of the emergent general managerial cadre to place constraints around professional control over workflow? Who, for instance, decides on the overall volume of activity? Since the Griffiths Report (1983), there has been a continuing concern to engage clinicians with questions of management. Some and perhaps an increasing number of clinicians recognize the importance of management and have been engaged through such initiatives as the roll-out of Resource Management and clinical directorates, but for many others there is little interest in management. As Fitzgerald (1990) points out, there are still few incentives for clinicians to participate in management and there may indeed be some disincentives resulting from the nature of current medical education and rigid career structures.

For Harrison and Schulz (1989), the notion of clinical autonomy is at the heart of medicine's claim to professional status built up over many years and undisturbed in the 1948 settlement. Traditionally NHS administration has been seen as facilitating the work of clinical professionals, rather than exercising control over them, but in the NHS of the mid 1980s a raft of measures (Management Budgeting, Performance Indicators, controls over drug prescribing) emerged in addition to the introduction of general management which marked a significant challenge to dominant professional interests. However, such professionals would be likely to fight vigorously to defend traditional notions of clinical freedom:

> Respondents regard overall financial limitations as being legitimate restrictions on their autonomy, and indeed a majority accept the principle of individual clinicians being given budgets which may not be exceeded. In sharp contrast, respondents did not see a legitimate role for any mechanism, such as peer review or quality assurance, which restricted their freedom to decide how to treat individual patients. (Harrison and Schulz, 1989)

Another study of clinicians and resource management (Pollitt et al., 1988) found profound resistance among clinicians to any development which admitted managers to direct discussions concerning clinical workload. Hardly any of the consultants interviewed felt that general management had significantly lessened their autonomy, and most declared themselves ready to fight such incursions in the future. For managers, however, much of the variability in expenditure can be seen as attributable to the behaviour of clinicians. Bed reductions, for example, may not achieve their expected savings because clinicians change their workflow (by, for example, increasing day surgery) so as to increase throughput. While these studies suggest that the 1980s were marked by a rising managerial challenge to professional power bases, they also indicate that there has as yet only been modest change. Our case studies in this chapter should be able to shed some further light on this argument.

Some Implications of the Literature Review for the Case Studies

The literature that is available on the organizational and managerial problems of DGHs is surprisingly thin and diffuse in comparison with many other health care issues, despite the societal importance of the national programme of DGH construction that has taken place over the past 30 years. There is a range of possible definitions of what the problem might be, both from policy-based and more theoretical perspectives.

The policy system – through such arenas as the Public Accounts

Committee – has been taking recurrent looks at what have been seen as weaknesses in this programme of DGH construction. Three problems have been highlighted: failure to open on time; failure to open to cost; and failure to meet revenue consequences or to prevent 'overspends' from emerging. A 'quality' theme has also emerged, but has not been substantively developed within this literature. Nor has it always been recognized that performance on these indicators may be competitive rather than complementary.

Two more theoretical themes were also identified for further examination. The first was the birth and early development of new organizations, where the 'organizational template' argument developed by authors at the University of Aston such as Vann-Wye (1991) was introduced which suggested that substantial continuity could coexist with surface radicalism. The nature of institutionalization processes in new settings and of possible Organizational Development input was also discussed. The second theme related to the generic question of clinical–managerial relationships, of professionalization processes and the extent to which challenges to professionally based concepts of 'clinical freedom' might be effective. Early evidence suggested profound resistance among clinicians to any development which admitted managers to direct discussion concerning clinical workload.

Milton Keynes: a Vision Fades

Milton Keynes District Health Authority is one of the smaller Districts in the Oxford Region, constituted as a separate DHA in 1982. The District population is substantially younger than the country as a whole, has a socio-economic profile broadly similar to the national average, and there is a high rate of childbirth. Milton Keynes is a modern, planned city and the bulk of NHS facilities (along with the rest of Milton Keynes) are new. The Milton Keynes Development Corporation (MKDC) (due to be wound up in 1992) had a social as well as a physical planning role and is a key lobbyist and facilitator in health care politics locally, for example reserving land for a hospital campus.

Managing up to Oxford Region was important as the District had done well out of the targeted 1984 Regional Strategic Plan where the Milton Keynes DGH was identified as a key priority. Between 1974 and 1982 health services in Milton Keynes were run from Aylesbury Vale. On its formation as a separate District in 1982, a consensus-based DMT was formed in the usual way and opinions varied as to its effectiveness. Some, particularly consultants or administrators who held to a public service ethos, felt that it performed its job well, for instance opening the new DGH on time. But others felt that difficult internal dynamics within the DMT and lack of a clear leadership structure meant that decisions were not always made.

The transition to general management in the District was seen as evolutionary: the DGM and the two UGMs were all inside appointments. The DHA was generally unassertive, except when highly visible service reductions were made. The DGM had a clinical background (the ex-DMO), and was interested in service development, particularly for priority groups where he had played a lead role in much of the strategic planning. There was a premium on innovation (managers did not want to be seen as 'dull') in what was a growing District in a growing Region, and financial control was seen more in terms of a necessary evil. There was a hidden expectation that Region would tolerate some level of overspend given the growing population, but the tricky judgement lay in assessing the point at which progressive loss of financial control was likely to set in.

Developing a Vision and Early Strategic Planning, 1967–1974

The announcement of the Milton Keynes Development Corporation in 1967 gave the NHS an opportunity to learn from the earlier failure to introduce comprehensive health care planning in the first generation of New Towns. The initial energy very much rested at Regional level, as the first RGM (who had been deputy SAMO in 1967) recalled:

> *Int*: Is Milton Keynes a personal project for you?
> *Resp*: Oh, yes, the very day that Milton Keynes was announced on the 9 o'clock news, by 11 we were up at the DHSS, my colleagues and I, saying how we would need additional funding to develop a health service in a city of that size.

An early 1968 report – in keeping with the prevailing ideology of social planning – proclaimed as its bold objective the development of a comprehensive health service, which was seen as easier to achieve in a green field setting. Clarity about values and objectives was seen as central:

> It is important to resist an early desire to draw squares on the map of a New Town, labelling some as health centres, and one or more as hospital sites. Instead, planning must begin by discussing the philosophy of the proposed health service. (Gooding and Reid, 1970)

> Milton Keynes is probably the first New Town in which health service planning has been an integral part of the overall planning ab initio. (Reid, 1973)

The early vision began to take on flesh and form, as six main principles for service development were identified (Reid, 1973): there should be a community orientation; primary care should be supplied through health centres (rather than single-handed GPs); there should be a single District General Hospital (rather than a cluster of small DGHs as suggested by DHSS, perhaps another example of a local 'template'); there should be integrated staffing and blurring between primary and secondary care (through GP Clinical Assistantships in hospital settings); there should be a better balance between prevention and cure; there should be close liaison not only with the Development Corporation but also with the social and educational services. Vann-Wye's (1986) argument that professional norms will serve to restrict change even in periods of organizational reproduction thus needs qualification. However, much of this new thinking was contained within the more conceptual specialty of public health and was to experience difficulty in effecting a transition to a more routine capital planning process.

Strategic Planning in a Time of Capital Scarcity, 1974–1986

There were now attempts to ensure that Phase 1 retained a secure place at the top of an overloaded Regional capital programme in the face of successive wobbles. The attention shifted to the mainstream Regional capital planning process and some of the early vision seemed to fade (although the changes projected outside the hospital sector lasted better as a network of modern health centres was built up and as the importance of joint planning became more widely accepted across Milton Keynes). For the new DGH, the litmus test of success was the timing of the start, and even minor delays could produce a political storm. The ad hoc machinery which had previously been used for health service planning in Milton Keynes was phased out during 1974 and in November 1974 an Area Planning Team was created. It was the Regional tier which in reality took much of the decisions, where a Combined Planning Team was set up in 1975. In November 1974, a joint press statement of the Oxford RHA and the Milton Keynes Development Corporation had stated that there should be a start on site in 1978 and an implied opening in 1982 (Cooper, 1978). But the mid 1970s were a time of severe pressure on capital investment in the NHS and the 1977–8 Regional capital programme contained such gloomy statements as: 'resources expected to be available in the next two or three years are insufficient to meet the objectives then [in the previous plan] set'; and 'significant slippage on most schemes is inevitable'.

Significant slippage began to creep into the Milton Keynes scheme as well. Much of the key planning was undertaken at Regional level on a normative basis, including specification of the basic configuration of beds. Much of the earlier vision appears to have been lost at this point given the need for economy. Oxford RHA (1976) made it clear that the reduction of demands on the capital programme would be crucial, and whereas some of the early thinking was retained (the tying of developments in priority group services to local social care services), other themes (such as integration of GPs in the hospital) began to fade. The Regional planning was essentially based on the application of Regional norms, with financial constraints to the fore, and there was little emphasis on medical staffing, infrastructure or developmental concerns. The aim was rather to establish a first phase of a DGH which gave priority to clinical services, was operationally viable, produced functional solutions attracting significantly less than the conventional Building Note Cost Allowances, was compatible with the Regional investment strategy and provided as economical a revenue solution as possible (Oxford Regional Health Authority, 1976).

Region committed itself to a 1980 start in June 1977, and set up a design team to develop a more detailed brief for the physical planning. However, planning was once more disrupted by a new hiatus in the Regional capital programme in July 1978 which implied further slippage, because, it was reported, of shortage of Regional design staff. This further slippage provoked an embarrassing public statement by the Chair of the MKDC. The Development Corporation had, he said, been repeatedly assured that the DGH planning process was on time and in 1975 the MKDC had given the RHA a confidential undertaking to underwrite planning costs in view of ministerial support for the hospital.

Region commissioned an inquiry into the successive slippage (Cooper, 1978) which blamed an overloading of the capital programme, understaffing in the Regional Works Department and administrative fragmentation at Region:

> The idea that an RTO can go out and sense trouble and then do something about it like a chief executive dies hard. It is just not the way that consensus management works. Officer Teams process by consultation matters which come before them and do not interfere in each other's departments. It is a non-authoritarian system, probably appropriate to the health service, but it does not lead to decisive executive action. (Cooper, 1978)

Given this pressure, opinion at Regional level was in favour of 'doing something' to protect Milton Keynes. In order to protect timetables, a management contractor was to be used. The planning process now moved into budget cost submission stage, approved by the RTO in October 1979, retaining the key target dates. Different accounts were received of the 'real' reasons why these decisions were finally made. Regional respondents argued that the Region had always been keen to start on site just as soon as the population levels were viable, and the planning process proceeded in the normal way. Others saw central political influence as accelerating the process (Margaret Thatcher had opened Milton Keynes's new shopping centre in 1979 and had been heavily lobbied by the Chairman of the Development Corporation).

This drama cemented still further Region's commitment to Milton Keynes. Overcommitment of the Regional capital programme was again apparent in 1980, but it was taken for granted by Region that it would respond to the 'special needs' of Milton Keynes. In 1982, there was pressure from every other District in the Region to postpone the opening of the DGH for a year because of the Region's financial difficulties, but again the line was held.

Precommissioning and Commissioning, 1980–1984

The Commissioning Team (CT) met for the first time on 17 December 1980, and although dedicated commissioning resources were small scale (a part-time Commissioning Officer, a Commissioning Nurse and subsequently a Commissioning Assistant), there was a good lead-in time as the Regional Project Team retained formal responsibility for the project until the site was handed over. A peculiar feature of Milton Keynes was that the team was planning from scratch as there were no acute services at all to re-provide and therefore no consultant or nursing body or local body of practice. The administrators were in the field before the professionals, and early clinical advice was obtained from the more distant Aylesbury consultants (which caused some problems). There was no clear clinical product champion for the hospital.

The Commissioning Team was expected to produce reports for the DTO, ATO and RTO on different subjects, with any equipment over £15,000 going to Region for assessment. After 1982, the new Milton Keynes DMT emerged as the monitoring body, checking the progress of the Commissioning Team. There sometimes seemed concern that the Commissioning Officers were taking long-term policy decisions without reference to the rest of the District. An October 1982 paper identified some key issues.

1 *Ensuring that the building would be handed over by the contractors in April 1983* In the end the site was not handed over until September 1983, and the commissioning process had to be telescoped from 12 into six months to meet the original April 1984 deadline. This shortening of timescale increased the pressure on team members, and there was some feeling that 'it was all done in a rush', or that 'the hospital opened too early', that some people felt confused or out of their depth, and that many of the operational policies that supposedly existed on paper did not take root.

2 *Medical staff* This potentially critical issue was being deal with by Region. District was pushing Region to accelerate the timetable, although Region felt that it was on course and that the District was a little over-anxious. The large number of last minute appointments made it difficult, however, to get consultant advice during commissioning. The medical member of the CT was only appointed in October 1983, had no previous experience of commissioning, and was unsure whether he should speak for his department or for the hospital as a whole. One view was that there should have been a consultant representative in post from April 1983, with a team of consultants from October 1983, to give advice on equipment and policies.

Many of the new consultants were appointed from time-expired senior registrars available elsewhere in the Region, with these posts being squeezed out of the other Districts through the Regional manpower committees. Although the hospital was originally envisaged as being 'consultant led', the number of junior staff ended up varying between departments, with some criticism that Region was unable to 'get off the fence' and enforce a clear medical staffing policy.

3   *Revenue funding*   The Regional allocation was initially less than District's allocation. While the CT was asked to prepare contingency plans to reduce running costs, in the end augmented sums were negotiated from Region.

The hospital opened in full and on time in April 1984, which could be seen as a great success, especially as the original contract completion overran by six months. The hospital soon scored extremely highly on certain Performance Indicators. However, while the original budget cost was £12.68m, the final cost came in at £15.52m (including £1.67m for fluctuations).

Assessment of the Commissioning Process

Yet alongside these successes, there were also doubts expressed about the quality of the commissioning process. Respondents varied widely in their rating of the quality of the commissioning process: broadly speaking, the further they were from the hospital, the more likely they were to see it as a 'success'. Some of the criticisms were:

- Thin resourcing and inadequate lead-in times; difficult team dynamics ('all a bit vague'); no sense of direction; unclear leadership structures despite the formal appointment of a Commissioning Officer; little clinical input.
- Unclear role definition: 'muddle rather than direction'. Team members who lacked experience of commissioning could find it very difficult to cope with a wide brief and very tight timescales.
- 'The hospital was opened too early': there was no time to set up a proper Works Department or to ensure real operational policies had been developed.
- An unclear relationship with an overcontrolling DMT. While the DMT suspected that there were weaknesses in the CT which could threaten the timetable, the DMT also became embroiled in detailed disputes about budgets which were often resolved through brinkmanship.
- Mixed feelings about Region. While Region was seen as supportive and some departments (such as computing) gave an excellent service, they were also seen as overcontrolling in capital planning, and unwilling to delegate even minor decisions.
- There was insufficient planning for people. Despite the early vision, Phase 1 planning in the end was dominated by questions of physical plant. A good example would be housing. Accommodation for junior medical staff was not ready on time, council houses were not always popular with nurses; there were difficult transport problems for nurses living off site. Within the hospital, there was inadequate provision for relatives' rooms, poor rest room facilities for nurses, and no night meal

service. Phase 1 was seen by some as a cold and unwelcoming place to work.

- Failure to learn: there was no debriefing and although nurse middle management had a wealth of operational knowledge, this had not been scripted in. So mistakes may be repeated in Phase 2.

Int: What was the quality of the commissioning for Phase 1 like?

Resp: I don't think it was very high. I think more worryingly, the lessons that should have been learnt from Phase 1 have not been. Phase 2 is proceeding in exactly the same bumbling way as Phase 1. (Consultant)

Post-opening Difficulties: the First Confrontation

The period after opening was a difficult one. People were seen as 'living off the euphoria of how they had opened the hospital successfully, they had not said "well, we have done that, now where do we go to?" The thing had opened and then slipped back, instead of opening and going forward' (Unit General Manager). Keen, young clinicians were getting through the work but increasingly running up against financial constraints (Watson, 1985). There was also an important change in leadership in the unit with the introduction of general management. The first UGM (Acute) was appointed in late 1985. He had previously been District Treasurer, came to the job with a clear managerial orientation ('a manager, not an administrator'), as well as a keen interest in financial control. Relations with the two surviving members of the Commissioning Team were not so good, and both left the District. It was the first change of managerial leadership for the hospital.

The District's acute sector strategy was implicitly expansionist, centred on building up plant, and managerial behaviour could oscillate between financial control and planning for expansion. The DGM, however, had gained most experience in developing priority group strategies, and acute sector issues were new to him. One perception was of a 'vacuum at the centre' with vague and possible contradictory objectives. The big problems were the burst of activity (Accident and Emergency attendances in particular were much higher than projected) and an emerging overspend, so that by December 1984 a £242,000 overspend was already apparent in the acute unit (Watson, 1985). Region was concerned that the high efficiency levels already achieved should not be put in jeopardy (especially as they could be used as targets for other hospitals in the Region) and was sympathetic to the argument that these activity levels represented higher than anticipated levels of need. Thus in early 1985 the RGM advised that no steps need to be taken to reduce services in the current year and that additional funding could be made available. The pattern was set for a series of uplifts in revenue in response to a local crisis, either through general development monies or from an advance on Phase 2 monies:

What has happened on numerous occasions is that there has been an overspend, the hospital or unit has said 'look, in order to save money we have to do this, are you prepared to take the political consequences?' and the health authority have fudged it, have backed down, and said 'well, perhaps you can overspend a bit longer and the money will appear' and to be fair to Oxford Region it has to a large extent. (Consultant)

Despite a further uplift in 1986, the overspend re-emerged in the winter of 1986–7, with the Treasurer projecting a £350,000 overspend by February 1987. This was seen within the District as a potential signal to Region of a serious escalation which could herald progressive loss of financial control: 'an overspend of £250,000 was to be expected . . . but if it was clearly going to be double that they wanted to see things happening. There was pressure therefore from the RHA' (District General Manager).

Approval was sought from January 1987 for managers to take vaguely worded 'corrective action', with the bulk of the savings (£120,000) falling on the Acute UGM where the overspend was concentrated. Moreover this target was to be met with only two months left in the financial year. As an accountant and an ex-treasurer, 'overspending was anathema' to the Acute UGM and he took firm action to meet these targets. Firm action meant that non-emergency surgery was stopped for two months and 40 beds closed, these decisions being made with minimal consultation with clinicians. These closures did in fact achieve the requisite savings by April, when the beds were re-opened. Admissions had in turn to be policed to ensure that the ban on elective surgery was maintained:

This patient with the hip got through the front door. I had to send someone out and say 'I am sorry but you can't come in.' Now the consultant was annoyed by that, but equally I was annoyed that he was not playing by the rules. (Unit General Manager)

The UGM became enmeshed in deciding who was an emergency and who was not, and this was seen by some as difficult terrain on which to fight.

The result was uproar at the Hospital Medical Advisory Committee in February and clinicians went straight to the DGM – as a clinician – to win his support about 'interference' in clinical judgements. The result was that the UGM was forced to back down on the monitoring of patient admissions, while the DGM ruled that admission was a clinical matter but also insisted that the 40 beds should remain closed despite 'banging of the table' from the clinicians until necessary savings were made. This was perceived as a major defeat for unit general management by the UGM. This sprang perhaps from a firm commitment at Unit level to financial objectives despite the wider ambiguity in the system and the dangers of interference in clinical judgement.

This is not to say that changes in bed use did not continue. Indeed that summer a five-day ward was introduced while, in the next winter, planned closures around Christmas were extended. The solution adopted the next year was to employ a nurse as 'bed manager', who had control of admissions, and was supported by a clinician who was given authority to decide priorities if the need arose. Some felt that the closure of beds was in fact useful in demonstrating both to the Region and the Consultants that the DHA would take necessary action. Of course accounts of these events vary. Some felt that the 'Unit Manager had to manage' while others felt that this led to a battle being fought on the wrong battleground when the war was being won in any case!

A second managerial objective was to 'stabilize' Phase 1, given the perception at least among nursing staff that Phase 1 had opened in a vacuum. A new Assistant UGM/Director of Nursing Services was appointed (February 1987) who saw a clear need to define structures and develop nursing middle management: 'It is pointless going into Phase 2 if Phase 1 is not right. This was my whole objective, stabilizing Phase 1, never mind Phase 2, let's get Phase 1 right, standards raised and working . . .' (Assistant UGM).

Moving on to Phase 2

Much of the early planning for Phase 2 had been done in the early 1980s, with an important input from Region, and the scheme was inherited by the Unit. Originally projected for a 1984–5 start, in the end Phase 2 started on site in 1988 because of the overcommitment of the Regional capital budget and the need to trim costs. 'Phase 2 is slipping faster than time itself' became a Milton Keynes saying. The District was under pressure not to endanger the timetable still further by challenging weaknesses such as the rather odd siting of facilities like theatres:

> clinicians have had no link with Phase 2 planning, none, and you probably know that the capital programme for Region was overspent and economies had to be made in Phase 2. These were done without any reference to clinicians, none, and it was only at the very last minute that we were able to stop the really crass, idiotic, things. (Consultant)

> They showed me the Phase 2 plans, and I said, 'I do not believe it', and then they said, 'obviously we can't do anything about it', so it was just a matter of sitting on my hands and doing nothing, just in case I would put Phase 2 behind – which I think is quite a big price to pay for something that I think personally is very badly planned. (Assistant Unit General Manager)

There was once more lack of clarity about the revenue which would be available for Phase 2, with Region likely to argue that not all the beds would be needed for acute care. District's objective, by contrast, was to get Phase 2 built, and worry about the revenue later.

Postscript: Stabilization

By 1991, many of the anxieties apparent in the mid 1980s seemed overdone. Phase 2 was due to be handed over in August 1990, but in fact this occurred in March 1991. With the new methods of funding the NHS, it will take a couple of years yet before the District is funded on a per capita basis, and the reversing of flows from other hospitals is 'allowed' by Region. This may mean that at least two of the new wards will not be affordable for two years, and this spare capacity will need to be marketed.

The hospital has applied for self-governing trust status by 1992. The DHA was due to be amalgamated with the other two Buckinghamshire DHAs by April 1992. There have been overspends in the acute unit, but financial control has been retaining, by delaying developments, waiting list initiative monies and virement from other budgets. The 'bed manager' has helped, but not solved, the difficulties arising from the delay in opening Phase 2 and the pressures brought about by other nearby DGMs closing beds for financial reasons.

Discussion

Clearly any account of the creation of the Milton Keynes DGH which was confined to the commissioning process by itself would be misleadingly narrow. There was an important prior history, stretching back to the late 1960s, and many of the key decisions were taken Regionally if not nationally, rather than locally. The political process played an important role in securing scarce investment, and the existence of a key player such as the Milton Keynes Development Corporation – with its own lines to centres of power – helped change the rules of the game. While there had been initially a 'growth idea' or broad vision generated in specialist planning machinery, much of it seemed to fade given the transition to mainstream planning processes where the dominant pressures were to build to time and to cost. Capital planning responsibility was split between the tiers, hindering the ability of the DHA to generate a strategic grasp of the whole process: it was better to build something flawed than not to build anything. Milton Keynes was such a green field site, and there was so little local capacity to begin with, that it proved difficult to generate a 'growth idea' locally, and indeed it was the senior levels of Regional administration who more than anyone acted as a champion for the project, over a long timescale (20 years), helping protect Milton Keynes's position against competitor Districts.

This is not to say that the commissioning process itself was unimportant and indeed there were difficulties experienced in forming a small group which could guide commissioning effectively. The difficult dynamics in the group, the confusion about roles, the difficulty in obtaining effective clinical advice, and the failure to debrief and to learn, all represented weaknesses in the commissioning process. The DMT was seen as acting in an overcontrolling fashion – which made it even more difficult to build the group – suspecting weakness and desperate to meet the target for opening, which had politically become a litmus test for success.

No cohesive mixed group of managers and clinicians had emerged in the commissioning period, given continuing confusion in role. But while the hospital opened to some extent in a vacuum, social structures quickly formed. The emergent differences in perspective between the newly appointed clinicians and the new generation of general managers were highlighted in the handling of the emerging Unit overspend which resulted in a defeat for Unit general management. Imposed retrenchment was in the end not acceptable to clinicians, the DGM or the DHA. Relations between clinicians and managers soured rapidly: was the new DGH fast becoming more similar than different, despite early hopes that major change in role could be achieved on a green field site with a new consultant body? Underlying this unwillingness to retrench was a perception that financial targets were ambiguous, and that with enough lobbying the goal posts could be moved by Region. Whether this is a viable long-term strategy for financial control remains to be seen.

Finally, the case study illustrates once more the difficulties of performance assessment in the NHS. Could the new hospital be seen as a 'success' or not? Alongside important indicators of 'success' (opening in full and on time), there were also weaknesses (the failure to obtain consultant input; poor team dynamics; overcommitment of the Regional capital programme; lack of control and direction at District level). Moreover there was a failure to generate learning for Phase 2. Respondents themselves used very different success criteria, with broadly speaking those furthest from the hospital most likely to see it as a success. Moreover, performance assessment is vulnerable to the timescale chosen, as between 1987 and 1991 there appear to have been important processes of stabilization and recovery apparent in the District.

Bromsgrove and Redditch: a Clinical Product Champion

Bromsgrove and Redditch is one of the smaller Districts in the West Midlands Region (with a population of about 170,000), previously part of the Hereford and Worcester AHA but becoming an autonomous District in 1982. The two main towns have a history of rivalry: Redditch is a New Town established in the 1960s, whereas Bromsgrove is an old-fashioned market town with more gradual growth. Up to the opening of the new DGH, the bulk of the District's acute services were provided at Bromsgrove at the General. However, the siting of the new hospital at Redditch reversed this historic position. Unlike Milton Keynes, therefore, there were pre-existing institutions and a medical and nursing workforce which was drawn into the new organization.

Those who looked at the District before 1982 described it as a poor performer (Bromsgrove General had only 61 per cent bed occupancy for example) and as having a history of management instability and turbulence: substandard buildings; a history of little capital investment and Area neglect; poor management infrastructure, with a strong finance function but weak on planning and intensely bureaucratic and 'admini-stration-bound'. There was a tradition of long service, dependability and strong local attachment, with little experience of external recruitment or of training. In 1981 a series of patient care issues resulted in adverse press coverage and so when the District was formed in 1982 there was a search for new blood. The DA (later DGM) who took up the post was aware of the bad history and saw himself as having a 'rescue role'. The DA set about strengthening the senior management and brought in staff whom he characterized as 'young, career motivated, progressive thinking, prepared to work very long hours and bring a lot of commitment'. New medical and professional staff were also being brought in as the prospect of a new DGH began to exercise a significant pull.

Pressure for Development and the Problem of Siting, 1948–1977

There were long-standing pressures for redevelopment as Bromsgrove General Hospital had been built as an Emergency Medical Service war time hospital, and by the 1970s the fabric had badly decayed:

> The hospital was built during the course of the Second World War for treating mainly American servicemen who had been injured in battle and they are single storey huts. They were built to last about 15 years. Ours was built in 1940 and there we still were in 1976.

The need for redevelopment is said to have been recognized at the inception of the NHS in 1948. The *Hospital Plan* White Paper (Cmnd 1604, 1962) included Bromsgrove and Redditch in its programme of intended developments, envisaging that the new DGH would be built on the Bromsgrove General site. The West Midlands RHA capital strategy programme (for financial years 1974/84) had developed a Regional commitment to build DGHs in each District, with the Bromsgrove and Redditch scheme being scheduled to start in the early 1980s.

The situation was changed by the creation of Redditch New Town with ambitious population targets. Redditch planners intended that the new hospital should be sited in Redditch, and earmarked a site on the southern boundary of the designated area (Cmnd 3000, 1966). Rivalry between the two towns threatened to stall the whole process, and in 1977 the Secretary of the Medical Executive Committee (who later became Chairman of the Commissioning Executive) became involved, producing a memorandum to 'tell the people of both towns what we were trying to do and that if they did not agree a site shortly we would not get a hospital at all'.

There were prolonged negotiations between Region and DHSS on the siting issue, but in June 1977, the RHA produced its definitive consultation document which resolved the siting issue (the Redditch site was chosen), and clarified that the new DGH would imply the change of use or closure of some existing hospitals. The new hospital was to be designed as a 'first phase Nucleus hospital of about 300 beds with capability of growth and change up to 600–900 beds'. Bromsgrove was, however, to be compensated by the creation of a community hospital on the BGH site. The basic configuration of services was also outlined. The document cited recent DHSS guidance that the expansionist period of public expenditure was at an end, and that given limited capital budgets, there were to be fewer whole hospital schemes. Building on this guidance, West Midlands RHA elected for smaller building phases and a more modest scale. The Redditch site was agreed at an RHA meeting (16 November 1977) and planning could begin in earnest.

The Planning Phase, 1978–1981

The initial Regional document originally had seen the hospital as an exercise in relocation rather than expansion: for example, 'the new hospital is a splendid replacement of the services in the old Bromsgrove General and not an additional service, on old planning norms, except the A and E, and trauma beds'.

> It was very much what we have got in Bromsgrove General Hospital at the moment, and what are we going to move in and most of it was staying at that. And we'll need some more children's beds because we've got a lot of children now coming into the District – almost seat-of-the-pants, gut reaction, decision making.

But a strong planning lead was now being given by some local clinicians, as those who had exerted pressure on the Region to resolve the siting issue remained involved. One clinician in particular – a consultant anaesthetist – was active and assertive, determined to influence the shape and direction of the new hospital. He was instrumental in getting the MEC to produce a detailed discussion document in June 1978 spelling out the stages in developing the hospital, the decision-making arrangements, the functional content of the new hospital and a local philosophy. This same consultant was then the Secretary of the MEC, later to become the consultant member on the RHA Project Team (1978–81/2) and then Chairman of the District Commissioning Executive (1982–5/6). It would seem that the MEC document became the working brief for the Region and the District, and that the MEC Secretary from this time on became the local clinician champion of the hospital, having both an important and enduring executive position and a personal sense of mission to get the new hospital.

The document contained strong statements about values, such as a patient-centred environment and public involvement:

> We should bear in mind the need to produce a building and an ambience which will inspire trust and affection . . . we are not building a showplace; but on the other hand, architecture, interior decoration, and landscaping – not necessarily costly in themselves – can make all the difference between a soulless mausoleum and a place fit for human habitation. The modern vogue for flat roofs, concrete, stainless steel and plate glass may not be the best approach to the design of the hospital.

One way to promote the friendly ambience so necessary to a patient's confidence and recovery is to involve the local community in the planning of the hospital right from the start. It is, after all, their hospital.

The philosophy and values laid down at this stage were rehearsed and defended throughout the entire commissioning process, providing a touchstone for decisions. It is also worth noting a plea for better financial information and efficiency. The document asked that:

In order to run the new hospital efficiently, consultants should be:

(a) given financial responsibility for clinical budgets;
(b) provided with appropriate information about costs;
(c) offered incentives to encourage them to act in an economic manner.

This contradicts the commonly held view that clinicians are universally change-resistant, profligate with money and reactive.

In 1982 DHSS pressure led to a sudden and critical debate concerning the level at which the hospital would run and the revenue required to run it. The accounts suggest that this was a period of extreme crisis when it seemed as if the DGH was once again in jeopardy. There was pressure on the Region from the DHSS (there had been embarrassing failures to open other new DGHs such as in Nottingham), through a letter asking for Regional assurances that the new hospital would be opened in full and that arrangements would be made to meet any shortfall in revenue should local closures fail to raise sufficient funds.

An accelerated programme of closures now had to be devised as the goalposts shifted, as the new District Administrator made clear:

The main contract for building the hospital was due to be let, and I had started in April, and about August, we were given about a week to give an assurance jointly with the RHA that when the hospital opened it would open in full, and to indicate precisely how that would be done. And within a week we virtually decided how we were going to restructure our hospital services within the District, which . . . naturally accelerated the closure of hospitals that would not otherwise have closed. We persuaded the Department to build two extra wards to facilitate the closure of the other units.

With such high stakes, the DA was able to mobilize the support of key constituencies, with managers and clinicians forming an alliance (the consultant member on DMT was seen as particularly influential and supportive). Moreover, closure was linked to securing other planning gains for potential 'losers', such as the general practitioners. While Regional officers worked hard with the District to achieve a solution, there was confusion about what precisely was agreed about funding revenue consequences (and this confusion resurfaced in 1986–7). Nevertheless, the crisis was averted and in November 1982 the contract for the new DGH was let.

The Commissioning Process, 1982–1986

While there had been some early efforts to secure a commissioning focus in the District, the 1982 reorganization created a hiatus as new managers came into post. But prompting from the newly appointed Unit Administrator in November 1982 led to discussion at DMT, out of which the concept of two groups emerged, namely a core executive group (Commissioning Executive, CE) and an operational group (Commissioning Team, CT). The CT was to report to the CE, and the CE to the DMT on a quarterly basis. The CE was to be chaired by the consultant member of the RHA Project Team, and it was to be accountable for 'the overall development and promulgation of the commissioning programme' and for identifying policy issues. The CE's first report (February 1983) identified some critical issues for the commissioning process such as:

• Preparation of a commissioning programme was seen as essential on the basis of a network programme.
• The value of research on other District experiences was noted.
• Emphasis was placed on public relations throughout because of the 'two towns' factor.
• Departmental working groups were to be established to prepare operational policies and manpower requirements. Seminars would explain roles of groups to key people.
• Concern was expressed about revenue allocation when compared to activity levels and Nucleus design.

The CE remained a stable body until the approach of the opening of the DGH and the introduction of general management. In March 1986 the CE was replaced by the DGH Opening Steering Committee, now chaired by the DGM, but otherwise with substantial continuity. However, the meeting procedures were to be streamlined with agendas having standing items, monthly progress reports were to be introduced and there was to be increased delegation of specific tasks to individuals. The CT had a more chequered history, with much greater turnover of staff. The hospital opened in full and on time in September 1986.

How does the case study stand on the variety of Performance Indicators identified? The District can be proud of the fact that the hospital opened in full and on time, despite a tortuous prehistory. There was however a significant overshoot on the capital budget (£2.2m on a £15.3m contract) although the impression of some managers in the District was that they undershot the capital budget! A Public Accounts Committee investigation concluded:

> The overrun at Bromsgrove [*sic*] stemmed mainly from delays in providing information for which the engineering design consultants were reprimanded by the Department. Another factor was the design changes which became necessary to accommodate additional legionella precautions. (Public Accounts Committee, 1990)

The CHC Report for 1985–6 praised the way that commissioning had been undertaken:

> The Secretary has been privileged to be on the Commissioning Executive – now the Steering Group for Opening – as a consumer representative . . . he has been impressed by the dedication and commitment of the Commissioning Team and everyone else connected with the project to make sure that as much as possible is as right as possible.

There were of course some problems: equipping had brought 'major headaches', and rumours about equipping difficulties led to staff taking things into their own hands, secreting pieces of equipment from their old units, and transferring them, sometimes without permission. Operational policies were sometimes not implemented, left unfinished, poorly formulated or inoperable. Very often staff had to perform new tasks, and adopt new practices, as well as adjust to a new physical environment. There was also a mix of new recruits, experienced staff and staff from two old local hospitals who had different conventions and habits. Staffing levels were also overambitious, especially medical and nursing staffing budgets, both of which had to be pulled back at a time of escalating activity which caused great difficulty within the Unit.

Into an Overspend

> I think for the future there needs to be (and I think this is a lesson for Region as well) a very clear understanding on the level of revenue resourcing for the new hospital when it is to open and linking that to activity.

There was a sense in Bromsgrove and Redditch that the Milton Keynes experience could be theirs: indeed it was. The Watson (1985) article on the Milton Keynes experience found its way into the Bromsgrove and Redditch archives, yet despite this knowledge the District seemed unable to prevent an overspend from building up there too. From very early on after the opening of the new DGH, it was apparent that there had been an underestimate of activity levels (a throughput of 16,400 was being realized against an expectation of 14,200), and this steep increase in activity seems to have taken everyone by surprise ('the workload was like an avalanche'). The fast acceleration of activity raised issues about strength of data, and the role of information systems in resource management. This escalation also put a strain on some of the weaker departments (such as medical records), created pressure for staff who had been used to a different pace of work in other hospital (such as Smallwood), and threatened the organizational stability of the hospital as a whole:

> the quality of the data was very dubious. We were on very shaky grounds and we had a lot of cries going up throughout the organization – 'I can't cope; I can't cope' – and you had nothing scientific to quantify 'I can't cope' on.

> Smallwood is a very different hospital to BGH. It was an oil and water job . . . I think it was very much, we didn't do this in Smallwood, or we didn't do this in BGH.

Unlike the Preston case, the crucial interface for District management was up rather than down the organization. There were complex discussions and negotiations with the RHA, and a compromise solution on the agreed level of revenue funding was not reached until mid 1987. The differences concerned the adequacy of service planning, and the interpretation of the meaning of earlier agreements about 'opening in full'. In the end Region agreed to increase the budget, but leaving District to find £0.5m through reductions in establishments and service rationalization. The explanations for why the activity levels increased include not only national trends towards faster throughput but also local factors: the behaviours of new clinical enthusiasts; a new pace of work; new technologies and drugs; the impact of A and E; changed referral patterns from GPs; increased public expectations following the 'selling' of the hospital; and changing cross-boundary flows.

Discussion

As in the Milton Keynes case, the creation of a new DGH can only be understood as a long-term process (starting well before commissioning), involving the accumulation of support at a number of different levels. The handling of politics was important not only at Regional level, but also locally, given the history of rivalry between two local towns. Region played a role throughout the process, yet the District perhaps retained a greater degree of control over the growth process. As in Milton Keynes, there was an underestimate of activity levels and an overspend quickly emerged (although negotiations to resolve it seemed less confrontational).

As far as the commissioning process itself was concerned, the quality of the working relationships and performance of the CE and the CT was praised: both groups were seen as dedicated, professional and willing to learn from the experience of other Districts (including Milton Keynes). Exploratory visits were encouraged to other sites, and 'away days' were used to forge a group identity. The impression is one of determined enthusiasts and specialists, united in their campaign to get the best facility up and running. The two-tier process linked by the District Commissioning Officer had advantages and disadvantages. Executive members had high status and therefore problems could be sent up the line: 'I would take the DGM out one evening and say, "Look we have got this problem, what do we do now?" And we would talk about it. I could talk to anyone.' The CE could provide guidance and help to the CT members, appraise performance and also engage in problem solving. However there was also uncertainty about the role, and there were some personality clashes between the Chairmen of the two bodies. Some members in the groups also acted as professional lobbyists, talking up their own staffing bids.

The CT had particular difficulties as there were delays in getting the team assembled and then the team disbanded as a unit before the commissioning task was complete. Not only did the commissioning resources dwindle, but the staff took with them much insight and knowledge that could not be replaced. The resource was thin in the first place, and the contractual position and security of tenure of the CT was also commented upon, as was the relationship of the CT to the future management of the DGH. The fact that the CT was grafted on to the District, rather than having a clear stake in managing the new hospital, was felt to be mistaken by some respondents.

What was the role of management in commissioning? While the process was kick-started by the DA, he played less of a role once the CE had been established. The CE had a very strong clinician chairman and almost provided 'shadow' management of the new scheme. Within consensus management, it could prove difficult to tackle potentially troublesome issues. For example, the DA was worried about the low levels of drug, medical and surgical budgets, as against nursing and medical staffing, but was overruled by the professionals on the DMT. With the introduction of general management, the new DGM was concerned to keep to time and took the chair of the new Steering Group. This was the point at which the new general managers assumed control and assimilated the special groups into mainstream structures. While on the one hand, general management brought a sharpening focus and increased discipline, it also destabilized previous arrangements and created some confusion.

The case study also produces interesting evidence about the role of individuals. While there was strong evidence of teamwork, three individuals were variously accredited with leading the development (the CE Chairman, the DGM and the DCO). The CE Chairman provided the critical link between the medical staff and the project, helping to promote good clinical practice and high quality patient care. He was seen as the 'visionary' of the team, with radical ideas, strong opinions and the verve to tackle hierarchies. His commitment to the DGH spanned eight years, soaking up enormous personal energy, persistence and resolve.

The DGM, by contrast, took on 'foreign policy', negotiating with Region and the DHSS, and keeping in touch with the local community. He also helped ensure that the project kept to time, and that targets were met. His profile oscillated between high and low at different points of the process, and he often worked through his officers or the CE Chairman.

The DCO received credit for maintaining the operational thrust of the project, and had a lead role in managing the day-to-day activities of the CT where there was a need for experience, attention to detail, accessibility and visibility in the organization and external contacts in the world of commissioning.

Preston: Clawing Back the Overspend

Preston DHA (with a small population of 127,000) is part of the North West RHA, and the old Lancashire AHA. It is situated north of the Chorley and South Ribble DHA, with which it has had historic service links. While there are some rural and suburban areas, and some urban renewal is evident, there remain many streets of small stone or brick-built terrace houses, and parts of the District are characterized by very high levels of unemployment, housing problems and multiple deprivation. The population experiences more ill health than the national average and in particular rates of lung cancer, respiratory and cardiovascular disease are high. The District contains a major new acute hospital (the Royal Preston which opened in 1981) with more than 700 beds.

The introduction of general management brought radical change, with a new DGM, three UGMs and a new District Management Board where continuity was only provided through the medical membership. The District has witnessed several changes in senior management, in 1982 and again in 1985, and indeed there was a period of considerable instability and unfilled senior management posts prior to 1985. For example, no full-time Treasurer had been in post in the District for 18 months prior to the introduction of general management. Some described the period 1982–5 as a time of weak financial management, which was radically changed by the introduction of general management. As one long serving officer put it:

> I think there has been a complete shake up. I think some Districts managed to introduce the philosophy and principles of general management with very little change in the existing structures and very little change in the existing personnel. In other Districts, and I think that Preston must be included, general management was only introduced with massive changes to the existing structures, massive changes to personnel.

Some of the essential features of the District's management style have already been outlined in Chapter 6.

The Royal Preston Hospital

Opened in 1981, the Royal Preston Hospital (757 beds) provided the bulk of acute services both for Preston and for what became in 1982 Chorley and Ribble Health District. The new hospital was to replace obsolescent plant on several sites, but several of these sites remained open until well into the 1980s. When this case study opens, in 1985, with the appointment of the first DGM, the District General Hospital had become the health authority's most pressing and urgent problem, contributing the bulk of a District recurring revenue overspend of £3m per annum.

An interesting feature of the Royal Preston is the paucity of managers' experience of its early history. By 1988 very few top managers had been working in Preston during commissioning, with the result that the Unit had been separated from its own early history. Moreover the absence of Unit management in 1981–5 with prior experience of running a large and complex acute unit was another important weakness:

> There had been several small hospitals in Preston, when I say small, one of them was, of course, the Royal Infirmary, which was *the* hospital, but it was only about 400 beds, maybe less. So it is really smallish, although people don't

really see it that way. And the rest are even smaller. So there was nobody at all who had got large hospital experience and it showed. And in fact, not a lot of large hospital experience had gone into the planning, so some of the problems that they are experiencing are, in my view, directly related to that. (Unit Manager)

This absence of a cohesive managerial lead perhaps contributed to the fragmented nature of the early hospital administration. Respondents characterized it as running as an assemblage of small fragmented units, with no coordination of activity and control. Without a lead either at Area or District, the Royal Preston's early history was of drift rather than of planned development. After commissioning, the agreed capacity and activity of the hospital was not controlled, and there was a relaxation of the pressures to accomplish the transfers and bed closures that were inherent in the funding agreed with Region:

> Beds didn't alter, proposed usage of beds never materialized, they were used for more cheaper services. So all of those changes had a knock on effect on this underfunding. And we have never really recovered from that. (Unit Accountant)

After the 1982 reorganization, the District would appear to have let the 'development drift' continue at the Royal Preston, funding the growing overspend from virement of the revenue provided for psychiatric services and from joint finance.

The Origins of the Overspend and the Pressures for Change, 1981–1985

By 1985, services at the Royal Preston were costing the District some 15 per cent above the original projection agreed between Area and Region. What were the causes of this progressive lack of financial control?

The NHS Planning Process and its Impact   The commissioning of Royal Preston Hospital coincided with a tight financial climate for the service nationally in the 1980s, such as underfunding of pay increases and the rapid escalation of some non-pay items such as the drugs budget. DHSS and Regional guidance on activity levels in new acute hospitals seems to be lower than the demand forecasts of acute sector clinicians, and demand shot up in Preston as in Milton Keynes and Bromsgrove and Redditch – theatre cases for instance rising from 10,200 in 1983 to 11,400 in 1984, to 16,800 in 1985 and 20,300 in 1986:

> Royal Preston was a new hospital and took some time to establish itself in its new role, then the sheer momentum was built up and it is almost impossible to immediately switch that off . . . It must be even more difficult with a brand new hospital that everyone wants to use . . . 'why can't they use this brand new hospital that's just gone up?' (Regional Officer)

Inadequate cost and information systems were also a generic weakness across much of the NHS in this period. Specialty costs were not known;

activity was not recorded in sufficient detail and budgets were not spent by those who held responsibility for controlling them. There were also few incentives for clinicians, who controlled much of the spending, to become involved in the management process and there was no effort to integrate consultants or management staff into the management structure.

The problems which arose in agreeing the revenue consequences of capital schemes between Area and Region are also common to many new developments and were seen in the previous two case studies considered in this chapter. While Region bargained Area's bid downwards, the administration of the new District tried to find revenue from elsewhere in their budgets to make up for this shortfall.

District-Specific Features Respondents also argued, however, that District's own management and decision processes bore much of the responsibility for the overspend, which had escalated to £3m by 1985 (a much greater level of overspending and over a more extended period of time than in the other two cases studied). There had been poor financial control after the break-up of Area in 1982, with a part-time Treasurer in post and the new District taking on some of Area's old role:

> I am sure that a lot of the problem was that Preston took on the old AHA role. I can see how it arose . . . They [Preston] are much more competent than they [AHA] were, in that you can tend to trust their figures and so on. (Regional Officer)

> We have never really recovered from that [initial underfunding]. There was a legacy. But it does not mean to say that management should not have addressed the problem . . . management should have tightened its belt and planned accordingly. (Unit Officer)

There was also a problem of managerial overload across the District, with a major change agenda in psychiatric as well as acute services. By contrast, the management resource at that stage was thin and directionless: the top tier was seen as lacking in initiative, and the middle tier as undistinguished. The new general managers, appointed in 1985 after a period in which the Chair was vacant, and the DGM post had been twice readvertised, faced a daunting task.

Preston's response to the early problems in the acute sector was to evade the issue of underfunding, by funding the overspend through virement from the psychiatric and joint finance budgets. Not only did such virement augment strategic planning blight in the priority group sector, but such measures proved to be of a short-term and palliative nature. Eventually the day of reckoning came as the Region clawed the money back: 'The NWRHA will also be looking for £500,000 to be withdrawn from Royal Preston Hospital, which is the sum funded out of earmarked Ring Fence monies' (Preston DHA, Agendum 4, December 1987).

There were also weaknesses at hospital level. Several respondents criticized the physical design of the new hospital – expensive to maintain, 'it soaks up staff to an unnecessary degree'. The old hospitals which were to be replaced by the new DGH were not closed either as quickly or as cheaply as planned. Weak hospital administration had been intertwined with the failure of clinicians to involve themselves in management and a fragmentation of the Unit into a collection of unorganized, compartmentalized, subunits, with uncoordinated decision making. A senior nurse who joined the hospital in 1983 observed that:

> I came into several small hospitals under one roof really . . . the small hospitals that had moved in here had been encouraged to retain their identity within this one . . . but I feel that you have to have a cohesive service, you can't have a fragmented service, you lose a tremendous amount, it is wasteful. So one of the things that I felt I had to do was to make it into *A* hospital, to become one cohesive unit, not just to do that, but also to make sure that people realized that a big hospital is actually a very different organism from a small one.

The cooperation of the clinicians was not secured prior to the DGM/UGM's appointments. The clinician body itself was relatively large, with 80 consultants, and the history of relations with District management was of detachment. The clinicians were respected, but saw their role as purely clinical, not in terms of service control:

> Perhaps the clinicians initially switched off. Perhaps they were familiar and happy with the old set-up, the old DA and the old District Treasurer, who in management terms were not very good, but in terms of pleasing the clinicians were pretty good, and everything was a bit loose . . . (Regional Officer)

> Probably the biggest problem is the fact that the consultants object to managership. Certainly in this patch they have not shown any willingness to work. When we have asked them to be budget holders, are they interested in coming in on to the management side to be a budget holder? They haven't been prepared to . . . Some will say they don't know enough about the financial side of things and they are not accountable, but it is a simple factor of book-keeping really. (District respondent)

So prior to 1985 the old District Administration had failed to bring a large group of independent-minded clinicians into the management process who subsequently behaved as if the overspend was none of their business.

Sensing the Problem and Steps towards Managing the Overspend, 1985–1986

Upon appointment in 1985, the first task of the DGM was to contain the problem and prevent a spiralling of the overspend, given that action had been shelved until he arrived in post. By 'Day 2' the decision to freeze all posts and vacancies was taken; by 'Week 2' 14 ambulances had been withdrawn. These measures alone shaved £1.5m off the overspend.

Of course, much longer-term measures needed to be taken, which required the development of information systems sophisticated enough to act as an effective management tool. Some potentially important problem areas could be identified very quickly (Performance Indicators showed the average length of stay in general medical beds to be well above the national average). But such corrections were necessarily long term, and in the shorter term other actions were taken with the rapid closure of the old, obsolescent, hospitals:

> Having come into general management determined not to be seen in any way as associated with being a financial person, I wanted to get away from my roots as an accountant, I was immediately seen as the wicked accountant who was cutting right, left and centre. (District General Manager)

While there have been initiatives in quality assurance and developing services for ethnic minorities, it is the management of the overspend which has held the stage. Beds were withdrawn following a protracted and controversial efficiency audit of bed usage. This audit entailed complex negotiations with the MEC, trade unions and members and demonstrated a new general managerial commitment to cost control, budget scrutiny and examination of clinical medical practice:

> There has been pressure all across the board. Each of the UGMs who was appointed in the summer of 1986 was clear that we'd got some fairly stringent financial targets, and at the same time there were service developments which they had to create, and there had to be a far rougher approach taken across the board in terms of a need for particular jobs.

Legitimation of Management Action, 1986–1988

At Unit level, general management had to tackle the log jam of clinical resistance, inadequate data systems and the historic lack of any managerial leadership. General management was seen as enhancing cost consciousness (clinicians might have mixed feelings about this), and resulting in speedier decision taking and clearer accountability.

Yet a less noticed aspect of the managerial task was the legitimation of action undertaken. Previously the fragile clinician–manager interface would have been unlikely to withstand the draconian measures taken in reining in the Unit overspend in 1986–8. The task of legitimating such retrenchment has been crucial, and there has been active and detailed attention to this by the UGM and DGM. Understanding and acceptance of closures have only come through patient lobbying of the consultants, to draw them into understanding and participating in the management task. This began with education about the management dilemma, with planning meetings of officers and members to provide legitimacy to officers' proposals at the DHA. The UGM succeeded in gaining access to the Specialty Management Teams, with the MEC Chairman as the formal UMB representative, and the DGM had by December 1987 gained access to the MEC (and the new MEC Chairman in 1989 appeared to have a wider remit in management matters.) These advances were hard won:

> *Resp*: I think in some ways we are moving forward. There is no doubt that in certain specialties the consultants are talking more actively and progressively with myself and [the DGM].

Int: Can you analyse why?
Resp: Hard work on behalf of (the DGM) and myself. (Unit General Manager)

> I would say that the DGM has got a lousy job to try and balance all these
> things, and to balance the various opinions, and I think it is fair to say that,
> can I say that the more enlightened of my colleagues, who see these things have
> got to be, will agree that he is not doing a bad job . . . (Consultant)

Even the formation of lines of communication – to the Teams, to the
MEC, to newly appointed consultants – takes time and effort. The
managers have had to move slowly and patiently, and there are still limits:
'I think they are more willing to actually talk to us. I think we have got
a long way to go. I don't think that they would want resource management at this stage' (District finance officer). There were some signs,
however, of an acceleration of the pace of change:

> We do have some clinicians who are budget holders in the paramedical area,
> which is surprising, and they are very keen and enthusiastic. I think that in the
> last 12 months there has been a change of attitude and a greater appreciation
> of the Health Service problems shown by clinicians . . . it is early stages, a lot
> of ground still to be covered, but I think the seeds have been sown. (Unit
> accountant)

General managers have also had to engage in extensive and time consuming lobbying of DHA members, trying to engage them – especially the
local authority members – with managerial action. The minutes and
agendas of the DHA make clear the repeated references to control of the
overspend, the presentation of information about where additional funds
were being generated, and the reasons why funds were being withdrawn.
By December 1987, the projected overspend at the hospital was down to
£300,000. However, the withdrawal of vired ring-fence money by the
Region threatened to lift the overspend back up to £710,000, indicating
that these issues were recurrent and not about to go away.

Discussion

While the previous two case studies illustrated the long prehistory to
commissioning, this case study considers in particular the post-
commissioning period, where considerable financial difficulties presented.
Region once more emerged as an important arbiter of financial flows,
determining which of District's strategies were in the long run acceptable
and which not.

The Preston case study indicates once more the difficulties of ensuring
organizational development and learning in the NHS: the new DGH
became quickly separated from its early history, and by 1988 few of the
managers in the District had a direct sense of why the hospital had
developed as it had. The hospital had opened, but then had slipped back
into an escalating overspend, in part because of the way in which
administrative and clinical roles had been constructed in the Unit. Clearly

there was an early transition from a growth- to a retrenchment-based agenda, yet the systems or shared sense which might have enabled the hospital to cope with such pressures were not in place and had to be painfully developed. In the initial post-opening period there appears to have been 'development drift' financed by the viring of earmarked money for psychiatric services and joint finance, yet such a strategy was not in the end acceptable to Region. The rationalizations promised in order to secure the hospital were also not implemented until there had been a considerable lag.

The introduction of general management appeared to make much more of an immediate difference in this District than the other two considered. The new general managers appointed were outsiders, came in after a long period of internal drift, were keen to re-establish internal financial control, yet also to construct alliances with at least some of the clinicians (even getting access to the MEC). The new hospital seemed instead to be dominated by a collection of semi-independent groups, with little cross-linkage or shared understandings. Some of the key problems lay in renegotiation of roles such as the manager/clinician interface, given traditional clinical distance from management. The apparent expansion of the role of the MEC Chairman is another case in point. There is an interesting contrast here with the experience of Milton Keynes, where the difficulties might be thought to have been less severe.

Developing New Organizations: Conclusions

We will first of all make some comparative observations across the case studies before moving on to consider how general analysis could be taken further. To recapitulate briefly the findings of the literature review at the beginning of the chapter: the policy system was seen to be utilizing a number of indicators (opening to time, opening to cost, control of revenue expenditure and more vaguely, quality) with which to assess the performance of new DGMs. While more theoretical literature highlighted the questions of the birth and early development of new organizations and of the pattern of clinical–management relations in respect of financial control, as interesting themes.

Comparing and Contrasting

The first observation is that the case study hospitals performed differently on the various performance criteria surfaced by the policy system – no hospital performed badly or well on all indicators. This highlights the complexity of performance assessment in this field, especially as different raters might attach very different weights to the possible measures. Table 8.3 outlines the performance of DGHs in the study against a basket of indicators (although the Preston case is less directly comparable on some

Table 8.3 *New DGHs assessed against possible performance criteria*

	Opened to time	Opened in full	Opened to cost	Revenue overspend	Quality of the process
Milton Keynes	Yes	Yes	No	Yes	Lower
Bromsgrove and Redditch	Yes	Yes	No	Yes	Higher
Preston	n/a	n/a	n/a	Yes	Lower

indicators as it relates to a later period of development of the hospital).

Milton Keynes opened on time, but an overspend soon built up. Bromsgrove and Redditch perhaps enjoyed a higher quality process, but came in well above cost. In all three hospitals a substantial revenue overspend built up, and although the problem was sensed in Bromsgrove and Redditch on the basis of the Milton Keynes experience, the District seemed powerless to take action to prevent a similar overspending emerging there. Opening to time and to cost were the indicators which seemed to be privileged by the official system (failure to open to time or in full was bad news politically), yet far less attention was paid to the quality of the process which could, however, pervasively affect the ability of these new organizations to function. Little thought was given to the construction of such quality indicators. Was the planning process producing healthy young organizations, or was it breeding monsters? In our view, far more attention should be paid to the development of such quality indicators, which would include as one component an awareness of the process. The three case studies outlined in this chapter all indicate the importance of such a process analysis in understanding the pattern of development in each site.

One common feature was the emergence of a revenue overspend, essentially activity-driven with a faster than expected increase in workload. The transition to a new DGH did seem to produce some important organizational discontinuities which should be set against the emphasis on continuity derived from the organizational template model: young, keen consultants; perhaps more flexible patterns of medical staffing; the introduction of new forms of medical intervention such as day surgery and faster throughput; heightened expectations among the community and GP referrers. Despite these common problems, between-District learning seemed rudimentary. However, the overspend drifted highest and for longest in Preston, where prior to the introduction of general management there seemed little organizational focus which could have tackled the budgetary problem.

This highlights the importance of role and culture construction in these new settings. What about the argument that in these new settings surface change coexists with underlying continuity? While there were some important sources of discontinuity (as outlined above) in these new organizations, in two of the cases (Preston and Bromsgrove and Redditch) it is fair to say that some of the old cultural and organizational characteristics of the old hospitals survived transportation – at least initially – to green field sites. At Preston a hospital-wide culture only slowly emerged, and hence there were problems with fragmentation among the subunits as a corporate perspective did not take shape. At Milton Keynes the keynote was one of anomie in a substantially cultureless institution which was crying out for 'stabilization', rather than the survival of vivid organizational and cultural forms.

The roles associated with the construction of these new organizations varied widely from one locality to another. Normann (1977) explores the processes of growth management and develops the concept of a 'growth idea', which may be vision- rather than goal-led: 'visions are not goals. They are intuitive ideas of reasonable (although in relation to the present state, sometimes highly deviating) future states of the system, which sometimes only exist as subjective states.' Indeed, in Bromsgrove and Redditch the exercise was animated and linked to operational action by a clinical product champion, working well in conjunction with other power centres such as the DGM and the DCO. A vision may start to take root as it accumulates a critical mass of political support: 'thus a crucial element in every growth idea is a strategy for effecting the necessary changes in the various power relationships' (Normann, 1977).

Perhaps this was the case which best exemplified the concept of a locally generated vision guiding the process of strategic growth. Nor did the clinicians here seem parochial in their vision, but more broadly concerned to introduce some qualitative change in the form of the new hospital, a view supported by the local CHC. Perhaps the really interesting developments are those which contain qualitative shifts in the type of work undertaken as well as the provision of a new physical shell. So 'templates' may not be as incremental or narrowly professionally based as some have argued. In Milton Keynes, by contrast, the early vision had been held by community medicine specialists who found it difficult to survive the transition to Regionally dominated, capital-led and normative planning. The vision did not lead in the end to substantial qualitative shifts within the new DGH. In Preston, the managerial problem was one of reconstructing the roles which had already emerged in a young organization – which were seen as inappropriate by management – so as to engage clinicians with management and resource control. There seemed in the early years there to be neither a managerial nor a clinical focus, but rather a loose confederation of disparate professionals. Here managers paid careful attention to legitimation of retrenchment by building channels of communication and encouraging the formation of more hybrid roles; the Milton Keynes case demonstrated that a general manager could end up as a sacrificial change agent if this legitimating activity were not undertaken.

Discontinuous Change in New Organizations

What can we say about some of the more general theoretical work introduced at the beginning of this chapter? While little research has been conducted, the concept of an 'organizational template', associated with recent work at the University of Aston, now draws attention to the social, political and cognitive elements in building new organizations. This is a welcome corrective to some of the aprocessual and ahistorical perspectives which hitherto have been evident, stressing the need that decision makers have to make sense of an uncertain world in exhibiting rule- and precedent-bound behaviour. Local histories compete against standard design packages and the outcome is an uncertain product of negotiations. But such a notion of 'an organizational template' also emphasizes substantial continuities in the organizational process, and is thus more sceptical about the impact of moments of discontinuity. Even 'green field sites' may develop on the basis of a set of taken for granted assumptions locally or generated by particular occupational groups which have national systems of inspection and accreditation. This argument would obviously also have implications for the private sector, where often 'green field sites' are preferred because it is thought easier to negotiate new working practices.

Our case studies, however, point to moments of discontinuity as well as continuity in the building of new organizations. 'Green field sites' do indeed appear to be different. In particular the opening of a new DGH seemed to produce some important breaks with the past in terms of the recruitment of new and younger staff, the introduction of new forms of work organization (such as day surgery) and a faster pace of work, leading to a rapid and unplanned for escalation of activity. The opening of the new Accident and Emergency Department in Milton Keynes, for instance, was described as producing a 'tidal wave' of work with a rapid build-up of activity levels. It is interesting to compare these case studies with the new universities which opened in the 1960s. These new universities were able to create their own curricula, build new buildings and plan for green field sites. But more fundamentally, there were certain ideas about the nature of higher education (such as new and cross-disciplinary subjects) which were seen as easier to introduce in 'new' institutions. We thus highlight moments of discontinuity as well as of continuity in these new organizations and believe this has more general resonance for the 'green field sites' debate.

Building New Organizations

We argued earlier that seeing the creation and early history of DGHs through an organizational transitions perspective could be helpful. We then stated that we needed to know more about the organizational and small group processes involved in the creation of these new organizations. What has been found?

First of all, the process of creating these settings has been partly routinized and standardized by higher tiers, although there was also local variation which might be in tension with such standard design packages.

Inter-organizational negotiations seemed much more central to the success of the project than in many accounts of new settings, and there was the related danger that a strong local vision of the new service would or need not be created and defended. There were long processes of gestation, reflecting the complexity of the political environment in which these new organizations operated. There also seemed (at least in two of the case studies) to be more attention paid to the physical shell of the new hospital than to constructing the new organizational order. This confirms Sarason's 1976 analysis of the dynamics involved in the creation of new settings within human service organizations which highlighted the dangers apparent when such physical planning ('monumentalism') displaced concern for organizational relationships. Preston seemed rapidly to have become separated from its own history, and to display little organizational memory; while Milton Keynes DGH was seen by staff as an anomic organization where the problem was not too strong a culture (compare this with the chapter on HIV/AIDS) but the lack of one.

A second point is that early vision and plans for innovation could be initially generated but then fade (the Milton Keynes case was a good example of this). Kimberly's (1980) analysis of the birth of an innovative medical school has also highlighted the rapid pace of institutionalization and routinization of an originally innovative organization, alerting us to the possible question of 'drift'. There is also some evidence (Van de Ven, 1980) of relationships between the ways in which human service organizations were planned and the subsequent implementation 'success'. Lodahl and Mitchell (1980) have taken special interest in the process of 'institution-building', distinguishing between standard technical skills and 'institutional skills', involving the manipulation of structure and process to ensure that the organization becomes an 'institution'. Drift and lack of commitment – they argue – may result in developing organizations where technical matters are given priority over institutional ones.

Only in one of the case studies (Bromsgrove and Redditch), did a high status clinical product champion emerge, maintaining involvement over a long time period, articulating and defending a vision for the hospital and perhaps acquiring a 'founder' role. Otherwise the prime motor seemed to be a top-down mandate for this organizational form, namely the national programme for constructing new DGHs. It seemed difficult to sustain a local vision for development and this highlights the need to consider institution-building much more carefully. This may also be true of new organizations in other sectors.

Clinical–Managerial Relationships

We now turn to another analytic theme identified, namely the pattern of clinical–managerial relationships as it evolves in these new organizations, especially as it relates to core questions of financial control and the capping of levels of clinical activity. The new hospital can be seen as a good example of a setting where management and powerful professionals negotiate for control. In all three settings 'overspends' emerged and managers were drawn into the question of how to influence the behaviour of the clinicians who were the key resource allocators. Deriving such influence was a long and difficult task, as clinicians would fight direct and unlegitimated managerial action to control clinical activity.

It seemed that social orders form within these developing organizations as a result of negotiations between the participating groups. Thus the imposed – and non-negotiated – order briefly apparent in the Milton Keynes case proved fragile, and broke down as clinicians successfully mobilized against general managerial fiat. These negotiation processes are of course influenced by local histories, group ideologies and power relations, but also contain a more substantial degree of local variation than is often implied in crude accounts of the professionalization process. The pattern of manager–clinician relations, for example, varied substantially across the three sites studied, and more surprisingly managers varied in their perception that influencing clinicians was a core part of their managerial brief.

Special problems may arise in new settings such as these where there are few standard rules, and a greater potential for conflict, ambiguity or novelty (Strauss, 1978). Nor are social orders immutably fixed, but may change over time reflecting shifts in power or in strategy. Thus while the introduction of general management was seen nationally as a means of increasing managerial influence vis-à-vis the previously dominant position of clinicians, national change also had to be played out in local settings and changes were more radical in some localities than others. The Preston case perhaps illustrates the use by the new general managers of tactics of persuasion as well as negotiation in renegotiating the pattern of clinical–managerial relations. This echoes Strauss's finding (1978) that much of the content around the negotiation process related to what was and was not a legitimate action, and periodically agreements would have to be renegotiated. This suggests questions for other new organizations (such as the new universities, new forms of legal practices, R & D laboratories and 'high tech' firms) where management coexists with powerful professionals.

Receptive and Non-receptive Contexts for Change

The 1980s were marked by sustained top-down pressure to change not only the structure of the NHS, but also its ruling assumptions and much of the service culture. The new cadre of general managers created by the Griffiths Report (1983) was seen as perhaps one of the most important mechanisms for achieving these changes. Behind this new managerialism were concerns about strategic drift; many policies, including those discussed in previous chapters relating to acute, mental illness and mental handicap services, were being only falteringly implemented.

This book reports evidence on progress in implementing service changes at District Health Authority level. The key questions guiding the study include, did the top-down changes of the 1980s secure change at local levels, and if so, why and how? Was there evidence of variability in the rate and pace of change in Districts facing broadly similar change objectives? Where such differential movement occurred, why did it occur and how? What features of the outer and inner context of each District caused change to occur, and how did those features of context interweave with the change strategies used in the different localities? What mixture of top-down and bottom-up pressure provided momentum and energy for change, and how was early progress maintained, increased, or lost?

Such questions are not specific to the NHS, nor indeed to public bureaucracies in general. The questions raised throughout this book about why, how and when change occurs are of universal significance at all levels in both the private and public sectors. Thus in this final chapter we not only seek to connect some of the key empirical findings in the study, but also discuss their managerial significance alongside that wider set of theoretical and empirical literature now emerging from the private sector.

The comparative case study analyses in Chapters 4–8 demonstrate that DHAs addressing the same strategic change problem display both differences as well as similarities in their experience of the strategic change process. Therefore we need to confront the key generic question: why is it that the rate and pace of strategic change differs across DHAs?

The starting point was that the rate and pace of change could be explained by a subtle interplay between the content of change, the context of change and the process of change. Context may therefore be a critical shaper of process: Pettigrew (1985a) explores within the same firm (ICI) differences between the Agriculture Division (situated north of the River Tees) and Petrochemicals (situated south of the River Tees). Although

these were divisions of the same company, situated in the same geographical region, with broadly similar technologies and recruiting from
the same graduate pool, their processes of handling change were substantially different. The different experiences of Parkside and Bloomsbury
DHAs – neighbouring, Inner London, teaching Districts – both in managing acute sector rationalization and developing a response to HIV/AIDS
reinforce this argument. We conclude, therefore, that the management of
change is likely to be contextually very sensitive; that there is no 'quick
fix' or simple recipe; and that there is no one way of effecting change in
such a pluralist organization as the NHS, where the introduction of
general management has not been at all general, and there seemed almost
as many general managements as general managers.

With these broad caveats, is it possible to begin to see any patterns in
the way that strategic service change occurs? A good focus for this
analysis is the distinction between receptive and non-receptive contexts for
change where we mean by the term 'receptive context' that there are
features of context (and also management action) that seem to be
favourably associated with forward movement. On the other hand, there
is in non-receptive contexts a configuration of features which may be
associated with blocks on change.

The next section of this chapter develops the theme of receptive
contexts for change, drawing on earlier literature which alludes to this
distinction. We then go on to reveal a set of eight highly interrelated
factors which produced receptivity for change in the DHAs we have
studied. The final section draws attention to some major implications of
our findings.

Receptive Contexts for Change

Analytical Underpinnings

In Chapter 1 we argued that despite the substantial literature which now
exists on change in health care organizations, there is a need for more
research which is:

- processual – an emphasis on action as well as structure;
- comparative – a range of studies of local health care agencies;
- pluralist – describe and analyse the often competing versions of reality
  seen by actors in change processes;
- historical – take into account the historical evolution of ideas and
  actions for change as well as the constraints within which decision-
  makers operate.

Behind these important conclusions about research approach lay a
considered view of the short-comings and gaps of much research and
writing on health care decision making and change.

Although the issue of policy implementation failure has fascinated researchers for some time, the focus on priority groups and community care has been narrow, the development and rationalization of acute services has been given much less attention. But if the content of change has been limited, so has the level of analysis. Many public policy studies (Hunter, 1980; Korman and Glennerster, 1985, 1990) and the diffusion-based work of Stocking (1985) have had a unitary or single change issue focus. Little attempt has been made to study how management tackles a larger, interrelated change agenda, juggling time, energy and effort between change issues.

The problems within these studies of a single change issue focus have been exacerbated by the narrow treatment of context in such research. There is a tendency for research on management process in the NHS to concentrate on one tier of management or a single configuration of decision-making. Public policy analysts meanwhile tend to provide explanations which emphasize national barriers to implementation of policy without highlighting local barriers or the differential progress in creating change in a national agenda at District and Unit levels.

Our own approach is to study change over time in a contextualist mode (Pettigrew, McKee and Ferlie, 1988; Pettigrew, 1990). A number of principles underpin such an approach. First, the importance of embeddedness, implying the need to study change in the context of interconnected levels of analysis. Secondly, the importance of temporal interconnectedness – the need to locate change in past, present and future time – should be stressed. Thirdly, the need to explore context and action (how context is a product of action and vice versa) is crucial. Finally, the central assumption about causation in this kind of holistic analysis is that causation of change is neither linear nor singular – the search for a simple and singular grand theory of change is unlikely to bear fruit. For the analyst interested in the theory and practice of changing, the task is to identify the variety and mixture of causes of change and to explore through time some of the conditions and contexts under which these mixtures occur.

But how are we to identify such variety and mixture of causes of change? The promise in our framework lies in the interdependent exploration of content, process and contexts. In the three-dimensional model utilized in this research, already referred to in Chapter 2, context refers to the 'why' and 'when' of change and concerns itself both with influences from the outer context (such as the prevailing economic, social, political and, for Districts, Regional environment) and influences internal to the focal organization under study (for example, its resources, capabilities, structure, culture and politics). Content is the 'what' of change, here the major service changes in the NHS. Finally, process is the 'how' of change and involves examination of how, and by whom change is formulated and managed, and what patterning occurs in this activity. The dimension of time is a fourth critical ingredient, as each of the dimensions is dynamic and changeable in itself. Links between the outer and inner context permit the analysis of national and local barriers to implementation. Analysing the fine shading of the inner context of Districts has permitted us to differentiate between receptive and less receptive contexts for change, highlighting the importance of management style, strategies and tactics as well as structural, political and cultural features of particular locales. Thus we are now able to explain why Districts facing similar environmental and policy pressures behave differently, and sometimes achieve different outcomes at variable rates.

Aspects of the Literature on Receptivity

Pick up any textbook on managing change, for example, Beckhard and Harris (1977) or Plant (1987), or even a more research-based monograph such as Kilmann et al. (1986) or Tichy (1983), and much of the logic of presentation assumes sets of driving or inhibitory forces explaining change and continuity. Such approaches are helpful in stimulating thought around the general question of why change occurs or does not. However, much less attention has been given in the literature on change to the more specific question, why does the rate and pace of change differ across different localities? It is rarer still for questions of rate and pace to be posed in the context of research studies and settings where the content of change is broadly similar, and where there may be some equivalence in the outer context framing the change process.

So far as we are aware, there is no social science research explaining rates and pace of change in varying localities which explicitly uses the language of receptivity and non-receptivity. However, the theme of differential receptivity and how to create it does emerge in sections of the literature on innovation. Thus Roberto Unger (1987) has written a whole treatise on change in social and political institutions which is organized around the language of 'smashing and remaking contexts' (p. 37). In the narrower field of management, Kanter (1985, 1989) has characterized integrative structures and cultures as 'innovation stimulating' and segmented structures and cultures as 'innovation smothering'. There is also a tradition of writing on innovation exemplified, for example, by Rothwell and Gardiner (1985) and Delbecq and Mills (1985) which links the rate and pace of the product development process to various characteristics of the firm.

Scholars interested in why and how human resource changes occur in organizations have begun to tease out the features of context and action which drive, inhibit and stabilize such changes (Goodman and Dean, 1982; Beer et al., 1990; Pettigrew and Hendry, 1991). Finally, there is now an emerging literature which not only seeks to connect features of context and action to rates of adaptation and change, but then posits a relationship between capabilities to change and learn and variations in the competitive performance of firms (Smith and Grimm, 1987; Pettigrew and Whipp, 1991, 1992).

What can be learned from this literature? Kanter's position (1985) seems clear. It is environment, more than the person, which makes the biggest difference in the level of innovative managerial activity. The environment here is defined narrowly as those features of the structure and culture of firms which are described as integrative or segmented. Thus integrative structures and cultures with their holistic problem-solving, team-orientated and cooperative environments, strong mechanisms for idea generation and exchange, sense of purpose and direction, and capability to overthrow and yet use history and precedent, are innovation stimulating. Meanwhile, segmented structures and cultures with their features of compartmentalized problem-sensing and problem-solving, preoccupation with hierarchy and rules, inhibit entrepreneurial spirit and energy and become innovation-smothering situations.

But if certain characteristics of structure and culture provide the desire and energy for innovation, what are the additional sufficient conditions for the delivery of innovation? Here Kanter (1985) takes us into the important process parts of her argument and data. Innovation is certainly a market place for ideas, but it is also only possible where processes of bargaining and negotiation can accrue support and legitimacy for the new order of things. So campaigning, lobbying, coalition-building and the sharing of information, rewards and recognition are all fateful for innovation, together with the stability of key actors championing the evolving idea through the various unpredictable stages and loops of project completion.

Kanter continues this argument in her latest book, *When Giants Learn to Dance* (1989). The research base is less secure and the presentation looser and more didactic, but the quality of writing and argument demands attention. A theme of the book is the need for organizations to create new levels of flexibility to compete more effectively in the ever changing 'global corporate Olympics'. Networks inside the firm and between firms are seen as part of the answer. Hierarchies are now dead. Flexibility and adaptability will come from being person- not position-centred, creation- not efficiency-orientated, results- not rules-orientated, a team and not a hierarchical preoccupation, and from a drive for leverage and experimentation and not a search for ownership and control (Kanter, 1989, p. 353). Aspects of Kanter's developing thesis will be confirmed in what we have discovered about receptive contexts for change in the NHS.

Research on training and human resource management in organizations has also confronted the question of differential rates and depth of change. For Goodman and Dean (1982) the key questions were: why does change persist, and indeed why does change persist more in some settings than others? The results of their research on the persistence of planned change programmes paint a pessimistic picture: 'Change has been successfully introduced, some benefits appeared; but over time the majority of programs had become deinstitutionalized' (p. 268). But what factors precipitated deinstitutionalization of change efforts? The crucial ones appeared to be the disjuncture between the content of the changes and key features of the inner context of the organization, such as the prevailing structures and management philosophy. The early departure of a key sponsor of the change programme and the over reliance on external consultants also destabilized change efforts. Greater progress was also made in implementation when there had been explicit attempts to buffer the change programme from energy-sapping short-term pressures. Again we shall see these patterns evident in our receptive and non-receptive contexts.

The Harvard Business School study of human resource change in organizations also reports noteworthy patterns in the evolution and impact of change programmes (Beer et al., 1990). They conclude that many of the corporate programmes to alter culture or the management of people in the firm are inherently flawed even when supported by top management. Prescriptively they end up by arguing that organizations should start corporate revitalizations by targeting small, isolated, peripheral operations, not large, central core operations.

Work at the Centre for Corporate Strategy and Change at the University of Warwick on human resource change also provides additional clues about change receptivity. Drawing on a sample of 20 UK organizations (Pettigrew, Hendry and Sparrow, 1990; Pettigrew and Hendry, 1991) report on why firms train, what stops them and how and why certain organizations are able to develop their human resources on a continuous basis. The clear message of the research is that those firms that have made developments in their human resources, including new levels of concern for and activity in training, did so under competitive pressures. Human resource change was precipitated by strong pressures from the outer context of the firm which led to business strategy changes which in turn brought a new consciousness of human resource deficiencies and the consequent human resource change. However, the triggering effect of business strategy changes was in itself insufficient to bring necessary levels of receptivity for sustained training and human resource change. The three other positive factors were the external/internal labour market; internal product champions for human resources and availability of appropriate systems, philosophies and management organizations; and external human resource stimuli and support, including funding. Conversely, decay/inertia in human resource change efforts was the result of decline in any number of these forces along with additional specifically negative forces, or contraindicators. Crucially, attention to broader human resource issues (such as career moves and development, appraisal and reviews of organization development and culture change processes) was necessary to cement attention to training. Training alone, for most firms, represented a tap which could too readily be turned on and off. Thus the most effective way to build a receptive context for training in an organization is successfully to address a broader range of human resource issues directly, not to dwell solely on training issues.

Building and sustaining a receptive context for human resource change is an extremely complex process. It involves the weaving together of competences across a wide range of human resource specialisms together with the necessary process skills to develop the activities in specific situational contexts. This interweaving and orchestration of contextual forces and pressures through adroit human action is another key sub-theme in our synthesis of service change developments in the NHS.

The final set of empirical findings linkable to our interest in receptive and non-receptive contexts for change makes the connection between differential capabilities in learning and change and the differential performance of firms. At its most general level in, for example, the work of Teece, Pisano and Shuen (1990), the competitive advantage of the firm is seen to derive from 'its routines, its skills, its organization, and its capabilities' (1990, p. 30). Such intangible assets as technological or managerial know-how, are often tacit, hard to imitate, difficult to develop quickly and yet can be fateful for sustaining advantage in a particular business. Firms that can build situationally specific capabilities, or in Prahalad and Hamel's terms, core competences, will be able quickly to grasp opportunities 'to spawn unanticipated products' (1990, p. 81).

Evidence linking the possession and use of intangible assets to performance is at the moment still confined to a few studies. Drawing on a sample of eight firms from four sectors, Pettigrew and Whipp (1991, 1992) set out to determine if the way a firm managed strategic change made a demonstrable difference to its competitive performance. The main conclusion to be drawn from examining the firms in the four sectors is twofold. First that a common pattern emerges from the key features of managing strategic and operational change among the firms; and second, that there is an observable difference in the way the higher performing firms manage change from their counterparts over time. The pattern is best represented by a model composed of five interrelated factors, the five central factors are shown in Figure 9.1.

Each of the five factors is built upon a combination of conditioning features and secondary mechanisms. The conditioning features and secondary mechanisms gain their power from being developed in combined form. Their potency is built up through repeated application and across differing circumstances. This building process is measured in years rather than months. In terms of competitive success, the management of strategic change is the result of an uncertain, emergent and iterative process. There are no grand blueprints for long-term success or quick fixes for immediate salvation. The process of change relies on the development and use of the less immediately visible organizational capabilities (and particularly those to do with learning and change) called intangible assets. Managing such an uncertain process places heavy demands on the ability of firms to learn and adapt over time in relation to all five factors described and analysed in the Pettigrew and Whipp (1991) model.

Without using the language of receptivity, the Pettigrew and Whipp

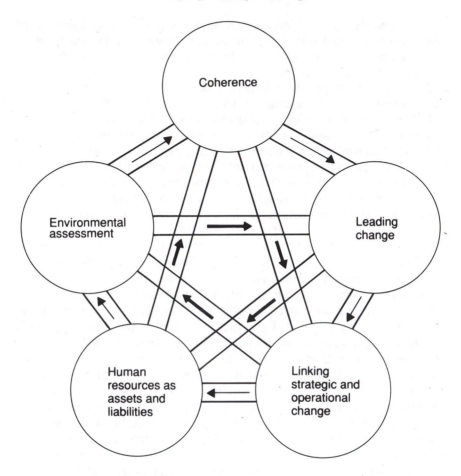

Figure 9.1 *Managing change for competitive success: the five central factors*

(1991, 1992) study points to a clear set of interrelated factors which provide both high energy around change and in turn contribute to performance. All five of the factors are echoed in our higher change Districts, and there are clear parallels between the private sector observations of the change process as uncertain, emergent and iterative, and what we have observed in the NHS.

Roberto Unger's treatise *False Necessity* (1987) provides the most extended, abstract and theoretical elaboration of the reform of what he calls formative contexts. His book is an explanatory theory of society and a programme for social reconstruction underpinned by an avowedly voluntarist perspective.

> False Necessity shows how we may carry forward the radical project of freeing our practical and passionate dealings from the constraints imposed upon them by entrenched social roles and hierarchies . . . the best hope for the advancement

of this radical cause lies in a series of evolutionary reforms in the organization of governments and economies and in the character of our personal relations. (1987, p. 1)

But Unger's radical optimism is tempered by his contextualism. Some settings are more capable of disturbance, some more open to revision than others. History does not have pre-arranged and programmatic scripts. Reforms have to be crafted to challenge the institutional arrangements and assumptions of particular formative contexts.

Having set up a clear argument about variations in receptivity for change, Unger (1987) is regrettably much less explicit in outlining patterns in the process of transformation. However, where his thesis is transparent it shows remarkable similarities to Kanter's perspective on changing (1985). Thus opportunities for transformation will more likely occur from a challenge which itself has a framework of shared understandings and practices, and which itself has to be revisable. The ends of challenge require specification in a framework of understanding, but so indeed do the means, through tasks, targets and other operational activities. Reforms may also necessitate cultural changes to weaken the influence of established roles and hierarchies, and thereby enable conditions of local self-assertion and empowerment. In so far as there is a key to 'transformative practice', that lies in the quality of direct relations among people (1987, p. 397), their capability to alter formative contexts of power, and skill in encouraging and consolidating 'opportunities for grass roots collective militancy' (p. 402).

Receptivity and Change in the NHS: the Eight Factors

The rather scattered and eclectic literature review in the previous section has established there is not a strong social science tradition of theorizing about receptive context for change. Neither is there a great welter of empirical studies in organizational settings seeking to describe and explain differences in the rate, pace and depth of change in contrasting contexts. Before going on to synthesize our own findings about why Districts facing similar environmental and policy pressures behave at times similarly and at times differently in achieving outcomes, there are some final intellectual caveats to be made about the structure of our argument.

First, the eight factors outlined in Figure 9.2, which are derived inductively from our studies of strategic service change in the NHS, should be seen as providing a linked set of conditions which provide high energy around change. This energy and the capabilities which underpin it cannot be conjured up over a short period of time through the pulling of a single lever. The past weighs a heavy hand in determining local perceptions, and layers of competence emerge only slowly to enable and protect champions of change. The factors represent a pattern of association rather than a simple line of causation, and should be seen as a series of loops rather

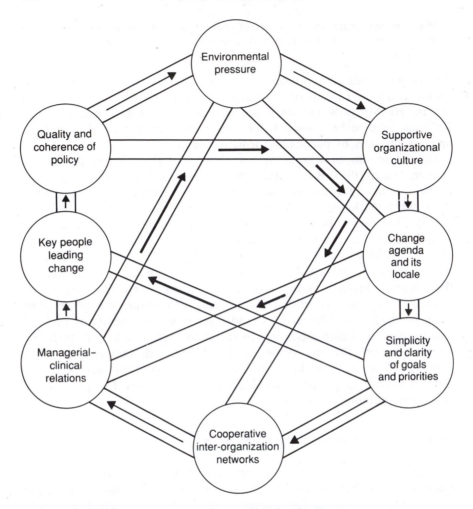

Figure 9.2 *Receptive contexts for change: the eight factors*

than a causal path between independent and dependent variables (Pettigrew, 1990).

Secondly, notions of receptivity and non-receptivity are dynamic not static concepts. Receptive contexts for change can be constructed through processes of cumulative development but such processes are reversible, either by the removal of key individuals or ill considered or precipitous action. But movement from non-receptivity to receptivity is equally possible (the Preston acute sector case study perhaps illustrated the beginnings of such a process), encouraged either by the environment or 'policy' changes at higher tiers and by managerial and professional action at local level.

Thirdly, in the way that continued processes are reversible so they are also indeterminate in their outcomes and implications. We are presenting a view of change processes which recognizes emergence, possibility, precariousness and iteration. Although it is possible to identify patterns in such processes (and our eight factors organize such patterns), those factors have to be constructed, maintained, elaborated and fashioned idiosyncratically in particular localities.

Finally, our observations may be limited as our sample has been drawn from Districts selected as carrying a high strategic service change load as defined in the terms current in the mid 1980s. Our Districts may not be typical, and we need to test the robustness of our findings against successor managerial change agendas (see, for example, Pettigrew et al., 1991).

Factor 1: The Quality and Coherence of 'Policy' – Analytical and Process Components

The quality of 'policy' generated at local level was found to be important, both from an analytic and a process perspective. It was not always enough to take perhaps dated central policy 'off the shelf', and the policy as well as the managerial process was important. Analytically, data played a major role in substantiating a solid case, especially in relation to convincing scientific publics, and we would not generally support the argument of 'paralysis by analysis' (Peters and Waterman, 1982). The ordering of such data within clear conceptual thinking helped frame strategic issues, especially where they were initially characterized by complexity and uncertainty, and gave direction. Strong testing of initial thoughts was also important in ensuring that a strategic framework considered questions of coherence between goals, was feasible (a strategy should not create unsolvable problems) and complemented the service strategy with parallel functional strategies (such as finance, human resources, communications).

Perhaps analytical considerations represent necessary conditions, while sufficient conditions relate to attention to processes of negotiation and change. Here the starting point was critical: a broad vision seemed more likely to generate movement than a blueprint. Such broad visions were found to have significant process and implementation benefits in terms of commitment-building and allowing interest groups to buy into the change process, and allowing top-down pressure to be married with bottom-up concern as the field gets scripted in rather than scripted out.

The role of broad, rather imprecise visions in stimulating change processes has also been reported by Pettigrew (1985a), Baier, March and Saetren (1986) and Pettigrew and Whipp (1991). Baier et al. note that policy support may increase with the ambiguity of proposed policies, but at the cost of administrative complications. There may be a threshold effect in operation here. Our own studies of attempts to close psychiatric hospitals demonstrate that the absence of a shared world view at the front end of the policy process can cause inertia.

It was also important to marry strategic and operational change by breaking a strategy down into actionable pieces. Policy had also to be matched to a realistic and achievable financial framework, and wobbling Regional capital budgets in particular could destabilize strategic change exercises. Finally, long-term issues (such as psychiatry) needed to be kept on change agendas, which could be difficult in the NHS where there is a tendency for every issue to be famous for 15 minutes.

Example: Acute Sector Strategy in Paddington This case study demonstrated both the importance of analytical soundness in generating the data (how many empty beds were there in the District?) and framing the issue ('Three into Two Will Go') to convince the many sceptics in the District. The District was pioneering service planning, at a time when narrow capital planning dominated in much of the NHS as it had hitherto in Paddington. But in addition, attention was paid to the negotiating and political requirements, and the proposal for redevelopment was presented as a broad vision ('the objective was so imprecise it was not that troublesome') around which concessions could be made to interest groups. The crucial decisions were taken in an informal study group with no Chair, and the Capricode planning procedures which followed on mechanistically were of secondary importance. The strategy generated in the 1976–8 period had far reaching consequences: the District was operationalizing the strategy throughout the 1980s, and ensuring that those peripheral acute hospitals that were planned to close did close.

Factor 2: Availability of Key People Leading Change

An important factor which makes change highly contextually sensitive is the availability of key people in critical posts leading change. We do not here refer to heroic and individualistic 'macho managers', but rather leadership exercised in a much more subtle and pluralist fashion. The small group – as well as one individual – could be an effective vehicle, so conscious team-building could be important, with selectors (such as District Chairs) pulling together officers from diverse constituencies and providing complementary assets or skills. There was a critical role for continuity: paradoxically there is a requirement for a substantial degree of stability in the effective management of strategic change and the case studies do not support the argument that posts should rotate every two years, at least where there is a strategic change exercise underway.

The link between the unplanned movement of key personnel and the draining of energy, purpose, commitment and action from major change processes has now been established from a whole series of research studies (Klein, 1976; Goodman and Dean, 1982; Kanter, 1985; Pettigrew, 1985a). What is rarely mentioned as a corollary of the problem is that the change process or programme then goes into a period of regression leaving the newcomer manager to start again but now possibly in a soured and non-receptive context for change.

The diversity of leadership was also apparent both in terms of its occupational base (clinicians as well as managers) and hierarchical level. Many frontline workers (for instance in HIV/AIDS) demonstrated great commitment and skill in the development of services. Often it was personalities not posts that were important: personal skills were more important in managing change than formal status or rank within the organization. Recent research (Pettigrew and Whipp, 1991) and writing (Nadler and Tushman, 1990) in private sector strategic change processes also points to the need to broaden and deepen the leadership cadre if long-term results are to be achieved in change processes.

Pettigrew and Whipp (1991) specifically use the term 'leading change' rather than 'leadership' to denote the collective, complementary and multi-faceted aspect of leading change. Leadership, they suggest, has too many connotations of individualism, and too often, one-dimensional heroism. The tasks of leading change are about the resolution of a pattern of interwoven problems, not the tackling of single great issues. The problems of maintaining simultaneous action over a long-term process are at their sharpest in leading change. The need appears to be for not boldness nor decisiveness, as much as for a combination of planning, opportunism and the adroit timing of interventions. The task of leading change is as difficult if not more difficult in the NHS, and we saw a similar pattern of diversity and complementarity being fashioned and used in our receptive contexts.

Example: Mental Handicap Services in Huddersfield DHA   This strategic change exercise was effectively carried forward by a small group or perhaps even a looser network which spanned occupational and agency divisions. There was a new consultant who was seen as 'an enthusiast' who maintained the momentum to community services. There was also a DHA Chairman with a strong personal interest in the service and also the use of organizational development, and who was consciously fostering innovation through the use of development groups or planning teams acting as change agents. Team-building was another feature of his style, promoting the gradual emergence of a collective of dedicated experts from different functions, specialisms and organizations.

There were allies too at senior levels in Social Services and the voluntary sector (Mencap), prepared to enter into partnership with the NHS. Stress was placed on the existence of powerfully placed innovators in different organizations: 'Personalities do come into it . . . It is personalities that count as opposed to posts quite often.'

It was a 'critical mass' of 'enthusiasts' with shared values that was important, rather than one individual champion of change. Partly this network formed organically, partly it was being orchestrated by the Chairman and was aided by stability in management, tempered by judicious appointments.

Factor 3: Long-term Environmental Pressure – Intensity and Scale

Studies of strategic change outside the NHS (Pettigrew, 1985a; Tushman and Romanelli, 1985) have highlighted the significant role of intense and large-scale environmental pressure in triggering periods of radical change. The picture in the NHS is more complex, as in some instances excessive pressure can deflect or drain energy out of the system. Goodman and Dean (1982) have noted the same phenomenon in private sector change. They note that inadequate environmental buffering is a key factor in helping to drain energy out of major change processes. In other cases environmental pressure can produce movement, especially if the pressure is skilfully orchestrated. Perhaps the use to which financial pressure is put depends on the prevailing distribution of power, history and assumptions of each District. In some of our Districts, financial crises produced a wide range of pathological organizational reactions such as delay and denial, collapse of morale and energy and the scapegoating and defeat of managers (Dutton, 1987). Financial crisis was here seen as a threat to the organization, rather than as an opportunity for radical reconfiguration. In others (such as Paddington in the late 1970s) financial crisis was even played up and skilfully orchestrated by management in order to accelerate the process of rationalization.

Example: The Acute Sector in Paddington and Bloomsbury In Paddington, the DMT accepted that the District was losing money under RAWP very early on ('we just faced the reality') and managed to assemble a strategy which combined retrenchment and redevelopment, winning support from the key clinicians at the W2 site. The DMT even used pseudo-financial crises (such as the 1979 'VAT disaster') as a means of accelerating retrenchment within the agreed strategy:

> That was the year of discontent when we had to start making very unpalatable decisions and the Area was very unhelpful, because there were a number of things that we could have done like competitive tendering, but they would not hear of competitive tendering so we cut services. (Paddington respondent)

Radical reduction proposals were pursued at the W9 site even given an improvement in the financial situation, with the District Administrator arguing that although the proposals originated in the now defunct 1979 crisis, the savings were still needed to finance backlog maintenance and new developments.

In the neighbouring District of Bloomsbury, on the other hand, management was unable to form a dominant coalition and was increasingly diverted into a series of short-term palliative measures to meet its financial targets. The requirement in the 1984 Regional Plan to get £14m out of Bloomsbury during the strategic period produced a target which the District was unable or unwilling to meet but which did not go away. Cost improvement savings were not met; only marginal reconfigurations to service took place and by 1985/6 a significant overspend built up which resulted in both unplanned bed cuts in the core campus (two teaching hospitals) and a humiliating appeal to Region for relief. The managerial action taken to reduce clinical activity only reinforced the resolve of oppositionist members on the DHA and management effectively lost control over District strategy in 1987 as the DMB felt it increasingly difficult to generate cohesion. Far from producing radical change, severe financial pressure in Bloomsbury produced paralysis and loss of managerial control.

Factor 4: A Supportive Organizational Culture

'Organizational culture' is a currently fashionable term and remains a fascinating but difficult topic to study. 'Culture' refers to deep-seated assumptions and values far below surface manifestations (who gets to park in front of the hospital?), officially espoused ideologies, or even patterns of behaviour. The past weighs a heavy hand in shaping these values, setting expectations about what is and what is not possible. This may be both a strength (as in Parkside's experience in the acute sector) or a weakness, as difficult experiences in the past are projected forward.

Lorsch (1986) has discussed the invisible barrier of culture causing strategic myopia and therefore inertia in organizations. For him, a supportive organizational culture is about challenging and changing beliefs about success and how to achieve it. This factor and requirements to encourage flexibility were illustrated in our case data.

Broadly our studies in both the public and the private sector conclude that tremendous energy is required to effect cultural change. Programmatic change strategies contain important weaknesses (Beer et al., 1990), but there are some other clues about how culture change management is being attempted. One avenue is through the use of leaders as role models for a wider diffusion process. Another feature is the attempt to create a general managerial cadre as opposed to a small number of general managers (in one District the three general managers met for lunch once a week with no other officers present). There may be a role for action as a demonstration effect as behavioural change may precede attitudinal change (the Rainhill case demonstrates this philosophy). We know that rewards – broadly defined – may be important, and that there is an extremely important role for Human Resource Management policies and practices, somewhat neglected perhaps in the NHS in the past.

It is not possible in the NHS to talk of a single culture, but rather of a collection of different subcultures which may inhabit the same District. If we concentrate on the managerial subculture, we can select out some features of a District culture associated with a high rate of change:

- Flexible working across boundaries with purpose-designed structures rather than formal hierarchies; non-representational mode of working; focus on skill rather than rank or status.

- An open, risk-taking approach. Some innovations may fail, but it is important that the innovators are not punished.
- Openness to research and evaluation.
- A strong value base which helps give focus to what otherwise might be a loose network.
- Strong positive self-image and sense of achievement.

Such features of local culture do not, of course, develop by accident. They develop characteristically from the values and change experiences of key leaders in the District, interlinked with environmental pressure and effective managerial–clinician relations.

Example: The Response to HIV/AIDS in Bloomsbury The early response to HIV/AIDS was developed through ad hoc advisory machinery ('the kitchen cabinet') which brought together a small team of people from different backgrounds, often with high energy levels and a strong value base. It was much easier to get a decision in HIV/AIDS than in other District fora, where issues would often get bogged down, and informal channels of communication across traditional boundaries were stronger. Unexpected networks formed as specialties which had never had contact with each other started gong to the same meetings (such as STD, drugs and dentistry) encouraged by the appointment of a designated AIDS Coordinator. A series of innovations was launched, some of which did not do as well as expected, but were transformed rather than disbanded. A strong sense of achievement enabled the core group to move on to quite new White Paper issues where they were quick to think, for example, about the implications of contracting for open access services. The self-confidence of the 'bubble' of HIV/AIDS service is in marked contrast to the experience historically apparent in the acute sector in the District. However, such a culture emerged organically more than it was consciously created.

Factor 5: Effective Managerial–Clinical Relations

The managerial–clinical interface was obviously critical. The pattern found was one of wide variation in the quality of such relations, and when clinicians had gone into opposition, they could exert a powerful block on change. Perhaps more surprisingly managers varied in the extent to which they saw relationship-building and trading with clinicians as a core part of their brief.

The importance of effective managerial–clinical relations in stimulating strategic change has also been reported in studies of the US health care system. Shortell, Morrison and Friedman (1990) present this as a dominant theme in their work, emphasizing the significance of looking for common ground, involving selected physicians early on in planning, carefully identifying the needs and interests of key physicians, and working on a daily basis to build a climate of trust, honesty and effective communications (1990, p. 237). Hocking (1991) has identified a similar pattern in the university sector, where relationships between professionals and administrators can be a stimulant or block to major change.

Manager–clinician relations were easier where negative stereotypes had broken down, perhaps as a result of the emergence of mixed roles or perspectives. For managers, it was important to understand what clinicians valued (medical records may be not so important to managers, but are of great importance to clinicians), and hence what they had to do to engage in effective trading relations. Those managers who were best were those semi-immersed in the world of clinicians, which was a great advantage enjoyed by those general managers who had been previously NHS Administrators. It is helpful to understand the implications of medical workflow for the design of a hospital, and perhaps even help clinicians to do their own planning (such as Approvals in Principle) as a way of earning trust.

From a clinical perspective, there is an important group of clinicians – who have often come up through the MEC – who think managerially and strategically. Clinical directors may increasingly form a second such hybrid group, and they will be directly linked to their business managers. These are clinicians who think across the patch, and may even be able to speak for the medical community as a whole. Such strategic clinicians are critical people for management to identify, foster and encourage and under no circumstances should they be driven into opposition by trivia. Considerable managerial acumen was needed to foster positive alliances and managers sometimes had to enter into deals, offering incentives while holding on to the core objective, and enforcing penalties where this was seen as politically possible.

Upward and downward spirals in the pattern of managerial clinician relations were evident in some of the case studies: relationships could quickly sour (as in Milton Keynes) but were slow to build up.

Example: Role Change in the Royal Preston Hospital Historically clinicians had not been involved in management in the Royal Preston, yet by 1985 there was a requirement on general management to rein back a significant overspend. The task of legitimating such retrenchment has been crucial, and understanding and acceptance of closures have only come about through the patient lobbying of consultants, so as to draw them into understanding of and participation in the management task. The Unit General Manager succeeded in gaining access to clinicians via the Specialty Management Teams, with the MEC Chairman as the formal UMB representative, and the District General Manager had by December 1987 gained access to the MEC. Since 1988, a medical representative has sat on the UMB, and in 1989 a new MEC Chairman appeared to have a wider remit in management. These were hard-won breakthroughs, and the introduction of budgeting responsibilities to such a large and historically hostile or indifferent group of consultants is necessarily a gradual process.

The formation of lines of communication – to teams, to the MEC, to newly appointed clinicians – itself takes a long period of time.

Factor 6: Cooperative Inter-organizational Networks

Many changes in the priority group sector in particular were underscored by the development and management of inter-organizational networks with such agencies as Social Services Departments and voluntary organizations. DHAs had little power in such settings, but rather had to win influence. A number of features could enrich these networks, such as the existence of boundary spanners who crossed agency divides (e.g. DHA members who also served on SSD Committee) and clear referral and communication points.

The most effective networks were both informal and purposeful (rather than self-absorbed and narcissistic), but – as a consequence of the personalities not posts argument – also fragile and vulnerable to turnover. One Director of Social Services might be interested in mental handicap, the next in the elderly. But at their best such networks provided opportunities for trading and education, for commitment and energy-raising and for marrying top-down and bottom-up concerns. The significance of purposeful networks and their role as arenas for trust-building, bargaining and deal making is a key part of Rosabeth Kanter's (1985) perspective and data on how substantial change occurs.

Example: Psychiatric Services in Milton Keynes   Milton Keynes DHA is a receiving District in the closure of St John's psychiatric hospital in Aylesbury. This means that it will have to build up new mental health services to care for patients discharged from the old hospital. Not only has this required liaison with Region and the other Buckinghamshire health authorities, but a major part of the change consists of a transfer from medical to social care. Effective links over to senior Social Services Department management are therefore fundamental to the whole undertaking. While the closure is now well advanced, in the early 1980s the SCM who was given the task of developing a strategy was only able to secure DMT support and base budget money through joint finance, which entailed doing deals with the Director of Social Services:

> not strategic funding at that stage, it was quite hard work, really trying to get our small planning group well linked into the joint care planning structure to get the joint finance. And if you look at what happened in those two or three years you will see that the vast majority of joint finance in mental health actually came to Milton Keynes.

So the SCM got himself on the Joint Finance Group of the JCPT and also ensured that the Milton Keynes Treasurer became Treasurer of Buckinghamshire Joint Finance. The early links forged in this period helped pave the way for the choice by Region in 1984 of St John's as the first psychiatric hospital in the region to close.

Factor 7: Simplicity and Clarity of Goals and Priorities

This focusing issue arises from the conclusion that managers varied greatly in their ability to narrow the change agenda down into a set of key priorities, and to insulate this core from the constantly shifting short-term pressures apparent in the NHS. The danger was that the number of 'priorities' would escalate until they became meaningless. Rather, persistence and patience in pursuit of objectives over a long period seemed to be associated with achieving strategic change. So managers may be wise to ignore or minimize some of the ever-changing sources of pressure, while using others to amplify their pre-existing change objectives. Skills in complexity and conflict reduction could also be important here, in trying to contain complex problems in simpler organizational frameworks.

The question of simplicity and clarity of goals and priorities is one aspect of a much more general analytical and practical problem of how the nature of the context of change influences the rate and pace of change. Dufour (1991) cites Van Meter and Van Horn (1976) and Grindle (1980) as important contributors to the debate about how implementation gaps are linkable to variability in the content of change. Thus Van Meter and Van Horn (1976) argue the implementation process is likely to be influenced by the amount of change involved and the extent of goal consensus among the participants. Grindle (1980) indicates that changes with long-range objectives, requiring considerable behavioural adaptation, and depending on networks of widely dispersed units (characteristics present in our cases of psychiatric hospital closure) will be far more difficult and onerous to implement. Dufour's own research (1991) on factors influencing the rate and pace of closure of general practitioner maternity units also contributes to the debate about how content may influence pace of change. He is able to show in some of his cases how the shrinking and de-escalation of the change content brought sudden movement in previously contentious and deadlocked processes. Thus one way to simplify and clarify is to shrink the problem at the outset, or alternatively to break the problem into more manageable and actionable pieces once the change process is underway.

Example: The Action Bias at Rainhill Hospital, St Helens and Knowsley There were, of course, disadvantages as well as advantages to the style adopted at Rainhill, but at least there was no doubt that early managerial behaviour there signalled that this time closure was actually going to happen. Behavioural change in this case study preceded attitudinal change. The Unit General Manager had been faced on appointment with a daunting array of possible interpretations of his role, and had clearly decided that achieving closure on time was the key target. The introduction of general management also provided focal points for inter-District negotiation, as the three UGMs emerged as a core group.

*Factor 8: The Fit between the District's Change Agenda and its
Locale*

Private sector research on, for example, human resource change has
indicated that various features of the locale where change is to occur may
inhibit or accelerate change. Thus Hardy's studies (1985) of organizational closures demonstrate how and why climate building for such
changes is linkable to high levels of unemployment and consequential
changes in the power balance between managers and trade unionists.
There is also evidence (for example, Bassett, 1986; Marchington, 1989)
that the incidence and timing of joint consultative arrangements is often
linked to the enhanced opportunities afforded by 'green field sites'.

In the NHS the nature of the locale also had an impact on how easy
it was to achieve change:

- The degree of coterminosity with SSDs.
- Whether there is one large centre of population or two or more major
  towns.
- Whether there is a teaching hospital presence.
- The strength and nature of the local political culture.
- The nature of the local NHS workforce.

While many of these factors may appear beyond management control,
awareness of their influence could nevertheless be important in anticipation of potential obstacles to change. Some of them may also be reshaped
in the long term by higher tiers (boundary changes, removal of local
authority and trade union representatives from the DHA) or locally
through Human Resource Management activities.

*Example: Inter-organizational Mental Health Networks in Milton
Keynes* The strong emphasis on the joint planning of mental health
services between the NHS, SSD and the voluntary sector in Milton Keynes
in part reflected the emerging civic culture of the New Town:

> There have been a lot of exciting and unusual developments in Milton Keynes.
> Everyone says we accept that we work together and the voluntary sector is
> working very closely . . . that is the climate in Milton Keynes, because it is a
> new city, because of the Development Corporation, to build that user participa-
> tion in. (SSD respondent)

The voluntary sector itself was lively and well developed, both generally
and in the field of mental health, with one of the first Advocacy Groups
in the country. Moreover it had secured representation on at least some
of the planning fora. These strong networks, and in particular the links
with the Director of Social Services built up through joint care planning,
helped explain Region's decision in 1984 to target the closure of St
John's, Aylesbury, as a Regional flagship.

Some Implications of the Findings

We repeat that the eight features of receptivity should not be seen as a shopping list or as discrete factors but, as Figure 9.2 indicates, they represent a highly intercorrelated combination which taken together may raise energy levels around change in ways which are highly District-specific. Thus, in, for example, Paddington the timing and rate and pace of change was influenced by the combined and additive effect of seven of the eight features in our model. Environmental pressure over a long period of time was a constant stimulus for change to rationalize acute service provision. For this pressure to be recognized and effectively orchestrated a team of change leaders had to be built and an evolving sense of focus, direction and purpose created. The team over time learned progressively how to evolve and negotiate a pattern of agreement with key clinicians, and work with key actors in and outside the Districts in ways which additively constructed stepping stones for change. The small movements forward further enhanced the receptivity for change and allowed further action to occur, sometimes occasioned by chance, and other times as a result of planned activity. The fact that, compared with Bloomsbury, there was a simpler political and structural context for change (there being only one teaching hospital in Paddington, compared with two in Bloomsbury) also eased the on-going process of change and learning. But even in this relatively receptive setting for change, the process was full of complexity, indeterminism and simultaneity. Dead ends and blocks emerged. Sudden opportunities for movement had to be exploited on a constantly moving stage. Energy once orchestrated had to be sustained. We repeat there is no simple recipe, no quick fix in managing complex change.

We have also recognized that there may be a link between the criteria of receptivity and the content of the change issue or agenda, and future work (Pettigrew et al., 1991) will give an opportunity to test the robustness of these findings derived from one change agenda to that apparent in the new era. But they may at least provide some clues about why it is that certain localities seem to demonstrate a faster rate and pace of change in an organization such as the NHS where there are dangers of 'process without memory', where priorities unpredictably shift, where past learning is too easily lost, and where wheels are constantly being reinvented.

But our research findings have other related implications and we will examine these under the following themes:

- Turning problems and panics into sustainable action.
- Managing incoherence.
- Incentives and the politics of exchange.
- Combining top-down pressure and bottom-up concerns.
- Dualities and dilemmas in managing change.

Turning Problems and Panics into Sustainable Action

In the NHS 'panics' and 'crises' are legion. It is a management system which features endemic short-termism and over reaction Few of the disturbances which are labelled as crises are, of course, organizationally life-threatening, most are just bubbles of short-term excitement which managers and professionals at all levels have come to expect, perhaps even need to convince themselves of the profundity of their task and position.

What are some of the pathologies associated with a culture of self-generated panics, and what has produced such a culture? One of the most obvious pathologies is that managers and professionals in the NHS find it very difficult to disentangle the urgent from the important. When everything is 'crucially important' few things get done; or rather they start to get done and then action is overwhelmed by the searing but ephemeral heat of the next panic. But if endemic failure to see priorities and hold on to them is a pathology of effectiveness, then the most obvious pathology of efficiency is the sparse respect afforded people's time in the NHS. Meetings are called and individuals cry off at the last moment and do not appear, or they appear for a short period and then leave to sweep off to the next panic.

Few managers we have encountered in the NHS query the veracity of this characterization of a culture of panics. But why has it arisen and what sustains it? There are several possible explanations. One is that it is a reflection of the top-down and short-term pressure from the politicians who drive the NHS. Ministers are compelled amongst other things by political advantage and by requirements to hold on to power and we know, for example, that the heat is turned on and off hospital closure activities after and before general elections (Dufour, 1991). Ministers also have to defend themselves in Parliament on a daily basis, and need to be seen to be doing something about the latest panic being orchestrated by the many interest groups who operate in and around the goldfish bowl of publicity surrounding the NHS. So pressures and panics from ministers are then relayed through the NHS management executive right down the hierarchy of Region and District to the Unit level of management.

There is a developing tradition in the social sciences (e.g. Hill, 1982; Beyer et al., 1983; Barrett and Hill, 1984; Brunsson, 1985, 1986, 1989) which would explain the culture of panics as symbolic decision making (Dufour, 1991). Thus panics and decisions associated with them are deemed to be ceremonial, or are empty promises designed to cool down strong oppositions from various interest groups. Brunsson (1986) writes of public organizations 'exploiting problems and employing rationalistic decision procedures, and they produce hypocritical outputs in the shape of talk (the spoken and written word) . . . but these inconsistencies, which thus serve a useful purpose, also represent an obstacle to organizational action' (1986, p. 165). Korman and Glennerster, in their study of the closure of a large mental handicap hospital, pursue a similar theme:

> the reason why some policies are not implemented is that no one ever expected them to be. Acts are passed or ministerial speeches made to satisfy some party pressure or awkward interest group but civil servants know that they need not strain themselves too hard to achieve results. The policy is symbolic. (1985, p. 7)

So reforms become symbolic routines and 'many public organizations have concentrated on problems and have been stronger in talk and decisions than in action' (Brunsson, 1986, p. 183; 1989).

But if the driving force for the culture of panics has been the highly politicized outer context of the NHS, what are the other factors that nourish and sustain such a culture? One undoubtedly is the politics of reward and recognition among managers in the NHS. There is no centrally designed and orchestrated internal labour market in the NHS, no system that plans and develops people's careers in the way now regarded as essential to the functioning of most private sector firms (see, for example, the GKN, IMI and Pilkington Glass experiences discussed by Hendry, 1990). The consequence of no managed internal labour market is that most managers and professionals have to make their own careers. One pathological by-product of this is that people move around the system in ways which are uncoordinated with the tasks of the service, cycles of activity get started but often not finished, and as we have seen in some of our Districts, long-term inertia is the result. Another implication of individuals having to construct their own careers is that areas for public display of virtue have to be found and effectively used. Panics represent regular opportunities for public display. Even though the consequences of such searches for reward and recognition may lead to unintended as well as intended outcomes, the social dramatic impact of the panic is thereby reinforced as a vehicle for career development. And so the symbolic organizational function of the panic, combined with individual motives for display, the ever-present difficulty in the NHS of obtaining hard information as to what is going on, and habit, conspire to puff bubbles of panic regularly into the management process.

In a world of panics and problems how does one disentangle the urgent from the important? More crucially, perhaps, how does one turn what is important into action? Factor 7 in our model of receptive contexts for change (simplicity and clarity of goals) directly addressed this issue. In addition to the points made under Factor 7, there are a number of other important considerations. Research in the private sector reported in Pettigrew and Whipp (1991, 1992) demonstrates that the starting point for strategic focusing and change derives from a firm's skill in environmental assessment. In general terms that research shows that it is insufficient for companies to regard the creation of knowledge and judgements of their external competitive work as simply a technical expertise. Rather the need is for organizations to become open learning systems which acquire, interpret and process information about their environment. Such process-ing is more likely to occur when various conditioning features are in place and in use. These include the extent to which key actors are prepared to champion assessment techniques; the structural and cultural character-istics of the firm; skill in recognizing and exploiting environmental distur-bances; and the extent to which assessment is seen as a multi-function and multi-level activity and not the preserve of a single individual or a particular specialist function such as planning. For the conditioning factors to work, however, they need to be stabilized and impelled by a further set of organizational features. Of these the most crucial are the incorporation of planning and marketing; the availability of purposive inter-organizational and intra-organizational networks, and the use of multi-functional task forces and teams.

Our case study data (and especially the Paddington acute sector and Huddersfield mental handicap processes) have demonstrated the role and value of environmental assessment in the conduct of change processes in the NHS. The quality of networking in each of those contexts made it easier for the groups championing change to disentangle the panics from the significant issues and data, and thereby focus in on their key priority and the critical people and information which could help to sustain that priority for change.

But turning panics and problems into sustainable action is more than a question of how and when to focus, we also know that critical aspects of the change process relate to energy raising and energy sustaining activities, and the avoidance of the debilitating reversals associated with regression.

Crisis-as-opportunity (Starbuck et al., 1978) as distinct from the negative consequences of crisis-as-threat (Jick and Murray, 1982) is a crucial mechanism for turning problems into live issues. Major change is seen as taking place when the perception of crisis forces a panic or problem up the issue agenda. The process of strategic change in ICI (Pettigrew, 1985a) would be one example where concern was skilfully orchestrated by the new leadership in the company.

Looking across our NHS cases a range of factors and behaviours helped with energy mobilization. These included: the mobilization of crisis; the articulation of broad visions; the role of leadership in challeng-ing old assumptions and behaviours; the encouragement of deviants and heretics to say the unsayable and think the unthinkable; the importance of early action to signal new changes of direction; the building of complementary teams and networks of leaders; and the positive reinforce-ment of early if limited successes in the change process. Our cases of the development of services for HIV/AIDS illustrate many of the above points. The role of medical product champions in spotting the problem and turning it into a rising issue; the continuing pressure from those pioneers; the formation of special groups which reach out to the rest of the organization; high energy and commitment levels from the activists;

strong integration mechanisms through special coordinating machinery and a sense of shared purpose: 'The perception of crisis, in other words, facilitates rapid learning, consciousness raising and mobilization' (Ferlie and Bennett, 1992). However, in the way that the NHS finds it difficult to disentangle panics and problems from issues, and to turn the former into the latter, there is the additional difficulty (shared by many institutions) that issues themselves may have an attention cycle (Downs, 1972, Hogwood, 1987). Public, media and organizational attention may shift to ever newer issues, and old ones may fade even if unresolved. This is the great challenge now for the HIV/AIDS issue. How to reinvigorate the issue, provide momentum through a period when ear-marked funds may be withdrawn; early medical product champions are suffering from burn-out or marginalization; and yet patient load may be increasing as the iceberg of HIV turns into presenting AIDS (Bennett et al., 1990; Ferlie and Bennett, 1992).

Managing Incoherence

The NHS is an extremely large and complex organization. It is also an extraordinarily segmented and incoherent series of interlocking systems and groups divided on every conceivable axis: political and managerial; professional and managerial; professional and professional; Regional, District and Unit levels of management; and, of course, geography and care group. Overlaid on top of this mosaic are the vagaries of changing political ideologies, the instabilities caused by the political economy of resource allocation; the changing interfaces with local government and the voluntary sector; and the ever present difficulties of determining and evaluating ends and means in health care. The culture of panics and problems and the dispersion of power all add to the picture of fragmentation and incoherence.

Research in the US and UK private sectors by Kanter (1985) and Pettigrew and Whipp (1991, 1992) has clearly linked segmentation and incoherence to organizational inertia, and integration and coherence to change capability. The cases in this book provide further confirmation of those links. The clearest examples of incoherence are in the studies of the closure of Rainhill and Whittingham psychiatric hospitals (Chapter 6) and the long difficulties in effecting the rationalization of acute services in Bloomsbury DHA (Chapter 4). What are some of the factors which made those such non-receptive localities for change?

In Bloomsbury structural complexity was an issue. Unlike its neighbour Parkside (where the rate and pace of change was much faster and more sustained) Bloomsbury had two elite teaching hospitals on its patch (in Parkside there was one), a vast array of specialist services, three postgraduate medical groups and a more politicized health authority. Bloomsbury had a more incoherent and unstable set of senior managers, poorer links with clinicians, weaker information systems and thus greater problems in building a consensus around a strategy of retrenchment. When the beginnings of a consensus began to emerge around a service strategy, those service aims were only sketchily linked to an enabling financial strategy and the consequent poor operationalization of action led to a series of confidence sapping strategic flip-flops as one attempt after another to produce movement ended in deadlock.

In Rainhill and Whittingham we could identify different degrees of incoherence, with, for a time, Rainhill producing movement around a top-down focused process. Again structural complexity was difficult to overcome. The Rainhill closure involved linkages with two Districts other than the host District of St Helens, two local authorities, and St Helens itself was composed of two metropolitan boroughs. Divisions in the structure of the psychiatric medical community and the geographical inaccessibility of both Rainhill and Whittingham from local management and centres of population added to problems of focusing and service planning. In Whittingham a further crucial gloss of incoherence was provided by poor linkages between Regional, District and Unit levels of management and perhaps by weak organizational capacity for change. But as Grindle (1980) suggests, the content of the change problem can also be crucial in explaining implementation gaps. The psychiatric changes and closures described in this book represent long-range objectives, long waves of change not driven so much by emergencies or crunch points but evolving from protracted historical movement. Focusing, energy-raising and sustaining momentum are much more difficult in such cases, and the process is likely to be that much more susceptible to reverses, unexpected opportunities for movement (as indeed was orchestrated in Rainhill) and the politics of precariousness, conflict and uncertainty.

Nevertheless, managing incoherence remains the most wide-ranging challenge in producing change in the NHS, as indeed it was in our high performing private sector organizations (Pettigrew and Whipp, 1991). This ability to hold an organization together while simultaneously reshaping it was for a time a feature of the Rainhill story. It was also a key factor in the more sustained examples of receptive contexts witnessed in the Paddington and Parkside cases (Chapter 4) and Huddersfield (Chapter 7). We can perhaps signal some of the inputs and dynamics of producing that coherence by focusing on the role of incentives and of combining top-down pressures and bottom-up concerns in change processes.

Incentives and the Politics of Exchange

It has long been recognized that incentives and rewards of various kinds have a role in reinforcing and sustaining change processes (Goodman and Dean, 1982; Kanter, 1985). More recent research (Pettigrew, Hendry and Sparrow, 1990) has also established that the selective use of a variety of human resource factors, such as performance review criteria and systems, career development pathways, and reward and recognition systems, can help to reinforce early behavioural change in cultural change processes.

However, this research on service change demonstrates the critical role of incentives and the politics of exchange in both the energy mobilization and energy sustaining aspects of change processes. Our Paddington–Parkside case illustrates the importance of using the incentive of redevelopment to progress essentially retrenchment policies. The significance of political language at the front end of change processes needs emphasizing. Closures can be labelled as redevelopments. Problems can be re-coded into opportunities with, as happened in Paddington, broad positive visions being articulated to build early coalitions between managers and senior clinicians. A similar tactic was used in some of Dufour's cases (1991) of GP maternity unit closures.·

With the broad direction determined by an exchange of retrenchment for redevelopment, the climate was then set for a range of subsidiary deal making and trading as the change process evolved. So the original deal had two major pay-offs. The broad vision set the framework of the content of the change (what would happen), and built a purposive and positive climate for change in the early coalition which enabled subsequent negotiations to occur. The more operational trading between managers and clinicians in Paddington–Parkside was also assisted by a range of contextual and managerial factors. Thus there were actually quite a number of small hospitals in the Paddington area which could act as tradeable plant 'to be sold down the river' in exchange for the big new glossy development at St Mary's, W2.

Coherence was achieved by the simplicity of the original deal; the top team coherence among the senior managers in the District; the relationships of informality and trust between key managers and clinicians; the stability of the managerial group in the District; the effective linking of the broad service vision down into operational change targets, and the positive energy fed back into the process by a succession of these targets being realized on or before the expected date.

Combining Top-down Pressure and Bottom-up Concerns

In Chapter 3 we reviewed available research and writing on the top-down restructuring of the NHS, and other UK public sector institutions. That review revealed different assessments of the impact of the Thatcherite era of top-down institutional reform. One view was that sustained and consistent pressure over 11 years had consolidated and a new action-orientated management style had indeed been created. A more sceptical view (Harrison et al., 1989a) is that superficial change hides underlying continuity as the same people largely remained in post, relabelling themselves as appropriate to survive. A third argument, by Gunn (1989), was that subtle and mixed processes of change were emerging and that a new public management culture was developing with the survivors in this new managerial cadre revealing a different self-image, power position and pattern of behaviour.

Even from the limited data set in this study it is apparent that top-down pressures have not produced similar shifts in this balance of power, across all localities and change processes. Our whole argument has been that there are as many general managements as there are general managers. However, we are able to report accelerated processes of change in our receptive contexts, and indeed even a greater sense of purpose and action, if not yet total accomplishments, in our less receptive Districts and issues. A similar pattern is also evident in Dufour's (1991) study which describes managerial action before and after the Griffiths Report (1983) in four localities in the Oxford RHA.

Top-down pressure has been evident in our Districts, and most fundamentally where that pressure has been selectively and astutely orchestrated at local level and linked in a coherent and sensitive fashion to bottom-up concerns. Big pressures require refocusing and transmitting at local levels. The content of grand reforms requires customization at lower tiers in order to match local circumstances and to script in local commitment and psychic energy. But all this requires considerable managerial skill. Korman and Glennerster (1990) take a similar view, arguing that the final result achieved in closing the large mental handicap hospital at Darenth Park (after long delays) was a product of a new approach combining central pressure with the freedom of the District to produce its own solutions.

What were the interlocking set of features; of context and action, of top-down and bottom-up pressure, which produced substantial movement in mental handicap service change in Huddersfield? Again we see this pattern of a web of interlocking external pressures, some from the Department of Health and the Region, and others from the *Care in the Community* report (DHSS, 1981b) marrying with an active DHA Chairman and a new mental handicap consultant to slowly evolve a broad and purposive vision. There was no attempt to create a local blueprint for change, but a culture of experimentation was encouraged which set in train early action and a conscious process of learning by doing. 'We needed to get some action before we knew where we were going.' Parents and the voluntary organization Mencap were quickly encouraged into the process. A variety of projects, planning groups and educational and consulting groups, and educational and consultational activities were built up and the whole process was guarded and energized by a senior coalition of managers and professionals who stayed together as a team for several years. Informal and purposive networks were built with Social Services and voluntary organizations and attention was given to matching service and financial strategies. Early progress was reinforced by further flexibility and at times opportunism of response. Sustained progress began to create a feeling that 'we are getting ahead of the field' and a virtuous cycle was created.

The cumulative yet uncertain character of the Huddersfield change process shows parallels with the Whipp and Pettigrew (1990a) data on the bridging of strategic and operational change in the private sector. They report that the process of translating strategic intent into operational form does not occur by a single step or conversion, or even a neat sequence of steps into a logical outcome. It has an especially rich set of temporal dimensions for managers. The process may need repeated attempts to even begin; it may include clusters of iterative action in order to break through ignorance or resistance; it often requires the enduring of aborted effects or the build-up of slow incremental phases of adjustment which then allow short bursts of concentrated action to take place. The process is iterative and cumulative with a strong element of learning by doing, which may lead to the original intentions being overwhelmed.

Pettigrew and Whipp (1991) present strong evidence for this pattern of continuous but at times indeterminate and unpredictable learning and change in their publishing case of Longman. In the period from the mid 1970s to the mid 1980s in Longman the direction of change in the company was towards greater internationalization and greater market mindedness, a set of moves which involved complementary traditional editorial publishing skills and new marketing expertise (mostly from outside publishing), and a widening of the geographical spread and depth of Longman's involvements. Such changes were partly engineered by their Chairman, Tim Rix, but also demanded the extension of his personal learning about strategic analysis and marketing into the creation of a more general culture of learning in various levels and corners of the company.

In Chapter 2 we noted how there had been a falling away of interest in diffusion based research, perhaps as interest switched to top-down restructuring as the dominant motor of institutional change. Such a switching of interest may be misplaced for two reasons. First of all top-down strategies need to co-exist not only with a certain minimum level of readiness and capability at local levels, but also with sound links between higher and lower tiers. Secondly, current policy initiatives are recognizing the need to link top-down 'revolution' with local 'evolution', thus implying a return to diffusion based models of change. Examples include the Resource Management Initiative and the Localities Project where 'leading edge' Districts are to experience a faster pace of change and act as role models for the wider population. The evolutionary approach to NHS Trusts will also be helped by the speedy diffusion of learning and best practice from the first to the second generation of self-governing trusts.

There is now a considerable body of evidence from private sector research (e.g. Walton, 1975, 1980; Goodman and Dean, 1982) that evolutionary processes of change that rely on diffusion through 'pilot sites' or 'experiments' or other forms of diffusion strategies rarely spread to a wider set of the population. Pilot experiments may be successful on their own site but that very success may generate tension and therefore rejection elsewhere, often with cries of 'but we're different here'. Sometimes pilots also fail because they are too small scale and not cumulative, because timescales have been extremely short with poorly worked out logics and targets; or because the experiment has been under resourced.

But there is a wider set of considerations than these, considerations which are fateful to diffusion strategies of change. One obvious one is that the evolution at the local level is critically dependent upon consistently visible pressure from the revolutionary higher tier. This is not just a question of skill in digging out best practice early from the first generation of sites (for without that there will be nothing to diffuse), but persistent and consistent pressure from the higher tier. A key to success in managing change is the effective linking of the tier leading the change and the lower tiers carrying through operational implementation. The negotiation of customized solutions at lower tiers is very dependent also on the leadership role and pressure being consistently maintained. If a District is close to accepting hard targets for change, that deal could be undermined and even destroyed by a weakening of the leadership position at higher tiers.

Another critical question is where are choices made about intervention points? The notion of receptive contexts may be helpful here. It is important to ensure that early interventions are made in receptive contexts which increase the probability of success in the early phases of the change process, providing further momentum, energy and experience for later sites.

But implementation is not just about 'picking winners'. Attention needs to be given to how change can spread out from any initial (perhaps rather unusual) sites. It may be helpful to think of localities not just as 'receptive' or 'unreceptive', but as high, medium or low. Some sites lie in the middle ground where there are some features of receptivity, but not others. The crucial issues relate to the diffusion of learning from higher to medium sites and the upgrading of capacity in the middle ground. In planning change it can also be extremely valuable to know which localities should be left more or less alone. Thought also could be given to devising effective diffusion and learning mechanisms. Twinning may be possible between a 'medium' or highly receptive site, and managers seconded across to develop role models, can receive mentoring and practise newly recognized skills in a safer environment.

In selecting sites we also recognize the importance of 'soft' and 'hard' data. Given the importance of background history, relations and assumptions will vary from one locality to another, pervasively affecting the probability of successful implementation. The importance of 'soft' data was acknowledged in the initial Resource Management Initiative evaluation. Buxton et al. (1989) clearly identified capacity for change management as crucial to implementation, and their report noted the significance of powerful 'local champions' and associated changes in structure and information systems as fateful to implementation.

But the implications of our findings for the new change agenda in the NHS go beyond using our features of change receptivity as a heuristic device and trigger for a problem solving process. The results of this research on managing service change also point to critical organizational and managerial skills for managers, clinicians and human resource specialists. In particular, our findings signal the importance of analytical and conceptual skills in policy analysis, of political and negotiating skills, and skills of networking and managing across inter-organizational boundaries. There is also a continuing need to select and develop individuals for leadership roles, and to encourage effective team building where the complementary assets provided by several people can energize and bring results. Finally and most obviously, skills and conceptual knowledge in the management of change remain critical requirements for those trying to take the NHS into yet another new era of change.

Dualities and Dilemmas in Managing Change

The methodology used in this study has been that of the longitudinal and processual comparative case study. The analytical approach has been an interdependent exploration of content, process and contexts. Studying temporal processes at different levels of context, outer and inner, has been the leitmotif of the research approach. Historical antecedents and the chronology of change are considered vital in this style of research and we have sought to capture retrospective change, real time analysis and prospective or anticipated change. The design choice has been to conduct intensive analysis of a relatively few cases, rather than a more superficial analysis of many. Such are the complexities of both the strategic change issues and of the host systems that such superficial analyses would be in danger of missing key components of the explanation.

Our desire to capture contextual realism has shaped our observations of the character of the change process. We have not seen change moving forward in a direct, linear way, nor through easily identifiable phases or stages. History appears not to have pre-arranged paths or easily predictable scripts. Change processes are better conceptualized in the language of probability, indeterminacy, precariousness and reversibility (with perhaps the single most significant cause of reversibility being the changing priorities and attention spans of the power figures who often champion the original idea for change).

In other studies (Pettigrew and Whipp, 1991), change has been described as intentional and emergent, with the additive effects of implementation sometimes overwhelming the original intentions. Changes are reformulated as they proceed, and managers are engaging with activities which are inseparably analytical, political and educational. Development is often uneven with interruptions and periods of acceleration sometimes contrasting with dead-ends and periods of planned and unexpected slow down. There is also evidence of cumulative development, of periods of explicit and implicit learning by doing. Simultaneity is also a key characteristic of managing change. There are many tasks to do, many decisions to be made in parallel as well as in sequence, and all in the changing context of the political economy of the UK in the 1980s and 1990s.

It is to this complexity and simultaneity in managing change we now wish to turn. Leading change calls for the resolution of not so much great single issues but rather a pattern of interwoven problems (Whipp and Pettigrew, 1990b). The skill in leading change therefore centres on managing a series of dualities and dilemmas.

But what are these dualities and dilemmas? The broadest, of course, relates to the need to handle what Berman (1978) calls the macro and micro aspects of implementation. There are also requirements to mobilize energy for change and to sustain early momentum; to handle change projects and longer-term processes; to balance needs for continuity and for change; and to use formal hierarchies and informal purposive networks. We have also discussed needs to dovetail top-down pressures and bottom-up concerns, and occasions when the escalation of problems into issues becomes a necessity. However, at other times, de-escalation, the shrinking of the content of a change issue, becomes important in order to quieten opposition and start building support.

For central government there is the unrelenting task of developing strategies which incorporate the macro and micro aspects of implementation. As Berman (1978, p. 164) puts it, policy has to influence local delivery organizations to behave in desired ways and in response to central actions, the local organizations have to devise and carry out their own internal policies. The dilemma here, of course, is how to orchestrate and sustain generalized pressure while leaving some freedom to build customized solutions at local levels which are sensitive to different and changing contexts. The commitment building aspect of this dilemma we have tried to describe as a process of marrying top-down pressures and bottom-up concerns. But it is never easy for higher tiers to set frameworks for action when the intellectual and emotional pressure is ever present to set blueprints for action, and especially if as intended the framework leaves space for creativity and collective insubordination at lower tiers. The fact that such judgements are taking place in a shifting context adds to the complexity. This dynamic complexity has been portrayed as like juggling lots of balls in the air while the platform on which the juggler stands is moving all the time (Lorenz, 1991).

Change processes rarely gather momentum in entirely receptive contexts and there is always the duality of raising and sustaining energy. But the crises which can help to mobilize change can be both opportunities and threats. Those crises can create a fragmented and defensive atmosphere which can inhibit change, as well as a purposive and coherent environment that can drive change. One of the great dilemmas of change management is how to create zones of disturbance, to energize a process of creative destruction, while also building a zone of comfort for new directions to be constructed and legitimacy and support built. Elsewhere Whipp and Pettigrew (1990a) have catalogued how costly bold and precipitous action can be in change processes. The dual task is to build a climate for leading change while at the same time raising energy and tension levels and setting out new directions *before* precise action is taken. We have also emphasized in this book that sustaining pace and momentum in change processes has its own requirements. Momentum cannot be taken for granted.

A further duality involves how managers conceptualize change. Is change seen as an episode, a project or programme which is arbitrarily driven down on to an organization, or is change conceptualized as a process of continuous improvement, where leadership in change management requires ongoing skill in timing perhaps small interventions so that the force of natural organizational processes amplifies those interventions? This duality is linked to the ever present practical problem in change management of how to avoid the debilitating effects of regression. One way to maintain momentum in the change process and avoid significant regression is to ensure that key change leaders stay in position long enough to see through the change process. Where this is impossible, it is very important to appoint successors who have the same value position and vision as their predecessor, if not the same personal style. Behind such actions may be the more fundamental view that changes are not best thought of as episodes or events. Regression is more likely to occur when change is seen in episodic terms.

There is also the duality of simultaneously managing continuity and change. The development of a receptive context for change has to share its influence with needs for continuity. Part of the task of leading change is to specify frameworks and boundaries as well as painting a picture of a better world, although part of the canvas may itself need to be revised as the context unfolds. Pettigrew (1985a) has argued that a key part of managing continuity and change is coping with the dilemma of exclusivity and inclusivity. Innovators may need to focus on certain areas of action, to express implacable energy and openly to criticize the status quo – to behave exclusively.

However, there is also the requirement for inclusivity. To change the world one must live with it. The politics of generating support and legitimacy for a new order normally require keeping one foot in the present while the other stretches forward.

Finally, there is the requirement to build commitment, energy and action from hierarchies and networks. Contrary to a current management fad (e.g. Kanter, 1989), large bureaucratic organizations will not be able to switch from hierarchies to networks, rather they will have to build and use both. Our case studies have demonstrated that in a pluralistic and multi-level system like the NHS, change can arise from the generalized pressure of hierarchies linking up to the customized needs and solutions coming out of local networks. But there is no quick fix, no remission from the varieties of fashioning that need to occur at higher and lower tiers. No respite from the ever present duality of holding together an organization while simultaneously re-shaping it.

Appendix
Research Aims and Methodology

The project was funded by the NHSTA and a consortium of eight RHAs,* hence funders had a variety of rather different needs (national and Regional; practitioner and education centre interests; general managerial and personnel) which the team had to satisfy. The idea for the project initially sprang from the implementation of the Griffiths Report (1983) general managerial reforms and the early consultancy work around the management of change of Professor Pettigrew in 1984–5 in three Regions. The subsequent desire of the funders to generate larger-scale research findings which would help to develop practice formed the starting point for the project.

Research Aims

The project aims were formally described as follows:

To Study Strategic Service Change in the NHS The team had to decide upon a clear focus of analysis, given the potentially extremely wide-ranging nature of the initial brief. A fundamental research design decision was not to study the Griffiths management reforms in isolation but rather to treat them as a means to an end and assess how they impacted on the service system. There is one answer to the question: but what is general management for? There are of course many ways of examining changes to the system of service (for example, we could have concentrated on the pattern of doctor–manager relations), but the approach we adopted was to track the influence of general management on strategic service change processes which were ongoing and which were high on managers' agendas.

An important unit of analysis is thus the strategic change process: all the results reported in Chapters 5–8 relate to long time frames, some (such as the closure of asylums) having their roots in the Victorian era when these institutions were constructed; the issue with the shortest time frame is the management of HIV/AIDS but nevertheless even here it is important to go back to the late 1970s when the early research groups emerged around hepatitis B which were subsequently to shift across to HIV. The section on methodology below will outline how our sampling frame was constructed.

To Focus on 'High Change' Districts A second decision was to select Districts which were tackling many of the major strategic issues. Our sample therefore may not reflect the 'average' District but rather those processing high change agendas, and therefore one should be cautious in extrapolating from the sample to the whole population. The decision to select 'high change' Districts was made for two reasons. First, questions of managerial capacity to handle change would stand out

---

* Mersey RHA, North East Thames RHA, North West Thames RHA, North West RHA, Oxford RHA, South West Thames RHA, West Midlands, RHA, Yorkshire RHA.

in much sharper relief in these Districts where changes of major substantive importance were proceeding and where critical dramas would be likely to emerge which could condense and illuminate wider processes of negotiation. Secondly, such change processes would be likely to engage interest among funders and readers in their own right: the closure of Victorian asylums and the construction of new District General Hospitals are societal processes of great importance where general management faces a stern and visible test.

To Identify Motors of, and Barriers to, Change   Case studies of strategic service change in these 'high change' districts should not only be descriptive (although the empirical base should be sound) but also analytic. That is to say, it is important to interrogate the case material to identify both the motors of, and barriers to, change. This is not only a question of assessing the impact of general management, which may represent only one source of change, or may play no role in the case at all, or indeed have a negative role. We therefore need a conceptual framework which will alert us to a much wider array of potential sources of change.

To Explore the Skills Associated with Change Management   Many of these motors of, and barriers to change will be outside the role of action, but some will be more amenable to skilled intervention. There may even be skills in change management which are discernible in these case studies, although it should not be assumed that general managers offer any more than one basis for leadership in such a pluralist organization as the NHS.

Case Study Methodology – Comparative, Longitudinal and Processual

The basic methodology used has been that of longitudinal and processual comparative case study. The best statement of this approach is found in the present authors' literature review (Pettigrew, McKee and Ferlie, 1988; and see Chapter 9 above).

The methodological approach adopted here has allowed for the analysis of retrospective change, real time analysis and prospective or anticipated change. Historical antecedents and the chronology of change are considered vital. The design choice in this study has been to conduct intensive analyses of a relatively few cases, rather than a more superficial analysis of a larger number. Such are the complexities of both the strategic change issues and the host systems that such superficial analyses would be in danger of missing key components of the explanation.

Clearly a variety of data sources has been used in these case studies. Archival material was often used most in the early stages, sensitizing the researcher to the key questions and supplying a chronology of change. Although minutes have often been criticized as being bland and formalistic accounts, ephemera such as internal memos or annotations in margins could yield interesting insights. Secondary (or routinely available) statistics (such as on bed state or financial flows) were also used. Site visits were also undertaken in order to get a 'feel' for the issues. Meetings were attended (between five and ten per District) in order to observe group dynamics which were different from those of one-to-one interviews. Semi-structured interviews were undertaken with about 50 respondents per District (400 altogether), with respondents selected either because of their lead position in the organization or because they were involved directly in the change process. A wide range of respondents was interviewed: different functional groupings; different hierarchical levels; and from outside as well as inside the NHS (such as Social Services). Finally, there was informal observation while the researcher was in the District.

Table A.1 *District–issue matrix*

District Health Authority	Acute sector		Priority groups	
	Development	Rationalization	Development	Rationalization
St Helens and Knowsley		Across two-sited DGH		Mental illness closure by 1992
Paddington and North Kensington	AIDS*	Closure, achieved 1986		
Preston	DGH – 5 years on: overspend			Mental illness reduction
Bloomsbury	AIDS*	General strategy Also Accident and Emergency closure		
Bromsgrove and Redditch	New DGH		Mental handicap community provision	
Milton Keynes	New DGH		Mental illness community provision	
Mid Downs			Mental handicap community provision	Mental handicap closure by 1990
Huddersfield			Mental handicap community provision	Mental handicap reduction/closure

* This issue subsequently acquired a community – as well as a hospital-based focus.

There was intensive fieldwork of about four months in each District, followed up by limited monitoring. Two Districts in London funded a follow-up out of their own resources, and very high quality data have now been generated there.

Sample Selection

The first task was to select the key dimensions of strategic service change. Acute sector and priority group changes were chosen as the substantive basis of the research after a comprehensive literature review, discussion with key academics and Regional personnel, and a survey of the 1984–5 Regional Strategic Plans. This was further subdivided into the expansion or contraction of services and a matrix developed allowing for a spread or combination of issues and changes across Districts and Regions. We selected two change issues in each District as a minimal means of forcing the question of the interrelatedness of, and competing pressures on the managerial agenda. The reality is that management is not trying to achieve just one goal, but rather a series of different and potentially contradictory goals. Does progress on one issue make it easier to achieve change elsewhere within a District, or do managers have to choose their targets carefully? (The Preston case study is a good example of such a trade-off.) Do Districts handle different change issues in roughly the same way, or are issue characteristics much more important? (See Table A.1.)

The second task was to select the Districts. Regions were usually asked to provide some documentation on a shortlist of three, after which the final decision would be made in order to avoid too heavy a Regional steer. Additionally we tried to 'pair' Districts at least to some extent to facilitate comparison: Bromsgrove and Redditch can be seen as some sort of comparator for Milton Keynes; Bloomsbury for Paddington and North Kensington.

References

Acheson Report (1988) *Public Health in England*. Report of the Committee of Inquiry into the future development of the Public Health function. Cm 289. London: HMSO.

Ackroyd, S., Hughes, J.A. and Soothill, K. (1989) 'Public Sector Services and their Management', *Journal of Management Studies*, 26(3), pp. 603–19.

Adler, M. (1986) 'AIDS and Intravenous Drug Abusers', *British Journal of Addiction*, 81, pp. 307–10.

Aiken, M. and Hage, J. (1971) 'The Organic Organisation and Innovation', *Sociology*, 5, pp. 63–81.

Alexander, E.R. (1974) 'Decision Making and Organisational Adaptation: Proposed Model'. Paper presented to the 8th World Congress of Sociology in Toronto.

Alexander, J.A., Kaluzny, A.D. and Middleton, S.C. (1986) 'Organizational Growth, Survival and Death in the US Hospital Industry: a Population Ecology Perspective', *Social Science and Medicine*, 22(3), pp. 303–8.

Alford, Robert R. (1975) *Health Care Politics*. London: University of Chicago Press.

Alleway, Lynn (1987) 'Back on the Outside Looking In', *Health Service Journal*, 16 July, pp. 818–19.

Alvesson, M. and Melin, L. (1987) 'Major Discrepancies and Contradictions in Organizational Culture'. Paper to 3rd International Conference on Organizational Symbolism and Corporation Culture, June, Milan.

Arno, P. (1986) 'The Non Profit Sector's Response to the AIDS Epidemic: Community Based Services in San Francisco', *American Journal of Public Health*, 76(11), pp. 1325–30.

Arnold, P.E. (1988) 'Reorganisation and Regime in the United States and Britain', *Public Administration Review*, 48 (May/June), pp. 726–34.

Audit Commission (1986) *Making a Reality of Community Care*. London: HMSO.

Audit Commission (1989) *Developing Community Care for Adults with a Mental Handicap*. Occasional Paper No. 9. London: HMSO.

Bachrach, P. and Baratz, M.S. (1970) *Power and Poverty*. New York: Oxford University Press.

Baier, U.E., March, J.G. and Saetren, H. (1986) 'Implementation and Ambiguity', *Scandinavian Journal of Management Studies*, 2(3–4), pp. 197–212.

Bains Working Group (1972) *The New Local Authorities: Management and Structure*. London: HMSO.

Barnard, K., Mills, A. and Reynolds, J. (1979) *Towards a New Rationality: a Study of Planning in the NHS*. University of Leeds.

Barrett, S. and Fudge, C. (eds) (1981) *Policy and Action*. London: Methuen.

Barrett, S. and Hill, M. (1984) 'Policy, Bargaining and Structure in Implementation', *Policy and Politics*, 12(3), pp. 218–39.

Bassett, P. (1986) *Strike Free*. London: Macmillan.

Battle, Tim (1989) 'The Role of Management Development Strategies in Managing Organisational Change', *Health Services Management*, August, pp. 169–72.

Becker, M.H. (1970a) 'Sociometric Location and Innovativeness: Reformulation and Extension of the Diffusion Model', *American Sociological Review*, 35, pp. 267–82.

Becker, M.H. (1970b) 'Factors Affecting the Diffusion of Innovation among Health Professionals', *American Journal of Public Health*, 60, pp. 294–304.

Beckhard, R. and Harris, R. (1977) *Organization Transitions: Managing Complex Change*. Reading, MA: Addison Wesley.

Beer, M., Eisenstat, R.A. and Spector, B. (1990) *The Critical Path to Corporate Renewal*. Boston, MA: Harvard Business School Press.

Behn, R.D. (1988) 'The Fundamentals of Cutback Management', in K.S. Cameron, R.I. Sutton and D.A. Whetten (eds), *Readings in Organizational Decline*. Cambridge, MA: Ballinger.

Bennett, C. and Pettigrew, A. (1990) 'A Vision of Preventing the Holocaust: the Response to HIV Infection in Central Birmingham'. Centre for Corporate Strategy and Change, University of Warwick.

Bennett, C., Ferlie, E. and Pettigrew, A. (1990) 'Developing Services for HIV/AIDS: Organisational Learning in DHAs', in *Handbook of R & D, 1990*. London: DHSS.

Benson, J.K. (1982) 'Networks and Policy Sectors: a Framework for Extending Inter-organizational Analysis', in D. Rogers and D. Whitten (eds), *Interorganizational Coordination*. Ames, IA: Iowa State University Press.

Bentley, C. (1990) Consequences for HIV Services in Bloomsbury of the Changes Resulting from the NHS Review. Department of Public Health, Bloomsbury DHA.

Berg, P.O. (1979) *Emotional Structures in Organisations: a Study of the Process of Change in a Swedish Company*. Lund: Student Literature, University of Lund.

Berman, P. (1978) 'The Study of Macro and Micro Implementation', *Public Policy*, 26(2), pp. 157–85.

Best, G. (1987) *The Future of General Management – Where Next?* London: King's Fund.

Beyer, J.M., Stevens, J.M. and Trice, H.M. (1983) 'The Implementation Organization: Exploring the Black Box in Research in the Public Policy', in R.H. Hall and R.E. Quinn (eds), *Organization Theory and Public Policy*. Beverly Hills, CA: Sage.

Bidwell, C.E. and Vreeland, R.S. (1977) 'Authority and Control in Client-serving Organizations', in R. Blakenship (ed.), *Colleagues in Organization: the Social Construction of Professional Work*. New York: Wiley.

Bloomsbury DHA (1983) 'Finding the Frame', Strategy Document, Bloomsbury District Health Authority, November.

Bloomsbury DHA (1987) 'Meeting the Challenge', Strategy Document, Bloomsbury District Health Authority, June.

Boswell, J. (1973) *The Rise and Decline of Small Firms*. London: Allen and Unwin.

Bozeman, B. and Straussman, J. (1982) 'Shrinking Budgets and the Shrinkage of Budget Theory', *Public Administration Review*, 42, pp. 509–15.

Brecher, C. and Horton, R. (1985) 'Retrenchment and Recovery: American Cities and the New York Experience', *Public Administration Review*, 45, pp. 267–74.

Bromley, G. (1984) 'Hospital Closure: Death of Institutional Psychiatry?' MA thesis, University of Essex.

Brown, R.G.S. (1979) *Reorganising the NHS: a Case Study in Administrative Change*. Oxford: Basil Blackwell.

Brunsson, N. (1982) 'The Irrationality of Action and Action Rationality: Decisions, Ideologies, and Organisational Action', *Journal of Management Studies*, 19(1), pp. 29–44.

Brunsson, N. (1985) *The Irrational Organization*. Chichester: John Wiley.

Brunsson, N. (1986) 'Organizing for Inconsistencies: on Organizational Conflict, Depression and Hypocrisy as Substitutes for Action', *Scandinavian Journal of Management Studies*, 2(3–4), pp. 165–86.

Brunsson, N. (1989) 'Administrative Reforms as Routines', *Scandinavian Journal of Management Studies*, 5(3), pp. 219–28.

Bucher, R. and Stelling, J. (1977) 'Four Characteristics of Professional Organizations', in R. Blankership (ed.), *Colleagues in Organization: the Social Construction of Professional Work*. New York: John Wiley.

Burgelman, R.A. and Sayles, L.R. (1986) *Inside Corporate Innovation: Strategy, Structure and Managerial Skills*. London: Collier Macmillan.

Burns, T. and Stalker, G.M. (1961) *The Management of Innovation*. London: Tavistock.

Busfield, J. (1986) *Managing Madness: Changing Ideas and Practice*. London: Hutchinson.

Buxton, M., Packwood, T. and Keen, J. (1989) 'Resource Management: Process and

Progress – Monitoring the Six Acute Hospital Pilot Sites'. Health Economics Research Group, Brunel University.

Carrier, J. and Kendall, I. (1986) 'NHS Management and the Griffiths Report', in M. Brenton and C. Ungerson (eds), *Yearbook of Social Policy 1985–86*. London: Routledge.

Chandler, A.J. (1962) *Strategy and Structure: Chapters in the History of the American Industrial Enterprise*. Cambridge, MA: MIT Press.

Child, J. (1972) 'Organisation Structure, Environment and Performance – the Role of Strategic Choice', *Sociology*, 6, pp. 1–22.

Child, J. and Keiser, A. (1977) 'The Development of Organisations Over Time', in W.H. Starbuck (ed.), *The Handbook of Organisational Design*, vol. 2. Amsterdam: Elsevier.

Clark, B. (1972) 'The Organisational Saga in Higher Education', *Administrative Science Quarterly*, 17, pp. 178–84.

Cm 555 (1989) *Working for Patients*. White Paper. London: HMSO.

Cmnd 1604 (1962) *A Hospital Plan for England and Wales*. White Paper. London: HMSO.

Cmnd 3000 (1966) *The Hospital Building Programme*. London: HMSO.

Cmnd 8616 (1982) *Efficiency and Effectiveness in the Civil Service*. London: HMSO.

Cohen, M.D., March, J.G. and Olsen, J.P. (1972) 'A Garbage Can Model of Organizational Choice', *Administrative Science Quarterly*, 17, pp. 1–25.

Coleman, J.S., Katz, E. and Merzel, H. (1966) *Medical Innovation: a Diffusion Study*. Indianapolis, IN: Bobbs-Merrill.

Collin, A.J., Edmonstone, J.R. and Sturt, J.R. (1981) 'Commissioning District General Hospitals: the State of the Art', *Hospital and Health Services Review*, October, pp. 268–71.

Collin, T. and Wilson, D. (1985) 'Workshops for Commissioning Teams', *Health Service Manpower Review*, 11 (May), pp. 9–12.

Committee of Inquiry (1971) *Report of a Committee of Inquiry: Whittingham Hospital*. London: HMSO.

Committee of Inquiry (1979) *Report of a Committee of Inquiry: Rainhill Hospital*. London: HMSO.

Cooper, G. (1978) *Report of Inquiry into the Planning of the Proposed Milton Keynes DGH*. Oxford: Oxford RHA.

Copeland Report (1981) 'The Development and Organization of Rainhill Hospital'. Rainhill Hospital, Merseyside (mimeo).

Crispin, A. and Marslen-Wilson, F. (1986) 'Local Responses to Block Grant: The Case of Education', in M. Goldsmith (ed.), *New Research in Central-Local Relations*. Aldershot: Gower.

Davies, B.P. and Ferlie, E.B. (1982) 'Efficiency Promoting Innovation in Social Care: Social Services Departments and the Elderly', *Policy and Politics*, 19(2), 181–205.

Davies, B.P. and Ferlie, E.B. (1984) 'Patterns of Efficiency Improving Innovation: Social Care and the Elderly', *Policy and Politics*, 12(3), pp. 281–96.

Davies, C. (1987) 'Viewpoint: Things to Come: the NHS in the Next Decade', *Sociology of Health and Illness*, 9(3), pp. 302–4.

Day, P. and Klein, R. (1983) 'The Mobilisation of Consent (vs) the Management of Conflict: Decoding the Griffiths Report', *British Medical Journal*, 287 (10 December), pp. 1813–17.

Deal, T.E. and Kennedy, A.A. (1982) *Corporate Cultures: the Rites and Rituals of Corporate Life*. Reading, MA: Addison Wesley.

Delbecq, A.L. and Mills, P.K. (1985) 'Structure which Executives Can Implement under Conditions of Ambiguity to Increase Innovation', in L.R. Pondy, R.J. Boland and H. Thomas (eds), *Managing Ambiguity and Change*. Chichester: John Wiley.

DHSS (1979) *Patients First*. London: HMSO.

DHSS (1980) *Mental Handicap: Progress, Problems and Priorities*. London: HMSO.

DHSS (1981a) *Care in Action*. London: HMSO.

DHSS (1981b) *Care in the Community: A Consultative Document*. London: HMSO.

DHSS (1982) *The NHS Planning System*. HC (82)6. London: DHSS.

Douglas, M. (1987) *How Institutions Think*. London: Routledge.

Downs, Anthony (1967) *Inside Bureaucracies*. Boston, MA: Little, Brown.

Downs, A. (1972) 'Up and Down with Ecology – the Issue Attention Cycle', *The Public Interest*, 28, pp. 38–50.

Downs, G.W. and Mohr, L.B. (1976) 'Conceptual Issues in the Study of Innovations', *Administrative Science Quarterly*, 21 (December), pp. 700–14.

Dufour, Y. (1991) 'The Implementation of General Practitioner Maternity Unit Proposals in Hospitals'. PhD Thesis, Centre for Corporate Strategy and Change, University of Warwick.

Dutton, J. (1987) 'The Processing of Crisis and Non Crisis Strategic Issues', *Journal of Management Studies*, 23(5), pp. 501–17.

Edmonstone, J. (1982) 'From "Organisational Social Work" to Organisational Design', *Leadership and Organisation Development Journal*, 3(1), pp. 24–6.

Efficiency Unit (1988) *Improving Management in Government: the Next Steps*. London: HMSO.

Eisenhardt, K. (1989) 'Building Theory from Case Study Research', *Academy of Management Review*, 14(4), pp. 532–50.

Elcock, H. (1978) 'Regional Government in Action: the Members of Two RHAs', *Public Administration*, 56, pp. 379–97.

Evans, T. (1987a) 'Strategic Response to Environmental Turbulence', in B. Stocking (ed.), *In Dreams Begin Responsibility*. London: King's Fund.

Evans, T. (1987b) 'Managing Service Changes with Declining Resources', in B. Stocking (ed.), *In Dreams Begin Responsibility*. London: King's Fund.

Ferlie, E.B. (1990) 'Understanding Change in Psychiatric Services: Whose Change Agenda? Whose Organisation?' Centre for Corporate Strategy and Change. Working Paper, University of Warwick (mimeo).

Ferlie, E.B. and Bennett, C. (1992) 'Patterns of Strategic Change in Health Care: District Health Authorities Respond to AIDS', *British Journal of Management*, 3 (March), pp. 21–38.

Ferlie, E.B. and Judge, K. (1981) 'Retrenchment and Rationality in the Personal Social Services', *Policy and Politics*, 9(3), pp. 311–30.

Ferlie, E.B. and Pettigrew, A.M. (1990) 'Coping with Change in the NHS: a Frontline District's Response to AIDS', *Journal of Social Policy*, 19(2), pp. 191–220.

Feuer, L. (1975) *Ideology and the Ideologist*. Oxford: Basil Blackwell.

Fitzgerald, L. (1990) 'Management Development in the NHS: Crossing Professional Boundaries', *Public Policy and Management*, 10(1), pp. 31–5.

Flowers Report (1980) *London Medical Education – A New Framework*. Report of a Working Party on Medical and Dental Teaching Resources. London: University of London.

Flynn, A., Gray, A. and Jenkins, W. (1989) 'Management Reform in British Government: the Role of the Next Steps'. Paper presented to the EGPA Conference, Chester, September.

Flynn, N. (1989) 'The "New Right" and Social Policy', *Policy and Politics*, 17(2), pp. 97–109.

Foucault, M. (1967) *Madness and Civilization*. London: Tavistock.

Freidson, E. (1970a) *Profession of Medicine*. New York: Dodd-Mead.

Freidson, E. (1970b) *Professional Dominance*. Chicago: Aldine.

Fry, G. (1981) *The Administrative 'Revolution' in Whitehall*. London: Croom Helm.

Fry, G. (1984) 'The Development of the Thatcher Government's "Grand Strategy" for the Civil Service: a Public Policy Perspective', *Public Administration*, 62 (Autumn), pp. 322–35.

Fulton Report (1968) *The Civil Service*. Vol. 1, *Report of the Committee*. Cmnd 3638. London: HMSO.

George, A.L. and McKeown, T.J. (1985) 'Case Studies and Theories of Organizational Decision Making', in *Advances in Information Processing in Organizations*, vol. 2. Greenwich, CT: JAI Press.

Glennerster, H., Korman, N. and Marslen-Wilson, F. (1983) *Planning for Priority Groups*. Oxford: Martin Robertson.

Glennerster, H., Owens, P. and Kimberley, A. (1986) 'The Nursing Management Function after Griffiths in the North West Thames Region'. Interim Report. London School of Economics.

Goffman, I. (1968) *Asylum: Essays on the Social Situation of Patients and Other Inmates.* Harmondsworth: Penguin.

Golembiewski, R.T. (1990) 'The Boom in the Decline Literature: Surveying the Field and Detailing One Metaphor', *Public Administration Review*, 50(1), pp. 108–10.

Goodenough Report (1944) *Report of the Interdepartmental Committee on Medical Schools.* London: HMSO.

Gooding, D. and Reid, J.J. (1970) 'Health Service Planning in a New Town', *Medical Officer*, 123(14), pp. 177–80.

Goodman, P.S. and Dean, J.W. (1982) 'Creating Long-Term Organization Change', in P.S. Goodman (ed.), *Change in Organizations.* San Francisco: Jossey Bass.

Gordon, G. and Fisher, L. (1975) *Diffusion of Innovations in Medicine.* Cambridge, MA: Ballinger.

Greenwood, R. (1984) 'Incremental Budgeting: Antecedents of Change', *Journal of Public Policy*, 4(4), pp. 277–306.

Greenwood, R. and Hinings, C.R. (1986) 'Organisation Design Types, Tracks and the Dynamics of Change'. Department of Organizational Analysis, University of Alberta (mimeo).

Greenwood, R., Walsh, K., Hinings, C.R. and Ranson, S. (1980) *Patterns of Management in Local Government.* Oxford: Martin Robertson.

Grieco, M.S. (1988) 'Birthmarked? A Critical View of Analysing Organizational Culture', *Human Organization*, 47(1), pp. 84–7.

Grieco, M. (1991) 'Central Treatment: Contestation and Smuggled Innovation', in K. Starkey and R. Loveridge (eds), *Continuity and Crisis in the NHS: the Politics of Design and Innovation in Health Care.* Milton Keynes: Open University Press.

Griffiths Report (1983) *NHS Management Inquiry.* London: DHSS.

Griffiths Report (1988) *Community Care: an Agenda for Action.* London: HMSO.

Grindle, M.S. (1980) 'Policy Content and Context in Implication', in M.S. Grindle (ed.), *Politics and Policy Implementation in the Third World.* Princeton, NJ: Princeton University Press.

Grinyer, P. and McKiernan, P. (1990) 'Generating Major Change in Stagnating Companies', *Strategic Management Journal*, 11, pp. 131–46.

Grinyer, P.H., Mayes, D. and McKiernan, P. (1988a) 'Sharpbenders: the Process of Marked and Sustained Performance in Selected UK Companies', in A.M. Pettigrew .(ed.), *Competitiveness and the Management Process.* Oxford: Basil Blackwell.

Grinyer, P.H., Mayes, D.G. and McKiernan, P. (1988b) *Sharpbenders: the Secrets of Unleashing Corporate Potential.* Oxford: Basil Blackwell.

Gunn, L. (1989) 'A Public Management Approach to the NHS', *Health Services Management Research*, 2(1), pp. 10–19.

Hage, J. and Dewar, R. (1973) 'Elite Values versus Organisational Structure in Predicting Innovation', *Administrative Science Quarterly*, 18, pp. 279–90.

Hales, C. (1986) 'What do Managers Do? A Critical Review of the Evidence', *Journal of Management Studies*, 23(1), pp. 88–113.

Hall, P. (1980) *Great Planning Disasters.* London: Weidenfeld and Nicolson.

Hall, P., Land, H., Parker, R. and Webb, A. (1975) *Change, Choice and Conflict in Social Policy.* London: Heinemann Educational.

Ham, C. (1981) *Policy Making in the NHS.* London: Macmillan.

Hannan, M.T. and Freeman, J. (1977) 'The Population Ecology of Organizations', *American Journal of Sociology*, 82, pp. 929–64.

Hannan, M.T. and Freeman, J. (1984) 'Structural Inertia and Organizational Change', *American Sociological Review*, 49 (April), pp. 149–64.

Hardy, B., Wistow, G. and Rhodes, R.A.W. (1990) 'Policy Networks and the Implementation of Community Care Policy for People with Mental Handicaps', *Journal of Social Policy*, 19(2), pp. 141–68.

Hardy, C. (1985) *The Management of Organisational Closure*. Aldershot: Gower.

Hardy, C. (1987) 'Using Content, Context and Process to Manage University Cutbacks', *Canadian Journal of Higher Education*, 27(1), pp. 65–82.

Harrigan, K.H. (1988) 'Strategies for Declining Industries', in K.S. Cameron, R.I. Sutton and D.A. Whetten (eds), *Readings in Organizational Decline*. Cambridge, MA: Ballinger.

Harrison, S. (1982) 'Consensus Decision Making in the NHS: a Review', *Journal of Management Studies*, 19(4), pp. 377–94.

Harrison, S. (1988) *Managing the NHS: Shifting the Frontier*. London: Chapman and Hall.

Harrison, S., Hunter, D., Marnoch, G. and Pollitt, C. (1989a) 'General Management and Medical Autonomy in the National Health Service', *Health Services Management Research*, 2(1), pp. 38–46.

Harrison, S., Hunter, D.J., Marnoch, G. and Pollitt, C. (1989b) *General Management in the NHS: Before and After the White Paper*. Report no. 2. Leeds: Nuffield Institute.

Harrison, S. and Schulz, R. (1989) 'Clinical Autonomy in the UK and the US: Contrasts and Convergence', in G. Freddi and J.W. Bjorkman (eds), *Controlling Medical Professionals: the Comparative Politics of Health Governance*. London: Sage.

Harrow, J. and Willcocks, L. (1990) 'Public Services Management: Activities, Initiatives, and Limits to Learning', *Journal of Management Studies*, 27(3), pp. 281–304.

Hart, G. (1989) 'State Policy, Drug Users and Needle Exchange: Say No to Drugs, but Yes to Clean Syringes'. Paper presented as BSA Conference, Plymouth Polytechnic, March.

Haywood, S. (1974) *Managing the Health Service*. London: Allen and Unwin.

Haywood, S.C. (1977) 'More Democracy for the NHS', *Hospital and Health Services Review*, April, pp. 123–6.

Haywood, S. and Alasweski, A. (1980) *Crisis in the Health Service*. London: Croom Helm.

Haywood, S. and Ranade, W. (1985) *District Health Authorities in Action Two Years On: a Progress Report*. Birmingham: University of Birmingham HSMC.

Haywood, S. and Ranade, W. (1986) 'Resources and Innovation in Health Care', *Policy and Politics*, 14(4), pp. 461–74.

Heclo, H. and Wildavsky, A. (1974) *The Private Government of Public Money*. London: Macmillan.

Hedberg, B.L.T. (1981) 'How Organisations Learn and Unlearn', in P.C. Nystrom and W.H. Starbuck (eds), *Handbook of Organisational Design*. Vol. 1, *Adapting Organisations to their Environments*. Oxford: Oxford University Press.

Hedberg, B.L.T., Nystrom, P.C. and Starbuck, W.H. (1976) 'Camping on Seesaws: Prescription for a Self Designing Organisation', *Administrative Science Quarterly*, 21 (March), pp. 41–65.

Hendry, C. (1990) 'The Corporate Management of Human Resources under Conditions of Decentralization', *British Journal of Management*, 1 (July), pp. 91–105.

Hennessy P. (1988) 'Demystifying Whitehall: the Great British Civil Service Debate, 1980s Style', in C. Campbell and G. Peters (eds), *Organizing Governance: Governing Institutions*. Pittsburgh, PA: University of Pittsburgh Press.

Hermann, C.F. (1963) 'Some Consequences of Crisis which Limit the Viability of Organisations', *Administrative Science Quarterly*, 8(1), pp. 61–82.

Hill, M. (1982) 'Street Level Bureaucracy in Social Work and Social Services Departments'. Research Highlights no. 4, 'Social Work Departments as Organizations', University of Aberdeen.

Hinings, C.R. and Greenwood, R. (1988) 'The Normative Prescription of Organizations', in L. Zucker (ed.), *Institutional Patterns and Organizations: Culture and Environment*. Cambridge, MA: Ballinger.

Hocking, J. (1991) 'Managing in the Market Place: Universities and Institutional Change in the Late 1980s and Early 1990s'. MBA dissertation, University of Warwick.

Hogwood, B. (1987) *From Crisis to Complacency*. Oxford: Oxford University Press.

Hunter Report (1972) *Report of the Working Party on Medical Administrators*. London: HMSO.

Hunter, D. (1980) *Coping with Uncertainty*. Chichester: Research Studies Press.

Hunter, D. (1984) 'NHS Management: is Griffiths the Last Quick Fix?', *Public Administration*, 62 (Spring), pp. 91–4.

Hunter, D. (1986) *Managing the NHS in Scotland: Review and Assessment of Research Needs*. Edinburgh: Scottish Home and Health Department.

Hunter, D. (1989) 'Organising and Managing Health Care: a Challenge for Medical Sociology', in S. Cunningham-Burley and N. McKeganey (eds), *Readings in Medical Sociology*. London: Tavistock/Routledge.

Hunter, D. and Williamson, P. (1989) 'Perspectives on General Management in the NHS', *Health Services Management Research*, 2(1), pp. 2–9.

Hunter, D. and Wistow, G. (1987a) *Community Care in Britain: Variations on a Theme*. London: King's Fund.

Hunter, D. and Wistow, G. (1987b) 'The Paradox of Policy Diversity in a Unitary State: Community Care in Britain', *Public Administration*, 65, pp. 3–23.

Hurley, R.E. and Kuluzny, A.D. (1987) 'Organisational Ecology and Health Care Research', *Medical Care Research*, 44(2), pp. 235–55.

Illich, I. (1976) *Limits to Medicine*. London: Marion Boyars.

Jelinek, M. and Schoonhoven, C. (1990) *The Innovation Marathon: Lessons from High Technology Firms*. Oxford: Basil Blackwell.

Jick, T.D. and Murray, V.V. (1982) 'The Management of Hard Times: Budget Cutbacks in Public Sector Organisations', *Organisation Studies*, 3(2), pp. 141–69.

Johnson, A.M., Adler, M.W. and Crown, J.M. (1986) 'AIDS and Epidemic of Infection with HIV: Costs of Care and Prevention in an Inner London District', *British Medical Journal*, 293, pp. 489–92.

Johnson, A.M. and Miller, D. (1988) 'Health Care Planning and Social Policy Issues', in A.J. Pinching, R.A. Weiss and D. Miller (eds), *AIDS and HIV Infection: the Wider Perspective*. London: Churchill Livingstone.

Johnson, G. (1987) *Strategic Change and the Management Process*. Oxford: Basil Blackwell.

Johnson, G. (1990) 'Managing Strategic Change: The Role of Symbolic Action', *British Journal of Management*, 1, pp. 183–200.

Johnson, T. (1972) *Professions and Power*. London: Macmillan.

Kanter, R.M. (1985) *The Change Masters: Corporate Entrepreneurs at Work*. London: Allen and Unwin.

Kanter, R.M. (1989) *When Giants Learn to Dance*. New York: Simon and Schuster.

Kelly, A. (1989) 'An End to Incrementalism? The Impact of Expenditure Restraint on SSDs, 1979–1986', *Journal of Social Policy*, 18(2), pp. 187–210.

Kervasdoue, J. de (1981) 'Institutions, Organisations, Medical Disciplines and the Dissemination of Research Results', *Organisation Studies*, 2/3, pp. 249–66.

Kervasdoue, J. de and Kimberly, J.R. (1979) 'Are Organizations Culture Free?', in G. England, A.R. Negandhi and B. Wilpert (eds), *Organizations Functioning in a Cross Cultural Perspective*. Kent, OH: Kent State University Press.

Kilmann, R.H., Saxton, M.J. and Serpa, R. (1986) *Gaining Control of the Corporate Culture*. San Francisco: Jossey Bass.

Kimberly, J.R. (1980) 'Initiation, Innovation and Institutionalization in the Creation Process', in J.R. Kimberly and R.H. Miles (eds), *The Organizational Life Cycle*. San Francisco: Jossey Bass.

Kimberly, J. (1987) 'The Study of Organizations: Toward a Biographical Perspective', in J.W. Lorsch (ed.), *Handbook of Organizational Behaviour*. Englewood Cliffs, NJ: Prentice Hall.

Kimberly, J. (1989) 'Change in the NHS: a View from America'. Presentation to CCSC Open Seminar 'Managing Change in Health Care Systems: Slogan or Reality?', University of Warwick, September.

Kimberly, J.R. and Evanisko, J.M. (1981) 'Organizational Innovation: the Influence of Individual Organizational and Contextual Factors on Hospital Adoption of Technological and Administrative Innovation', *Academy of Management Journal*, 24(4), pp. 689–713.

Kimberly, J. and Rottman, David (1987) 'Environment, Organisation and Effectiveness: a Biographical Approach', *Journal of Management Studies*, 24(6), pp. 595–622.

Kimberly, J. and Miles, R. (eds) (1980) *The Organizational Life Cycle*. San Francisco: Jossey Bass.

King's Fund (1987) *Planning Health Services for Inner London: Back to Back Planning*. London: King's Fund.

Klein, L. (1976) *A Social Scientist in Industry*. Epping, Essex: Gower Press.

Klein, R. (1983) *The Politics of the National Health Service*. London: Longman.

Klein, R. (1984) 'The Politics of Ideology (vs) the Realities of Politics: the Case of Britain's NHS in the 1980s', *Millbank Memorial Fund Quarterly, Health and Society*, 62(1), pp. 82–109.

Kogan, M. et al. (1978) *The Working of the NHS*. Research Report 1. Cmnd 7615. London: HMSO.

Korman, N. and Glennerster, H. (1985) *Closing a Hospital: the Darenth Park Project*. Occasional Papers on Social Administration no. 78. London: Bedford Square Press.

Korman, N. and Glennerster, H. (1990) *Hospital Closure*. Milton Keynes: Open University Press.

Korman, N. and Simons, H. (1979) *Hospital Closures*. Research Paper 1, Royal Commission on the NHS. London: HMSO.

Kotter, J. (1982) *The General Manager*. New York: Free Press.

Lant, T.K. and Mezias, S.J. (1990) 'Managing Discontinuous Change: a Simulation Study of Organisational Learning and Entrepreneurship', *Strategic Management Journal*, 11, pp. 147–79.

Levine, C.H. (1978) 'Organisational Decline and Cutback Management', *Public Administration Review*, 38 (July/August: 316–25.

Levine, C.H. (1988) 'Police Management in the 1980s: from Decrementalism to Strategic Thinking', in K. Cameron, R. Sutton and D. Whetten (eds), *Readings in Organizational Decline*. Cambridge, MA: Ballinger.

Levine, C.H., Rubin, I.S. and Wolohojian, G.G. (1981) *The Politics of Retrenchment: How Local Governments Manage Fiscal Stress*. London: Sage.

Levine, C.H., Rubin, I.S. and Wolohojian, G.G. (1982) 'Managing Organisational Retrenchment: Preconditions, Deficiencies, and Adaptations in the Public Sector', *Administration and Society*, 14(1), pp. 101–36.

Liddell, A. (1987) 'General Management in a DHA', in Barbara Stocking (ed.), *In Dreams Begins Responsibility: a Tribute to Tom Evans*. London: King's Fund.

Lindblom, C.E. (1959) 'The Science of Muddling Through', *Public Administration Review*, 19, pp. 91–9.

Lodahl, T. and Mitchell, S. (1980) 'Drift in the Development of Innovative Organisations', in J.R. Kimberly and R.H. Miles (eds), *The Organizational Life Cycle*. San Francisco: Jossey Bass.

Lorenz, C. (1991) 'Juggling Lots of Balls in the Air . . .', *Financial Times*, 9 January, p. 14.

Lorsch, J. (1986) 'Managing Culture: the Invisible Banner to Strategic Change', *California Management Review*, 28(2), pp. 95–109.

Louis, K.S., Blemerthal, D., Gluck, M. and Stoto, M. (1989) 'Entrepreneurs in Academe: an Exploration of Behaviours among Life Scientists', *Administrative Science Quarterly*, 34, pp. 110–31.

Louw, J. (1989) 'Positive Job Planning', *Health Services Journal* 31 (Aug), pp. 1062–3.

March, J.G. and Olsen, J.P. (1983) 'Organising Political Life – What Administrative Reorganisation Tells Us about Government', *American Political Science Review*, 77, pp. 281–96.

March, J.G. and Olsen, J.P. (1984) 'The New Institutionalism: Organisational Factors in Political Life', *American Political Science Review*, 78, pp. 735–49.

March, J.G. and Olsen, J.P. (1989) *Rediscovering Institutions: the Organizational Basis of Politics*. New York: Free Press/Macmillan.

Marchington, M. (1989) 'Joint Consultation in Practice', in K. Sisson (ed.), *Personnel Management in Britain*. Oxford: Basil Blackwell.

Marquand, D. (1988) *The Unprincipled Society*. London: Fontana.

Marsh, P. (1983) 'A Study of the Policy Process within a Health Authority'. MPhil. Thesis, University of Warwick.

Maxwell, R. (ed.) (1988) *Reshaping the NHS*. Policy Journals Series. Oxford: Transaction Books.

McCarthy, J. and Zald, M.N. (1976) 'Resource Mobilisation and Social Movements: a Partial Theory', *American Journal of Sociology*, 82, pp. 1212–41.

McKee, L. (1988) 'Conflicts and Context in Managing the Closure of a Large Psychiatric Hospital', *Bulletin of the Royal College of Psychiatrists*, 12(8), pp. 310–19.

McKee, L. and Ferlie, E. (1988) 'Planning for Alternative Futures in the NHS', *Health Service Management Research*, 1(1), pp. 4–18.

McKee, L. and Pettigrew, A.M. (1988) *A Case Study of Strategic Change in Psychiatric and Acute Services*. Centre for Corporate Strategy and Change, University of Warwick (mimeo).

McLachlin, G. and McKeown, T. (eds) (1971) *Medical History and Medical Care*. Oxford: Oxford University Press.

McMorrin, A., Sims, C. and Talbot, D. (1990) 'Department of Health Estates Directorate: Marketing Study'. Project Report, Warwick Business School, University of Warwick.

Merrison Report (1979) *Royal Commission on the National Health Service*. Cmnd 7615. London: HMSO.

Mersey RHA (1982) 'The Green Book: Strategies for Mental Illness and Mental Handicap Services'. Mersey Regional Health Authority (mimeo).

Metcalfe, L. and Richards, S. (1987) *Improving Public Management*. London: Sage.

Meyer, A.D. (1982) 'Adapting to Environmental Jolts', *Administrative Science Quarterly*, 27, pp. 515–37.

Meyer, M. (1990) 'Notes of a Sceptic: from Organisational Ecology to Organisational Evolution', in J.U. Singh (ed.), *Organisational Evolution: New Directions*. London: Sage.

Miles, R. and Randolph, A. (1980) 'Influence of Organisational Learning Studies on Early Development', in J. Kimberly and R. Miles (eds), *The Organizational Life Cycle*. San Francisco: Jossey Bass.

Millard, G. (1981) *Commissioning Hospital Buildings*. London: King's Fund/Pitman.

Miller, D. (1982) 'Evolution and Revolution: a Quantum View of Structural Change in Organisations', *Journal of Management Studies*, 19(2), pp. 131–51.

Miller, D. and Friesen, P. (1982) 'Structural Change and Performance: Quantum versus Piecemeal-Incremental Approaches', *Academy of Management Journal*, 25(4), pp. 867–92.

Miner, A. (1990) 'Structural Evolution through Idiosyncratic Jobs: the Potential for Unplanned Learning', *Organization Science*, 1(2), pp. 195–208.

Mintzberg, H. (1973) *The Nature of Managerial Work*. New York: Harper and Row.

Mintzberg, H. (1978) 'Patterns in Strategy Formation', *Management Science*, 24(9), pp. 934–48.

Mintzberg, H. (1990) *Mintzberg on Management*. London: Free Press.

Morgan, G. (1986) *Images of Organization*. London: Sage.

Mumford, E. and Pettigrew, A.M. (1975) *Implementing Strategic Decisions*. London: Longman.

Nadler, D.A. and Tushman, M.L. (1990) 'Beyond the Charismatic Leader: Leadership and Organizational Change', *California Management Review*, 32(2), 77–97.

National Audit Office (1989) *Hospital Building in England*. London: HMSO.

Navarro, V. (1976) *Medicine under Capitalism*. New York: Prodist.

NCVO (1986) *A Stake in Planning: Joint Planning and the Voluntary Sector*. London: Community Care Project.

NHSTA (1986) *Better Management, Better Health*. Bristol: National Health Service Training Authority.

Nodder Report (1980) 'Organisation and Management Problems of Mental Illness Hospitals'. London: DHSS.

Normann, R. (1977) *Management for Growth*. London: Wiley.

Norton, A. and Rogers, S. (1981) 'The Health Service and Local Government Services', in G. McLachlan (ed.), *Matters of Moment*. London: Nuffield Provincial Hospitals Trust.

Oakley, A. (1980) *Women Confined: Towards a Sociology of Childbirth*. Oxford: Martin Robertson.

Olsen, J.P. (1988) 'Administrative Reform and Theories of Organization', in L. Campbell and G. Peters (eds), *Organizing Governance: Governing Institutions*. Pittsburgh, PA: University of Pittsburgh Press.

Oxford RHA (1976) 'Milton Keynes DGH Phase 1: Stage 1G Submission' (draft). Oxford Regional Health Authority.

Paine, L.W.H. (ed.) (1978) *The Health Service Administrator: Innovator or Catalyst*. London: King's Fund.

Parston, G. (ed.) (1986) *Managers as Strategists*. London: King's Fund.

Parston, G. (1988) 'Evolution – General Management', in Robert Maxwell (ed.), *Reshaping the NHS*. Policy Journals Series. Oxford: Transaction Books.

Pascale, R. (1990) *Managing on the Edge*. London: Penguin.

Perrin et al. (1978) *Management of Financial Resources in the NHS*. Research Paper 2, Royal Commission on the NHS. London: HMSO.

Petchey, R. (1986) 'The Griffiths reorganisation of the NHS: Fowlerism by Stealth?', *Critical Social Policy*, 17, pp. 87–101.

Peters, G. (1988) 'Introduction', in Colin Campbell and Guy Peters (eds), *Organizing Governance: Governing Organizations*. Pittsburgh, PA: University of Pittsburgh Press.

Peters, J.P. and Tseng, S. (1983) *Managing Strategic Change in Hospitals – Ten Success Stories*. Chicago: American Hospital Publishing.

Peters, T.J. and Waterman, R. (1982) *In Search of Excellence: Lessons from America's Best Run Companies*. New York: Harper and Row.

Petrie, H.G. and Alpert, D. (1984) 'What is the Problem of Retrenchment in Higher Education?', *Journal of Management Studies*, 20(1), pp. 97–119.

Pettigrew, A.M. (1973a) 'Occupational Specialisation as an Emergent Process', *Sociological Review*, 21(2), p. 255–78.

Pettigrew, A.M. (1973b) *The Politics of Organisational Decision-making*. London: Tavistock.

Pettigrew, A.M. (1975) 'Strategic Aspects of the Management of Specialist Activity', *Personnel Review*, 4(1), pp. 5–13.

Pettigrew, A.M. (1976) 'The Creation of Organisational Cultures'. Paper presented to EIASM-Dansk Management Centre Research Seminar, Copenhagen (mimeo, University of Warwick).

Pettigrew, A.M. (1977), 'Strategy Formulation as a Political Process', *International Studies of Management and Organization*, 7(2), 78–87.

Pettigrew, A.M. (1979) 'On Studying Organisational Culture', *Administrative Science Quarterly*, 24(4), pp. 570–81.

Pettigrew, A.M. (1985a) *The Awakening Giant: Continuity and Change in ICI*. Oxford: Basil Blackwell.

Pettigrew, A.M. (1985b) 'Contextualist Research: a Natural Way to Link Theory and Practice', in E.E. Lawler (ed.), *Doing Research that is Useful in Theory and Practice*. San Francisco: Jossey Bass.

Pettigrew, A.M. (1985c) 'Examining change in the Long Term Context of Culture and Politics', in J. and M. Pennings and associates, *Organizational Strategy and Change*. San Francisco: Jossey Bass.

Pettigrew, A.M. (1990) 'Is Corporate Culture Manageable?', in D. Wilson and R. Rosenfeld (eds), *Managing Organizations: Text, Readings and Cases*. London: McGraw Hill.

Pettigrew, A.M. and Hendry C. (1991) 'Getting Training and Development into the Organisational Bloodstream', in M. Silver (ed.), *Competent to Manage: Approaches to Management Training and Development*. London: Routledge.

Pettigrew, A.M. and Whipp, R. (1991) *Managing Change for Competitive Success*. Oxford: Basil Blackwell.

Pettigrew, A.M. and Whipp, R. (1992) 'Managing Change and Corporate Performance', in V. Cool, D. Neven and I. Walter (eds), *European Industrial Restructuring in the 1990s*. London: Macmillan.

Pettigrew, A.M., Ferlie, E.B., FitzGerald, L. and Wensley, R. (1991) 'The Leadership Role of the New Health Authorities: an Agenda for Research and Development', *Public Money and Management*, 11 (Spring), pp. 39–43.

Pettigrew, A.M., Ferlie, E. and McKee, L. (1990) 'Managing Strategic Service Change in the NHS'. Final Report. Centre for Corporate Strategy and Change, University of Warwick.

Pettigrew, A.M., Hendry, C. and Sparrow, P. (1989) *Training in Britain: Employers' Perspectives on Human Resources*. London: HMSO.

Pettigrew, A.M., Hendry, C. and Sparrow, P.R. (1990) *Corporate Strategy Change and Human Resource Management*. Research and Development Paper no. 63. Sheffield: Department of Employment.

Pettigrew, A.M., McKee, L. and Ferlie, E. (1988) 'Understanding Change in the NHS', *Public Administration*, 66(3), pp. 297–317.

Pettigrew, A.M., McKee, L. and Ferlie, E. (1989) 'Managing Strategic Change in the NHS', *Health Services Management Research*, 2(1), pp. 20–31.

Pfeffer, J. (1981) *Power in Organizations*. Marshfield, MA: Pitman.

Pinching, A.J. et al. (1983) 'Studies of Cellular Immunity in Male Homosexuals in London', *The Lancet*, 16 July, pp. 126–30.

Plant, R. (1987) *Managing Change and Making It Stick*. London: Fontana Paperbacks.

Plowden Report (1961) *Control of Public Expenditure*. Report of a Committee of Inquiry chaired by Lord Plowden. Cmnd 1432. London: HMSO.

Pollitt, C. (1990) *Managerialism and the Public Services*. Oxford: Basil Blackwell.

Pollitt, C., Harrison, S., Hunter, D. and Marnoch, G. (1988) 'The Reluctant Managers: Clinicians and Budgets in the NHS', *Financial Accountability and Management*, 4(3), pp. 213–33.

Prahalad, C.K. and Hamel, G. (1990) 'The Core Competence of the Corporation', *Harvard Business Review*, 68 (May–June), pp. 79–91.

Public Accounts Committee (1980) *Standardisation of Hospital Design*. Session 79/80, 11th Report, HCP 498. London: House of Commons.

Public Accounts Committee (1981) *Financial Control and Accountability in the NHS*. Session 80/81, 17th Report, HCP 255. London: House of Commons.

Public Accounts Committee (1984) *Manpower Control, Accountability and Other Matters Relating to the NHS*. Session 83/84, 16th Report, HCP 113. London: House of Commons.

Public Accounts Committee (1990) *Hospital Building in England*. Session 1989/90, 18th Report, HCP 397. London: House of Commons.

Pugh, D.S. (1973) 'The Measurement of Organization Structures: Does Context Determine Form?', *Organizational Dynamics*, Spring, pp. 19–34.

Quinn, J.B. (1980) *Strategies for Change: Logical Incrementalism*. Homewood, IL: Irwin.

Quinn, J.B. (1982) 'Managing Strategies Incrementally', *Omega*, 10(6), pp. 613–27.

Quinn, R.E. and Anderson, D.F. (1984) 'Formalisation as Crisis – Transition Planning for a Young Organization', in J.R. Kimberly and R.E. Quinn (eds), *Managing Organizational Transitions*. Homewood, IL: Irwin.

Quinn, J.B., Mintzberg, H. and James, R. M. (1988), *The Strategy Process: Concepts, Contexts, and Cases*. Englewood Cliffs, NJ: Prentice Hall.

Rainey, H.G. (1983) 'Public Organisation Theory: the Rising Challenge', *Public Administration Review*, March/April, pp. 176–82.

Ranade, W. (1985) 'Motives and Behaviours in DHAs', *Public Administration*, 63 (Summer), pp. 183–200.

Reid, J.J. (1973) 'Milton Keynes – Problem and Opportunities', in *Milton Keynes Symposium, 1972*. Milton Keynes: Update Publications.

Renshaw, J., Hampson, R., Thomason, C., Darton, R., Judge, K. and Knapp, M. (1988) *Care in the Community: the First Steps*. Aldershot: Gower.

Renshaw, L.R., Kimberly, J.R. and Schwartz, J.S. (1990) 'Technology Diffusion and

Ecological Analysis', in S.S. Mick and associates, *Innovations in Health Care Delivery*. San Francisco: Jossey Bass.

Rhodes, R.A.W. (1981) *Control and Power in Central–Local Government Relations*. Farnborough: Gower.

Rhodes, R.A.W. (1986) *The National World of Local Government*. London: Allen and Unwin.

Roderick, P. and Stevens, A. (1989) 'Fighting the Fire in Paddington and North Kensington', in M. Pye, M. Kapila, G. Buckley and D. Cunningham (eds), *Responding to the AIDS Challenge*. Harlow: Health Education Authority/Longman.

Rogers, E. (1962) *The Diffusion of Innovations*. New York: Free Press.

Rogers, E. (1983) *Diffusion of Innovations*, 3rd edn. New York: Free Press.

Rothwell, R. (1976) 'Intracorporate Entrepreneurs', *Management Decision*, (13) 3, pp. 142–54.

Rothwell, R. and Gardiner, P. (1985) *Innovation*. London: Design Council.

Rothwell, R. and Zegveld, W. (1982) *Innovation and the Small and Medium Sized Firms*. London: Frances Pinter.

Rubin, I. (1989) 'Aaron Wildavsky and the Demise of Incrementalism', *Public Administration Review*, 49(1), pp. 78–81.

Salaman, G. (1979) *Work Organisations: Resistance and Control*. London: Longman.

Sarason, S. (1976) *The Creation of Settings and the Future Societies*. San Francisco: Jossey Bass.

Schein, E.H. (1985) *Organisational Culture and Leadership*. San Francisco: Jossey Bass.

Schön, D. (1973) 'Champion for Radical New Inventions', *Harvard Business Review*, 51 (March/April).

Schultz, R. and Harrison, R. (1983) *Teams and Top Managers in the NHS*. Project Paper 41. London: King's Fund.

Scott, A. (1990) *Ideology and the New Social Movements*. London: Unwin Hyman.

Scott, W.R. (1986) 'Organizational Barriers to Innovation'. Department of Sociology, Stanford University, CA.

Scott, W.R. (1987) 'The Adolescence of Institutional Theory', *Administrative Science Quarterly*, 32, pp. 493–511.

Scull, A.T. (1979) *Museums of Madness: the Social Origins of Insanity in Nineteenth Century England*. London: Allen Lane.

Sharifi, S. (1988) 'Managerial Work: a Diagnostic Model', in A.M. Pettigrew (ed.), *Competitiveness and the Management Process*. Oxford: Basil Blackwell.

Shilts, R. (1987) *And the Band Played On . . .*. London: Penguin.

Shortell, S. (1988) 'The Evolution of Hospital Systems: Unfulfilled Promises and Self-fulfilling Prophesies', *Medical Care Review*, 45(2), pp. 177–214.

Shortell, S.M., Morrison, E.M. and Friedman, B. (1990) *Strategic Choices for America's Hospitals*. San Francisco: Jossey Bass.

Simon, H.A. (1953) 'Birth of an Organisation: the Economic Cooperation Administration', *Public Administration Review*, 13, pp. 227–36.

Singh, J.V. (1990) 'Future Directions in Organisational Evolution', in J.V. Singh (ed.), *Organisational Evolution: New Directions*. London: Sage.

Singh, J.V., House, R. and Tucker, D. (1986) 'Organisational Change and Organisational Mortality', *Administrative Science Quarterly*, 31, pp. 587–611.

Smart, C. and Vertinsky, I. (1977) 'Designs for Crisis Decision Units', *Administrative Science Quarterly*, 22, pp. 640–55.

Smith, J. (1981) 'Conflict without Change: the Case of London's Health services', *Political Quarterly*, 52, pp. 426–40.

Smith, K.G. and Grimm, C.M. (1987) 'Environmental Variation, Strategic Change and Firm Performance: a Study of Railroad Deregulation', *Strategic Management Journal*, 8, pp. 363–76.

Smith, R.P. and Perry, J.L. (1985) 'Strategic Management in Public and Private

Organisations: Implications of Distinctive Contexts and Constraints', *Academy of Management Review*, 10(2), pp. 276–86.

Social Services Select Committee (1984) *Griffiths NHS Management Inquiry Report*. Session 83/84, HCP 209. London: House of Commons.

Social Services Select Committee (1987) *Problems Associated with AIDS*. Session 86/87, 3rd Report, HCP 182. London: House of Commons.

Starbuck, W.H. (1965) 'Organizational Growth and Development', in James G. March (ed.), *Handbook of Organizations*. Chicago: Rand McNally.

Starbuck, W.H., Greve, Arent and Hedberg, B.L.T. (1978) 'Responding to Crisis', *Journal of Business Administration*, 9, pp. 111–37.

Starkey, Ken and Wright, Mike (1990) 'Strategic Flexibility and Corporate Strategy'. Department of Industrial Economics, University of Nottingham.

Stewart, J.D. (1980) 'From Growth to Standstill', in M. Wright (ed.), *Public Spending Decisions: Growth and Restraint in the 1970s*. London: Allen and Unwin.

Stewart, J.D. and Ranson, S. (1988) 'Management in the Public Domain', *Public Money and Management*, 8(2), pp. 13–19.

Stewart, R., Smith, P., Blake, J. and Wingate, P. (1980) *The District Administrator in the NHS*. Oxford: Oxford University Press/King's Fund.

Stewart, R. and Smith, P. (1986) 'Confused DGMs Speak Out', *Health Service Journal*, 6 March, pp. 316–17.

Stewart, R., Gabbay, J., Dopson, S., Smith, P. and Williams D. (1987a) *DGMs and the DHA: Working with Members*. Templeton Series no. 3. Bristol: National Health Service Training Authority.

Stewart, R., Gabbay, J., Dopson, S., Smith, P. and Williams D. (1987b) *Role and Progress of DGMs: an Overview*. Templeton Series no. 8. Bristol : National Health Service Training Authority.

Stinchcombe, A.L. (1965) 'Social Structure and Organizations', in J. March (ed.), *Handbook of Organizations*. Chicago: Rand McNally.

Stocking, B. (1985) *Innovation and Inertia in the NHS*. London: Nuffield Provincial Hospitals Trust.

Stocking, B. (ed.) (1987) *In Dreams Begin Responsibility: a Tribute to Tom Evans*. London: King's Fund.

Strauss, A. (1978) *Negotiations: Varieties, Contexts, Processes and Social Order*. San Francisco: Jossey Bass.

Strauss, A., Schatzman, L., Bucher, R., Elrich, D. and Sabstin, M. (1964) *Psychiatric Ideologies and Institutions*. London: Collier Macmillan.

Street, J. (1988) 'British Government Policy on AIDS', *Parliamentary Affairs*, 41, pp. 490–508.

Strong, P. (1990) 'Epidemic Psychology', *Sociology of Health and Illness*, 12(3), pp. 249–59.

Strong, P. and Robinson, J. (1988) 'New Model Management: Griffiths and the NHS'. Nursing Policy Studies Centre, University of Warwick.

Strong, P. and Robinson, J. (1990) *The NHS: Under New Management*. Milton Keynes: Open University Press.

Sutton, R. (1989) 'Organisational Decline Processes: a Social Psychological Perspective', in B.M. Straw and L.L. Cummings (eds), *Research in Organizational Behaviour*, Vol. 12, Greenwich, CT: JAI Press.

Taylor, R. (1981) 'The Contribution of Social Science Research to Health Policy', *Journal of Social Policy*, 10(4), pp. 531–48.

Teece, D.J., Pisano, G. and Shuen, A. (1990) 'Firm Capabilities, Resources, and the Concept of Strategy'. Working Paper no. 90-8. Center for Research in Management, University of California, Berkeley.

Thomas, D. (1988) 'Managing Change in Mental Handicap Services: a Comparative Study'. MBA dissertation, University of Warwick.

Thompson, D. (1987) 'Coalitions and Conflict in the NHS: Some Implications for General Management', *Sociology of Health and Illness*, 9(2), pp. 127–53.

Thunhurst, C. (1982) *It Makes You Sick: the Politics of the NHS*. London: Pluto Press.

Tichy, N. (1983) *Managing Strategic Change: Technical, Political and Cultural Dynamics*. New York: John Wiley.

Todd Report (1968) *Royal Commission on Medical Education*. Cmnd 3569. London: HMSO.

Tomlinson, D. (1988) 'Let the Mental Hospitals Close', *Policy and Politics*, 16(3), pp. 179–95.

Touraine, A. (1981) *The Voice and the Eye: an Analysis of Social Movements*. Cambridge: Cambridge University Press.

Turner, B. (1976) 'The Organisational and Interorganisational Development of Disasters', *Administrative Science Quarterly*, 21, pp. 378–97.

Tushman, M.L. and Romanelli, E. (1985) 'Organizational Evolution: a Metamorphosis Model of Convergence and Reorientation', in B.M. Staw and L.L. Cummings (eds), *Research in Organizational Behaviour*. Vol. 7. Greenwich, CT: JAI Press.

Unger, R.M. (1987) *False Necessity*. Cambridge: Cambridge University Press.

Van de Ven, A.H. (1980) 'Early Planning, Implementation and Performance of New Organizations', in J.R. Kimberly and R.H. Miles (eds), *The Organizational Life Cycle*. San Francisco: Jossey Bass.

Van de Ven, A.H. and Huber, G.P. (1990) 'Longitudinal Field Research Methods for Studying Processes of Organizational Change', *Organization Science*, 1(3), pp. 213–19.

Van Meter, D.S. and Van Horn, C.E. (1976) 'The Policy Implementation Process: a Conceptual Framework', *Administration and Society*, 6(4), pp. 445–88.

Vann-Wye, G. (1986) 'Designing Technical Change: a Study within the National Health Service'. PhD Thesis, University of Aston, Birmingham.

Vann-Wye, G. (1991) 'Hospitals in Britain: a Study of their Physical Design and Work Organisation', in K. Starkey and R. Loveridge (eds), *Continuity and Crisis in the NHS: the Politics of Design and Innovation in Health Care*. Milton Keynes: Open University Press.

Walker, A. (1982) 'The Meaning and Social Division of Community Care', in A. Walker (ed.), *Community Care: the Family, State, and Social Policy*. Oxford: Basil Blackwell.

Walton, R.E. (1975) 'The Diffusion of New Work Structures: Explaining Why Success Didn't Take', *Organisational Dynamics*, 3 (Winter), pp. 3–22.

Walton, R.E. (1980) 'Establishing and Maintaining High Commitment Work Systems' in J. Kimberly and R. Miles (eds), *The Organizational Life Cycle*. San Francisco: Jossey Bass.

Walton, R.E. (1987) *Innovating to Compete*. San Francisco: Jossey Bass.

Warren, D.L. (1984) 'Managing in Crisis: Nine Principles for Successful Transition', in J.R. Kimberly and R.E. Quinn (eds), *Managing Organizational Transitions*. Homewood, IL: Irwin.

Watson, N. (1985) 'Hamstrung by their own Enthusiasm: a Cautionary Tale from Milton Keynes', *British Medical Journal*, 290 (23 March), pp. 945–6.

Wertheimer, A. (1986) *Hospital Closures in the 80s*. London: Campaign for People with Mental Handicaps.

Whetten, D.A. (1980) 'Sources, Responses and Effects of Organizational Decline', in J. Kimberly and R. Miles (eds), *The Organizational Life Cycle*. San Francisco: Jossey Bass.

Whetten, D.A. (1988) 'Organizational Growth and Decline Processes', in K. Cameron, R. Sutton and D. Whetten (eds), *Readings in Organizational Decline – Frameworks, Research and Prescription*. Cambridge, MA: Ballinger.

Whipp, R. and Pettigrew, A.M. (1990a) 'Managing Change for Competitive Success: Bridging the Strategic and the Operational'. Paper presented to the 10th International Conference on the Strategic Management Society on Strategic Bridging, Stockholm, September.

Whipp, R. and Pettigrew, A.M. (1990b) 'Leading Change and the Management of Competition'. Paper presented to Strategic Management Society Workshop on Leadership and the Management of Strategic Change, Robinson College, Cambridge University, December.

Whipp, R., Rosenfeld, R. and Pettigrew, A.M. (1989) 'Culture and Competitiveness: Evidence from Two Mature UK Industries', *Journal of Management Studies*, 26(6), pp. 561–86.

Whittingham Hospital Management Committee (1973) 'Whittingham Hospital – One Hundred Years 1873–1973'. Whittingham, Lancs.

Wilson, B.R. (ed.) (1967) *Patterns of Sectarianism*. London: Heinemann.

Wilson, D.C., Butler, R.J., Cray, D., Hickson, D.J. and Mallory, G.R. (1986) 'Breaking the Bounds of Organisation in Strategic Decision Making', *Human Relations*, 39(4), pp. 309–32.

Wistow, G. (1985) 'Community Care for the Mentally Handicapped: Disappointing Progress', in A. Harrison and J. Gretton (eds), *Health Care UK*. Newbury: Policy Journals.

Wistow, G. and Fuller, S. (1984) *Collaboration since Restructuring*. Birmingham: National Association of Health Authorities.

Young, H. (1989) *One of Us*. London: Macmillan.

Zald, M.N. and Ash, R. (1966) 'Social Movement Organisations: Growth, Decay and Change', *Social Forces*, 44, pp. 327–39.

Zald, M.N. and Berger, M. (1978) 'Social Movements in Organizations: Coup d'état, Insurgency and Mass Movements', *American Journal of Sociology*, 83(4), pp. 823–61.

Zucker, L.G. (1983) 'Organizations as Institutions', in S.B. Bacharach (ed.), *Research in the Sociology of Organizations*, Vol. 2. Greenwich, CT: JAI Press.

Zucker, L.G. (1987) 'Normal Change or Risky Business: Institutional Effects on the "Hazard" of Change in Hospital Organisations, 1959–1979', *Journal of Management Studies*, 24(6), pp. 671–700.

Zucker, L.G. (ed.) (1988) *Institutional Patterns and Organizations: Culture and Environment*. Cambridge, MA: Ballinger.

Index